SOCCERNOMICS

D0352570

SOCCERNOMICS

WHY ENGLAND LOSE, WHY GERMANY, SPAIN AND FRANCE WIN, AND WHY ONE DAY THE REST OF THE WORLD WILL FINALLY CATCH UP

SIMON KUPER AND STEFAN SZYMANSKI

HarperCollins*Publishers*

HarperCollins*Publishers*
1 London Bridge Street
London SE1 9GF

www.harpercollins.co.uk

First published by HarperCollins*Publishers* as
Why England Lose in 2009
This revised and updated edition published 2018

5 7 9 10 8 6 4

© Simon Kuper and Stefan Szymanski 2009, 2010, 2012, 2014, 2018

Simon Kuper and Stefan Szymanski assert the moral right
to be identified as the authors of this work

A catalogue record of this book is
available from the British Library

ISBN 978-0-00-823664-9

Printed and bound in Great Britain by CPI Group (UK) Ltd, Croydon

All rights reserved. No part of this publication may be
reproduced, stored in a retrieval system, or transmitted,
in any form or by any means, electronic,
mechanical, photocopying, recording or otherwise, without
the prior written permission of the publishers.

MIX
Paper from
responsible sources
FSC
www.fsc.org
FSC™ C007454

FSC™ is a non-profit international organisation established to promote
the responsible management of the world's forests. Products carrying
the FSC label are independently certified to assure consumers that they
come from forests that are managed to meet the social, economic and
ecological needs of present and future generations,
and other controlled sources.

Find out more about HarperCollins and the environment at
www.harpercollins.co.uk/green

CONTENTS

DRIVING WITH A DASHBOARD: IN SEARCH OF NEW TRUTHS ABOUT FOOTBALL

A few years ago, the data department at Manchester City carried out a study of corner kicks. City hadn't been scoring much from corners, and the analysts wanted to find out the best way to take them. They watched more than four hundred corners, from different leagues, over several seasons, and concluded: the most dangerous corner was the inswinger to the near post.

The beauty of the inswinger was that it sent the ball straight into the danger zone. Sometimes an attacker would get a head or foot to it and divert it in from point-blank range. Sometimes the keeper or a defender stopped the inswinger on the line, whereupon someone bashed it in. And occasionally the ball just swung straight in from the corner. Of course, you wouldn't want to take every corner as an inswinger. It's a good idea to hit the odd outswinger too, just to keep the opponents guessing. This is what's known as a mixed strategy. But all in all, the analysts found, inswingers produced more goals than outswingers.

They took their findings to the club's then manager, Roberto Mancini, who like almost all managers is an ex-player. He heard them out politely. Then he said, in effect: 'I was a player for many years, and I just know that the outswinger is more effective.' He was wrong, but we can understand why he made the mistake: outswingers tend to create beautiful goals (ball swings out, player meets it with powerful header, ball crashes into net) and beautiful goals stick in the memory. The messy goals generally produced by inswingers don't.

At first Mancini didn't change his thinking. But sometime around 2011, when City were again having trouble with corners, his assistant David Platt came to chat with the club's data department. The analysts told Platt about the corners study. They heard nothing more about the matter, but soon they noticed that City had begun taking inswinging corners. In the 2011/2012 season City scored 15 goals from corners, more than any other team in the Premier League. Ten of those goals came from inswingers, including the header from Vincent Kompany against Manchester United that effectively sealed the title for City.

It's a story that captures where football is today. On the one hand, the March of the Geeks has advanced fast since we first published *Soccernomics* in 2009. Football is becoming more intelligent. The analysts who now crunch 'match data' at almost all big European clubs (and at many smaller ones) are just one symptom of the shift.

Today's plugged-in clubs know stats like 'pass completion rates in the final third of the field', miles run in each phase of the game and pace of sprints for all their players. These numbers increasingly inform decisions on which players to buy and sell.

On the other hand, as Mancini's initial rejection of the data about corner kicks shows, there is still widespread suspicion of numbers in football. John Coulson of the data provider Opta told us, 'There are still maybe a lot of teams that view data as a threat rather than as a tool.' Statisticians don't always make the best communicators. Baseball has had its *Moneyball* revolution, but in football, the transformation is still just in its first phase.

This new, updated, expanded edition of *Soccernomics* uses data to clarify our thinking on topics ranging from tackles through transfers to why England lose and why China might start winning. We have a new chapter on crooked business; one on how the biggest clubs might now finally be turning into serious businesses, and why that isn't a good thing; and a final chapter arguing that the game has never had it so good (though the smartphone could bring everything down). We have also expanded our thoughts on some mystifying questions, such as: 'How do clubs use data to judge, buy and sell players?' and 'How powerful are agents in the transfer market?' In every chapter of the book we have found stories and analyses to update, and new thoughts to add.

We've watched fans and media shift to our point of view on certain issues: most people now recognize that hosting big tournaments doesn't make you rich, and also that England shouldn't expect to win those tournaments. (We wish we could claim responsibility for shifting global opinion, but we can't.) On other issues, we've changed our mind somewhat. In 2009 we were confident that the rest of the world would soon catch up with the best Western European nations. That hasn't happened, so we've had to rethink what's going on. We're with the economist John Maynard Keynes: when the facts change, we change our minds.

It's a long way from *Soccernomics*'s beginnings in the Hilton in Istanbul one winter's day in 2007. From the outside the hotel is squat and brutalist, but once the security men have checked your car for bombs and waved you through, the place is so soothing you never want to go home again. Having escaped the 14 million-person city, the only stress is over what to do next: a Turkish bath, a game of tennis, or yet more over-eating while the sun sets over the Bosphorus? For aficionados, there is also a perfect view of the Besiktas football stadium right next door. And the staff are so friendly, they are even friendlier than ordinary Turkish people.

The two authors of this book, Stefan Szymanski (a sports economist) and Simon Kuper (a journalist), met here. Fener-bahce football club was marking its centenary by staging the '100th Year Sports and Science Congress' and had flown us both in to give talks.

The two of us had never met before, but over beers in the Hilton bar we found that we thought much the same way about football. Stefan as an economist is trained to torture the data until they confess, while Simon as a journalist tends to go around interviewing people, but those are just surface differences. We both think that much in football can be explained, even predicted, by studying data – especially data found outside football. We decided to write a book together.

When we began writing, Stefan lived in London and Simon in Paris, so we spent a year firing figures, arguments and anec-dotes back and forth across the Channel. As we talked more and began to think harder about football and data, we buzzed around all sorts of questions. Why was football such a terrible business? Might the game somehow deter people from killing themselves? And are fans really monogamous?

Applying data to these questions felt like a new project. Until very recently, football had escaped the Enlightenment. Football clubs are still run mostly by men who do what they do because they have always done it that way. These men used to 'know' that black players 'lacked bottle', and they therefore overpaid mediocre white players. Today they discriminate against black managers, buy the wrong players, and then let those players take corners and penalties the wrong way. (We can, incidentally, explain why Manchester United won the penalty shoot-out in the Champions League final in 2008. It's a story involving a secret note, a Basque economist and Edwin van der Sar's powers of detection.)

Entrepreneurs who dip into football also keep making the same mistakes. They buy clubs promising to run them 'like a business' and disappear a few seasons later amid the same public derision as the previous owners. 'I screwed up,' Tony Fernandes, chairman of Queens Park Rangers, told us. Fans and journalists aren't blameless, either. Many media headlines rest on false premises: 'Newcastle Land World Cup Star', 'England Underachieve' or 'World Cup Will Be Economic Bonanza'. The game is full of unexamined clichés: 'Football is becoming boring because the big clubs always win', 'Football is big business' or 'The big money will turn fans off'. None of these shibboleths has been tested against the data.

Most male team sports have long been pervaded by the same overreliance on traditional beliefs. Baseball, too, was until quite recently an old game stuffed with old lore. Since time immemorial, players had stolen bases, hit sacrifice bunts and been judged on their batting averages. Everyone in baseball just knew that all this was right.

But that was before Bill James came along. James was from the rural state of Kansas in the middle of the US. He hadn't done much in life beyond keeping the stats in the local children's baseball 'Little League' and watching the furnaces in a pork-and-beans factory. However, in his spare time he had begun to study baseball statistics with a fresh eye and discovered that 'a great portion of the sport's traditional knowledge is ridiculous hokum'. James wrote that he wanted to approach the subject of baseball 'with the same kind of intellectual rigor and discipline that is routinely applied, by scientists great and poor, to trying to unravel the mysteries of the universe, of society, of the human mind, or of the price of burlap in Des Moines'.

James told us that baseball set the trend for the global data revolution, because the game's record-keepers had begun gathering stats in the nineteenth century – before almost any other human activity. James explained: 'So when the computer revolution started 100 years later, we were ahead of the game. We had 100 years of really interesting data to play around with. So the analytical revolution hit in baseball before places where sensibly you would think it would hit.'

In self-published mimeographs masquerading as books, the first of which sold seventy-five copies, James began demolishing the game's myths. He found, for instance, that an extremely telling statistic in batting was the rarely mentioned 'on-base percentage' – how often a player manages to get on base. James and his followers (statisticians of baseball who came to be known as sabermetricians) showed that time-honoured strategies like sacrifice bunts and base stealing didn't make any sense.

His annual Baseball Abstracts turned into real books; eventually they reached the best-seller lists. One year the cover picture showed an ape, posed as Rodin's Thinker, studying a baseball. As James wrote in one Abstract: 'This is outside baseball. This is a book about what baseball looks like if you step back from it and study it intensely and minutely, but from a distance.'

Some Jamesians started to penetrate professional baseball. One of them, Billy Beane, general manager of the little Oakland A's, is the hero of Michael Lewis's earth-moving book *Moneyball* and the film starring Brad Pitt. In recent years Beane, like so many Americans, has become a football nut. He has spent a lot of time thinking about how his insights into baseball might apply to football, and in 2015 he made his first official foray into the game, as adviser to AZ Alkmaar in the Netherlands. In December 2017 he was one of a consortium of foreign investors that took over Barnsley. (We'll say more later about Beane's gaming of baseball's transfer market and its lessons for football.)

For several seasons Beane's Oakland A's did so well using Jamesian ideas that eventually even people inside baseball began to get curious about James. In 2002 the Boston Red Sox appointed him 'senior baseball operations adviser'. That same year the Red Sox hired one of his followers, the twenty-eight-year-old Theo Epstein, as the youngest general manager in the history of the major leagues. (Beane had said yes and then no to the job.) The 'cursed' club quickly won two World Series. Today large statistical departments are the norm at American baseball clubs. Now football has embarked on its own Jamesian revolution.

A NUMBERS GAME

It's strange that football always used to be so averse to studying data, because one thing that attracts many fans to the game is precisely a love of numbers.

The man to ask about that is Alex Bellos. He wrote the magnificent *Futebol: The Brazilian Way of Life*, but has also written several books about maths. 'Numbers are incredibly satisfying,' Bellos tells us. 'The world has no order, and math is a way of seeing it in an order. League tables have an order. And the calculations you need to do for them are so simple: it's nothing more than your three-times table.'

Though most fans would probably deny it, a love of football is often intertwined with a love of numbers. There are the match results, the famous dates, and the special joy of sitting in a coffee shop with your phone on a Sunday morning 'reading' the league table. Fantasy football leagues are, at bottom, numbers games.

In this book we want to introduce new numbers and new ideas to football: numbers on suicides, on wage spending, on countries' populations, on passes and sprints, on anything that helps to reveal new truths about the game. Though Stefan is a sports economist, this is not a book about money. The point of football clubs is not to turn a profit (which is fortunate, as few of them do), nor do we get particularly excited about any profits they happen to make. Rather, we want to use an economist's skills (plus a little geography, psychology and sociology) to understand the game on the field, and the fans off it.

Some people may not want their emotional relationship with football sullied by our rational calculations. On the other hand, the next time their team loses a penalty shoot-out at the World Cup these same people will probably be throwing their beer bottles at the TV, when instead they could be tempering their disappointment with some reflections on the nature of binomial probability theory.

We think it's a good time to be rewriting this book. The amount of information available is expanding exponentially. In recent years the world has entered the era of 'big data'. The phrase describes the unprecedented mountain of information that is now collected every day. This information comes mostly from the internet (from innumerable search terms, Facebook pages and emails), and from sensors that are attached to ever more physical objects – among them, footballers during training sessions. We have much more data to help us understand events than human beings could gather using only their eyes and ears. Moreover, all this data can be stored and faithfully reproduced, without the annoying tendency that humans have to misremember or just plain forget. Computing can identify patterns in datasets that would not be visible to a person 'reading' the data. We believe the data revolution enhances the capacity of humans to make good decisions. Note that we say *enhance*, not *replace*. Cyborgs replacing humans is, for now, still science fiction. But humans can make better decisions if aided by data analysis.

That's true in football too. For the first time in the game's history, there are a lot of numbers to mine. Traditionally the only data that existed in the game were goals and league tables. (Newspapers published attendance figures, but these were unreliable.) In 1979, after Steve Daley was transferred for a then record £1.43 million, from Wolves to Manchester City (where he flopped), the Treasury considered a tax on football transfers. The problem was that it couldn't find any reliable financial data on the topic. In the end a young civil servant had to page through the *Rothmans Football Yearbook* to work out more or less how much clubs had spent on transfers the previous season.

Now the game is drowning in information. Data companies such as Opta can collect millions of observations (facts) about a single game. Clubs, which used to rely on gut alone, now use the new stats to analyse games and players. Every day, data analysts collect ever more information about every player's every move on the field, the training ground, and even in bed – they know how well he slept last night.

Academics are pitching in as well. At the end of the 1980s, when Stefan went into sports economics, only about twenty or thirty academic articles on sports had ever been published. Now countless academics work on football. Many of the new truths they have found have not yet reached most fans. Much of what we argue in the book – for instance, that a club's wage bill is an excellent predictor of its league position – is taken from Stefan's academic work. Other insights come from his colleagues' work. Generally speaking, we are more confident of what we assert when it is backed up by research that we believe is credible: meaning that the methods are clear, the data is adequate, and the results carefully explained and preferably peer-reviewed. You could still disagree with the work, but it has a solid foundation. Peer-reviewed academic research is, for us, the gold standard.

However, this book is more than just academic work rewritten for laypeople. Simon has been covering football as a journalist for over thirty years. He has met and interviewed many of the people who have shaped the modern game. This kind of knowledge is not always susceptible to formal statistical tests, but it is knowledge just the same. It informs our understanding of the sport. For instance, Simon came up with our theory of football networks: that Western Europe keeps winning World Cups because the countries of this little region are constantly exchanging knowhow with each other. We have much less data for this theory than, say, for Stefan's insight that coaches have little impact on results. However, we think the network theory is plausible – and Stefan has set his economist's brain to developing it. We think our combination of data and experience is the best way to understand social activities.

Like Stefan, Simon has also drawn on the knowledge of his colleagues – the growing number of people who write football books. When Pete Davies published *All Played Out: The Full Story of Italia '90*, there were probably only about twenty or thirty good football books in existence in English. Now – thanks partly to Davies, who has been described as John the Baptist to Nick Hornby's Jesus – there are thousands in untold languages. Simon, in his office in Paris, has a library containing a large proportion of them. Many of these books contain truths about the game that we try to present here.

What has happened in football mirrors a trend across all sports. Michael Lewis, author of *Moneyball*, wrote in 2009: 'The virus that infected professional baseball in the 1990s, the use of statistics to find new and better ways to value players and strategies, has found its way into every major sport. Not just basketball and [American gridiron] football, but also soccer and cricket and rugby and, for all I know, snooker and darts – each one now supports a subculture of smart people who view it not just as a game to be played but as a problem to be solved.'

In football, these smart men (it's still part of the game's own 'ridiculous hokum' that they have to be men) have even begun taking key roles at some of Europe's biggest clubs. European football, professional on the field for over a century, is finally creaking into professionalism off the field, too. Given the global obsession with the game, there could come a time when some of the best and brightest young people are working in the front offices of football clubs. Already the rising generation of club executives understands that in football today, you need data to get ahead. If you study figures, you will see more and win more.

One early harbinger of the Jamesian takeover of football was the Milan Lab. Soon after it began work, AC Milan's in-house medical outfit found that just by studying a player's jump, it could predict with 70 per cent accuracy whether he would get injured soon. Later the Lab began testing, almost day by day, each player's muscle weaknesses, the movement of his eyes, the rise and fall of his heart-rate, his breathing, and many other obvious and less obvious indicators. Jean-Pierre Meersseman, the Lab's cigarette-puffing director, was given a power of veto over the club's prospective signings. 'The last signature on the contract before the big boss signs is mine,' he told us in 2008. By 2013 the Lab had performed 1.2 million physical tests on Milan's players, collected millions of pieces of data on computers, logged even the slightest injury to every player, and in the process had stumbled upon the secret of eternal youth.

Most of Milan's starting eleven who beat Liverpool in the Champions League final of 2007 were thirty-one or older: Paolo Maldini, the captain, was thirty-eight, and Filippo Inzaghi, scorer of both of Milan's goals, was thirty-three. (After the final whistle, Inzaghi still had enough juice to kick a ball around on the field for fun.) In large part, that trophy was won by the Milan Lab and its database. It is another version of the March of the Geeks story. In the last few years, cash-strapped AC Milan have reduced the Lab's funding and power. However, other big clubs all over Europe now lead the data-driven quests to reduce injuries, and to predict which twelve-year-old will grow up to be the next Xavi. Meersseman says data-driven scientists seem to be better than experienced youth coaches at making those predictions. He told us: 'In football, they say, "You know about football or you don't." And when you go and test the ones who "know", it's surprising how little they know. It's based on the emotion of the moment.'

What started in Istanbul in 2007 as a book idea has turned into a long-term collaboration. These days our contact is transatlantic: Simon is still in Paris, but Stefan is now at the University of Michigan. Together with Ben Lyttleton we have also founded the Soccernomics consultancy. On its website, Soccernomics-agency.com, we publish an occasional blog with our thoughts on football. And we have kept rewriting and updating this book. It has sold a total of about 250,000 copies in over two dozen languages. We've had the chance to influence the opinions of lots of people, some of whom work in the game.

All the while, we have continued to distrust every bit of the game's ancient lore, and tested it against the numbers. As Meersseman says, 'You can drive a car without a dashboard, without any information, and that's what's happening in football. There are excellent drivers, excellent cars, but if you have your dashboard, it makes it just a little bit easier. I wonder why people don't want more information.' We do.

PART I

THE CLUBS

Racism, Stupidity, Bad Transfers,
Capital Cities, the Leicester Fairy Tale and
What Actually Happened in that Penalty
Shoot-out in Moscow

GENTLEMEN PREFER BLONDS: HOW TO AVOID SILLY MISTAKES IN THE TRANSFER MARKET

In 1983 AC Milan spotted a talented young black forward playing for Watford just outside London. The word is that the player the Italians liked was John Barnes and that they then confused him with his black teammate Luther Blissett. Whatever the truth, Milan ended up paying Watford a 'transfer fee' of £1 million for Blissett.

As a player Blissett became such a joke in Italy that the name 'Luther Blissett' is now used as a pseudonym by groups of anarchist writers. He spent one unhappy year in Milan, before the club sold him back to Watford for just over half the sum it had paid for him. At least that year gave football one of its best quotes: 'No matter how much money you have here,' Blissett lamented, 'you can't seem to get Rice Krispies.' More on the beloved British breakfast cereal later.

In summer 2017 alone, clubs worldwide spent $4.71 billion on transfers (about £3.6 billion), reported FIFA Transfer Matching

System (TMS), the department of FIFA that oversees international transfers. The sum includes the world record fee of £198 million that Paris Saint-Germain paid Barcelona for Neymar.*

Unfortunately, much of the money thrown around in the transfer market is wasted. Newcastle have long been a particularly humorous example, but in fact the net amount that almost any club spends on transfer fees bears little relation to where it finishes in the league. We studied the spending of forty English clubs between 1978 and 1997, and found that their net outlay on transfers (i.e. each club's transfer fees paid minus transfer fees received) explained only 16 per cent of their total variation in league position. In other words, taken over many years, the mere fact of being a 'buying club' in the transfer market didn't help a team perform significantly better than being a 'selling club'.[1]

By contrast, clubs' spending on salaries was extremely telling. The size of their wage bills explained a massive 92 per cent of variation in their league positions, if you took each club's average for the entire period. That correlation shows little sign of going away. We show almost exactly the same result below using data for the Premier League and the Championship for the decade to 2016. In that period, wage spending still explained more than 90 per cent of the variation in league position. It seems that over the long term, high wages help a club much more than do spectacular transfers.

Obviously we don't believe that if you took a random bunch of players, and doubled their salaries, they would suddenly play twice as well. It's not that high pay *causes* good performance. Rather, we think that high pay *attracts* good performers. Chelsea can afford to pay Eden Hazard's wages, whereas Burnley cannot.

* A note about currencies: almost always in this book, we have cited sums of money in pounds. When converting from euros or other currencies, we have used the pound equivalent at the time the sum was spent. (The pound's value is always changing – and since Brexit, chiefly in a downward direction.)

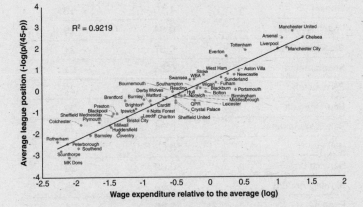

Premier League and Championship teams 2007–2016 performance and wage expenditure

THE MORE YOU PAY YOUR PLAYERS, THE HIGHER YOU FINISH: 2007–2016

Club	Wage spending relative to the average	Average league position
Manchester United	3.40	3
Chelsea	3.97	3
Arsenal	2.92	3
Manchester City	3.13	5
Liverpool	2.74	5
Tottenham Hotspur	1.69	6
Everton	1.28	7
Aston Villa	1.54	12
West Ham United	1.31	14
Stoke City	0.91	14
Newcastle United	1.44	14
Sunderland	1.19	15
West Bromwich Albion	0.79	16
Swansea City	0.75	16

Fulham	1.10	18
Wigan Athletic	0.84	19
Blackburn Rovers	0.87	21
Southampton	0.83	21
Portsmouth	1.47	22
Bournemouth	0.58	22
Bolton Wanderers	0.94	23
Hull City	0.63	24
Norwich City	0.69	24
Birmingham City	0.59	25
Reading	0.66	25
Middlesbrough	0.66	25
Leicester City	0.60	25
Wolverhampton Wanderers	0.53	25
Burnley	0.38	27
Cardiff City	0.50	27
Queens Park Rangers	0.80	27
Brentford	0.28	27
Crystal Palace	0.60	27
Watford	0.41	27
Sheffield United	0.60	28
Brighton & Hove Albion	0.37	29
Derby County	0.42	29
Ipswich Town	0.33	31
Nottingham Forest	0.40	32
Blackpool	0.24	33
Preston North End	0.25	33
Charlton Athletic	0.44	34
Sheffield Wednesday	0.23	34
Leeds United	0.36	34
Bristol City	0.29	34
Plymouth Argyle	0.19	36

Colchester United	0.15	37
Millwall	0.23	37
Huddersfield Town	0.23	38
Coventry City	0.26	39
Barnsley	0.17	40
Rotherham United	0.10	41
Peterborough United	0.12	41
Southend United	0.14	42
Scunthorpe United	0.11	42
MK Dons	0.12	43

And if you have Hazard and other good players, you will win lots of matches. Rich clubs pay high salaries to get good players.

In short, wages buy success (something Stefan has been banging on about since his first published article on football in 1991). We have yet to see anyone produce a credible alternative theory. Did Manchester City or Roman Abramovich's Chelsea hire great managers who won titles, but then also decide out of the goodness of the owners' hearts to pay the players exorbitant wages? No, they had to hire players whose pay predicted their ability to win games.

True, some players are paid either more or less than they are worth. In fact, it's an agent's job to persuade clubs to pay excessive salaries. The former Dutch defender Rody Turpijn has written up a lovely vignette showing how this works. In 1998, the young Turpijn's career at Ajax Amsterdam was falling apart. The player had only one thing going for him: he was represented by Mino Raiola, a chubby little Dutch-Italian former pizza restaurateur who was becoming one of Europe's most powerful agents.

Raiola and Turpijn drove to a motorway hotel (classic venue of football deals) to meet the chairman of the small Dutch club De Graafschap. Raiola kicked off by impressing the chairman with some gossip about Juventus's Pavel Nedved. Then the chairman wrote on a piece of paper the salary he was offering Turpijn. It was more than Turpijn earned at Ajax.

But to Turpijn's surprise, Raiola shouted: 'Do you know what he earns at Ajax? This isn't a serious offer! Come, Rody, we're not going to waste our time on this.' Raiola stood up as if to walk out, so Turpijn hesitantly rose too. The chairman anxiously persuaded them to sit down. Twenty minutes later, Raiola had negotiated a lucrative four-year contract. As Turpijn wrote years later in the Dutch literary magazine *Hard Gras*, that meeting secured his future 'for just about the rest of my life'.

So Turpijn was overpaid. However, the overpayment didn't last. Over his four years at De Graafschap it became clear that he wasn't worth the salary. When his contract ended, the club let him go. Rather than joining another club at a lower and more rational wage, he retired from football aged 25 and happily went off to university. The salary market had corrected itself.

Conversely, in 2012, the teenage Paul Pogba was underpaid at Manchester United, relative to what he could be earning at other clubs. Raiola, who represented him too, went to Alex Ferguson to negotiate a higher salary. One afternoon at his little office in the Dutch town of Haarlem, where Raiola had grown up working in his immigrant family's pizza restaurants, he reconstructed the pay talks for us:

Ferguson to Raiola: I don't talk to you if the player is not here.
Raiola: Get the player out of the locker room and sit him here.

Enter Pogba.

Ferguson to Pogba: You don't want to sign this contract?
Pogba: We're not going to sign this contract under these conditions.
Ferguson to Raiola: You're a twat.

Raiola was unfazed, partly because he didn't know the word.

Raiola: This is an offer that my chihuahuas – I have two chihuahuas – don't sign.
Ferguson: What do you think he needs to earn?
Raiola: Not that.
Ferguson: You're a twat.

Ferguson's published verdict on Raiola: 'I distrusted him from the moment I met him.' Pogba left for Juventus, who paid him what he was worth. Once again, the salary market had corrected itself – but in this case upwards rather than downwards.

And so, over the long run, most footballers earn what they deserve, at least measured by their contribution to winning matches. (If you measured their contribution to society, you might end up with very different salaries, but that's true of almost every profession from bond trader to nurse.) Generally, a player's salary is a good gauge of his ability to play football. The same is true at a team level: the higher the total wage bill, the better the squad, and the higher the team will finish in the league.

At this point the reader is probably jumping up and down and shouting, 'But what about Leicester?' In 2016, the club defied odds of 5,000–1 against (for the handful of punters who bet on this outcome pre-season) to win the only title of its 132-year history with the Premier League's fifteenth-highest wage bill. To find a comparable achievement you would need to go back to Brian Clough and Peter Taylor's triumphs with Derby County in 1972 and Nottingham Forest in 1978.

The popular theory of Leicester's title at the time was that it was mostly down to the manager, Claudio Ranieri, who had supposedly instilled the players with the self-belief and will to win, but was too modest to claim any credit. Later in the book we will attempt to demolish this theory but, anyway, you hear rather less of it since Ranieri was sacked six months into the next season with Leicester fighting relegation.

Rather, we would identify two main causes of Leicester's victory: 1) a very good goalkeeper and defence; 2) luck.

Let's start with luck. Leicester won the title without performing exceptionally. The team's goal difference that season was +32 (scored sixty-eight goals, conceded thirty-six). On average over the previous ten seasons, the English champions had a goal difference of +53. Only one champion in the previous thirty-nine years had scored fewer goals than Leicester: Manchester United in 1992/93, with sixty-seven goals.

So Leicester didn't perform as well as the typical champions. The team's goals for and goals against were both two standard deviations better than its expected performance, which is a fancy way of saying: much better than expected, but not amazing. Nobody might have noticed Leicester except for another random event: all the usual title contenders had bad seasons simultaneously. That allowed an overachieving mid-table team to end up champions. It's reasonable to expect an outcome like that once every fifty years or so. In technical terms, Leicester's triumph was an extreme random event. These things happen. In a single season, the correlation between salaries and league position is weaker than over the long term. That's because in such a short period, luck plays a big role in performance. Injuries, dodgy referees, poor form and a host of other factors cause big swings in performance from year to year. For any one given season, clubs' wage spending explains only about 70 per cent of the variation in league position.* A team can therefore get a big extra lift from luck.

---

* In statistics the measure of correlation can be squared in order to derive a percentage of the variation that is explained. Thus if the correlation (called 'r') between league position and wages is +0.84, then the 'r squared' is 0.7 or 70 per cent.

Yet the human mind tends to resist the notion of luck, of stuff just happening. Even Einstein said, 'God does not play dice with the universe.' Instead, most people like to seek explanations in human actions. Hence the view that Ranieri suddenly revealed himself as a genius.

Still, the fact remains that Leicester played remarkably well that season. Patrick Lucey, of the data science company STATS in Chicago, has written a good paper pinpointing exactly why. He says that while Leicester's attacking stats were unexceptional, the team 'had by far the most effective defense'. In fact its defensive numbers were the best of any team in the previous five Premier League seasons. STATS calculates that the keeper, Kasper Schmeichel, saved about 4.6 goals more than expected over the season – better than any other keeper in the division except Watford's Heurelho Gomes. (It seems that the richest English clubs had been missing some tricks on the goalkeepers' transfer market.) Meanwhile Leicester's defence did a very good job of forcing opponents to try difficult passes from wide areas. And Leicester had a couple of excellent pass-interceptors. STATS ranked Manchester City's Nicolas Otamendi first in the league for improbable interceptions, but Leicester's Christian Fuchs was third and N'Golo Kanté fifth.

Kanté in midfield was clearly crucial. Steve Walsh, Leicester's then assistant manager and chief scout, famously remarked, 'People think we play with two in midfield, and I say "No". We play with Danny Drinkwater in the middle and we play with Kanté either side, giving us essentially 12 players on the pitch.' The next season at Chelsea, Kanté ran more miles than any other player in the Premier League except Tottenham's Christian Eriksen. He won another league title, and was voted England's Players' Player of the Year.

In other words, excellent players win titles, and they rarely need managers to inspire them. Ranieri himself recognized Kanté's importance at Leicester's very first training session.

He later told the Players' Tribune website, 'He was running so hard that I thought he must have a pack full of batteries hidden in his shorts. . . . I tell him, "One day, I'm going to see you cross the ball, and then finish the cross with a header yourself."'

We won't be betting on Leicester to shock the world again. The team just doesn't spend enough. True luck (i.e. statistical randomness) tends to even out over the years. So if you track each club's performance over a longer period – fifteen or twenty years, say – then salaries explain about 90 per cent of the variation in league position. Leicester was an exception.

Simon's colleagues at the *Financial Times* ranked sixty-nine clubs from Europe's biggest leagues by how well they did relative to their wage bills from 2011 through 2015. Atlético Madrid emerged from the exercise as 'Europe's "smartest" spending club,' while Everton, Spurs, and Southampton also excelled. Among the worst underachievers were Cesena, Queens Park Rangers and the two Milan clubs. Real Madrid and Paris Saint-Germain also ranked in the *FT*'s bottom fifteen, largely as an effect of 'the sheer size of their wage bills'.

But on the whole, the market for players' wages is pretty efficient: the better a player, the more he earns. By comparison – and this is our focus in this chapter – the transfer market is inefficient. Much of the time, clubs buy the wrong players. Even now that they have brigades of international scouts, they still waste fortunes on flops like Blissett.

As a case study of bad transfer policy, let's take Liverpool from 1998 to 2010. The club's managers in this period, Gérard Houllier and Rafael Benitez, kept splashing out on big transfer fees, yet Liverpool hardly ever even threatened to win the league. Jamie Carragher, who played for Liverpool throughout these years, provides a dolefully comic commentary on some of the club's misguided signings in his excellent autobiography, *Carra*:

- ⚽ 'Sean Dundee was not a Liverpool footballer.'
- ⚽ 'The signing I didn't rate was Sander Westerveld. . . . I thought he was an average goalkeeper who seemed to think he was Gordon Banks.'
- ⚽ 'What about Josemi? He struggled to find a teammate six yards away. Djimi Traore had the same weakness.'
- ⚽ 'To be blunt, [Christian] Ziege couldn't defend.'
- ⚽ 'The names El-Hadji Diouf and Salif Diao now make the legs of the toughest Liverpudlians shudder in fear. . . . The first concern I had with Diouf was his pace. He didn't have any. . . . Do you remember being at school and picking sides for a game of football? We do this at Liverpool for the five-a-sides. Diouf was "last pick" within a few weeks.'
- ⚽ '"You paid ten million for him and no one wants him in their team," I shouted to Gérard.'
- ⚽ 'If Diouf was a disappointment, Diao was a catastrophe. . . . But even he wasn't the worst arrival of this hideous summer [of 2002]. Houllier also signed Bruno Cheyrou.'
- ⚽ On the expensive French striker Djibril Cissé: 'He was supposed to be a strong, physical target man who scored goals. He was neither one nor the other.'
- ⚽ 'The greatest disappointment was Fernando Morientes. . . . He was a yard off the pace.'

When Benitez replaced Houllier in 2004, writes Carragher, the Spaniard encountered 'a host of poor, overpaid players and expectations as great as ever'. But the new man didn't do much better than his predecessor. Carragher's book is gentler with Benitez than with Houllier, presumably because the Spaniard was still his boss when he wrote it, but the waste of the Benitez years is remarkable. Most strikingly, perhaps, in 2008 Benitez handed Tottenham Hotspur £20 million for the twenty-eight-year-old forward Robbie Keane. The much-touted fact that Keane was a lifelong Liverpool fan turned out not to help much. Six months after buying the player, Benitez decided that Keane wasn't the thing after all and shipped him back to Tottenham (who themselves would soon regret buying him) at a loss of £8 million. Virgin Trains took out newspaper advertisements that said, 'A Liverpool to London return faster than Robbie Keane'.

For all the spending, most of Liverpool's best performers during the Houllier–Benitez years were home-grown players who had cost the club nothing: Steven Gerrard, Michael Owen and Carragher himself. Another stalwart for a decade, centre-back Sami Hyppiä, had come for only £2.6 million from little Willem II in the Netherlands. In short, there didn't seem to be much correlation between transfer spending and quality.

In October 2009, after Benitez's sixth and last summer masterminding Liverpool's transfers, Britain's *Sunday Times* newspaper calculated the damage. It found that in those six years at Anfield, Benitez had spent £122 million more than he had received in transfer fees. Alex Ferguson's net spend at Manchester United in the same period was only £27 million, yet in those years United had won three titles to Liverpool's none. Arsène Wenger at Arsenal had actually received £27 million more in transfer fees than he had spent during the period, the newspaper estimated. From 2005 through 2009, Benitez had outspent even Chelsea on transfers. Yet at the end of this period he had the nerve to complain, 'It is always difficult to compete in the Premier League with clubs who have more money.' Ferguson later commented that he hadn't been able to see any 'strategy' in Benitez's buying. 'It amazed me that he used to walk into press conferences and say he had no money to spend,' Ferguson wrote in his 2013 autobiography. 'He was given plenty. It was the quality of his buys that let him down. If you set aside Torres and Reina, few of his acquisitions were of true Liverpool standard. There were serviceable players – Mascherano and Kuyt, hard-working players – but not real Liverpool quality.' (Mind you, with hindsight, Ferguson's assessment of Mascherano wasn't perfectly judged either.)

Benitez's failure at Liverpool was partially disguised by one night in Istanbul: the victory in the Champions League final of 2005, after having been 3–0 down to Milan after 45 minutes. However, as we'll discuss later in the book, a large chunk of luck is involved in winning knockout competitions – even leaving aside the fact that Benitez got his tactics wrong going into the game and had to turn his team upside down at half-time. The most reliable gauge of a team's quality is its performance in the league, and here Houllier and Benitez failed. Their expensive transfers didn't bring commensurate results. If you add in agents' fees, taxes on transfers and the constant disruption to the team, all this wheeling and dealing helps explain how Liverpool got left behind by Manchester United. To quote Carragher, 'As I know to my cost at Anfield, having money is no guarantee of success. The skill is spending it on the right players.'

The question, then, is what clubs can do to improve their status. If you are Liverpool now, owned by the American commodities trader John Henry, who understands statistics, and you have this knowledge of the relative importance of wages and unimportance of transfers, how can you win more matches? The obvious answer is to spend less of your income on transfers and more of it on wages. In general, it may be better to raise the pay of your leading players than to risk losing a couple of them and have to go out and buy replacements. Benitez had a net transfer spend of minus £122 million in six years. If he had merely balanced his transfer budget in that period, let alone made a profit as Wenger did, he could have raised his team's salaries by £20 million a year. In the 2008–2009 season, that boost would have given Liverpool a slightly larger wage bill than Manchester United. United won the title that year.

Clubs need to make fewer transfers. They buy too many Dioufs. But they will keep buying players, and the transfer market is probably the area in which clubs can most easily improve their performance. They need to learn from the few clubs and managers who have worked out some of the secrets of the transfer market.

Any inefficient market is an opportunity for somebody. If most clubs are wasting most of their transfer money, then a club that spends wisely is going to outperform. Indeed, a handful of wise buyers have consistently outperformed the transfer market: Brian Clough and his assistant-cum-soul mate Peter Taylor in their years at Nottingham Forest, Wenger during his first decade at Arsenal (though not since) and, most mysteriously of all, Olympique Lyon, who rose from obscure provincial club to a period of dictatorial rule over French football. From 2002 through 2008, Lyon won the French league seven times running. That era is now over, and the club subsequently made mistakes, as it tried and failed to compete with clubs with much higher revenues, such as Real Madrid or Manchester United. Lyon got tempted into paying big transfer fees for supposed 'stars' – for instance, gambling £18 million on the slow playmaker Yoann Gourcuff in 2010. It is now recovering through a new strategy focused on youth development. However, its seven-year reign remains an extraordinary feat. The usual way to win things in football is to pay high salaries. These clubs found a different route: they worked out the secrets of the transfer market.

There is a fourth master of the transfer market who is worth a look, even if he works mostly in a different sport across an ocean: Billy Beane, general manager of the Oakland A's baseball team. In his book *Moneyball*, Michael Lewis explains how Beane turned one of the poorest teams in baseball into one of the best by the simple method of rejecting what everyone in the sport had always 'known' to be true about trading for players. Lewis writes, 'Understanding that he would never have a Yankee-sized checkbook, Beane had set about looking for inefficiencies in the game.' It's odd how many of the same inefficiencies exist in football, too.

MARKET INCOMPETENCE

If we study these masters of transfers, it will help us uncover the secrets of the market that all the other clubs are missing. First of all, though, we present a few of the most obvious inefficiencies in the market. Although it doesn't take a Clough or a Beane to identify these, they continue to exist.

⚽ A New Manager Wastes Money

Typically the new manager wants to put his mark on his new team. So he buys his own players. He then has to 'clear out' some of his predecessor's purchases, usually at a discount.

Strangely, it's Tottenham during its years under a famously tight-fisted chairman, Alan Sugar, that provides the worst example. In May 2000 the club's manager, George Graham, paid Dynamo Kiev £11 million – nearly twice Spurs's previous record fee – for the Ukrainian striker Sergei Rebrov. Clearly Rebrov was meant to be a long-term investment.

But nine months later, Sugar sold his stake in Tottenham, whereupon the new owners sacked Graham and replaced him with Glenn Hoddle. Hoddle didn't appreciate Rebrov. The record signing ended up on the bench, was sent on loan to a Turkish team and in 2004 moved to West Ham on a free transfer.

This form of waste is common across football: a new manager is allowed to buy and sell on the pretence that he is reshaping the club for many years to come, even though in practice he almost always leaves pretty rapidly. A great example was Paolo Di Canio at Sunderland in 2013: in the six months and thirteen games that he managed the club, he spent £23.5 million on transfers, brought in fourteen players and let fifteen leave. When he was sacked, he left his successor, Gus Poyet, a team in last place in the Premier League. Tony Fernandes, the Queens Park Rangers chairman who spent a net £40 million on transfer fees while getting relegated from the Premier League in 2012/2013, told us mournfully: 'Sunderland's going through, in some ways, what we went through. The manager comes in, he changes everyone. If you change a manager, I don't care who they are, they're going to have a different opinion, right? Mark Hughes liked a certain player, Harry [Redknapp] doesn't like a certain player.'

But why couldn't a chairman just say no to a shopaholic new manager? 'You yourself see the results,' replied Fernandes, 'and you think, "God, we need some change."'

A manager typically doesn't care how much his wheeler-dealing costs: he doesn't get a bonus if the club makes a profit. Billy Beane told us: 'When you think of the structure of most sports teams, there is no benefit to a head coach in the NFL or a soccer manager to think years ahead. The person who has access to the greatest expenditure in the business has no risk in the decision-making.' He added that the exception to this rule was Wenger. Beane said, 'When I think of Arsène Wenger, I think of Warren Buffett [the billionaire investor]. Wenger runs his football club like he is going to own the club for one hundred years.'

⚽ **Stars of Recent World Cups or European Championships Are Overvalued (and so Are Superstars in General)**

The worst time to buy a player is in the summer when he's just done well at a big tournament. Everyone in the transfer market has seen how good the player is, but he is exhausted and quite likely sated with success. As Ferguson admitted after retiring from United: 'I was always wary of buying players on the back of good tournament performances. I did it at the 1996 European Championship, which prompted me to move for Jordi Cruyff and

Karel Poborský. Both had excellent runs in that tournament, but I didn't receive the kind of value their countries did that summer. They weren't bad buys, but sometimes players get themselves motivated and prepared for World Cups and European Championships and after that there can be a levelling off.'

Moreover, if you buy a player because of a good tournament, you are judging him on a very small sample of games. Take, for instance, Arsenal's purchase of the Danish midfielder John Jensen in July 1992. The previous month, Jensen had scored a cracking long-range goal in the European Championship final against Germany. Arsenal's then manager, George Graham, told the British media that Jensen was a goal-scoring midfielder.

But he wasn't. The goal against Germany had been a one-off. Jensen would go years without scoring for Arsenal. Over time this failing actually turned him into a cult hero: whenever he got the ball, even in his own penalty area, the crowd at Highbury would joyously shout, 'Shoot!' By the time Jensen left Arsenal in 1996, he had scored one goal in four years. (Arsenal fans printed T-shirts saying, 'I was there when John Jensen scored.') Graham's mistake had been to extrapolate from that single famous goal against Germany. This is an example of the so-called availability heuristic: the more available a piece of information is to the memory, the more likely it is to influence your decision, even when the information is irrelevant.

Signing these shooting stars fits what *Moneyball* calls 'a tendency to be overly influenced by a guy's most recent performance: what he did last was not necessarily what he would do next'.

Real Madrid are of course the supreme consumer of shooting stars. This is largely because the club's fans demand it. Madrid (or Spurs, or Marseille) probably aren't even trying to be rational in the transfer market. The club's aim is not to buy the best results for as little money as possible. When it bought the Colombian James Rodríguez for about £63 million in 2014, it may well have suspected it was paying more for him than the benefit it was likely to get in results or higher revenues. But big signings of this type (like Newcastle buying fragile Michael Owen from Madrid for £17 million in 2005) are best understood as marketing gifts to a club's fans, its sponsors and the local media. (It's hugely in the interest of *Marca*, the Spanish sports newspaper, for Real always to be buying players, or else hardly anyone would bother reading the paper over the three-month summer break.) As Ferguson explained Real's purchase of Cristiano Ronaldo in 2009: 'Madrid paid £80 million in cash for him, and do you know why? It was a way for Florentino Pérez, their president, to say to the world, "We are Real Madrid, we are the biggest of the lot."'

In 2013, Madrid's purchase of Gareth Bale for £85 million (a bit more than the club admitted to) made the same statement. Probably nobody at Madrid believed that the Welshman was twice as good a player as Mesut Özil – sold to Arsenal for half Bale's transfer fee – but he was deliciously new. His record fee only enhanced his glamour. There was a high risk that the money paid would not bring commensurate reward, but Real probably didn't care very much. The club is not a business. It's a populist democracy. Few football clubs pursue bean-counting quests for return on investment.

Raiola is so wary of Real's tendency to buy a player just for his name that in 2016 he advised Pogba not to move there. Real Madrid had just won the Champions League, and Raiola realized that although the club was keen to sign Pogba, it didn't actually need him. 'Another player for the cabinet. A trophy player, I call it.' By contrast, United needed Pogba.

Buying a big name (even if you don't need him) makes every person in the club feel bigger. Christoph Biermann, in his pioneering German book on football and data, *Die Fussball-Matrix*, cites the president of a Bundesliga club who said his coach got very excited whenever the club paid a large transfer fee.

Biermann explains, 'For this coach it was a status symbol to be allowed to buy players who cost many millions of euros. My car, my house, my star signing!' In short, it's conspicuous consumption. The very pointlessness of the purchase emphasizes that the purchaser is a prestigious high roller who can afford to waste money.

Buying names also gives supporters the thrill of expectation, a sense that their club is going somewhere, which may be as much fun as actually winning things. Buying big names is how these clubs keep their customers satisfied during the summer shutdown. (And some managers buy players to make themselves some illicit cash on the side, as George Graham did when he signed Jensen, but that's a subject for Chapter 5.)

Yet it turns out that the superstar isn't necessarily the player who has the biggest impact on a team's performance. (Note that Spurs didn't obviously suffer from losing Bale.) Nor is the decisive player the team's weakest link. Chris Anderson and David Sally argue in their book *The Numbers Game* that the best way to improve a team is to replace the worst player. But when Stefan and his University of Michigan colleague Guy Wilkinson looked at which players in the team had the biggest impact on results, they found it was neither the best nor the worst. Instead, it was the transfer fee of the second-best player that was most decisive. Here, they argue, is the best way to allocate a club's transfer budget across the eleven starters:

Best-paid player: 25.76%
Number two: 25.76%
Three: 18.41%
Four: 9.80%
Five: 9.80%
Six: 9.80%
Seven: 0.14%
Eight: 0.14%

Nine: 0.14%

Ten: 0.14%

Eleven: 0.14%

In other words, they found it would make sense for a club to spend almost nothing on its five cheapest players, since they have very little impact on results, and instead to devote about 70 per cent of the budget to the three best players. But in fact, clubs don't do this. Clubs in the Premier League in 2012–2013 typically spent more than 1 per cent of the budget even on the team's cheapest player, and about 8 per cent on the seventh cheapest. In short, they spread the money around more equally than they should. This might be because they think that massive differences in status within a team could unsettle the locker room. It might be because they want to keep some good players in reserve in case the best get injured. Or perhaps there just aren't enough stars in the sport to go around, especially not for smaller clubs, so relatively little money is spent on the top players. Still, we think an innovative club could do well by concentrating its budget upwards. Chris Anderson recently added an interesting nuance, saying that rather than target scarce superstars, clubs should try to assemble productive combinations of two, three or four players. 'Who plays well with whom?'

⊛ Certain Nationalities Are Overvalued

Clubs will pay more for a player from a 'fashionable' football country. American goalkeeper Kasey Keller says that in the transfer market, it's good to be Dutch. 'Giovanni van Bronckhorst is the best example,' Keller told Christoph Biermann. 'He went from Rangers to Arsenal, failed there, and then where did he go? To Barcelona! You have to be a Dutchman to do that. An American would have been sent straight back to DC United.'

For decades the most fashionable nationality in the transfer market was Brazilian. As Alex Bellos writes in *Futebol: The Brazilian Way of Life*: 'The phrase "Brazilian footballer" is like the phrases "French chef" or "Tibetan monk". The nationality expresses an authority, an innate vocation for the job – whatever the natural ability.' A Brazilian agent who had exported very humble Brazilian players to the Faroe Islands and Iceland told Bellos: 'It's sad to say, but it is much easier selling, for example, a crap Brazilian than a brilliant Mexican. The Brazilian gets across the image of happiness, party, carnival. Irrespective of talent, it is very seductive to have a Brazilian in your team.'

That sentiment may have been dented by Brazil's 1–7 defeat to Germany in the semi-final of the 2014 World Cup in a Belo Horizonte. In recent years Belgians have been coming into fashion, and after the 2014 World Cup Costa Ricans suddenly became the hot new items in every self-respecting club's wardrobe. After the little country got within a penalty shoot-out of reaching the semi-final, the total value of transfer fees for Costa Rican players moving internationally rose from $922,000 in 2013 to almost $10 million in 2014, said FIFA TMS. A wise club will buy unfashionable nationalities – Bolivians, say, or Belorussians – at discounts.

⚽ Gentlemen Prefer Blonds

One big English club noticed that its scouts who watched youth matches often came back recommending blond players. The likely reason: when you are scanning a field of twenty-two similar-looking players, none of whom yet has a giant reputation, the blonds tend to stand out (except, presumably, in Scandinavia). The colour catches the eye. So the scout notices the blond boy without understanding why. The club in question began to take this distortion into account when judging scouting reports. We suspect the bias towards blonds disappears when scouts are

assessing adult players who already have established reputations. Then the player's reputation – 'World Cup hero', say, or
perhaps 'Costa Rican' – guides the scout's judgement.

Similarly, Beane at the Oakland A's noticed that baseball
scouts had all sorts of 'sight-based prejudices'. They were suspicious of fat guys or skinny little guys or 'short right-handed
pitchers', and they overvalued handsome, strapping athletes
of the type that Beane himself had been at age seventeen.
Scouts look for players who look the part. Perhaps in football,
blonds are thought to look more like superstars.

This taste for blonds is another instance of the 'availability
heuristic': the piece of information is available, so it influences
your decision. Blonds stick in the memory.

* * *

The inefficiencies we have cited so far are so-called systemic
failures: more than just individual mistakes, they are deviations
from rationality. There is now decades of research by psychol-
ogists showing that even when people try to act rationally they
are prone to all sorts of cognitive biases that lead them astray.
If decision-makers are aware of these biases, they stand a better chance of avoiding them. All this is what you might call Transfer Market 101. To learn more about how to play the market, we
need to study the masters.

DRUNKS, GAMBLERS AND BARGAINS: CLOUGH AND TAYLOR AT FOREST

Probably nobody in English football has ever done a better job of
gaming the transfer market than Nottingham Forest's manager
Brian Clough (or 'Old Big Head', as he fondly called himself) and
his assistant Peter Taylor. As manager of Forest from 1975 to
1993, Clough managed to turn the provincial club into European
champions while turning a profit on the transfer market (and, as

we'll see in the next chapter, making enough on deals to slip the odd illegal bonus into his own pocket on the side).

Clough and Taylor met while playing in a 'Probables versus Possibles' reserve game at Middlesbrough in 1955. They seem to have fallen in love at first sight. Pretty soon they were using their free time to travel around the north watching football and coaching children together. Taylor never became more than a journeyman keeper, but Clough scored the fastest 200 goals ever notched in English football. Then, at the age of 27, he wrecked his right knee skidding on a frozen pitch on Boxing Day 1962. Three years later he phoned Taylor and said: 'I've been offered the managership of Hartlepool and I don't fancy it, but if you'll come, I'll consider it.' He then immediately hung up. Taylor took the bait, though to get in he had to double as Hartlepool's medical department, running on with the sponge on match days. It was the prelude to their legendary years together at Derby and Nottingham Forest.

David Peace's novel *The Damned United* – and Tom Hooper's film of it – is in large part the love story of Clough and Taylor. The men's wives only have walk-on parts. As in all good couples, each partner has his assigned role. As Peace's fictional Clough tells himself: 'Peter has the eyes and the ears, but you have the stomach and the balls.' Taylor found the players, and Clough led them to glory.

The relationship ended in 'divorce' in 1982, with Taylor's resignation from Forest. It seems that the rift had opened two years before, when Taylor published his excellent but now forgotten memoir *With Clough by Taylor*. More of this in a moment, because it is the closest thing we have to a handbook to the transfer market.

But clearly the couple had other problems besides literature. Perhaps Clough resented his partner because he needed him so badly – not the sort of relationship Clough liked. Indeed, the film *The Damned United* depicts him failing at Leeds partly because Taylor is not there to scout players, and finally driving down to Brighton with his young sons to beg his partner's forgiveness. He finds Taylor doing the gardening. At Taylor's insistence, he gets down on his knees in the driveway, and recites: 'I'm nothing without you. Please, please, baby, take me back.' And Taylor takes him back, and buys him the cut-price Forest team that wins two European Cups. Because, whatever their precise relationship, the duo certainly knew how to sign footballers. Here are a few of their coups:

⚽ Buying Gary Birtles from the non-league club Long Eaton for £2,000 in 1976, and selling him to Manchester United four years later for £1.25 million. A measure of what a good deal this was for Forest: United forked out £250,000 more for Birtles than they would pay to sign Eric Cantona from Leeds twelve years later, in 1992. Birtles ended up costing United about £86,000 a goal, and after two years was sold back to Forest for a quarter of the initial fee.

⚽ Buying Roy Keane from an Irish club called Cobh Ramblers for £47,000 in 1990, and selling him to Manchester United three years later for £3.75 million, then a British record fee.

⚽ Buying Kenny Burns from Birmingham City for £145,000 in 1977. Taylor writes in *With Clough by Taylor* that Burns was then regarded as 'a fighting, hard-drinking gambler . . . a stone overweight'. In 1978, English football writers voted Burns Footballer of the Year.

⚽ Twice buying Archie Gemmill cheaply. In 1970, when Gemmill was playing for Preston, Clough drove to his house and asked him to come to Derby. Gemmill refused. Clough said that in that case he would sleep outside in his car. Gemmill's wife invited him to sleep in the house instead. The next morning at breakfast Clough persuaded Gemmill to sign. The fee was £60,000, and Gemmill quickly won two league titles at Derby. In 1977 Clough paid Derby £20,000 and the now forgotten goalkeeper John Middleton to bring Gemmill to his new club, Forest, where the player won another league title.

If there is one club where almost every pound spent on transfers bought results, it was Forest under Clough. In the 1970s the correlation must have been off the charts: they won two European Cups with a team assembled largely for peanuts. Sadly there are no good financial data for that period, but we do know that even from 1982 to 1992, in Clough's declining years, after Taylor had left him, Forest performed as well on the field as clubs that were spending twice as much on wages. Clough had broken the usually iron link between salaries and league position.

Clough himself seemed to think that what explained Forest's success was his and Taylor's eye for players, rather than, say, any motivational gift or tactical genius. Phil Soar, the club's chairman and chief executive for four years at the end of the 1990s, told us: 'In hours of musings with Clough (I had to try to defend him from the bung charges) I obviously asked him what made this almost absurdly irrelevant little provincial club (my home town of course) into a shooting star. And he always used to say, "We had some pretty good players you know . . ."'

It's hard to identify all of the duo's transfer secrets, and if their rivals at the time had understood what they were up to, everyone would simply have imitated them. Taylor's book makes it clear that he spent a lot of time trying to identify players (like Burns) whom others had wrongly undervalued owing to surface characteristics; but then everyone tries to do that. Sometimes Forest did splash out on a player who was rated by everybody, like Trevor Francis, the first 'million-pound man', or Peter Shilton, whom they made the most expensive goalkeeper in British history.

Yet thanks to *With Clough by Taylor* we can identify three of the duo's rules. First, be as eager to sell good players as to buy them. 'It's as important in football as in the stock market to sell at the right time,' wrote Taylor. 'A manager should always be looking for signs of disintegration in a winning side and then sell the players responsible before their deterioration is noticed by possible buyers.' (Or in Billy Beane's words: 'You have to always be upgrading. Otherwise you're fucked.')

The moment when a player reaches the top of his particular hill is like the moment when the stock market peaks. Clough and Taylor were always trying to gauge that moment, and sell. Each time they signed a player, they would give him a set speech, which Taylor records in his book: 'Son, the first time we can replace you with a better player, we'll do it without blinking an eyelid. That's what we're paid to do – to produce the best side and to win as many things as we can. If we see a better player than you but don't sign him then we're frauds. But we're not frauds.' In 1981, just after Kenny Burns had won everything with Forest, the club offloaded him to Leeds for £400,000.

Second, older players are overrated. 'I've noticed over the years how often Liverpool sell players as they near or pass their thirtieth birthday,' notes Taylor in his book. 'Bob Paisley [Liverpool's then manager] believes the average first division footballer is beginning to burn out at thirty.' Taylor added, rather snottily, that that was true of a 'running side like Liverpool', but less so of a passing one like Forest. Nonetheless, he agreed with the principle of selling older players.

The master of that trade for many years was Wenger. Arsenal's manager is one of the few people in football who can view the game from the outside. In part, this is because he has a degree in economic sciences from the University of Strasbourg in France. As a trained economist, he is inclined to trust data rather than the game's received wisdom. Wenger is obsessed with the idea that in the transfer market clubs tend to over-value a player's past performance. That prompts them to pay fortunes – in transfer fees and salaries – for players who have passed their prime. FIFA TMS analysed the pay of players who moved internationally to Brazil, Argentina, England, Germany, Italy and Portugal in 2012, and found, remarkably, that the aver-age man earned his peak fixed salary at the ripe old age of 32.

Seniority is a poor rationale for pay in football (and probably in other industries). All players are melting blocks of ice. The job of the club is to gauge how fast they are melting, and to get rid of them before they turn into expensive puddles of water. Wenger often lets defenders carry on until their mid-thirties, but he usually gets rid of his midfielders and forwards much younger. He flogged Thierry Henry for £16 million aged twenty-nine, Patrick Vieira for £14 million aged twenty-nine, Emmanuel Petit for £7 million aged twenty-nine and Marc Over-mars for £25 million aged twenty-seven, and none of them ever did as well again after leaving Arsenal.

The average striker has peaked by age twenty-five, at least as measured by goals scored, as the French economist Bas-tien Drut has shown – think of Michael Owen, Robbie Fowler, Fernando Torres and Patrick Kluivert. Zlatan Ibrahimovic and Didier Drogba, who improved after their mid-twenties, are exceptions, probably because they never relied much on pace in the first place. Yet many clubs still insist on paying for past performance. Forty per cent of players bought by Premier League clubs from 2010 to 2016 were signed after passing their prime age, says Blake Wooster, chief executive of 21st Club, which advises football clubs. Manchester United's hiring on loan of the twenty-eight-year-old Colombian striker Radamel Falcao just after severe injury was an especially bad decision, as was Chelsea's repetition of United's mistake a year later. English clubs particularly overvalue Premier League experi-ence, says Wooster – it just isn't that important.

The same overvaluation of older players exists in baseball, too. The conventional wisdom in the game had always been that players peak in their early thirties. Then along came Bill James from his small town in Kansas. In his mimeographs, the father of sabermetrics showed that the average player peaked not in his early thirties, but at just twenty-seven. Beane told us, 'Nothing strangulates a sports club more than having older players on long contracts, because once they stop performing, they become immovable. And as they become older, the risk of injury becomes exponential. It's less costly to bring a young player. If it doesn't work, you can go and find the next guy, and the next guy. The downside risk is lower, and the upside much higher.'

Finally, Clough and Taylor's third rule: buy players with personal problems (like Burns, or the gambler Stan Bowles) at a discount. Then help them deal with their problems.

Clough, a drinker, and Taylor, a gambler, empathized with troubled players. While negotiating with a new player they would ask him a stock question, 'to which we usually know the answer,' wrote Taylor. It was: 'Let's hear your vice before you sign. Is it women, booze, drugs, or gambling?'

Clough and Taylor believed that once they knew the vice, they could help the player manage it. Clough was so confident of his psychological skills that in the early 1970s he even thought he could handle Manchester United's alcoholic womanizing genius George Best. 'I'd sort George out in a week,' he boasted. 'I'd hide the key to the drinks cabinet and I'd make sure he was tucked up with nothing stronger than cocoa for the first six months. Women? I'd let him home to see his mum and his sisters. No one else in a skirt is getting within a million miles of him.'

Taylor says he told Bowles, who joined Forest in 1979 (and, as it happens, failed there), 'Any problem in your private life must be brought to us; you may not like that but we'll prove to you that our way of management is good for all of us.' After a player confided a problem, wrote Taylor, 'if we couldn't find an answer, we would turn to experts: we have sought advice for our players from clergymen, doctors and local councillors.' Taking much the same approach, Wenger helped Tony Adams and Paul Merson combat their addictions.

All this might sound obvious, but the usual attitude in football is, 'We paid a lot of money for you, now get on with it,' as if mental illness, addiction or homesickness should not exist above a certain level of income.

It should be added that often the shrewdest actors in the transfer market are not managers at all, but agents. Raiola told us that he tries to decide which club a player should join, and then sometimes persuades the club to make the move happen. In his words, 'I always try to formulate a goal with a player: "That is what we want. We're not going to sit and wait and see where the wind blows."' For instance, in 2004, when his client Zlatan Ibrahimovic was a wayward young striker at Ajax, Raiola decided that the best place for him to learn professionalism (while earning good money) was Juventus. Juve may believe that it chose Zlatan, but that ain't necessarily so. In 2006 Raiola told his player that Juve's ship was sinking and it was time to join Inter. In 2009 he moved Ibrahimovic to Barcelona, then to Milan, and in 2012 (very much against the player's will) to Paris Saint-Germain. There the Swede earned €14 million a season in a top-class team while underfunded Milan sank.

In 2016, Raiola brought Ibrahimovic, Pogba and Henrikh Mkhitaryan to Manchester United. Why join a club that hadn't qualified for the Champions League and had underperformed for three years? Raiola told us: 'Because I think: you have to go to the club that needs you. This club needed them.'

He claims to have foreseen United's need as early as 2015, when the club signed the young forwards Anthony Martial and

Memphis Depay. Raiola insists he knew they wouldn't succeed. 'Not if you have to perform now,' he says, slapping a fat fist into a fat hand. 'Martial and Depay come in and say, "We have to carry Manchester United, a giant institution?" So already last year [2015] I told the people at United, "You'll have to put in a guy like Zlatan to restore the balance. Then the attention goes to Zlatan. He has the experience, and he dares to take the responsibility."'

Raiola continues, 'At clubs that understand me, I have three or four players. Now at United, and before at Juventus, Milan, Paris Saint-Germain.' In these cases, he says, he becomes a club's 'in-house consultant'. He then effectively shares a seat with the club's top management. No wonder that in 2017, Manchester United paid Everton £75 million (plus potential bonuses) for his client Romelu Lukaku.

Some readers may be surprised to hear us praise agents, who are always accused of breaking laws and sucking money out of the game. True, some of them are criminals (who often act in cahoots with clubs) but most agents get an unfair rap. We understand why clubs wish they didn't exist. A club would love to be able to tell a twenty-year-old player from a poor background who hasn't had any financial education, 'Here's your contract, congratulations. Now run up and see the chief executive, and he'll tell you your salary.' This sort of talk plays well with the fans. However, football needs professional agents, who will take a closer long-term interest in their players' well-being than any club ever will.

RELOCATION, RELOCATION, RELOCATION: THE RICE KRISPIES PROBLEM

Clough and Taylor understood that many transfers fail because of a player's problems off the field. In a surprising number of cases, these problems are the product of the transfer itself.

Moving to a job in another city is always stressful; moving to another country is even more so. The challenge of moving from Rio de Janeiro to Manchester involves cultural adjustments that just don't compare with moving from Springfield, Missouri to Springfield, Ohio. An uprooted footballer has to find a home and a new life for his family, and gain some grasp of the social rules of his new country. Yet European clubs that pay millions of pounds for foreign players are often unwilling to spend a few thousand more to help the players settle in their new homes. Instead the clubs have historically told them, 'Here's a plane ticket, come over, and play brilliantly from day one.' The player fails to adjust to the new country, underperforms, and his transfer fee is wasted. 'Relocation', as the industry of relocation consultants calls it, has long been one of the biggest inefficiencies in the transfer market.

All the inefficiencies surrounding relocation can be assuaged. Most big businesses know how difficult relocation is and do their best to smooth the passage. When a senior Microsoft executive moves between countries, a relocation consultant helps his or her family find schools and a house and learn the social rules of the new country. If Luther Blissett had been working for Microsoft, a relocation consultant could have found him Rice Krispies. An expensive relocation might cost £20,000, or 0.05 per cent of a large transfer fee. But in football, possibly the most globalized industry of all, spending anything at all on relocation was until very recently regarded as a waste of money.

Boudewijn Zenden, who played in four countries, for clubs including Liverpool and Barcelona, told us during his stint in Marseille in 2009:

It's the weirdest thing ever that you can actually buy a player for 20 mil, and you don't do anything to make him feel at home. I think the first thing you should do is get him a mobile phone and a house. Get him a school for the kids, get something for his missus, get a teacher in for both of them straightaway, because obviously everything goes with the language. Do they need anything for other family members, do they need a driving licence, do they need a visa, do they need a new passport? Sometimes even at the biggest clubs it's really badly organized.

Milan: best club ever. AC Milan is organized in a way you can't believe. Anything is done for you: you arrive, you get your house, it's fully furnished, you get five cars to choose from, you know the sky's the limit. They really say: we'll take care of everything else; you make sure you play really well. Whereas unfortunately in a lot of clubs, you have to get after it yourself. . . . Sometimes you get to a club, and you've got people actually at the club who take profit from players.

For any foreign player, or even a player who comes in new, they could get one man who's actually there to take care of everything. But then again, sometimes players are a bit – I don't want to say abusive, but they might take profit of the situation. They might call in the middle of the night, just to say there's no milk in the fridge. You know how they are sometimes.

Raiola laughingly endorses Zenden's assessment of golden-age Milan: 'I always used to say, "I think they'll come and put a pill on your tongue if you have a headache." Whereas Inter would say, "Here's your contract, go and figure it all out yourself."'

In football, bad relocations have traditionally been the norm. In 1961, two fifteen-year-olds from Belfast took the boat across the Irish Sea to become apprentices with Manchester United. George Best and Eric McMordie had never left home before. When they landed at Liverpool docks, they couldn't find anyone from the club to meet them. So they worked out for themselves how to get a train to Manchester, eventually found the stadium, and wound up feeling so lonely and confused that on their second day they told the club: 'We want to go back on the next boat.' And they did, recounts Duncan Hamilton in his biography of Best, *Immortal*. In the end, Best decided to give Manchester one last try. McMordie refused. He became a plasterer in Belfast after leaving school, though he did later make a respectable football career with Middlesbrough. Just imagine how the botched welcome of Best might have changed United's history.

Yet bad relocations continued for decades, like Chelsea signing Dutch cosmopolitan Ruud Gullit in 1996 and sticking him in a hotel in the ugly London dormitory town of Slough, or Ian Rush coming back to England from a bad year in Italy marvelling, 'It was like another country.' Many players down the years would have understood that phrase. In 1995 Manchester City bought the Georgian playmaker Georgi Kinkladze, who spoke no English, and stuck him on his own in a hotel for three months. No wonder his early games were poor. His improvement, writes Michael Cox in *The Mixer*, 'coincided with the arrival of two Georgian friends and his mother, Khatuna, who brought some home comforts: Georgian cognac, walnuts, and spices to make Kinkladze his favourite dishes.'

But perhaps the great failed relocation, one that a Spanish relocation consultant still cites in her presentations, was Nicolas Anelka's to Real Madrid in 1999.

A half-hour of conversation with Anelka is enough to confirm that he is self-absorbed, scared of other people and not someone who makes contact easily. Nor does he appear to be good at languages, because after well over a decade in England he still spoke very mediocre English. Anelka was the sort of expatriate who really needed a relocation consultant.

Real had spent £22 million buying him from Arsenal. The club then spent nothing on helping him adjust. On day one the shy, awkward twenty-year-old reported to work and found that there was nobody to show him around. He hadn't even been assigned a locker in the dressing room. Several times that first morning, he would take a locker that seemed to be unused, only for another player to walk in and claim it.

Anelka doesn't seem to have talked about his problems to anyone at Madrid. Nor did anyone at the club ask him. Instead he talked to *France Football*, a magazine that he treated as his newspaper of record, like a 1950s British prime minister talking to *The Times*. 'I am alone against the rest of the team,' he revealed midway through the season. He claimed to possess a video showing his teammates looking gloomy after he had scored his first goal for Real after six months at the club. He had tried to give this video to the coach, but the coach hadn't wanted to see it. Also, the other black Francophone players had told Anelka that the other players wouldn't pass to him. Madrid ended up giving him a forty-five-day ban, essentially for being maladjusted.

Paranoid though Anelka may have been, he had a point. The other players really didn't like him. And they never got to know him, because nobody at the club seems ever to have bothered to introduce him to anyone. As he said later, all that Madrid had told him was, 'Look after yourself.' The club seems to have taken the strangely materialistic view that Anelka's salary should determine his behaviour. But even in materialistic terms, that was foolish. If you pay £22 million for an immature young employee, it is bad management to make him look after himself. Wenger at Arsenal knew that, and he had Anelka on the field scoring goals.

Even a player with a normal personality can find emigration tricky. Tyrone Mears, an English defender who spent a year at Marseille, where his best relocation consultant was his teammate Zenden, said, 'Sometimes it's not a problem of the player adapting. A lot of the times it's the family adapting.' Perhaps the player's girlfriend is unhappy because she can't find a job in the new town. Or perhaps she's pregnant and doesn't know how to negotiate the local hospital, or perhaps she can't find Rice Krispies ('or beans on toast', added Zenden, when told about the Blissett drama). The club doesn't care. It is paying her boyfriend well. He simply has to perform.

Football clubs never used to bother with anything like an HR department. As late as about 2005, there were only a few relocation consultants in football, and most weren't called that, and were not hired by clubs. Instead they worked either for players' agents or for sportswear companies. If Nike or Adidas is paying a player to wear its shoes, it needs him to succeed. If the player moves to a foreign club, the sportswear company – knowing that the club might not bother – sometimes sends a minder to live in that town and look after him.

The minder gives the player occasional presents, acts as his secretary, friend and shrink, and remembers his wife's birthday. The minder of a young midfielder who was struggling in his first weeks at Milan said that his main task, when the player came home from training frustrated, lonely and confused by Italy, was to take him out to dinner. At dinner the player would grumble and say, 'Tomorrow I'm going to tell the coach what I really think of him,' and the minder would say, 'That might not be such a brilliant idea. Here, have some more spaghetti alle vongole.' To most players, this sort of thing comes as a bonus in a stressful life. To a few, it is essential.

After international transfers became common in the 1990s, some agents began to double as player minders. When the Dutch forward Bryan Roy moved from Ajax to Foggia in Italy in 1992, Raiola's personal service included spending seven months with Roy in Foggia, and helping paint the player's house. He later said, 'I already realized then that that this kind of guidance was very important in determining the success or failure of a player.'

Many of Raiola's players still treat him as an all-purpose helpmeet. Mario Balotelli once phoned him to say his house was on fire; Raiola advised him to try the fire brigade. Nowadays Raiola's younger players Facetime him. He waddles around his office imitating them as they hold up their phones to show him objects they want to buy: '"I'm walking through the house. What do you think of it?"' He chuckles fondly. He considers it all part of his job.

But part of the history of football is that agents such as Raiola have tended to be cleverer than the people who run clubs. Most clubs took a long time to see the value of relocation. Drogba in his autobiography recounts joining Chelsea from Olympique Marseille in 2004 for £24 million. He writes, 'I plunged into problems linked to my situation as an expatriate. Chelsea didn't necessarily help me.' Nobody at the club could help him find a school for his children. All Chelsea did to get him a house was put him in touch with a real estate agent who tried to sell him one for £10 million. For 'weeks of irritation' the Drogba family lived in a hotel while Drogba, who at that point barely spoke English, went house hunting after training.

All Chelsea's expensive foreign signings had much the same experience, Drogba writes. 'We sometimes laughed about it with Gallas, Makelele, Kezman, Geremi. "You too, you're still living in a hotel?" After all these worries, I didn't feel like integrating [at Chelsea] or multiplying my efforts.'

Chelsea were no worse than other English clubs at the time. The same summer Drogba arrived in London, Wayne Rooney moved thirty-five miles up the motorway from Everton to Manchester United and had an almost equally disorienting experience. United had paid a reported £25.6 million for him but then stuck its eighteen-year-old star asset in a hotel room. 'Living in such a place I found horrible,' reports Rooney in his

My Story So Far. The nearest thing to a relocation consultant he found at United seems to have been a teammate: 'Gary Neville tried to persuade me to buy one of his houses. I don't know how many he has, or whether he was boasting or winding me up, but he kept telling me about these properties he had.'

At a conference in Rome in 2008, relocation consultants literally lined up to tell their horror stories about football. Lots of them had tried to get into the sport and been rebuffed. A Danish relocator had been told by FC Copenhagen that her services weren't required because the players' wives always helped one another settle. Many clubs had never even heard of relocation. Moreover, they had never hired relocation consultants before, so given the logic of football, not hiring relocation consultants must be the right thing to do. One Swedish relocator surmised, 'I guess it comes down to the fact that they see the players as merchandise.'

The only relocation consultants who had penetrated football happened to have a friend inside a club or, in the case of one Greek woman, had married a club owner. She had told her husband, 'All these guys would be happier if you find out what their needs are, and address their needs.'

Another relocator had entered a German club as a language teacher and worked her way up. She said, 'I was their mother, their nurse, their real estate agent, their cleaning lady, their everything. They didn't have a car; they didn't speak the language.' Did her work help them play better? 'Absolutely.' The club was happy for her to work as an amateur, but as soon as she founded a relocation company, it didn't want her anymore. She had become threatening.

And so countless new signings continued to flop abroad. Clubs often anticipated this by avoiding players who seemed particularly ill-equipped to adjust. For instance, on average Latin Americans are the world's most skilful players. Yet historically, English clubs rarely bought them, because Latin

Americans don't speak English, don't like cold weather and don't tend to understand the core traditions of English football, such as drinking twenty pints of beer in a night. Few Latin Americans adjust easily to English football.

Instead of Latin Americans, English clubs traditionally bought Scandinavians. On average, Scandinavians are worse footballers than Latin Americans, but they are very familiar with English, cold weather and twenty pints of beer. Scandinavians adapted to England, and so the clubs bought them. But the clubs were missing a great opportunity. Anyone who bought a great Latin American player and hired a good relocation consultant to help him adjust would be onto a winner. Yet few clubs did. Years used to go by without any English club buying a Latin American.

In 2008 Manchester City took a gamble on Robinho. As a Brazilian forward who had had his moments in the World Cup of 2006, he was bound to be overvalued, and was also very likely to relocate badly. So it's little wonder that City paid a then British record transfer fee of £32.5 million for him, or that eighteen months later it gave up on him and sent him home to Santos on loan. Robinho never returned to English football. The experience obviously taught City a lesson, because for the next two years the club switched to a policy of buying only players who had already established themselves in England. It also finally began to take relocation seriously.

Bit by bit in recent years, the football business has become more intelligent. Way back in the mid-1990s, Liverpool had become one of the first clubs to hire some sort of employee to help new players settle. Ajax Amsterdam was another pioneer. The woman who first handled relocations at Ajax found that some of the problems of new players were absurdly easy to solve. When Steven Pienaar and another young South African player came to Amsterdam, they were teenagers, had never lived on their own before and suddenly found themselves sharing an apartment in a cold country at the other end of the earth. Inevitably, they put their music speakers on the bare floor and cranked up the volume. Inevitably, the neighbours complained. The South Africans had a miserable time in their building, until the woman from Ajax came around to see what was wrong and suggested they put their speakers on a table instead. They did. The noise diminished, their lives got easier, and that might just have made them better able to perform for Ajax.

Most clubs in the Premier League now have 'player care officers' – football code for relocation consultants. Some of these officers are full-timers, others not. Some do a serious job. Manchester City in particular learned from Robinho's failure. When we visited the club's training ground in 2012, on a wall just behind reception we saw a map of Manchester's surroundings, designed to catch the eyes of passing players. The map highlighted eight recommended wealthy towns and suburbs for them to live; not on the list was Manchester's city centre with its vibrant nightlife.

These recommendations are just the start. City's 'player-care department' aims to take care of almost every need a new immigrant might have, whether it's a nanny or a 'discreet car service'. Even before a new player signs, the club has already researched his off-duty habits and his partner's taste in restaurants. When he arrives for pre-season training, the club might say to him, 'Well, you're going to be busy for a couple of weeks, but here's a little restaurant your girlfriend might like.' It's not true that behind every successful footballer there is a happy woman (or man), but it probably does help.

In 2011 City signed the young Argentine striker Sergio Agüero. Nobody doubted his talent. However, many doubted whether he would adapt to English football and rainy provincial life. His transfer fee of £38 million seemed a gamble, even for Manchester City. But Agüero scored twice on debut. He finished his first English season with 30 goals, including the last-second strike in the last game of the season against QPR that won City their first league title since 1968. In part, Agüero succeeded thanks to City's excellence at relocation. Gavin Fleig, the club's head of performance analysis, told us: 'The normal transition time for a foreign player is considered in the industry to be about a year. Normally those players are in a hotel for the first three months. We were able to get from agreeing a fee to Sergio living in his house within two weeks, with a Spanish sat-nav system in his car, linked to the Spanish community in Manchester. We had our prize asset ready to go from day one.'

Then there was City's signing of Kevin De Bruyne from Wolfsburg in 2015. The Belgian was flown to Manchester in a private jet. 'It was like in a film,' his agent Patrick De Koster later recalled. 'We thought we'd have a lot of work finding a new house, opening a bank account, phone cards, a car. But everything was sorted in three hours. Incredible.'

Raiola says, 'In England the clubs have kept getting better at it. But it's just that in Italy it's done in a very Italian way, human: "Lovely, and we'll go and get a bite to eat, and how are the children?" In England it's much more businesslike. There's something to be said for both ways.'

Still, a few clubs continue to undervalue or even neglect relocation. One player care officer in the Premier League told us, 'Some very well-known managers have said to me they can't understand why you can possibly need it. They have said, "Well, when I moved to a foreign country as a player I had to do it myself." Well, yes, but that doesn't mean it's right. You probably had to clean boots, too, but nobody does that now.'

THE NICEST TOWN IN EUROPE: HOW OLYMPIQUE LYON BOUGHT AND SOLD

If you had to locate the middle-class European dream anywhere, it would be in Lyon. It's a town the size of Oakland, about two-thirds of the way down France, nestled between rivers just west of the Alps. On a warm January afternoon, drinking coffee outside in the eighteenth-century Place Bellecour where the buildings are as pretty as the women, you think: nice. Here's a wealthy town where you can have a good job, nice weather and a big house near the mountains.

Lyon also has some of the best restaurants in Europe, known locally as bouchons, or 'corks'. Even at the town's football stadium you can have a wonderful three-course pre-game meal consisting largely of intestines or head cheese, unless you prefer to eat at local boy Paul Bocuse's brasserie across the road and totter into the grounds just before kick-off. And then, for a remarkable decade or so, you could watch some very decent football, too.

Until about 2000 Lyon was known as the birthplace of cinema and nouvelle cuisine, but not as a football town. It was just too bourgeois. If for some reason you wanted football, you drove thirty-five miles down the highway to gritty proletarian Saint-Étienne. In 1987 Olympique Lyon, or OL, or les Gones (the Kids), was playing in France's second division on an annual budget of under £2 million. It was any old backwater provincial club in Europe. From 2002 to 2008 Lyon ruled French football. The club's ascent was in large part a story of the international transfer market. Better than any other club in Europe, for a while Lyon worked out how to play the market.

In 1987 Jean-Michel Aulas, a local software entrepreneur with the stark, grooved features of a Roman emperor, became club president. Aulas had played fairly good handball as a young man and had a season ticket at OL.

'I didn't know the world of football well,' he admitted to us in 2007 over a bottle of OL mineral water in his office beside the stadium (which he was already aiming to tear down and replace with a bigger one). Had he expected the transformation that he wrought? 'No.'

Aulas set out to improve the club step by step. 'We tried to abstract the factor "time",' he explained. 'Each year we fix as an aim to have sporting progress, and progress of our financial resources. It's like a cyclist riding: you can overtake the people in front of you.' Others in France preferred to liken Aulas to 'un bulldozer'.

In 1987 even the local Lyonnais didn't care much about les Gones. You could live in Lyon without knowing that football existed. The club barely had a personality, whereas Saint-Étienne was the 'miners' club' that had suffered tragic defeats on great European nights in the 1970s. Saint-Étienne's president at the time said that when it came to football, Lyon was a suburb of Saint-Étienne, a remark that still rankles. At one derby after Lyon's domination began, les Gones' fans unfurled a banner that told the Saint-Étienne supporters, 'We invented cinema when your fathers were dying in the mines.'

Aulas appointed local boy Raymond Domenech as his first coach. In Domenech's first season, OL finished at the top of the second division without losing a game. Right after that it qualified for Europe. Aulas recalled, 'At a stroke the credibility was total. The project was en route.'

It turned out that the second city in France, even if it was a bit bourgeois, was just hungry enough for a decent football club. The Lyonnais were willing to buy match tickets if things went well, but if things went badly, they weren't immediately waving white handkerchiefs in the stands and demanding that the president or manager or half the team be gotten rid of. Nor did the French media track the club's doings hour by hour. It's much easier to build for the long term in a place like that than in a 'football city' like Marseille or Newcastle. Moreover, players were happy to move to a town that is hardly a hardship posting. Almost nothing they got up to in Lyon made it into the gossip press. Another of Lyon's advantages: the locals had money. 'It allowed us to have not just a "popular clientele", but also a "business clientele",' said Aulas.

Talking about money is something of a taboo in France. It is considered a grubby and private topic. Socially, you're never supposed to ask anyone a question that might reveal how much somebody has. Football, to most French fans, is not supposed to be about money. They find the notion of a well-run football club humourless, practically American.

It therefore irritated them that Aulas talked about it so unabashedly. He might have invented the word 'moneyball'. Aulas's theme was that over time, the more money a club makes, the more matches it will win, and the more matches it wins, the more money it will make. In the short term you can lose a match, but in the long term there is a rationality even to football. (And to baseball. As *Moneyball* describes it, Beane believes that winning 'is simply a matter of figuring out the odds, and exploiting the laws of probability. . . . To get worked up over plays, or even games, is as unproductive as a casino manager worrying over the outcomes of individual pulls of the slot machines.')

In Aulas's view, rationality in football works more or less like this: if you buy good players for less than they are worth, you will win more games. You will then have more money to buy better players for less than they are worth. The better players will win you more matches, and that will attract more fans (and thus more money), because Aulas spotted early that most football fans everywhere are much more like shoppers than like religious believers: if they can get a better experience somewhere new, they will go there. He told us in 2007, 'We sold 110,000 replica shirts last season. This season we are already at 200,000. I think Olympique Lyon has become by far the most beloved club in France.'

Polls at the time suggested that he was right: in Sport+Markt's survey of European supporters in 2006, Lyon emerged as the country's most popular club just ahead of Olympique Marseille. This popularity was a recent phenomenon. In 2002, when Lyon first became champions of France, the overriding French emotion towards the club had still been, 'Whatever.' The editor of *France Football* magazine complained around that time that when Lyon won the title, his magazine didn't sell. But as the club won the title every year from 2002 to 2008 – the longest period of domination by any club in any of Europe's five biggest national leagues ever – many French fans began to care about them.

With more fans, Lyon made more money. On match days you could get a haircut at an official OL salon, drink an OL Beaujolais at an OL café, book your holiday at an OL travel agency and take an OL taxi to the game – and many people did. Lyon used that money to buy better players.

But for all Aulas's OL mineral water, what made the club's rise possible was the transfer market. On that warm winter's afternoon in Lyon, Aulas told us, 'We will invest better than Chelsea, Arsenal or Real Madrid. We will make different strategic choices. For instance, we won't try to have the best team on paper in terms of brand. We will have the best team relative to our investment.' Here are Lyon's rules of the transfer market:

⚽ *Use the wisdom of crowds.* When Lyon was thinking of signing a player, a group of men would sit down to debate the transfer. Aulas would be there, and Bernard Lacombe, once a bull-like centre-forward for Lyon and France, who served from the late 1980s until 2017 as the club's sporting director and then Aulas's 'special adviser'. Lacombe was known for having the best pair of eyes in French football. He coached Lyon from 1997 to 2000, but Aulas clearly figured out that if you have someone with his knack for spotting the right transfer, you want to keep him at the club long term rather than make his job contingent on four lost matches. The same went for Peter Taylor at Forest.

Whoever happened to be Lyon's head coach at the time would sit in on the meeting, too, and so would four or five other coaches. 'We have a group that gives its advice,' Aulas explained. 'In England the manager often does it alone. In France it's often the technical director.' Lacombe told us that the house rule was that after the group had made the decision, everyone present would then publicly get behind the transfer.

Like Lyon, the Oakland A's sidelined their manager, too. Like Lyon, the A's understood that he was merely 'a middle manager' obsessed with the very short term. The A's let him watch baseball's annual draft. They didn't let him say a word about it.

Lyon's method for choosing players is so obvious and clever that it's surprising all clubs don't use it. The theory of the 'wisdom of crowds' says that if you aggregate many different opinions from a diverse group of people, you are much more likely to arrive at the best opinion than if you just listen to one specialist. For instance, if you ask a diverse crowd to guess the weight of an ox, the average of their guesses will be very nearly right. If you ask a diverse set of gamblers to bet on, say, the outcome of a presidential election, the average of their bets is likely to be right, too. (Gambling markets have proved excellent predictors of all sorts of outcomes.) The wisdom of crowds fails when the components of the crowd are not diverse enough. This is often the case in American sports. But in European football, opinions tend to come from many different countries, and that helps ensure diversity.

Clough and Taylor at least were a crowd of two. However, the traditional decision-making model in English football is not 'wisdom of crowds', but short-term dictatorship. At many clubs the manager is still treated as a sort of divinely inspired monarch who gets to decide everything until he is sacked. Then the next manager clears out his predecessor's signings at a discount. Lyon, noted a rival French club president with envy, never had expensive signings rotting on the bench. It never had revolutions at all. It understood that the coach was only a temp. OL won its seven consecutive titles with four different coaches – Jacques Santini, Paul Le Guen, Gérard Houllier and Alain Perrin – none of whom, judging by their subsequent records, was exactly a Hegelian world-historical individual. When a coach left Lyon, not much changed. No matter who happened to be sitting on the bench, the team always played much the same brand of attacking football (by French standards).

Emmanuel Hembert grew up in Lyon supporting OL when it was still in the second division. Later, as head of the sports practice of the management consultancy firm A. T. Kearney in London, he was always citing the club as an example to his clients in football. 'A big secret of a successful club is stability,' Hembert explained over coffee in Paris a few years ago. 'In Lyon, the stability is not with the coach, but with the sports director, Lacombe.'

Even a club run as a one-man dictatorship can access the wisdom of crowds. Ferguson at Manchester United would regularly consult his players on transfers. When he was thinking of buying Eric Cantona from Leeds in 1992, writes Michael Cox, he 'asked centre-backs Gary Pallister and Steve Bruce for their opinion after Leeds's visit to Old Trafford. Both men suggested he was a difficult opponent because he took up unusual positions.' Ferguson bought Cantona. A year later, after United's players unanimously vouched that Nottingham Forest's Roy Keane was top-class, Ferguson broke the British transfer record to sign him too. And most famously, in 2003, on the plane home from a friendly in Portugal, United's defenders told Ferguson what a handful Sporting Lisbon's little-known teenage winger had been. The manager promptly forked out £12.24 million for Cristiano Ronaldo.

✤ *The best time to buy a player is when he is in his early twenties.* Aulas said, 'We buy young players with potential who are considered the best in their country, between twenty and twenty-two years old.' It's almost as if he has read *Moneyball*. The book keeps banging away about a truth discovered by Bill James, who wrote, 'College players are a better investment than high school players by a huge, huge, laughably huge margin.'

Baseball clubs traditionally preferred to draft high school players. But how good you are at seventeen or eighteen is a poor predictor of how good you will become as an adult. By definition, when a player is that young there is still too little information on which to judge him. Beane himself had been probably the hottest baseball prospect in the United States at seventeen, but he was already declining in his senior year at high school, and he then failed in the major leagues. Watching the 2002 draft as the A's general manager, he 'punches his fist in the air' each time rival teams draft schoolboys.

It's the same in football, where brilliant teenagers tend to disappear soon afterwards. Here are a few winners of the Golden Ball for best player at the under-seventeen World Cup since the 1980s: Philip Osundo of Nigeria, William de Oliveira of Brazil, Nii Lamptey of Ghana, Scottish goalkeeper James Will, Mohammed al-Kathiri of Oman, Sergio Santamaria of Spain and the Nigerian Sani Emmanuel. Once upon a time they must have all been brilliant, but none of them made it as adults. (Will ended up as a policeman in the Scottish Highlands playing for his village team, while Emmanuel seems to have drifted out of professional football aged twenty-three.) The most famous case of a teenager who flamed out is American Freddy Adu, who at fourteen was the next Pelé and Maradona. Ben Lyttleton, our partner in the Soccernomics consultancy, points out in his book *Edge*: 'It can be a challenge for a youngster who is suddenly successful – maybe even harder than coping with failure.' Many gifted teenagers are probably destroyed by acclaim and money. Liverpool is now trying to deal with the problem by capping salaries for first-year professionals (who are typically seventeen years old) at £40,000 a year.

Yet there's a converse to all these early flameouts: some ugly ducklings become swans. When Helmut Schulte was head of Schalke 04's youth academy, he had to decide over the futures of the teenaged Manuel Neuer and Mesut Özil. He remembers the fourteen-year-old Neuer as 'a totally normal keeper' who, moreover, was small. Schalke's coaches and scouts recommended getting rid of him. Schulte agonized over the decision, and finally decided to keep him. 'I overruled the others on three or four occasions during my time at Schalke, and it never worked out, except with Manuel.'

Soon after Neuer's narrow escape, he had a growth spurt, and got better. By the time he was about eighteen, he was playing for German national youth teams. Schulte recommended that he be given a senior contract. Schalke's general manager, Rudi Assauer, came to watch the kid at training. It happened that the session was a passing exercise, and Neuer could pass as well as any outfield player. Assauer, whose main criterion was skill on the ball, decided instantly to give him a contract.

The teenage Özil was even skinnier than Neuer. Nor did he seem particularly brilliant. Schalke soon let him go to the smaller local club Rot-Weiss Essen. Later, Schalke was asked whether Özil could train with their youth players in the mornings. 'As long as he doesn't disrupt training, he can join in', was the verdict. Like Neuer, Özil belatedly got better. However, when his dad announced, 'Mesut isn't a player for Schalke. He's a player for Barcelona or Real Madrid,' Schalke's coaches laughed at him. In short, when it comes to teenage footballers, the famous phrase of the Hollywood scriptwriter William Goldman applies: 'Nobody knows anything.'

Only a handful of world-class players in each generation, most of them creators – Pelé, Maradona, Rooney, Lionel Messi, Cesc Fàbregas – reach the top by the age of eighteen. Most players get there considerably later. Almost all defenders and goalkeepers do. You can be confident of their potential only when they are more mature.

Beane knows that by the time baseball players are in college – which tends to put them in Lyon's magical age range of twenty to twenty-two – you have a pretty good idea of what they will become. There is a lot of information about them. They have grown up a bit. They are old enough to be nearly fully formed, but too young to be expensive stars. FIFA TMS analysed international transfers to England in 2013, and found that players moving aged twenty to twenty-two were 18 per cent cheaper than players aged twenty-five to twenty-seven. Moreover, the younger players tended to have lower salaries, and higher future resale values.

Lyon always tried to avoid paying a premium for a star player's 'name'. Here, again, it was lucky to be a club from a quiet town. Its placid supporters and local media didn't demand stars. By contrast, the former chairman of a club in a much more raucous French city recalls, 'I ran [the club] with the mission to create a spectacle. It wasn't to build a project for twenty years to come.' A team from a big city tends to need big stars.

Football being barely distinguishable from baseball, the same split between big and small towns operates in that sport, too. 'Big-market teams', like the Boston Red Sox and the New York Yankees, hunt big-name players. Their media and fans demand it. In *Moneyball*, Lewis calls this the pathology of 'many foolish teams that thought all their questions could be answered by a single player'. (It's a pathology that may sound strangely familiar to European football fans.) By contrast, the Oakland A's, as a small-market team, were free to forgo stars. As Lewis writes, 'Billy may not care for the Oakland press but it is really very tame next to the Boston press, and it certainly has no effect on his behaviour, other than to infuriate him once a week or so. Oakland A's fans, too, were apathetic compared to the maniacs in Fenway Park or Yankee Stadium.' But as Beane told us, English football is 'even more emotional' than baseball. 'It's the biggest sport in the world,' he said. 'And that's the biggest league in the world, and then you put in sixty million people and a four-hour drive from north to south, and that's what you have.'

That's why most English football clubs are always being pushed by their fans to buy stars. Happy is the club that has no need of heroes. Lyon was free to buy young unknowns like Michael Essien, Florent Malouda, Mahamadou Diarra or Hugo Lloris just because they were good. And unknowns accept modest salaries. According to *L'Equipe*, in the 2007–2008 season Lyon spent only 31 per cent of its budget on players' pay. The average in the English Premier League was about double that. Like Clough's Forest, Lyon for many years performed the magic trick of winning things without paying silly salaries.

⚽ *Try not to buy centre-forwards.* Centre-forward is the most overpriced position in the transfer market, perhaps simply because centre-forwards are the players who score most and therefore end up on TV. Strikers in general also cost the most in salaries. In Italy's Serie A between 2009 and 2014, forwards earned an average of €1.1m, midfielders €820,000 and defenders €700,000, calculates French economist Bastien Drut.

Admittedly Lyon 'announced' itself to football by buying the Brazilian centre-forward Sonny Anderson for £12 million in 1999, but the club mostly scrimped on the position afterwards. Houllier left OL in 2007 grumbling that even after the club sold Malouda and Eric Abidal for a combined total of £23 million, Aulas still wouldn't buy him a centre-forward.

By contrast, goalkeeper is the most underpriced position in football's transfer market. Keepers also earn less than outfield players (according to a study by German economist Bernd Frick), even though they make a very large contribution to results and have longer careers than strikers.

⚽ *Help your foreign signings relocate.* All sorts of great Brazilians have passed through Lyon: Sonny Anderson; the long-time club captain Cris; the future internationals Juninho and Fred; and the world champion Edmilson. Most were barely known when they joined the club. Aulas explained the secret: 'Ten years ago [in 1997] we sent one of our old players, Marcelo, to Brazil. He was an extraordinary man, because he was both an engineer and a professional footballer. He was captain of Lyon for five years. Then he became an agent, but he works quasi-exclusively for OL. He indicates all market opportunities to us.' As a judge of players, Marcelo was clearly in the Lacombe or Peter Taylor class.

Marcelo said he scouted only 'serious boys'. Or as the former president of a rival French club puts it, 'They don't select players just for their quality but for their ability to adapt. I can't see Lyon recruiting an Anelka or a Ronaldinho.'

After Lyon signed the serious boys, it made sure they settled. Drogba noted enviously, 'At Lyon, a translator takes care of the Brazilians, helps them to find a house, get their bearings, tries to reduce as much as possible the negative effects of moving. . . . Even at a place of the calibre of Chelsea, that didn't exist.'

Lyon's 'translator', who worked full time for the club, sorted out the players' homesickness, bank accounts, nouvelle cuisine, and whatever else. Other people at the club educated the newcomers in Lyon's culture: no stars or show-offs.

✪ *Sell any player if another club offers more than he is worth.* This is what Aulas meant when he said, 'Buying and selling players is not an activity for improving the football performance. It's a trading activity, in which we produce gross margin. If an offer for a player is greatly superior to his market value, you must not keep him.' The ghost of Peter Taylor would approve.

Like Clough and Taylor, and like Billy Beane, Lyon never got sentimental about players. In the club's annual accounts, it booked each player for a certain transfer value. (Beane says, 'Know exactly what every player in baseball is worth to you. You can put a dollar figure on it.') Lyon knew that sooner or later its best players would attract somebody else's attention. Because the club expected to sell them, it replaced them even before they went. Ferguson at United also pursued a strategy of early replacement: 'I did feel sentimental about great players leaving us. At the same time, my eye would always be on a player who was coming to an end. An internal voice would always ask, "When's he going to leave, how long will he last?" Experience taught me to stockpile young players in important positions.'

Bringing in replacements before they are needed avoids a transition period or a panic purchase after the player's departure. Aulas explained, 'We will replace the player in the squad six months or a year before. So when Michael Essien goes [to Chelsea for £24 million], we already have a certain number of players who are ready to replace him. Then, when the opportunity to buy Tiago arises, for 25 per cent of the price of Essien, you take him.'

Before Essien's transfer in 2005, Aulas spent weeks proclaiming that the Ghanaian was 'untransferable'. He always said that when he was about to transfer a player, because it drove up the price. In his words, 'Every international at Lyon is untransferable. Until the offer surpasses by far the amount we had expected.'

⚽ *Don't worry too much about buying or keeping superstars.* Media and fans tend to obsess about the team's best player (as Essien was) but in fact you can usually let him go without damaging performance too much.

In general, most clubs don't spend their transfer budgets very rationally. Here, as a free service, are the thirteen main secrets of the transfer market in full:

1. A new manager wastes money on transfers; don't let him.
2. Use the wisdom of crowds.
3. Stars of recent World Cups or European Championships are overvalued; ignore them.
4. Both superstars and weakest links are overvalued: your top three players matter most.
5. Certain nationalities are overvalued.
6. Older players are overvalued.
7. Centre-forwards are overvalued; goalkeepers are undervalued.
8. Gentlemen prefer blonds: identify and abandon 'sight-based prejudices'.
9. The best time to buy a player is when he is in his early twenties.

10. Sell any player when another club offers more than he is worth.

11. Replace your best players even before you sell them.

12. Buy players with personal problems, and then help them deal with their problems.

13. Help your players relocate.

Alternatively, clubs could just stick with the conventional wisdom.

NOTE

1. Our view of transfers has been challenged in the book *Pay as You Play: The True Price of Success in the Premier League Era*, written by three Liverpool fans, Paul Tomkins, Graeme Riley and Gary Fulcher. The book is a treasure trove of interesting financial facts, with the added benefit that the authors are donating all their royalties to the children's charity Post Pals.

Pay as You Play uses data on transfer fees put together by Riley, by day a senior accountant at Adecco, by night an accomplished football statto. He collected figures for transfer fees paid by Premier League clubs since 1992–1993 from newspapers and any other sources he could find. It's a true labour of love.

The authors' approach to transfers is very reasonable. As they point out, adding up the total transfer fees paid for all the players in a squad over many years is misleading because of inflation in transfer fees – the average spend per player has roughly doubled in a decade. The authors therefore convert past transfer fees into the 'current transfer fee purchase price' (CTPP), using average transfer fees as an index. For example, Thierry Henry cost Arsenal an estimated £10.5 million in 1999, which converts to a CTPP of £24.6 million. By giving every transferred player a value, they can compare a team's spending on transfers to performance in the league.

When Tomkins then published a blog by Zach Slaton headlined 'Soccernomics Was Wrong: Transfer Expenditures Matter', naturally we sat up and took notice.

Slaton argued that transfer fees were just as good a predictor of league position as is wage spending. One of us (Stefan) contacted Slaton and the authors to find out a bit more about what was going on. Riley kindly showed us the data he had used to calculate his index.

It then became clear where the differences lay. The *Pay as You Play* index refers only to transfer fees paid. But when we said that spending on transfers bears little relation to where a club finishes, we were referring to *net* transfer spending – transfer fees paid minus transfer fees received. (We have clarified that point in this edition.) The net figure is the crucial one, because hardly any clubs can just keep buying players without occasionally selling some to stop their spending from going too far out of whack. Once you look at net spending, it's clear that very few clubs run successful transfer policies: their net spending barely predicts where they finish in the league. If managers and clubs were valuing players accurately, you'd expect to see a significant correlation between net spending and performance, at least over time.

The reliability of the *Pay as You Play* data is also doubtful. Data on wages is pretty accurate: it's drawn from each club's audited financial accounts, which are publicly available in England. But transfer fees quoted in the media are less trustworthy. Take the following comparison of transfer fees paid for members of Arsenal's 2008–2009 squad from *Pay as You Play* data and from another reputable source, transfermarkt.co.uk:

Player	Pay as You Play (£)	transfermarkt.co.uk (£)
Mannone	350,000	440,000
Almunia	500,000	0
Silvestre	750,000	836,000
Song	1,000,000	3,520,000
Eboue	1,540,000	1,936,000
Fabiański	2,000,000	3,828,000
Vela	2,000,000	2,640,000
Fàbregas	2,250,000	2,816,000
Van Persie	3,000,000	3,960,000
Denilson	3,400,000	4,400,000
Diaby	3,500,000	2,640,000
Gallas	5,000,000	0
Ramsey	5,000,000	5,632,000
Sagna	6,000,000	7,920,000
Adebayor	7,000,000	8,800,000
Walcott	12,000,000	9,240,000
Nasri	12,800,000	14,080,000
Arshavin	15,000,000	14,520,000

There are clearly some big differences here. No wonder, as transfer fees are almost never officially disclosed, only leaked to the media by the club or the player's agent, generally with a spin. Nonetheless, and given these caveats, the *Pay as You Play* index does quite well at explaining the variation in team performance in the Premier League for the years covered.

That's hardly surprising. A club that spends a big transfer fee buying a player will almost always also spend a big sum on his wages. So in this sense, in the very short term, transfer fees can be almost as good an explanation of success as wages. However, real success in the transfer market means buying cheap and selling dear. For that you need to know a club's net spending, which shows very little correlation with team performance. The transfer market remains far from efficient.

THE WORST BUSINESS IN THE WORLD: WHY FOOTBALL CLUBS HAVEN'T MADE MONEY

A man we know once tried to do business with a revered institution of English football. 'I can do business with stupid people,' he said afterwards, 'and I can do business with crooks. But I can't do business with stupid people who want to be crooks.'

It was a decent summary of the football business, if you can call football a business. People often do. William McGregor, the Scottish draper who founded the English Football League in 1888, was probably the first person to describe football as 'big business', but the phrase has since become one of the game's great clichés. In fact, McGregor was wrong. For almost all the game's history, football was neither big business nor good business. It arguably wasn't even business at all. But that may now be changing. For the first time ever, the world's biggest clubs are starting to turn into decent-sized and reasonably well-run businesses.

'BIG BUSINESS'

Few people have heard of a British company called BBA Aviation. It started out in 1879 making conveyor belts in Dundee, but over time it morphed into a supplier to the aeroplane industry. Mostly it now helps fuel, clean, repair and maintain planes. This is pretty unglamorous work, and BBA is an unglamorous company. It's in the FTSE 250, meaning that it ranks as one of the 250 biggest companies on the London stock market. In 2016 it had revenues of £1.59 billion, and operating profits of £123 million. But BBA, whose headquarters are on a quiet street in Mayfair, is not big business. For comparison: in 2016 the biggest company on the London market, Royal Dutch Shell, had revenues that were 106 times larger.

But compared with any football club, BBA is a behemoth. Manchester United's revenues in 2015/2016 were £581.2 million. That's a tidy sum, the highest any English club has ever achieved. However, it's just over a third of BBA's revenues, and 0.3 per cent of Shell's. To put it very starkly: in terms of revenue, Manchester United would still only be the 74th largest company in Finland. (Just ahead of them on the Finnish list is something called Raha-automaattiyhdistys.)

Because hardly any clubs are quoted on the stock market anymore, it is hard to work out their value. But we can certainly say that not even Real Madrid or Barcelona would get anywhere near the S&P 500.

And if we ranked clubs by their profits, the results would be embarrassing. Most clubs make losses or meagre profits, and fail to pay any dividends to their shareholders. They are chasing glory, not riches.

Whichever way you measure it, no football club is a big business. Even the world's biggest clubs are dwarfed by BBA. As for all the rest, the author Alex Fynn noted in the 1990s that the average English Premier League club had about the same revenue as a British supermarket – not a chain of supermarkets, but one single large Tesco store. True, Premier League clubs have grown a lot since then. However, Fynn's comparison still remains relevant. UEFA's Club Licensing Benchmarking Report for the financial year 2016 stated that there were 48 clubs in Europe that had annual revenues above €100 million. Well, Tesco's 45 superstores in the UK have average annual sales of around the €100 million mark. Europe's ten biggest clubs probably have about the same revenues as the world's ten largest hypermarkets, but below that clubs are typically much smaller than supermarkets.

A good way to visualize the size of the football industry is to visit the headquarters of UEFA, the European football association, in the Swiss town of Nyon. The building has a lovely view of Lake Geneva, but it looks like the offices of a small insurance company. Football is small business.

This feels like a contradiction. We all know that football is huge. Some of the most famous people on earth are footballers, and the most watched television programme in history is generally the most recent World Cup final. Nonetheless, football clubs are puny businesses. This is partly a problem of what economists call appropriability: so far football clubs haven't been able to make money out of (haven't appropriated) more than a tiny share of our love of football.

It may be that season tickets are expensive and replica shirts overpriced, but buying these things once a year represents the extravagant extreme of football fanaticism. Most football is watched not from £1,500 seats in the stadium but on TV – sometimes at the price of a subscription, often at the price of watching a few commercials, or for the price of a couple of beers in a bar.

Compare the cost of watching a game in a bar with the cost of eating out or watching a movie, let alone going on vacation.

Worse still, football generates little income from reruns of matches. And watching football (even on TV) is only a tiny part of the fan's engagement with the game. There are internet sites to be trawled and a growing array of video games to keep up with. Then there is the football banter that passes time at the dinner table, the bus stop and above all on social media. All this entertainment is made possible by football clubs, but they cannot appropriate a penny of the value we attach to it. Chelsea cannot charge us for talking or reading or thinking about Chelsea. As the former Dutch international Demy de Zeeuw said, 'There are complaints that we [players] earn too much, but the whole world earns money from your success as a player: newspapers, television, companies.' In fact, the world earns more from football than the football industry itself does.

BAD BUSINESS

Football is not merely a small business. It has also historically been a bad one. Until very recently, and to some degree still today, anyone who spent any time inside football soon discovered that just as oil was part of the oil business, stupidity was part of the football business.

This became obvious when people in football encountered people in other industries. Generally the football people got exploited because people in other industries understood business better. In 1997 Peter Kenyon, then chief executive of the sportswear company Umbro, invited a few guests to watch a European game at Chelsea, the club he would end up running a few years later. After the game, Kenyon took his guests out for dinner. Over curry he reminisced about how the sportswear industry used to treat football clubs. Before the 1980s, he said, big English clubs paid companies like Umbro to supply their clothing. It was obviously great advertising for the gear makers to have some of England's best players running around in their clothes, but the clubs had not yet figured that out. And so sportswear companies used to get paid to advertise themselves.

In fact, when England hosted the World Cup in 1966, it hoped merely that its usual supplier would give it a discount on shoes and shirts, 'particularly in the opening ceremony . . . with the Queen present,' writes Mihir Bose in *The Spirit of the Game*. As it happened, the English did even better: Umbro offered to supply the team for free. The company must have been pleased when England won the tournament.

Ricky George saw the ignorance of football in those days from point-blank range. In 1972, when George scored the famous goal for little semi-professional Hereford that knocked Newcastle out of the FA Cup, he was working for Adidas as a 'football PR'. His job was to represent Adidas to England players, former world champions like Bobby Moore, Bobby Charlton and Gordon Banks. There was little need to persuade them to choose Adidas. Most of them wore the three stripes for free anyway. George says, 'It is quite a fascinating thing if you compare it with today. There were no great sponsorship deals going on. All that happened is that you would give the players boots. But even then, at the beginning of every season the clubs would go to their local sports retailer and just buy twenty, thirty pairs of boots and hand them out. For a company like Adidas, it was the cheapest type of PR you could imagine.'

Only on special occasions did George have to pay players. 'When it came to a big international, and the game was going to be televised, my job was to go to the team hotel, hang around there, make myself known, and a couple of hours before the game I would go into the players' rooms and paint the white stripes on their boots with luminous paint so it was more visible. My bosses used to be keenly watching the television to make sure the stripes were visible, and if they weren't I would be in for bollocking.'

For this service, an England player would receive £75 per match – not a princely sum even in 1972. George recalls, 'Bobby [Moore], the most charming of people, didn't take the money on the day of the game. He just used to say to me, "Let it build up for a few games, and I'll ring you when I need it." And that's what he did.' Then the most famous defender of the era would pocket a cumulative few hundred pounds for having advertised an international brand to a cumulative audience of tens of millions.

Only in the late 1980s did English football clubs discover that people were willing to buy replicas of their team shirts. That made it plain even to them that their gear must have some value. They had already stopped paying sportswear companies for the stuff; now they started to charge them.

Over time, football clubs have found new ways of making money. However, the ideas almost never came from the clubs themselves. Whether it was branded clothing, or the gambling pools, or television, it was usually people in other industries who first saw there might be profits to be made. It was Rupert Murdoch who went to English clubs and suggested putting them on satellite TV; the clubs would never have thought of going to him. In fact, the clubs often fought against new moneymaking schemes. Until 1982 they refused to allow any league games to be shown live on TV, fearing that it might deter fans from coming to the stadium. Clubs couldn't grasp that games on television meant both free money and free advertising. There is now a good deal of research into the question of how many fans are lost when a game is shown on TV. Almost all the evidence shows that the number is tiny, and that the gate revenue that would be lost is usually well below the amount that would be made from selling extra matches for television coverage.

It took clubs a long time to realize just how much football was worth to television. When Greg Dyke was chairman of the UK's ITV Sport in the 1980s, he offered five big clubs £1 million each for the TV rights for English football. In 2013, when

Dyke was chairman of the FA, he fondly recalled: 'It's funny now, when you look at the money that's involved: these chairmen had eyes bulging. They couldn't believe it.' In total, Dyke bought the entire TV rights for English professional football for £12 million a year. Soon afterwards, he went up to Nottingham to try to talk Brian Clough, Forest's then manager, into coming back on TV as a pundit. When Dyke arrived at the club, Clough came up to him and said: 'Thank you. I want to shake your hand, Mr Dyke, because you're the first person that's given football what it's due: twelve million quid.'

In 1992 Murdoch began paying about £60 million a season for the television rights to the new Premier League. As of 2018 the league is getting more than 25 times as much a season from British TV companies alone. 'I've been screwed by television,' admitted Sir John Hall, the then Newcastle chairman, one rowdy night at Trinity College Dublin in 1995. 'But I'll tell you one thing: I won't be screwed again.'

Or take the renovation of English stadiums in the early 1990s. It was an obvious business idea. Supermarkets don't receive customers in sheds built in the Victorian era and gone to seed since. They are forever renovating their stores. Yet football clubs never seem to have thought of spending money on their grounds until the Taylor Report of 1990 forced them to. They did up their stadiums, and bingo: more customers came.

All this proves how much like consumers football fans are. It's not just that they come running when a team does well (although they do). But in addition, it seems that football can quickly become popular across a whole country. All teams then benefit, but particularly those that build nice new stadiums where spectators feel comfortable and safe. That would explain why the three English clubs whose crowds grew fastest over the 1990s were Manchester United, Sunderland and Newcastle. Later, when Arsenal moved from Highbury to the much larger Emirates, the new stadium filled up despite the fact that the club stopped winning trophies. In other leagues, clubs such as Juventus, Ajax and Celtic have also drawn big new crowds to their new grounds. There is such a close link between building a nice stadium and drawing more spectators that the traditional fans' chant of 'Where were you when you were shit?' should be revised to 'Where were you when your stadium was shit?'

Yet like almost all good business ideas in football, the Taylor Report was imposed on the game from outside. Football clubs are classic late adopters of new ideas. Several years after the internet emerged, Liverpool, a club with millions of fans around the world, still did not have a website. As we'll see in Chapter 6, clubs were equally late onto social media. It's no wonder that from 1992 to May 2008, even before the financial crisis struck, forty of England's ninety-two professional clubs had been involved in insolvency proceedings, some of them more than once. The proportions have been even higher in Spanish football in recent years.

HOW THE TRIBE CHOOSES ITS CHIEFS

Rather than stack up endless examples of the historical dimness of football clubs, let's take one contemporary case study: how clubs have traditionally hired the person they believe to be their key employee, the manager. Fans are still asking themselves how Steve McClaren ever got to be appointed England manager in 2006, but in fact it is unfair to single him out. The profusion of fantasy football leagues, in which office workers masquerade as coaches, indicates the widely held suspicion that any fool could do as well as the people who actually get the jobs. The incompetence of football managers may have something to do with the nonsensical and illegal methods by which they are typically recruited.

Football 'is a sad business', says Bjørn Johansson, who runs a headhunting firm in Zurich. Like his colleagues in headhunting, Johansson is never consulted by clubs seeking managers. Instead a club typically chooses its man using the following methods.

⚽ The New Manager Is Hired in a Mad Rush

In a panel at the International Football Arena conference in Zurich in 2006, Johansson said that in 'normal' business, 'an average search process takes four to five months.' In football, a club usually finds a coach within a couple of days of sacking his predecessor. 'Hesitation is regarded as weak leadership,' explained another panellist in Zurich, Ilja Kaenzig, then general manager of the German club Hannover 96. Brian Barwick, the English Football Association's former chief executive, has noted that McClaren's recruitment 'took from beginning to end nine weeks', yet the media accused the FA of being 'sluggish'. If only it had been more sluggish. Succession planning, common in business, is almost unheard of in football.

One rare slow hire became perhaps the most inspired choice in the game's modern history: Arsenal's appointment of Arsène Wenger in 1996. The Frenchman, working in Japan, was not free immediately. Arsenal waited for him, operating under caretaker managers for weeks, and was inevitably accused of being sluggish. Similarly, in 1990 Manchester United's chairman, Martin Edwards, was derided as sluggish when he refused to sack his losing manager, Alex Ferguson. Edwards thought that in the long term, Ferguson might improve.

⚽ The New Manager Is Interviewed Only Very Cursorily

In 'normal' business, a wannabe chief executive writes a business plan, gives a presentation and undergoes several interviews. In football, a club rings an agent and offers the job.

⚽ The New Manager Is Always a Man

For over a century, it was unthinkable that the manager be a woman, as stupid fans and players would object. Only in

2014 did Clermont in France's Ligue 2 finally break that taboo, appointing Corinne Diacre. 'Hiring a woman as a coach has not changed my daily life,' Clermont's president Claude Michy told Ben Lyttleton years later. 'The sun still rises in the east. I don't feel like I'm an innovator, just because I hired someone with the competence and the skills to do a job.' In 2015 *France Football* magazine voted Diacre best coach in Ligue 2. In her first three seasons the team always finished higher in the table than its budget would have predicted. In August 2017 she was named coach of France's women's team.

But that was partly because no other team in male football – which, after all, is where the money is – seemed to want her. Almost all the world's men's football clubs still discriminate illegally against women.

In these clubs, the new manager is not only invariably male, but also almost always white, with a conservative haircut, aged between thirty-five and sixty, and a former professional player. Clubs know that if they choose someone with that profile, then even if the appointment turns out to be terrible they won't be blamed too much, because at least they will have failed in the traditional way. As the old business saying went, 'Nobody ever got fired for buying IBM.'

The idea is that there is something mystical about managing a team, something that only former players can truly understand. Naturally, former players like this idea. Once in the 1980s, when Kenny Dalglish was in his first spell managing Liverpool, a journalist at a press conference questioned one of his tactical decisions. Dalglish deadpanned, in his almost impenetrable Scots accent, 'Who did you play for, then?' The whole room laughed. Dalglish had come up with the killer retort: if you didn't play, you couldn't know.

A former chairman of a Premier League club told us that the managers he employed would often make that argument. The chairman (a rich businessman who hadn't played) never knew how to respond. He hadn't played, so if there really was some kind of mystical knowledge you gained from playing, he wouldn't know. Usually he would back down.

'Who did you play for, then?' is best understood as a job protection scheme. Ex-players have used it to corner the market in managerial jobs.

But in truth, their argument never made sense. There is no evidence that having been a good player (or being white and of conservative appearance) is an advantage for a football manager. Way back in 1995 Stefan did a study of 209 managers in English football from 1974 to 1994, looking at which ones consistently finished higher in the league than their teams' wage bills predicted. He reported:

> I looked at each manager's football career, first as a player (including number of games played, goals scored, position on the field, international appearances, number of clubs played for) and then as a manager (years of experience, number of clubs played for, and age while in management). Playing history provides almost no guide, except that defenders and goalkeepers in particular do not do well (most managers were midfielders, forwards are slightly more successful than average).

Dalglish finished at the top of Stefan's sample of 209 managers, just ahead of John Duncan, Bob Paisley, George Curtis, Ken Furphy and Bill Shankly. (Clough wasn't in the sample because no good financial data existed for his clubs, Derby County and Nottingham Forest, or else he'd have surely won. Stefan recently updated his study, and we'll say more about his new findings in Chapter 8.)

Dalglish was a great player and an overperforming manager. However, Bobby Moore, another great player, was 193rd on the managers' list. Taken overall, a good career as a player predicted neither success nor failure as a manager. The two jobs just didn't seem to have much to do with each other. As Arrigo Sacchi, a terrible player turned great manager of Milan, phrased it, 'You don't need to have been a horse to be a jockey.'

A horse's knowledge doesn't help a jockey. Here is one player-turned-manager testifying anonymously in *Football Management*, an insightful book by Sue Bridgewater of Warwick Business School:

> I got the job and on the first day I showed up and the secretary let me into my office, the manager's office with a phone in, and I didn't know where I was supposed to start. I knew about football, I could do the on-pitch things, but I had never worked in an office and I just sat there and I waited for something to happen but no one came in, so after a while I picked up the phone and rang my mum.

Even this man's claim that 'I knew about football, I could do the on-pitch things' is dubious. Does Diego Maradona know more about the game than José Mourinho? Did Roy Keane's knack for geeing up teammates on the field translate once he had become a jockey?

Playing and coaching are different skill sets. Mourinho, who barely ever kicked a ball for money, is match for match among the most successful coaches in football's history. When Milan's then coach Carlo Ancelotti noted his almost non-existent record as a player, the Portuguese replied, 'I don't see the connection. My dentist is the best in the world, and yet he's never had a particularly bad toothache.' Asked why failed players often become good coaches, Mourinho said, 'More time to study.' They also have to have provided some evidence that they are good coaches, because nobody is going to hire them based on their playing careers.

The problem with ex-pros may be precisely their experience. Having been steeped in the game for decades, they just know what to do: how to train, who to buy, how to talk to their players. They don't need to investigate whether these inherited prejudices are in fact correct. Rare is the ex-pro who realizes, like Billy Beane at the Oakland A's, that he needs to jettison what he learned along the way. Michael Lewis writes in *Moneyball*, 'Billy had played pro ball, and regarded it as an experience he needed to overcome if he wanted to do his job well. "A reformed alcoholic," is how he described himself.' Even Ancelotti seems to have changed his mind about the usefulness of a playing career. Once a canny midfielder with Milan, and now a longstanding A-list coach, he told us in 2013: 'Experience as a player can help you just in one situation: I can understand what the players are thinking. But the job is different. You have to study to be a manager.'

In the world's most innovative football country, Germany, ex-players have now lost their monopoly on managerial jobs. On the German football federation's annual training course to certify professional coaches, an average of 16 of the 24 places are reserved for people who didn't play professionally. The head of the course, Frank Wormuth, told the Dutch online newspaper De Correspondent that although it helps to know 'the smell of the stables' in professional football, 'that's only one aspect of being a coach. How are you pedagogically, analytically, communicatively? Ex-pros often have less of an eye for that.'

Successful German coaches of recent times include Thomas Tuchel, who played eight games in the Second Bundesliga, Roger Schmidt, who was a manager in a car factory, and Julian Nagelsmann, who didn't play a single professional game before becoming the successful coach of Hoffenheim aged twenty-eight. Nagelsmann's career would have been unthinkable in all other major football countries. It's their loss.

But even outside Germany, former great players like Roy Keane, Ruud Gullit, Marco van Basten, Tony Adams and Diego Maradona are no longer in demand as managers of serious clubs. This looks like another indication that football is becoming less stupid.

⚽ Immediate Availability

The new manager is appointed either because he is able to start work immediately (often as a result of having just been sacked), or because he has achieved good results over his career, or, failing that, because he achieved good results in the weeks preceding the appointment. McClaren became England manager only because his team, Middlesbrough, reached the UEFA Cup final in 2006 and avoided relegation just as the English Football Association was deciding who to pick. By the time Middlesbrough were thumped 4–0 by Sevilla in the final, McClaren already had the job.

The problem is that there is a lot randomness in results in the short term. The underlying patterns can only be identified once you let the law of large numbers do its work. Match results (like daily movements in share prices) are a random walk, and only after many observations can you start to see the trend. Consider the main candidates to manage England in 1996: Bryan Robson, Frank Clark, Gerry Francis and the eventual choice, Glenn Hoddle. Today none of them works as a manager, none had his last job in the Premier League and none will probably work that high again. They were in the frame in 1996 because they had had good results recently, had been good players and were English – another illegal consideration in hiring. Or think of the Football Association's back-to-back appointments of the immediately available Englishmen Sam Allardyce and Gareth Southgate in 2016.

⚽ Star Power

The new manager is traditionally chosen not for his alleged managerial skills but because his name, appearance and skills at public relations are expected to impress the club's fans, its players and the media. It was brave of Milan to appoint the unknown Sacchi, and Arsenal the unknown Wenger. Tony Adams, Arsenal's then captain, doubted the obscure foreigner on first sight. In his autobiography, *Addicted*, the player recalls thinking, 'What does this Frenchman know about football? He wears glasses and looks more like a schoolteacher. He's not going to be as good as George. Does he even speak English properly?'

A manager must above all look like a manager. Clubs would rather use traditional methods to appoint incompetents than risk doing anything that looks odd.

⚽ Bad Staff

The most obvious reason football was such an incompetent business for so long is that football clubs tended to hire incompetent staff. The manager is only the start of it. Years ago one of us requested an interview with the chairman of an English club quoted on the stock market. The press officer asked me to send a fax (a 1980s technology revered by football clubs well into the twenty-first century). I sent it. She said she never got it. On request I sent three more faxes to different officials. She said none arrived. This is quite a common experience for football journalists. Because football clubs are the only businesses that get daily publicity without trying to, they treat journalists as humble supplicants instead of as unpaid marketers of the clubs' brands. The media often retaliate by being mean. This is not very clever of the clubs, because almost all their fans follow them through the media rather than by going to the stadiums.

A month after all the faxes, I was granted permission to send my request by email. When I arrived at the club for the interview, I met the press officer. She was beautiful. Of course she was. Traditionally, football clubs recruited the women on their office staff for their looks, and the men because they played professional football or were somebody's friend.

When Mino Raiola entered football as an agent in his early twenties, straight out of his family's restaurant business, he 'was not impressed at all', he told us. 'It's a closed world, with a gigantic potential, and where a lot of money circulates, but it's often managed by people of whom I think, "What the fuck?" It's hard to understand that on the field there are people who have made it through sweat and tears, through a certain natural selection – but not at the top, in the boardroom. That's very strange.

'You have to have done something in the football world to get another job in the football world. The average level in the football world is low, and why is it low? Because we don't want outsiders to influence and change or improve our football world.'

A clever person who has never played professional football can (after rigorous study) become a brain surgeon, but however long that person studies, he can never become coach of Ajax Amsterdam, marvels Raiola. 'That's ridiculous, isn't it?' When a football director's job opens up, he notes, it's rarely advertised publicly. Nor do many clubs or federations scour the world for the best possible candidate. 'No,' scoffs Raiola, 'we'll take someone from within our own ranks. Incest makes this world weak.'

This is all the more bizarre because it would be easy for football clubs and federations to recruit excellent executives. Professors at business schools report that many of their MBA students (who in the UK in 2017 paid between £16,000 and £73,000 a year in tuition fees) dream of working in football for a pitiful salary. Often the students beg clubs to let them work for free as summer interns. Clubs seldom want them (though here again, as the football business gradually gets clever, more MBAs are creeping in). If you work for a football club, your goal is generally to keep working there, not to be shown up by some overeducated young thing who has actually learned something about business.

In part this is because much of the traditionally working-class football industry distrusted education. In part, says Emmanuel Hembert of A. T. Kearney, it is because many clubs are dominated by a vain owner-manager: 'Lots of them invested for ego reasons, which is never a good thing in business. They prefer not to have strong people around them, except the coach. They really pay low salaries.' If you work for a football club as anything but a player or manager, you typically get paid in stardust.

Historically, only Manchester United recruited respected executives from normal industries (such as Peter Kenyon from Umbro). Only after about 2010 did most of the other biggest European clubs start to do so, too.

Baseball for a long time was just as incompetent. In *Moneyball* Lewis asked why, among baseball executives and scouts, 'there really is no level of incompetence that won't be tolerated'. He thought the main reason was 'that baseball has structured itself less as a business than as a social club. . . . There are many ways to embarrass the Club, but being bad at your job isn't one of them. The greatest offense a Club member can commit is not ineptitude but disloyalty.' Club members – and this applies in football as much as in baseball – are selected for clubbability. Clever outsiders are not clubbable, because they talk funny, and go around pointing out the things that people inside the Club are doing wrong. 'It wasn't as simple as the unease of jocks in the presence of nerds,' wrote Lewis – but that unease does have a lot to do with it.

The staff of football clubs traditionally tend not merely to be incompetent. They are also often novices. This is because staff turnover is rapid. Whenever a new owner arrives, he generally brings in his cronies. The departing staff rarely join a new club, because that is considered disloyal (Kenyon, an exception, was persecuted for moving from United to Chelsea), even though players change clubs all the time. So football executives are always having to reinvent the wheel.

Worse, the media and fans often make it impossible for clubs to take sensible decisions. They are always hassling the club to do something immediately. If the team loses three games, fans start chanting for the club to sack the coach or buy a new player, in short tear up the plans it might have made a month ago. Tony Fernandes, the Malaysian businessman who had run a tight ship at his airline AirAsia, couldn't do the same after taking over QPR in 2011. 'Two things are different from AirAsia,' he told us in 2013. 'One is I can control almost everything in AirAsia. You can do whatever you want in football, but it's up to the eleven guys on the pitch at the end of the day, right? The second thing is, you have a very vocal bunch of shareholders – called fans. Everyone has an opinion. The plans get thrown out of the window when you start losing. The excitement you get when you win a football game is unbelievable. The downside is that when you lose you want to kill yourself.'

'Consumer activism in this industry is extreme,' agreed A. T. Kearney in its report 'Playing for Profits'. Hembert says, 'The business plan – as soon as you sign a player for £10 million, you blow up your business plan. Commercial employees have to fight for £100,000 of spending here or there, but then suddenly the club spends £10 million.'

Or more. Sven-Göran Eriksson once flew into Zurich to tell the International Football Arena a 'good story' about his time managing Lazio. 'The chairman I had was very good,' Eriksson recalled for an audience of mostly Swiss businessmen. 'If I wanted a player, he would try to get that player. One day I phoned him up and I said: "Vieri."'

Christian Vieri was then playing for Atlético Madrid. Eriksson and Lazio's chairman, Sergio Cragnotti, flew to Spain to bid for him. Atlético told them Vieri would cost 50 billion Italian lire. At the time, in 1998, that was about £17 million. Eriksson reminisced, 'That was the biggest sum in the world. No player had been involved for that.' He said the talks then went more or less as follows:

Cragnotti: That's a lot of money.
Eriksson: I know.

At this point Atlético mentioned that it might accept some Lazio players in partial payment for Vieri.

Cragnotti: Can we do that?

Eriksson: No, we can't give away these players.

Cragnotti: What shall we do then?

Eriksson: Buy him.

Cragnotti: Okay.

Eriksson recalled in Zurich: 'He didn't even try to pay 49. He just paid 50.'

Nine months after Vieri joined Lazio, Inter Milan wanted to buy him. Once again, Eriksson reported the conversation:

Cragnotti: What shall I ask for him?

Eriksson: Ask for double. Ask 100.

Cragnotti: I can't do that.

Eriksson recalled: 'So he asked 90. And he got 90. That's good business.' (Or the ultimate example of the greater-fool principle.)

Someone in the audience in Zurich asked Eriksson whether such behaviour was healthy. After all, Lazio ran out of money in 2002 when Cragnotti's food company, Cirio, went belly-up. Cragnotti later spent time in prison, which even by the standards of Italian football was going a bit far.

Eriksson replied, 'It's not healthy. And if you see Lazio, it was not healthy. But we won the league. And we won the Cup Winners' Cup. We won everything.'

The point is that football clubs, prompted by media and fans, have a tendency to make financially irrational decisions in an instant. They would like to think long term, but because they are in the news every day they have ended up fixating on the short term. As the British writer Arthur Hopcraft wrote in his book *The Football Man* in 1968, 'It is the first characteristic of football that it is always urgent.' Ferran Soriano, chief executive of Manchester City, advises, 'Do not take decisions on a

Monday' (i.e. based on the weekend's result). However, taking decisions on a Monday is the nature of professional football.

An executive with an American entertainment corporation tells a story about his long-arranged business meeting with Real Madrid. His company was hoping to build a relationship with the club. But on the day of the meeting, Madrid ritually sacked its manager. The usual chaos ensued. Two of the club officials scheduled to attend the meeting with the American executive did not show up.

Chris Anderson entered football specifically with the aim of making the game more thoughtful. Once a semi-professional goalkeeper in Germany, he became a professor of political science at Cornell University in the US, but his life changed in 2009 when his wife gave him a copy of *Moneyball*. Anderson read it open-mouthed. He began blogging about football data. Soon he was being asked to consult clubs. He wrote his book *The Numbers Game*, and in 2015 gave up his tenured job at Cornell in order to become managing director of Coventry City in League One. He lasted only eleven months at Coventry, but he came away with some insights into why clubs don't think very hard. Anderson told the world-class Dutch sportswriter Michiel de Hoog that he hadn't come across a single truly innovative club anywhere in football. A club could potentially use all the new knowledge from physiology, psychology, sports data, organizational science and so on, and come up with a completely different way of doing things, but, said Anderson, 'No one has really taken it and run with it.'

Why not? Anderson identified various reasons:

1. 'Time is the great luxury in football,' he told De Hoog. Coventry often played two matches a week. The constant pressure dissuades clubs from trying anything new.
2. In Europe at least, football clubs can be relegated, which means financial disaster. Clubs in American sports

leagues are free from that pressure, which is why you find innovators at some NBA teams such as the Houston Rockets and the Philadelphia 76ers.

3. If you do everything the same as all the other clubs, then you can't be blamed or humiliated if things go wrong.

4. Most football clubs are packed with people who have always done things the old way. So everyone keeps doing the same things they have done for ever, even if those things have never worked particularly well.

5. A 'masculine culture' in the 'working-class' football industry encourages stubbornness and certainty, argues Anderson. He says that in recent years the game's insiders, the gnarled old ex-players-turned-coaches, have recently become scared of losing their power to egg-headed data whizzes. That has made some of them even more stubborn.

Anderson concluded that the clubs with the most freedom to innovate were new clubs with no existing culture, such as RB Leipzig, which was founded in 2009, and eight years later finished second in the Bundesliga. But in the rest of the industry, he said, two basic rules applied: 'When you're doing well, why change? And when you're doing badly, why change?'

NOT BUSINESSES AT ALL

When businesspeople looked at football, they were often aston-ished at how unbusinesslike the clubs were. Every now and then one of them would take over a club and promises to run it 'like a business'. Alan Sugar, who made his money in computers, became chairman of Spurs in 1991. His brilliant wheeze was to make the club live within its means. Never would he fork out 50 billion lire for a Vieri. He was dismayed to discover that managers regularly stole from their clubs in the form of bungs (bribes, mostly paid by agents who wanted the manager to make a particular transfer). After Newcastle bought Alan Shearer for £15 million in 1996, Sugar remarked, 'I've slapped myself around the face a couple of times, but I still can't believe it.'

He more or less kept his word. In the ten years that he ran Spurs, the team lived within its means. But most of the fans hated it. The only thing Spurs won in that decade was a solitary League Cup. It spent most of its time in mid-table of the Premier League, falling far behind its neighbour Arsenal. Nor did it even make much money: about £2 million a year in profits in Sugar's first six years, which was much less than Arsenal and not very good for a company its size. Sugar's Spurs disappointed both on and off the field, and its experience also illustrated a paradox: when businesspeople try to run a football club as a business, not only does the football suffer, but so does the business.

Other businessmen have pursued a different strategy than Sugar's. They assumed that if they could get their clubs to win trophies, profits would inevitably follow. But they too turned out to be wrong. Even the best teams seldom generated profits. We plotted the league positions and profits of all the clubs that played in the Premier League from 1997 to the 2015–2016 season, as shown opposite.

The graph shows how spectacularly unprofitable the football business has been. Each point on the chart represents the combination of profit and position for a club in a particular year. One obvious point to note is that most of the dots fall below zero on the profit axis: these clubs were making losses. But the graph also shows that there was barely any connection between league position and making money. Although there is some suggestion that a few clubs at the top of the table made big profits, the graph also shows that some clubs in these positions made big losses. Manchester United's consistent

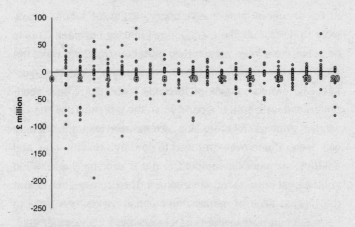

Pre-tax profit/loss of Premier League clubs by league position, 1997–2016

profitability is clearly the exception. In the thirty years before being taken over by the Glazer family in 2005, the club generated more than £250 million in pre-tax profits while also winning eight league titles. Indeed, other American owners might never have bothered buying into English football without United's example.

For most English clubs, our graph shows that there was not even a connection between changing league position and changing profits. In 45 per cent of all cases, when a club changed its league position, its profits moved in the opposite direction: higher position, lower profits, or lower position, higher profits. Only 55 per cent of the time did profits and position move in the same direction. Had there been no correlation at all between winning and making profits, that figure would have been much the same, namely, 50 per cent. Clearly, winning games was not the route to making money. As Francisco Pérez Cutiño noted in an MBA thesis at Judge Business School in Cambridge, it's not that winning matches can help a club make profits. Rather, the effect works the other way around: if a club finds new revenues, that can help it win matches.

For almost all of football's history, it proved almost impossible to run a club like a solid, profit-making business. This is because there were always rival owners – the Cragnottis, the Abramoviches, or the long-time ruling family of Libya, the Gaddafis, who owned a chunk of Juventus – who didn't care about profits and were free to spend whatever it took in the hope of winning trophies. All other club owners were forced to keep up with them. If one owner refused to pay large transfer fees and salaries, somebody else would, and that somebody else would get the best players and win trophies. The consequence is that the biggest slice of money that football makes has hitherto been handed over to the best players. As A. T. Kearney said, you could even argue that football clubs are nothing more than vessels for transporting football's income to players. 'The players are completely free to move [although as we will explain later, this is not quite true],' explained Hembert. 'They are a key factor in winning, and also in the ego, in pleasing the fans. And they all have pretty savvy agents who are able to maximize their bargaining power.'

This meant that even the cautious Sugar types could not make decent profits in football. In fact, because his team won fewer matches than its free-spending rivals, some fans deserted him. That ate further into his profits. From 1991 to 1998 average attendance in the Premier League rose 29 per cent, but Tottenham's crowds fell 5 per cent.

'I thought we could make it [QPR] profitable, definitely,' Fernandes admitted to us. 'I haven't yet,' he added, laughing. Even in the 2011–2012 season, when the club survived in the Premier League, it lost £22.6 million. The next season, when it kept buying players but got relegated regardless, it lost a lot more. 'On the pitch it was just a disaster,' said Fernandes. He mused: 'Football has survived on benefactors. Shareholders coming in and pumping money in, and then the next sucker comes in and pumps money in.' Did he consider himself a sucker, a benefactor, or a businessman in football? 'Now I would define myself as a sucker,' he replied. 'And benefactor. And I hope I will become a benefactor-stroke-businessman.' He hasn't. By 2016 QPR, still stuck in the Championship, had debts of nearly £200 million – the fifth-highest of all the clubs in Europe, according to UEFA.

In fact, very few club owners in history have even aspired to act like businessmen. Stefan and the Spanish economist Pedro Garcia del Barrio (of the Universidad Internacional de Cataluña) studied the behaviour of Spanish and English clubs between 1993 and 2005 to see whether the clubs were chiefly pursuing profits off the field or victories on it.

If a club wanted to make profits, clearly it would have to spend less than it earned. That would mean limiting its players' wages. Any club that paid players less would suffer on the field, because as we have seen, paying high wages wins football matches. It's a trade-off: if you want glory, you have to forget maximizing profits. If you want maximum profits, give up hope of glory. Stefan and Pedro estimated, for instance, that if Barcelona wanted to maximize profits, it would have to aim to finish fifteenth in the league, because it would need to slash its wages. A profit-driven Real Madrid should expect to finish a mere seventeenth, just above the relegation spots. Most other teams – such as Atlético Madrid, Athletic Bilbao, Sevilla or Villareal – would maximize their profit potential by playing in the second division. There they could save a lot of money on players' wages.

On the other hand, if a club's main aim was to win matches, it would have to spend every cent it earned (and borrow more besides). So what were clubs chasing, profits or wins?

Stefan and Pedro estimated how each club in the top two Spanish divisions would have behaved on average in the 1994–2005 period if it were pursuing profits, and how it would have behaved if it wanted wins. Then they looked at how clubs behaved in real life. Their unambiguous finding: clubs didn't care about profits. They were spending what it took to win games. 'On average,' Stefan and Pedro concluded, looking at ten years of league tables, 'the Spanish teams were twelve places above their profit-maximizing position over the sample period, but less than half a place below their win-maximizing position.' In short, club presidents were spending way more than they would have done if they were hard-headed businessmen out to make profits. Though many of the presidents were in fact hard-headed businessmen in real life, they weren't treating their football clubs as businesses. Nor was there any sign that any other actors – lending banks, say – were pressuring them to make profits.

Building magnates like Florentino Pérez and Jesús Gil y Gil seemed especially prone to blowing what looked like absurd sums of money on players. Possibly they were pursuing a business logic after all: they may have reasoned that making a name in local football would help them befriend bankers and get planning permission from local government for their construction projects. That would have boosted their non-football businesses. Fred Wilpon, the real estate developer who took over the New York Mets, discovered that a similar effect operated in baseball. To quote a profile of Wilpon in the *New Yorker* magazine:

> He didn't anticipate that owning the Mets would boost his seemingly unrelated business interests. 'No one had heard of us before we bought the Mets, and afterward the change was dramatic,' Wilpon told me. 'I don't think someone has not returned one of my telephone calls in thirty years. It's a small club, owning a baseball team, and people want to be near it.'

Owning a football team might help the owner's other businesses. But all Spanish football clubs tended to pursue wins rather than profits. In a sense, they had to. If your rivals are spending whatever it takes to win, then you must as well. Any team that pursued the highest possible profits would probably end up being relegated, because it wouldn't be spending enough to hire good players. And if the club got relegated, it would lose much of its revenues. So Spanish football became an arms race: every club overspent for fear of the neighbours.

No matter how much money Spanish clubs got their hands on, they spent it. In the decade that Stefan and Pedro studied, the average revenues of a club in the Spanish first division (Primera División) rose nearly fourteenfold, from €4.3 million in 1994 to €59 million in 2004. (By 2015 the figure was €130 million.) Yet the share of revenue that clubs spent on player wages didn't drop much throughout the period: in that decade, first-division clubs paid over an average of 62 per cent of their revenues to their players. In other words, the clubs weren't able to save all the additional money or do much else with it, such as build new stadiums or cut ticket prices. Most of the money that came in just went straight out again into players' bank accounts. In the second division, a whopping 93 per cent of clubs' revenues went to the players. These clubs really were just vessels for transporting money to players. The clubs weren't simply content with giving the players what money they had. They also gave them money they didn't have, and some clubs ended up seriously in debt.

By the standards of a normal business, this sort of spending is nuts. But for football clubs, it made sense: the only way to win matches was to overspend. Historically, nobody ran a football club to turn a tidy annual profit. However, as we'll explain in Chapter 6, at the very top end of the game at least, that is now changing. For the first time ever, big football seems to be turning into a good business.

SAFER THAN THE BANK OF ENGLAND: WHY FOOTBALL CLUBS ALMOST NEVER DISAPPEAR

On 15 September 2008, the American investment bank Lehman Brothers collapsed, followed almost immediately by the world's stock markets.

Any football club on earth was a midget next to Lehman. In the fiscal year ending in September 2007, the bank had income of $59 billion (148 times Manchester United's at the time) and profits of $6 billion (fifty times Manchester United's), and was valued by the stock market at $34 billion. If United's shares had been traded on the market at the time, they probably would have been worth less than 5 per cent of Lehman's. Yet Lehman no longer exists, while United very much does. So does almost every club in Europe that existed in 2008.

In the years before the global economic crisis, people worried a lot more about the survival of football clubs than that of banks. Yet it was many of the world's largest banks that disappeared. Then, after the recession began, worries about football clubs increased again. Many people pointed out that when Chelsea met Manchester United in the final of the Champions League in 2008, the two clubs had a combined net debt of more than £1.3 billion.

While Europe's biggest clubs are now becoming serious businesses, many small clubs still live from debt crisis to debt crisis. Yet the notion that football clubs are inherently unstable businesses is wrong. They virtually never go bust. Although large numbers of them are still incompetently run, they are some of the most stable businesses on earth.

First, some facts. In 1923 the English Football League consisted of eighty-eight teams spread over four divisions. In the 2016–2017 season, eighty-four of these clubs still existed (95 per cent),* and seventy-two remained in the top four divisions (82 per cent). Thirty-seven were in the same division as they had been in 1923. And only eight teams still in the top four divisions were two or more divisions away from where they had been in 1923. (Of the twenty-two teams in the First Division in 1923, only three were playing below the second tier in 2017: Bolton Wanderers and Sheffield United in the third tier and Notts County in the fourth tier.)

You would have expected the Great Depression of the 1930s, in particular, to pose the clubs something of a threat. After all, the Depression bit deepest in the north of England, where most of the country's professional clubs were based, and all romantic rhetoric aside, you would think that when

* The four lost clubs are Merthyr Town, Aberdare (disbanded 1928), New Brighton (which folded in 1983, was then reborn, but folded again in 2012) and South Shields (taken over by Gateshead in 1930). Both Merthyr and Aberdare are small towns that still possess a club today. Several other clubs have folded and been reborn, e.g. Accrington Stanley, Bradford Park Avenue, Durham City, Halifax Town, Merthyr Town, Nelson and Newport County.

people cannot afford to buy bread they would stop going to football matches.

Crowds in the Football League did indeed fall 12 per cent between 1929 and 1931. However, by 1932 they were growing again, even though the British economy was not. And clubs helped one another through the hard times. When Orient in east London hit trouble in 1931, Arsenal wrote its tiny neighbour a cheque for £3,450 to tide it over. Clubs know they cannot operate without opponents, and so unlike in most businesses, the collapse of a rival is not cause for celebration.

The Depression culled only a couple of clubs. Merthyr Town, after failing to be re-elected to the league in 1930, folded a few years later, the victim of economic hardship in the Welsh valleys (as well as competition from far more popular rugby). Wigan Borough went bankrupt a few games into the 1931–1932 season. It left the league, and its remaining fixtures were never played. Aldershot was elected to replace it, and sixty years later, in another recession, it became only the second English club in history to withdraw from the league with fixtures unplayed.

Almost equally hard as the Depression for English clubs was the 'Thatcher recession' of the early 1980s. Again many working-class fans lost their factory jobs. The league's attendance dropped from 24.6 million to 16.5 million between 1980 and 1986. Among those who continued to show up were lots of hooligans. Football seemed to be in terminal decline. As Ken Friar, then managing director of Arsenal, put it, 'Football is the oddest of industries. It sells one product and has ninety-two outlets for it. In any other business, if not all ninety-two outlets were doing well, there would be some talk of closing some of them down. But in football, all ninety-two outlets claim an equal right to survive.'

Many clubs in the early 1980s seemed to be dicing with death. If we look at one of the diciest, Bristol City, it will help us understand just how football clubs almost always survive.

Bristol City got into trouble in the same way that a lot of clubs do. In 1976 it had been promoted to the old First Division, then the highest tier in English football, a status the club had last enjoyed before the First World War. The fans were excited: attendance jumped from 14,000 per game in 1974–1975 to 24,500 in 1976–1977. The average ticket then cost less than £1, but the higher ticket sales still boosted the club's income from around £250,000 per year to £665,000. City survived three seasons in the top flight. As we've already seen, that took money. The club paid handsomely in the transfer market, and its wage bill doubled: all City's extra income was channelled straight to the players.

The money didn't do the trick. In the 1979–1980 season, the club was relegated just as Britain, in the first year of the new Thatcher government, was entering recession. First Division attendances dropped 5 per cent that season, but Bristol City's gates fell 15 per cent, while its wage costs rose 20 per cent.

Clearly the club needed to lose some of its expensive players. Unfortunately, the manager, Alan Dicks, who had just overseen the most successful period in Bristol City's modern history, had signed many of them on extraordinarily lengthy contracts – some as long as eleven years. Soon after relegation, Dicks was sacked. But by the end of the next season, 1980–1981, City's average attendance had collapsed to 9,700 per game (half the level of the previous season) and the club was relegated to the Third Division. Income was tumbling, yet most of the squad were still drawing First Division wages. When City's accounts were published on 15 October 1981 it was apparent that the club was in deep trouble, but the best that the new chairman could say in his report was that 'so much of this depends on success on the playing field'.

It is doubtful that promotion back to the Second Division would have improved the club's financial position materially in 1981–1982, but that's a purely academic question since by the end of 1981 Bristol City were heading for the Fourth Division. By now only 6,500 fans were showing up each week, about a quarter the number of four years earlier. An independent financial report produced that December showed that the club owed far more (over £1 million) than it could realistically repay in the foreseeable future. Early in 1982 Bristol City Football Club PLC – the limited company that owned the stadium at Ashton Gate, the players' contracts and a share in the Football League – was on the verge of appointing an official receiver to liquidate the company. That would have meant the end. In a liquidation all the players' contracts would have been void, the share in the League would have been returned to the League, the stadium sold, probably to a property developer, and any proceeds used to pay the creditors. Like so many British companies at the time, Bristol City seemed headed for extinction.

But football clubs command more love than widget-makers. Just before City could fold, Deryn Coller and some other local businessmen who were also fans offered to take over the club. It was at this point that the 'phoenixing' plan emerged.

Coller and his associates created a new company: BCFC (1982) PLC. It was to be a 'new' Bristol City: a phoenix from the ashes of the old club. The Coller group aimed to sell shares in the new company to fans. With the money, the group would buy Ashton Gate from the receiver. The group also asked the Football League for permission to acquire the old club's share in the League. Then the new Bristol City could 'replace' the old one in the Fourth Division. In short, the new company would take over almost everything of the old club – except, crucially, its debts and unaffordable players. Collier's group intended to ask City's most expensive players, left over from the First Division days, to tear up their contracts. You could see the appeal of the plan, as long as you were not one of the players.

The Football League said the plan was fine as long as Gordon Taylor, the head of the Professional Football Association

(PFA), would agree the deal on the players. Taylor was by no means sure that things were as bad at Bristol City as the directors said (after all, directors are always complaining about wages), but eventually he was convinced that the deal was the only way to save the club. No union wants to see an employer go bust, especially not an ancient employer loved by thousands of people.

The final decision was down to the players. Naturally, they were reluctant martyrs. But the pressure on them was intense, including some threats from fans. In the end, after some sweeteners were thrown in, the players agreed. Peter Aitken, Chris Garland, Jimmy Mann, Julian Marshall, Geoff Merrick, David Rodgers, Gerry Sweeney and Trevor Tainton are not the biggest names in football's history, but few players can claim to have given more for their clubs. On 3 February 1982 the 'Ashton Gate Eight' agreed to tear up contracts worth £290,000 and accept redundancy in order to save their employer. By the standards of the time, they were on very good pay. Most of them, nearing the end of their careers, would never earn as much again. They got a miserly pay-off of two weeks' wages, and afterwards they had to choose between retiring from football, moving abroad or joining lower-division clubs. The eight really deserve statues outside Ashton Gate. They gave Bristol City a future.

The phoenix rose from the ashes: the club was transferred from the ownership of Bristol City PLC, a company heading for liquidation, to BCFC (1982) PLC. The directors of the new business still faced the formidable task of finding the money to buy Ashton Gate. They had agreed a price with the receiver of just over £590,000. They raised £330,000 by selling shares in the new club to fans and well-wishers. They might have raised more, but they felt obliged to close the share offer early when rumours emerged that an unknown bidder was considering buying a majority of the shares on offer, possibly with the aim of selling off the ground to property developers. (Ashton Gate is handily located near the city centre.) The rest of the cash was raised from short-term loans.

Today Bristol City still play at Ashton Gate, in the Championship. (And Ashton Gate is now much more than a mere stadium. 'A premier conference and events venue, our stadium features a wide range of function rooms for both corporate and private hire,' proclaims Ashtongatestadium.co.uk.) The 'phoenixing' of Bristol City was the first of its kind in English football, and established a template that, like the club itself, survives to this day.

Other clubs quickly cottoned on to the joy of phoenixing. Between 1982 and 1984 Hereford, Hull, Wolves, Derby, Bradford and Charlton went through much the same experience as Bristol City. All these troubled clubs survived either by creating a new 'phoenix' company (Wolves, Bradford and Charlton) or by getting creditors to agree to suspend their claims (a moratorium), under the threat that a phoenix might be the alternative. In all cases, the bankrupt company was ditched, but the immortal club inside it salvaged.

Phoenixing – the creation of a new company – turned out to be an excellent way to escape creditors. Clearly there is something suspect about the method. Phoenixing allowed disastrous directors to escape the consequences of their decisions. Their clubs survived, but at the expense of creditors (often players, banks and the taxman), who never saw their money again.

Still, this was just what hapless football clubs needed. Many of them struggled in the 1980s, and several survived only thanks to a 'sub' – financial support – from the players' trade union, the Professional Footballers' Association. Charlton and Bristol City's neighbour Bristol Rovers had to move grounds because they could not pay the rent. However, nobody resigned from the league.

Soon after the Thatcher recession, a new law made it even easier for British clubs to survive. Historically in Western countries, attitudes to bankruptcy had been harsh. In nineteenth-century England, bankrupts were still being sent to prison. But over time, we have become more forgiving. Increasingly, people have come to recognize that bankruptcy can be caused by bad luck as well as bad judgement. As well as relaxing our moral stance, we have discovered some self-interested motives: bankruptcy destroys a company's value, often unnecessarily. By the 1980s, the UK's traditional method of liquidation – the bankrupt company's assets were sold, the debts repaid as far as possible and the company liquidated – had become discredited. Critics said it gave stricken companies little chance to recover. They praised the American approach, which treated failure as a frequently necessary precursor to eventual success. In 1979 the US had introduced the now famous Chapter 11 provisions. These protect a firm from its creditors, while it tries to work out a solution that saves the business. Britain – where insolvencies hit an all-time high during the Thatcher recession – wanted some of that. Later, Italy, Germany, Spain and eventually France too moved towards more forgiving, 'American', bankruptcy laws.

The UK's Insolvency Act of 1986 transformed a procedure known as 'administration'. Now when a company went into administration, an independent insolvency practitioner was called in and charged with finding a way to keep the business running, while repaying as much money as possible to the creditors. After the new law came in, stricken football clubs typically entered administration, struck deals with creditors and then swiftly emerged from administration. That's what Tranmere and Rotherham did in 1987, for instance. For most clubs, financial collapse was becoming something of a breeze.

True, Aldershot FC was liquidated in 1992, but supporters simply started a new club almost identical to the old one. The 'new' Aldershot Town FC has a badge that shows a phoenix in flames. Aldershot went into administration again in 2013, but now play in the National League, the fifth tier of English football. Other tiny British clubs that folded – Maidstone United, Newport County, Accrington Stanley – were also eventually resuscitated and now stumble on somewhere in the semi-professional or professional game. Accrington Stanley's rebirth was surely the most drawn-out: it resigned from the Football League in 1962 with debts of £63,000, got liquidated in 1966, was newly created by fans in 1968 and returned to the Football League in 2006, its brand still very much alive, probably even enhanced by the drama. 'Above the turnstiles now, the welcoming sign is, "The Club that Wouldn't Die",' Accrington's then chairman Ilyas Khan told us proudly in 2012.

The new British law was so kind to insolvent companies that ever more companies decided to enter insolvency. Some did it just to wipe off their debts. The method became more popular even as the economy improved. Company insolvencies in the recession of the early 1980s had run at an average of around 10,000 per year. In the boom period between 1994 and 2001 they ran at 16,000 per year. Football clubs, too, loved the new law: more of them went insolvent in the 1990s boom than in the early 1980s bust. They rarely even needed to bother to create a new 'phoenix' company anymore. Clubs would run up unpayable debts, go insolvent and, hey presto, months later would be fine and signing expensive players again. Better-run rivals complained that insolvency and phoenixing were giving the culprits an unfair advantage. In 2004 this argument prompted the league to introduce a ten-point penalty for clubs that went into administration. Still, it hasn't proved a huge deterrent.

There's something else to note about these near-death experiences: they almost only happen to small clubs. Big clubs almost never go bust.

Yes, there was a great kerfuffle in 2010 when Portsmouth of the mighty Premier League entered administration. The club had been on much the same journey as Bristol City thirty years earlier, just with larger sums. It had overspent on good players, won an FA Cup and ended up in trouble.

On the one hand, Portsmouth's story was all too familiar: football club goes bust and after many premature reports of its demise is reborn. The shared fan angst about their club disappearing has a useful psychological function: it's a communal ritual that gives people a chance to join together to affirm their love of the club. After administration, Portsmouth slid down the divisions and spent a few miserable years bumping along in League Two, the bottom tier of English football. In summer 2017 they celebrated an emotional promotion to League One, and were then taken over by Michael Eisner, former chief executive of Disney. Like almost every English professional club that has ever existed, Portsmouth still exist.

Yet in another way, Portsmouth's story is exceptional. They are the only club in the Premier League ever to go into administration. The other sixty-six cases of insolvency in English football from 1982 to 2010 involved teams in the lower divisions. That is something that doomsayers should note. They often complain about the debts of rich clubs, such as Manchester United. They ask how Chelsea would survive if Roman Abramovich falls under a bus.

In fact, though, big clubs are not the problem. Across Europe, lower-tier teams live on the edge of insolvency, while the top-tier teams, even though they too mostly lose money, seldom become insolvent. The highest risk of all in most countries is for recently relegated teams. We have been able to identify about a dozen Western European clubs that have disappeared from professional football during the post-2008 economic crisis: UD Salamanca, Lorca and CD Badajoz in Spain, Evian Thonon Gaillard in France, Haarlem, Veendam, AGOVV and RBC Roosendaal in Holland, FC Brussels and Beerschot in Belgium, MyPa in Finland and Gretna in Scotland. (Vanishing clubs are more common in poorer Eastern Europe, where almighty sugar daddies come and go, and especially common in Ukraine, where the Russian invasion hit several clubs very hard.)

None of the Western European clubs vanished after gambling tens of millions to compete with the big boys. Rather, they were midsized to tiny outfits (Badajoz in its 107 years of existence never once made it to Spain's top division) that had soldiered on gamely through the years. When the crisis hit, they were over-whelmed by their relatively puny debts. Haarlem, for instance, owed a fairly manageable €1.8 million when they folded in 2010. It's just that hardly anybody was interested enough to fight for the club's life. Anyway, several of the defunct clubs were immediately re-founded in a slightly different form. Gretna 2008 now plays amateur football in Scotland, as do RBC and AGOVV in Holland. Unionistas de Salamanca, the successor club to the one that died, now plays in Spain's third tier. MyPa are in the Finnish fourth division.

Perhaps because English professional clubs are older estab-lished brands than most continental teams, even the littlest among them survived the crisis. But if people are determined to worry about clubs going bust, it's the Accrington Stanleys they should worry about, not the Chelseas. And they probably shouldn't worry too much about the issue at all. If European foot-ball clubs really did collapse beneath their debts, there would now be virtually no European football clubs left. 'We must be sustainable,' clubs say nowadays, parroting the latest business cliché. In fact, they are fantastically sustainable. They survive even when they go bust. You can't get more sustainable than that. Match-fixing, say, is a much bigger problem for European football than bankruptcy. The near immortality of football clubs makes you wonder exactly what problem UEFA's rules on 'finan-cial fair play' are meant to solve.

Michel Platini, from 2007 until his ban from football in 2015, was always worrying about clubs' debts. But it's precisely because clubs are practically immortal that they have such large debts. They know from experience that they can take on whatever debt they like, and survive. If things go wrong, they simply don't repay their debt, the old directors walk away, and new ones come in promising to sweep up the mess (while also buying shiny new Brazilian centre-forwards). A club like Bayern Munich, which shuns debt, is in fact missing a trick. Bayern could easily borrow a few hundred million euros to make itself invincible against human opposition in the long term. Even if it flushed the money down the toilet and then said 'Nanananana' to the lenders, the club would survive. Right now Bayern is a marvellous self-sustaining debt-free business. But the point of a football club isn't to have nice accounts – after all, the clubs with horrible accounts survive, too. The point of a football club is to win trophies. From 1976 to 2017, Bayern won the Champions League just twice. That's a meagre return for the biggest club of Western Europe's biggest football country.

Once again, the comparison between football clubs and 'real' businesses breaks down. When clubs get into trouble, they generally 'do a Leeds', a manoeuvre named in honour of the spectacularly badly run Leeds United of the early 2000s. 'Doing a Leeds' means cutting your wages, getting relegated and competing at a lower level. Imagine if other businesses could do this. Suppose that Ford could sack skilled workers and hire unskilled ones to produce worse cars, or that British Airways could replace all its pilots with people who weren't as well qualified to fly planes. The government would stop it and, in any case, consumers would not put up with terrible products.

Football clubs have it easy. Recall that almost every English professional club has survived the Great Depression, the Second World War, recessions, corrupt chairmen, appalling managers and the post-2008 crisis. By contrast, economic historian Les Hannah made a list of the top one hundred global companies in 1912, and researched what had become of them by

1995. Nearly half the companies – forty-nine – had ceased to exist. Five of these had gone bankrupt, six were nationalized and thirty-eight were taken over by other firms. Even among the businesses that survived, many had gone into new sectors or moved to new locations.

What made these non-football businesses so unstable was, above all, competition. There is such a thing as brand loyalty, but when a better product turns up, most people will switch sooner or later. So normal businesses keep having to innovate or die. They face endless pitfalls: competitors pull ahead, consumers' tastes change, new technologies make entire industries obsolete, cheap goods arrive from abroad, the government interferes, recessions hit, companies overinvest and go bust, or simply get unlucky.

By contrast, football clubs are immune from almost all these effects:

A club that fails to keep up with the competition might get relegated, but it can always survive at a lower level. Some fans lose interest, but clubs have geographical roots.

A bad team might find its catchment area shrinking, but not disappearing completely.

The 'technology' of football can never become obsolete, because the technology is the game itself. At worst football might become less popular.

Foreign rivals cannot enter the market and supply football at a lower price. The rules of football protect domestic clubs by forbidding foreign competitors from joining their league. English clubs as a whole could fall behind foreign competitors and lose their best players, but foreign clubs have financial problems and incompetent management of their own.

Governments are not about to nationalize football.

Clubs often overinvest, but this almost never destroys the club, only the wealth of the investor. At worst, the club gets relegated.

A club's revenues might decline in a recession, but it can always live with lower revenues.

In most industries a bad business goes bankrupt, but football clubs almost never do. No matter how much money they waste, someone will always bail them out. This is what is known in finance as 'moral hazard': when you know you will be saved no matter how much money you lose, you are free to lose money.

There is a strange parallel here between professional football and communism. When we ask, 'Why do football clubs almost always survive?' we are echoing the great question asked about communism by one of our favourite economists, the Hungarian János Kornai. He grew up in Hungary, briefly worked for a communist newspaper despite knowing that the system was all nonsense, and after making his way to the West tried to answer the question: Why exactly did communism not work?

Kornai's answer could be summed up in four words: 'the soft-budget constraint'. Imagine that you are a tractor factory in communist Hungary. Each year the state gives you a budget. But if at the end of the year you've overspent the budget and haven't made any profits, the state just gives you a bit more money to make up the difference. In communism, bad companies were propped up forever. In other words, the 'budget constraint' on communist firms was soft. If they wanted to overspend their budgets, they could. The obvious consequence: unprofitable overspending became rife.

As scholars such as Wladimir Andreff and Rasmus Storm have noted, Kornai's 'soft-budget constraint' applies beautifully to football clubs. Like tractor factories in communism, clubs lose money because they can. They have no need to be competent. The professional investors who briefly bought club shares in the 1990s got out as soon as they discovered this.

Luckily, as we've seen, society can keep unprofitable football clubs going fairly cheaply. The total revenues of European professional clubs for the 2014–2015 season were €19.6 billion (about £15 billion), according to the business advisory firm Deloitte. For comparison: over about the same period, the struggling supermarket chain Sainsbury had annual revenues of £23.8 billion. The two-bit losses of football clubs hardly matter when set beside the enormous love they command. These tiny businesses are great enduring brands. Creditors dare not push them under. No bank manager or tax collector wants to say, 'The century-old local club is closing. I'm turning off the lights.' Society swallows the losses and lets even a Bristol City soldier on. In a sense, these clubs are too small to fail.

Unlike most businesses, football clubs survive crises because some of their customers stick with them no matter how lousy the product. Calling this brand loyalty is not quite respectful enough of the sentiment involved. To quote Rogan Taylor, a Liverpool fan and Liverpool University professor, 'Football is more than just a business. No one has their ashes scattered down the aisle at Tesco.'

CROOKED BUSINESS: FOOTBALL'S CORRUPTION AND THE HISTORY OF TECH

Remember what our friend said after trying to work with a revered English football institution: 'I can do business with stupid people, and I can do business with crooks. But I can't do business with stupid people who want to be crooks.'

Crookery has always been part of the football business. Powerful older men – working alone, or with friends – have traditionally run clubs and federations.

Their personal status encourages a sense of entitlement. The sums of money they handle have grown fast. They still mostly make decisions quickly and secretively. Their organizations have rarely had serious regulation. That creates opportunity.

Some types of corruption are eternal. However, each era also generates its own new crimes. The nature of football's scams has changed over time as technology changes. Here's a quick history of football crookery, and our views on why it has proved so hard to stamp out.

Before television discovered the game, football was a cash business. Every week, thousands of people would pay a few pennies each at the turnstiles, leaving the club with a large pile of cash on Saturday evening to be taken to the bank on Monday morning. This was a perfect opportunity for a money launderer. He might be a criminal who ran protection rackets, or perhaps a local business owner (a restaurateur, say) who didn't like paying tax. All the launderer needed to do was deposit as much cash as he wanted into the football club's account, claiming it was the gate receipts. If he was the chairman or some other club official with the power to sign cheques, he could then use the club's account to pay himself or an associate a sum for services. Hey presto, the money was laundered. And since most football clubs were unprofitable, they didn't pay much tax.

Clubs therefore attracted some unsavoury characters (not to mention egomaniacs) as well as the close attention of the tax authorities. Still, this was mostly small-time crookery – a few thousand pounds here or there. The club's business was limited by the size of the stadium. The amount of cash deposited in the bank had to be credible.

* * *

Then, in the 1970s, TV entered football. The device's first big impact was on the finances of FIFA. The global authority had always been a tinpot outfit. It had little power over clubs, which were mostly regulated by national federations. All FIFA had was the World Cup, and for decades that only generated peanuts. In 1970, the year of possibly the greatest World Cup ever played, FIFA's total declared income from all sources was just 1.5 million Swiss francs (then a little over £150,000).

But television transformed football. Between the early 1970s and 1990, the number of TV sets multiplied twenty times in Africa, ten times in Asia and four times in Latin America, writes David Goldblatt in his history of football, *The Ball Is Round*. The World Cup grew into arguably humanity's biggest party, watched from the Cook Islands to Iceland.

And so the rights to screen and sponsor the World Cup became ever more valuable. But the tiny FIFA set-up of the 1970s lacked the nous to market them. When João Havelange became FIFA's president in 1974, the organization's Zurich headquarters employed just twelve staff members. Horst Dassler, whose father had founded the boots manufacturer Adidas, a much larger operation, bought many of the rights directly from FIFA. Dassler paid Havelange kickbacks, and the Brazilian flew suitcases of cash first-class between Rio and Zurich. Nobody troubled him. Few journalists covered sports administration. Switzerland continued to treat FIFA as the sort of little not-for-profit sports association that it used to be, almost like a village hunting club. No wonder dozens of other sports federations right up to the International Olympic Committee found Switzerland a pleasant place to do business. Many of them became as corrupt as FIFA, albeit with less money.

The beauty of FIFA's business is that it's a monopoly. There is only one World Cup (nobody has ever credibly attempted to start a rival event) and only one global football association. Moreover, FIFA generally recognizes only one national association per country, and so in a sense it's a monopolistic association of monopolies. And a basic principle of economics says that monopoly creates profitability.

FIFA's revenues from TV and sponsors rose from $308 million in the four-year cycle to 1998, to $5.7 billion in the four years to 2014. This happened not because FIFA was run by geniuses, but because in an interconnected world ever more people from Shanghai to San Francisco wanted to watch World Cups.

What to do with all this money? FIFA has few costs of business, beyond the first-class flights and traditionally secret salaries of its officials. To organize a World Cup, it needs to do little more than let the host lay on some football matches. The host pays for the stadiums; FIFA takes almost all the income from TV and sponsors. That's what you call a business model.

So the FIFA president's main challenge is to get himself re-elected. His main weapon: FIFA's revenues.

In 1998, when Havelange retired, FIFA's congress in Paris elected Joseph 'Sepp' Blatter as his successor. The president of each national football federation has one vote in congress, Montserrat in the Caribbean (population: 4,900) the same as China. Many presidents proved corruptible. David Yallop, in his 1999 book How They Stole the Game, recounts how the emir of Qatar (then a little-known country) flew $1 million in cash on a private jet to Paris, where twenty voters each seem to have been handed envelopes stuffed with dollars.

That election set the template for Blatter's rule. He passed on chunks of TV money to national and continental football barons. This was typically veiled in the language of 'development': a grant, often handed over personally the night before a FIFA presidential election, was supposedly meant to fund facilities in the official's country. But if the official slipped the money into his jacket pocket, nobody would complain. In return, the happy officials voted for Blatter. Corruption was FIFA's system.

The organization's bribe-taker-in-chief was the Trinidadian Jack Warner, an alcoholic's son who had risen from college teacher to global football powerbroker. Warner put together a block of thirty-one mostly tiny Caribbean national associations. In a congress of a little over two hundred countries, this was often the swing vote. And so Warner and his friends filled their pockets. Banned for life from football, he lives prosperously in Trinidad while the FBI battles to have him extradited to stand trial in New York.

His biggest paydays came when FIFA's executive committee (Exco) got to choose a World Cup host. Indeed, for many Exco members, bribes were the main point of choosing a host.

The tradition of exchanging hosting for bribes probably goes back to the mists of time. However, we know that Germany in 2006, South Africa in 2010, and multiple bidders for the 2018 and 2022 World Cups paid members of Exco to vote for them. (Only Brazil in 2014 didn't have to stump up, simply because there were no other bidders.) The Exco members who took bribes didn't necessarily do what they had promised, but that's the risk every bribe-payer runs. In 2010, Exco chose Russia as host for 2018 and Qatar for 2022. Of the twenty-two men who voted on those bids, as of July 2017, seven had been charged or accused by US authorities of criminal wrongdoing; another, the German hero Franz Beckenbauer, is under criminal investigation in Switzerland and Germany regarding his country's 2006 bid; Spain's Angel Villar was arrested in an anti-corruption investigation; and five others have been sanctioned by FIFA's own ethics committee. Meanwhile Havelange resigned as FIFA's honorary president at age ninety-seven after new revelations about kickbacks. He died in 2016, aged one hundred.

Qatar undoubtedly sprinkled money and favours on some of these men, but so did the Western bidders. They just took care to sprinkle legally. England's bid, for instance, paid various sums into Warner's pet projects. He knew nobody was going to monitor how he spent the money.

None of this corruption was particularly secret. Yallop's book appeared in 1999 (Blatter sued), and journalists, led by Andrew Jennings, have been revealing wrongdoing at FIFA since the 1990s. Yet, for most of the time, they were ignored.

At dawn on 27 May 2015 it briefly looked as if the old FIFA system was crumbling. Swiss police working with the FBI raided Zurich's five-star Baur au Lac hotel and arrested seven senior international football officials. 'Some of them were led out of back doors into waiting cars, and shielded from photographers by thoughtful hotel staff holding Baur au Lac bed sheets in front of them,' writes David Conn in *The Fall of the House of Fifa*. One FBI official spoke of 'the World Cup of fraud'.

The dawn raids felt reassuring: the American global police officer, though getting doddery, still seemed able to enforce international legal norms.

But FIFA signalled almost immediately that it intended to soldier on unchanged. Days after the raids, while FIFA officials were shredding documents at headquarters, the seventy-nine-year-old Blatter was re-elected to his fifth presidential term in an election out of a Ruritanian farce. Some delegates photographed their supposedly secret votes for him as proof of loyalty. They liked his patronage system, and they didn't see anything wrong with it. After all, for most of them, it was how business and politics had always been done in their own countries. In much of the world – especially the developing world – crookery is normal.

It should be said that developed countries produce crooks, too, and fraud is not just about developing nations. According to the FBI, there were about 6 million criminals involved in 'white-collar crime' in the US in the period 1997–1999. There is no sign the numbers have fallen since. No wonder many football officials who are accused of fraudulent activities by Americans and Europeans dismiss this as just Western double standards.

In fact, Warner's main partner in football's criminal underworld was the fantastically obese New Yorker Chuck Blazer, who ended up living the grand life on an entire floor in Trump Tower in New York, with one apartment exclusively for his cats. His party ended one day in 2011 when the tax authorities tapped him on the shoulder as he trundled his mobility scooter down East 56th Street. Soon he was back on FIFA's luxury-hotel circuit, but now as an FBI informer wearing a wire in a key fob. Blazer died disgraced in 2017.

Developed countries often appear cleaner than poor ones. But that's partly because their forms of corruption tend to be legal rather than illegal. In the US, for instance, a former Congressman will lobby Congress for whatever company or country will pay him; meanwhile in a poor country, a politician pockets an illegal bribe. When Westerners watch FIFA, they see egregious forms of illegal corruption that (they often forget) were commonplace in their own countries in the nineteenth century, but have now been mostly wiped out. And frankly, with the election as president of a frequently bankrupted billionaire who allows his children to run his business while he runs the country and refuses to acknowledge conflicts of interest, the US's grip on the moral high ground is becoming tenuous.

Blatter resigned as FIFA's president in June 2015, only four days after being re-elected. The pressure from the media, the FBI and Switzerland (fed up with being embarrassed by FIFA) had become unbearable. Six months later he and UEFA's president Michel Platini were jointly banned from football. Their falls were in character: Blatter, who doesn't seem to have taken overt bribes himself, was found to have paid Platini two million Swiss francs. The Swiss claimed the money was for work that Platini had done for him thirteen years earlier. Platini doesn't seem to have had the sense to realize that there was anything wrong with the transaction. Blatter's demise felt cathartic, like the tumbling of Saddam Hussein's statue in Iraq in 2003. But this time, too, it turned out that the US hadn't restored a rules-based international order.

In February 2016, FIFA's congress elected as president another Swiss bureaucrat, Gianni Infantino, after he told the 209 national federation presidents, to loud applause, 'The money of FIFA is your money!' Most of these people had repeatedly elected Blatter and were still around, still keen on patronage. As we write in 2018, the FBI and Swiss police continue to investigate. However, FIFA has barely reformed, Qatar and Russia keep their World Cups, and Western countries seem powerless to force change. In fact, the shift of power from the West to the Gulf countries and Russia manifested itself in FIFA before it hit geopolitics.

Most of the heat is now off FIFA itself. Almost no journalists cover the organization full time. The US may pipe down about reforms now that it hopes to host the 2026 World Cup with Mexico and Canada. The Trump administration doesn't seem hugely bothered about foreign corruption.

In any case, US power has declined since 1999, when American authorities pushed the International Olympic Committee to reform after its Salt Lake City bribery scandal. The IOC listened then because at the time more than 60 per cent of its income came from US TV and sponsors. By contrast, FIFA's revenues today are spread worldwide. Sure, the federation has found sponsors harder to come by lately, what with all the scandals, and two straight World Cups being scheduled in unsexy non-democracies. But that won't bother FIFA much, because it's still a low-cost monopoly producer.

Reforming FIFA would have been quite easy had there been any will to do so. We know a lot by now about how to clean up organizations. For instance, you need an ethics unit that can investigate wrongdoing and is not under the president's control – which would imply a big change from the Blatter-era FIFA. The problem is that nobody on the outside has the power to change the organization.

For all this catalogue of misdeeds, football probably isn't an unusually corrupt sector by global standards. It might actually be cleaner than most, simply because journalists follow football. Criminals prefer to do their work when other people aren't watching. That's why most burglaries happen at night. So the corrupt will tend to prefer less transparent industries than football. If we studied other organizations in as much detail as we have scrutinized FIFA, we would probably find at least as much corruption.

HUMAN TRAFFICKING

'Cloughie likes a bung,' Alan Sugar told the High Court of England and Wales in 1993. Sugar's former manager at Spurs, Terry Venables, had told him so.

A 'bung' is football slang for an illegal under-the-table payment to sweeten a deal. The court heard that when Brian Clough bought or sold a player for Nottingham Forest, he expected to get a bung. In a perfect world, he liked it to be handed over at a lay-by. Clough denied everything – 'A bung? Isn't that something you get from a plumber to stop up the bath?' – and was never prosecuted.

Bungs are one of football's eternal forms of corruption. They have probably been around since the dawn of the professional game, and they still persist. An investigation by the UK's *Daily Telegraph* newspaper in 2016 found that eight Premier League managers were willing to take bribes to facilitate transfers. This corruption happens not because some people are bad, but because the transfer system is evil. It's essentially a system of human trafficking, which gives many people the right to control where a player works. Imagine for a moment that this applied to your own career. Imagine that if you wanted to change jobs, your employer could stop you moving for up to three years. In the meantime, it could threaten to make you do a job well below your qualifications, which could make your skills atrophy. These are the conditions under which footballers work.

The transfer system allows their employers to extort a fee for letting them move. That doesn't happen in any other industry we know of. When a player changes clubs, his agent and club manager (and who knows who else besides?) might dip their paws into the deal. The money that these criminals siphon out of the game is money that ought to go to the employee. And if the player's interests clash with theirs, he risks being mentally or physically abused. Workplace harassment is inevitable in a system that treats players as tradeable commodities.

The way to end these horrors is to close down the transfer system. FIFPro, the international players' trade union, has asked the European Competition Authority to do exactly that.

Some people will retort that making every player a free agent every day of his career would only serve to make multimillionaires even richer. But in fact, most players aren't rich. A majority of FIFPro members earn less than £50,000. Many earn much less. So don't think of Messi or Ronaldo, but of struggling family breadwinners in Poland or Croatia with short careers.

Some fans fear their clubs would collapse without income from transfers. However, the reality is that a large fraction of the money simply circulates among the big clubs, as Stefan pointed out in a study commissioned by FIFPro to support their case.

If the transfer system is abolished, there will be far fewer opportunities for stealing. True, if all players become free agents, some will move even more often than they do already. However, others will prefer the stability of staying with the same club as long as they are fairly treated. No longer will agents and managers have an incentive to move players in order to make some illegal cash in hand.

The transfer system seems necessary because it is familiar, while abolishing it seems like a step in the dark. We don't think abolition is nearly as risky as it sounds. But that is beside the point. Football's system of 'buying' and 'selling' players is unjust.

*   *   *

Match fixing was a well-known problem of the Olympic Games (original version) over 2,500 years ago. However, many people believe that this ancient scam has gotten a boost from the internet. Online betting sites have made it easy for punters to bet on any match anywhere on earth. Meanwhile, since about 2000 the giant gambling nation China has joined the global economy. The relatively small and regulated pre-internet world of sports gambling has become 'a jungle with no borders, populated by tens of thousands of operators', says the IRIS think tank in Paris.

In fact, sports gambling is now a bigger business than sport itself. The industry's estimated total value – counting both legal and illegal gambling – is 'anywhere between $700 billion and $1 trillion a year', Darren Small, of betting and sports data analysts Sportradar, told the BBC in 2013. As we've seen, the total revenues of European clubs in 2014–2015 were about £15 billion. In short, there's much more economic power in the betting market than in the football market.

But before we go any further, first a caveat. Stefan and Simon disagree a bit on match fixing. Simon is inclined to think it's a big problem for football. Stefan thinks it's a stain on the game's reputation, but not an existential threat.

One thing we agree on is that buying off your opponents in order to win (fixing to win) has always been common in football. One of the Bundesliga's most famous scandals broke in 1971 when the president of Kickers Offenbach played a tape at a garden party on which several players were heard offering to lose games for money to fix the league's relegation struggle. In 1993 Marseille was stripped of its first ever Champions League title for fixing a domestic league game so as to rest players for the final. And arguably the biggest match-fixing scandal of this century was Italy's Calciopoli scandal of 2006, in which Juventus was found guilty of fixing referees and rival teams in order to win titles.

There's a long history of fixing-to-win allegations associated with the World Cup. Most of us remember South Korea versus Italy at the World Cup 2002. The Ecuadorean referee Byron

Moreno gave the South Korean hosts a penalty, disallowed an apparently good Italian goal in extra time that would have won the match, and then gave Italy's Francesco Totti a second yellow card after a collision in the South Korean penalty area. From a distance of 35 yards, Moreno was sure that Totti had dived. South Korea beat a very good Italian side 2–1.

Afterwards Italy's minister for public offences, Franco Frattini, called Moreno 'a disgrace, absolutely scandalous'. The *Gazzetta dello Sport* newspaper said he was 'the worst referee, ever'. Soon afterwards, a set of new public toilets in Sicily was named after him.

Some Italians alleged that FIFA needed South Korea to reach at least the semis, in order to keep South Korean interest in the tournament alive as long as possible. Moreover, this was part of the well-known longstanding global conspiracy against the Italian people.

Many outsiders at the time thought the Italians were overdoing it. There have been weirder refereeing performances – for instance, the one by Egyptian Gamal Ghandour when South Korea beat Spain in the next round. Moreno seemed just your common-or-garden incompetent home ref.

But three months after the World Cup, the Ecuadorean FA gave Moreno a twenty-match ban for allowing thirteen minutes of extra time (when he had signalled only six) in a Liga de Quito–Barcelona Guayaqil match. In those thirteen minutes, Quito scored twice to win 4–3. The match also featured two controversial penalties and two sendings-off. At the time, Moreno happened to be running for a spot on Quito's city council.

Freshly returned from his ban in 2003, he was suspended again after sending off three Liga de Quito players in a match. He then resigned from refereeing, saying, 'I'm leaving through the front door with my head held high. I prefer to die standing up than to live kneeling down.'

In 2010, he suddenly popped up again at JFK airport in New York. After landing 'visibly nervous', Moreno was arrested when a customs official found 'hard objects on the defendant's stomach, back and both of his legs'. Italy's least favourite ref was carrying ten plastic bags of heroin. He was sentenced to thirty months in a New York jail, but was released after twenty-six due to good behaviour.

Few media noticed his arrest. Nonetheless, this looks like an interesting story about how World Cups sometimes work. Nor was Moreno necessarily an isolated case. In 2012, a Chinese referee named Lu Jun was sentenced to five and a half years in jail for taking nearly $130,000 to fix seven league matches. Hardly anyone abroad paid any attention. However, Lu Jun had refereed two games at the 2002 World Cup. Football's routine match fixing and FIFA's endemic corruption may be shaping outcomes of the game's biggest tournament.

But in recent years the focus of concern has shifted away from fixing-to-win towards fixing-for-gambling. Fixing-for-gambling, too, has a long history in sports. In baseball it goes back to the Black Sox scandal of 1919 and even beyond, while any serious basketball fan has heard of the City College of New York point-shaving scandal of 1951. One of football's earliest betting scandals, in 1962, involved three players from Sheffield Wednesday making sure they lost a game they were already expected to lose. Two facts stand out: the fix only came to light because the fixer (Jimmy Gauld) later sold his story to a newspaper; and the amounts paid to the fixers were tiny by modern standards. They only needed a small bribe because players back then earned little more than skilled labourers.

It's still cheaper to fix badly paid players and referees. (It's easiest of all to fix those who sometimes earn nothing at all, such as the many players in small national leagues whose wages are routinely paid late.) There's been a lot of evidence in recent years of gambling fixes happening at lower levels of the game. Wilson Raj Perumal from Singapore became notorious in 2011 when he was arrested and served time in a Finnish prison for fixing local games. He later co-authored a book explaining how fixes work, and pointing out the large number of meaningless friendly internationals played in obscure countries in front of tiny crowds. These games, he claimed, were largely vehicles for illegal Far Eastern betting syndicates.

But if big-name players have financial problems, they too can be targeted by fixers. Gambling addiction is an ancient problem in English football – just read Paul Merson's memoir *How Not to Be a Professional Footballer*. In fact, fixers corrupted the German second-division side Vfl Osnabrück after first helping its players run up gambling debts.

Even some players at World Cups – many of whom are middlingly paid journeymen – might not be immune. Simon was in the stands in Cologne at the World Cup 2006 when Brazil beat Ghana 3–0, and never for a moment imagined he was watching a fix. But Declan Hill, author of *The Fix*, the seminal book on match fixing and someone whose research we take very seriously, produced a pile of evidence to suggest that Asian gamblers meeting in a KFC in northern Bangkok bribed the Ghanaians to lose by more than two goals. FIFA never even investigated his allegations, which the Ghanaians denied.

Hill says that if you are a criminal looking for a money-making scheme, football gambling is now a relatively safe option. The online betting market is global, liquid and almost anonymous. Whereas smuggling drugs or people can get you shot or jailed, match fixing almost never does. As a bonus, it's a handy way to launder money. If fixers do it right, they will bet tens of thousands of dollars on a game – ideally spread over various bookmakers – without anyone noticing anything strange.

Hill goes so far as to say clubs themselves are now fixing games for gambling purposes. A club will decide: we'll lose on Saturday by more than two goals, or our striker will get sent off, or we'll concede a first-half penalty. It bets on that event, and its winnings help balance the budget. For some of Europe's indebted clubs, match fixing is part of the business plan.

Maybe, but Stefan argues that fixing-for-gambling is not a simple, costless or risk-free business. First, you have to work with accomplices (the players or referees) who have by defini-tion shown themselves to be untrustworthy. Second, the fixers have no legal comeback if the fix fails. This often happens – the best-laid plans, etc. What if you just can't find a way to let in that crucial fourth goal? It's almost impossible to fix all twenty-two players and the referee, so you may find some eager young thing scoring an inconvenient goal.

Third, the return on a successful fix might be small. The easier the fix, the more likely the game's outcome was anyway, and so the worse the betting odds. You can bet on whether the sun will shine in California tomorrow, but if you win you won't make much money. Fourth, if you fix the outcome to be some-thing that no one expects then the players or referee making the fix happen will charge a high price for the risk (reducing your profit), and the chances that the fix will be detected are greater. That means that you might get nothing. Legal book-makers do not pay on fixes, and we doubt that collecting is easy in illegal markets when the bookies suspect they have been conned.

Fifth, though the internet has made fixing easier, it also makes it easier for the good guys to uncover fixing. Legal book-makers have big incentives to find and stop fixes. Their busi-ness relies on punters believing that the outcomes of sports events are uncertain. Moreover, in many fixes the legal book-makers are the victims. So legal bookies – helped by gambling radar services – are always on the lookout for suspicious bet-ting patterns. There are also amateur sleuths looking for illegal patterns in the data of online gambling sites such as Betfair. In 2017 three academics – Christian Deutscher, Eugen Dimant

and Brad Humphreys – caused uproar in the German parliament when they published a working paper claiming to have
statistical evidence that there were irregular betting patterns
associated with two Bundesliga referees officiating between
2011 and 2015.

Here's a story which nicely illustrates Stefan's and Simon's
contrasting positions on the problem. In spring 2011, somebody whose name and job we are not allowed to mention
(because he is terrified of match fixers) showed Simon a legal
gambling website offering odds on the next weekend's Serie
A matches in Italy. 'What strikes you about those odds?' he
asked.

'That everyone already knows two results already,' said
Simon. For Chievo–Sampdoria, so much money had been bet
on a tie that you earned almost nothing for correctly predicting
that result. And for Brescia–Bologna, almost the whole market
had bet on a home win. That weekend, lo and behold, Brescia
beat Bologna and Chievo–Sampdoria ended in 0–0. 'Exactly as
predicted', reported the newspaper *Corriere della Sera*. 'Zero–
zero, zero real chances, zero desire to harm the opponent, zero
anything'.

Had the fix worked? From the fixers' perspective, probably
not. Rather, technology worked. Legal bookies had discovered
the fix from betting patterns, and the fixers probably won't have
made money out of it. If this is what usually happens, then fixers will go out of business. On the other hand, it still appeared
that a fix had taken place. Spotting odd betting patterns is not
enough to prove a fix in a court of law and so if there was a fix,
the fixers escaped unpunished.

Neither fixing-to-win nor fixing-to-gamble is easy to stop. The
media find any kind of organized crime difficult to cover. Tracking down match fixing is time-consuming, and few media organizations nowadays can afford to finance long investigations.
Given fixers' connections to the underworld, an eager journalist

can get hurt. It's also hard to find proof, and even if you do, libel laws in some countries would stop you publishing it.

The authorities likewise struggle to do much. Hard evidence of fixing usually requires intricate international cooperation. Europol, the European police agency, explained in 2013: 'One fixed match can involve up to 50 suspects in 10 countries, spanning different legal frameworks and definitions of match-fixing and betting fraud.' Given the complexities involved, the police have other priorities. A Western European policeman – one of the very few working on match fixing in his country – told us he had neither the budget nor the contacts to travel to China to investigate a case.

Sport's governing bodies do little better. Most major associations (FIFA, UEFA, the FA, the German DFB) have their own match-fixing units, but like the police and media, they rarely find evidence that would stand up in court. Sylvia Schenk of the anti-corruption NGO Transparency International says that governing bodies worry more about scandals than problems, and because match fixing is rarely revealed, it rarely produces scandals. Anyway, as we've seen, sporting authorities are themselves often corrupt too.

Nonetheless, there are ways to fight match fixing if the will to do so is there. The internet has spawned more gambling, but it has also created more data to reveal fixes. Some federations have set up anonymous hotlines for whistle-blowers to report match fixing. There is also some official 'match-fixing education', which teaches athletes to avoid any contact with gamblers or illegal bookmakers, because even friendly conversations can lead to crime. One practical step is to assign referees to games at the last minute, so that it is harder for fixers to get to them. All these things are being done. However, it's almost impossible to say how effective they are.

Neither of us doubts that if match fixing is widespread, it endangers football. After English football suffered a match-fixing scandal in 1994, the author Nick Hornby wrote that fixing dwarfed the game's other problems. 'Once we begin to doubt that what we are seeing is real, then we will cease to care,' he wrote, 'and without the caring, it is all over.' Of course, since then, caring about the Premier League has grown exponentially.

But what if people come to believe that there is systematic match fixing at the top of the game? Fool me once, shame on you; fool me twice and I'm switching channels. That has already happened in much of Eastern Europe and Asia, where fixing is believed to be common. Stadiums in these regions are mostly empty, and fans sit at home watching the Premier League, partly because they believe it is still fair. Even in Italy, the match-fixing clubs punished for the 'Calciopoli' scandal of 2005–2006 saw a significant fall in attendances afterwards, write the economists Babatunde Buraimo, Giuseppe Migali and Rob Simmons. In a global survey of fans by Transparency International in 2017, 66 per cent thought match fixing was the most troubling form of corruption in the game.

Fixing will probably always be part of football. But if there isn't much fixing in serious leagues, or at least if it's happening only in ways that no one can detect, then fixing in those leagues is only a small problem. Fans will continue to trust what they are seeing. Fixing would then be just one more ethical challenge to an already ethically challenged game. This might not be an ethically appealing conclusion, but it is like saying that for all the corruption at FIFA, the World Cup is still worth watching.

A DECENT BUSINESS
AT LAST?
BE CAREFUL WHAT
YOU WISH FOR

A few years ago, a rich Asian sent the former Israeli prime minister Ehud Olmert on a mission. The Asian, whom Olmert would describe to us only as an 'Eastern investor', wanted to buy Manchester United. A lot of people do. But for all of them, an early obstacle is the difficulty of actually meeting the Glazer family who own the club. The Glazers don't get out much.

That was where Olmert came in. The Glazers are great friends of Israel, and the Eastern investor suspected they would like to meet the country's former leader. So it proved. A meeting was arranged. At the Glazers' country club in Palm Beach, Florida, Olmert – a United fan since the Munich air crash of 1958 – handed the family a cheque from the Asian for about £1 billion to take over United.

Unfortunately, the Glazers said no straight away. 'This is the strongest brand name in the sports world,' they explained. They also expected the club to just get more valuable. And so far, they have been proven right. In 2005, they used borrowed money to buy United for £790 million. In January 2018, the club's market value on the New York stock exchange was $3.26 billion (£2.37 billion), exactly three times what the Glazers had paid for it.

In 2017 Olmert was released from jail after serving sixteen months for fraud and bribery. He must have walked out feeling pretty sunny. For different reasons the Glazers and other owners of football clubs will be feeling just as good. For the first time in history, Europe's largest clubs are making money. That is a transformation after all those decades of losses. However, we think it's bad news. We regret that the highest echelon of football seems to be becoming a profitable business, because football shouldn't be a business at all.

* * *

The most lucrative thing that ever happened to the football business was television. As long as the audience was restricted to the number of people who could fit inside a stadium there could never be much money in it. For example, when Arsenal won the English title in 1948 their total revenue for the season was £143,021. Allowing for inflation, that is worth about £5 million in 2017 money. By 2017, Arsenal's annual revenue was £424 million, or 85 times more.

As we've seen, TV began boosting football's revenues in the 1970s, but the big leap happened in the 1990s. Cable/satellite technology, digitization, encryption and flat-panel display made it possible to broadcast every game and charge customers premium prices for the privilege of watching on 72-inch screens in their own home.

TV also turned out to be the best showcase the game had ever had. It beamed the best of Western European football into living-rooms around the world. Pretty soon, some rich foreigners got interested in owning a piece of the game.

In 2003, Roman Abramovich bought Chelsea, sealing the deal with the departing owner Ken Bates over a bottle of Evian water in London's Dorchester Hotel. The Russian was then still happy to talk to journalists. When the *Financial Times* rang, he revealed that his favourite player was Thierry Henry (then at Arsenal), and explained why he had bought Chelsea: 'I'm looking at it as something to have fun with rather than having to realise a return. I don't look at this as a financial investment.' Abramovich has barely spoken another word in public since, but two things have become clear: 1) Buying a football club made this unknown billionaire world-famous; 2) as he predicted, the purchase hasn't been a 'financial investment'. In his first eight years as owner, he sank nearly £1 billion of his personal fortune into the club, money that he is unlikely ever to see again.

Despite the losses, Abramovich inspired the era of billionaire sugar daddies in football. After someone becomes a billionaire, he tends to want to convert some of that money into fun and prestige. A good way of doing that is buying into sports. Men such as Sheikh Mansour of Abu Dhabi – who bought Manchester City in 2008 – aren't like investors in normal businesses. They are willing to lose money just to be part of the game. They helped drive up wages and salaries for the best players to unprecedented levels. The sums involved didn't matter much to the sugar daddies: what's £40 million for a striker when your personal oil reserves are worth billions?

But pretty soon the sugar daddies hit obstacles. Much of European football said to them: we don't want your money, take it away.

Weirdly, this rejection of free money was done in the name of financial health. The Germans, in particular, have been regulating their clubs' spending since the 1960s. Clubs have to submit budgets for each forthcoming season, showing that they aren't spending more on wages than their expected revenues. Only 'healthy' clubs get licences. The French system is similar.

In the late 1990s and early 2000s, football officials began to worry more about clubs' health. In many European countries, clubs had long been kept afloat by public subsidies – often, a million here and there from the local town hall. Now these flows were drying up. Would lots of clubs suddenly disappear?

At this point UEFA – for decades a sleepy organization – began to wake up. The first thing it realized was that knowledge is power, and so, advised by lawyers, it began gathering information from clubs about their administrative and financial status. It then used this information to argue for European-wide regulation, otherwise known as club licensing. Who should be the regulator? UEFA, of course.

By 2009, UEFA was ready. Having worked to win the support of the big clubs and national associations, as well as some sympathetic journalists and fan lobby groups, it announced it would begin enforcing a set of regulations called Financial Fair Play. The aim, UEFA claimed, was to stop clubs spending more than they took in. Michel Platini, UEFA's then president (before he was banned from football for taking that suspicious payment from Sepp Blatter), sold FFP as a way of restoring European football to 'good health'. He had warned that half of Europe's professional clubs had financial troubles of some kind. 'If this situation goes on,' he added, 'it will not be long before even some major clubs face going out of business.'

From 2011 to 2013, the four English divisions adopted their own rules to stop their clubs overspending. The Premier League's rules, called 'Short Term Cost Control' (although often referred to as Premier League Financial Fair Play), involve a complex formula that broadly limits rises in player spending to a fixed amount per year. Spain, too, has tried to clamp down on profligate clubs.

Many fans seem to regard cost control as football's long-needed dose of sanity, but we disagree. We think cost controls are bad for the game. True, these rules are helping big clubs make money. However, that is happy news not for fans, or for players, but for a very select set of people: the rich men who own the big clubs. Cost controls will enrich them further. That is bad news for everyone else.

Cost control does do one thing that we applaud: it insists that every club must be solvent. Solvency means the capacity to pay your debts – that is, the reasonable expectation that your future income will be enough to pay what you owe. In most European countries, solvency is a basic requirement for doing business. If a company's directors know it is insolvent, then legally they should stop doing business until either solvency is restored or the company is shut down. Solvency can be restored if the creditors agree to write off some of their debts. If the creditors won't do that, then the business can be closed, the assets sold and the creditors paid off as far as is possible.

Insolvency is a very common business problem. Generally, the problem affects small businesses, and so these events go unnoticed by most of us. Occasionally, though, very large companies become insolvent, and it's headline news. However, as we showed in Chapter 4, football clubs almost never close down. They are practically always bailed out. This is one reason why European clubs have forever gone into debt: they overspend because they can. In the past many clubs restored their finances by refusing to pay small creditors, banks and the taxman – daring any of them to take on the label of the creditor that destroyed a club. Very few creditors have chosen to tread this path. And perhaps, in the days when there was almost no money in football, it didn't matter. Local banks can usually write off a debt of a few tens of thousands of pounds (not much money for a modestly sized bank).

In recent years, though, clubs' income has started to add up to something. These days, when a club can't pay, lots of creditors get hurt. Often the victims are small local businesses, such as the grocers who supply clubs with food. Clearly it's wrong for a club to pay its players millions and then stiff its creditors. So we think it's right that clubs should have to be solvent.

But there's one bit of the cost-control rules that we think is dangerous: the 'breakeven' rule, as it's called in UEFA's FFP. This aims to stop clubs spending more than they earn. If a club's annual revenues are £400 million, it is barred from spending £500 million even if some sugar daddy wants to give it the money.

Rich owners aren't allowed anymore to dip into their own pockets to balance a club's budget, as rich owners did for decades. Breakeven is not a solvency issue. It's not as if Chelsea faces any real risk that Abramovich will be unwilling or unable to cover losses as long as he owns the club. The aim of these rules seems to be, if not to drive the oligarchs out of football, at least to curb their spending. That allows rival clubs to spend less, and let them make profits at last. Wenger, for one, has welcomed the new rules. 'Financial fair play will make a big difference,' he has said, 'because you cannot imagine the world will go on just splashing money out without any return.' He calls the sugar daddies' money 'financial doping'. He seems to think it gives their clubs an unfair advantage.

Football's old 'aristocrats', the likes of Arsenal, Manchester United and Bayern Munich, love cost-control rules. No wonder, because these rules weaken their newer rivals such as Manchester City and Paris Saint-Germain, who rely on sugar-daddy funding to compete.

Let's compare the breakeven rule with the salary cap, widely used in American major-league sports. A salary cap generally restricts teams' spending on players to a fixed percentage of average club income (55 per cent, say). The key difference is that the US cap is the same for all clubs, whereas the European breakeven cap forces each club to keep spending in line with its current level of resources – which are obviously much larger for bigger clubs. So while the American salary cap encourages competitive balance between clubs (it stops the rich Dallas Cowboys from spending many times more than the poorer Jacksonville Jaguars), UEFA's breakeven rule cements inequality by making it harder for smaller clubs to compete with the aristocrats. This hardly seems fair, unless by 'fair' you mean the idea that big clubs should be protected from competition from upstarts.

Cost controls put downward pressure on salaries in two ways, directly and indirectly. The direct pressure works like this: Manchester City complies with breakeven by paying players less. But on top of that comes the indirect effect: by spending less, City becomes less of a competitive threat to other clubs. The cost of winning for these other clubs falls, and so they need to spend less on wages to achieve success. Manchester United, say, no longer has to worry that if it refuses a star a pay rise, he will run to the neighbours.

With sugar daddies unable to spend freely, other big European clubs can save on wages. Some people might think lower players' wages would be justification enough for cost control. But remember two things. First, cost control makes football at the top less competitive. Imagine if cost control had been in force since 2003, and Abramovich and Sheikh Mansour hadn't been allowed to buy English titles. What would have happened instead? Quite likely, Manchester United would have won the Premier League ten years running. With rules such as FFP, as the football writer Gabriele Marcotti has warned: 'Instead of football having a 1 per cent lording it over everyone else, it could become a 0.1 per cent.' Second, if cost controls do cut players' wages, there is no reason to think the savings will go back into football. More probably, they will go into the offshore accounts of billionaire owners.

So far, there is only limited evidence that cost controls are making big clubs more profitable. In 2015 UEFA boasted that 'following the onset of Financial Fair Play, wage growth slowed to the lowest rate in recent history (3%) in 2014.' Better yet, it said, 'European clubs generated the highest underlying operating profits in history in 2014.' But that turned out to be a blip. Clubs did briefly rein themselves in to adjust to cost control, but soon afterwards they went back to spending whatever it took to buy success. In 2015, by UEFA's own figures, European top-division clubs spent 63 per cent of their revenues on wages. In 2009, before cost control, that figure was almost identical: 64 per cent. In any case, FFP has been diluted. In 2015 UEFA agreed that clubs could spend more or less whatever they liked as part of a 'voluntary agreement', as long as they made some commitment to reducing spending.

The same pattern can be seen in the Premier League's data. Deloitte, the business advisory firm, found that in the decade up to 2012–2013 Premier League clubs had accumulated total pre-tax losses of £2.6 billion. Then, in 2013–2014, clubs reported an aggregate pre-tax profit of £187 million, followed by £121 million in 2014–2015. Talk of a new era abounded. But in 2015–2016, the clubs returned to aggregate losses of £110 million.

Still, while most small clubs continue to lose money as they always have, some of Europe's biggest clubs are now consistently making money. 'Economically our club is, I think, in the best position in its history,' Barcelona's president Josep Maria Bartomeu told us in 2015. Two years later Barça's annual revenues hit €708 million (£632 million), the highest for any club in the history of sports.

The rise in profits at the top of the game isn't chiefly thanks to cost controls. Instead, it has more to do with clubs' exposure to global TV audiences. In England, the revenues of Premier League clubs jumped more than twenty-five-fold in the twenty-five years from 1991 and 2016. (Think of your annual income today. Now imagine that in twenty-five years' time, your income had increased twenty-five times. Think how different your life would be.)

Some of these big clubs still manage to lose money, at least according to their accounts. However, it's crucial to understand that these losses are often more or less fictional. Whether a big club reports profits or losses need not say anything about its financial health. Manchester United reported a pre-tax loss of £2.3 million over 2014–2015, but the business is doing just fine, thank you very much. In 2015–2016, Premier League clubs as a group sank back from pre-tax profits into losses – and yet that scarcely mattered. These clubs were losing money on paper, but in reality they were cash machines. The key word to grasp here comes from accounting: amortization.

Until 1990, a club paying a transfer fee had to report it in its accounts as a one-off expense. If you paid another club £1 million for a player, that meant £1 million less profit for the season. Then in the 1990s British and European accounting rules changed. Clubs were allowed to 'amortize' – to write off – the cost of a transfer fee over the life of a player's contract. If you paid a £30 million transfer fee and signed the player to a three-year deal, you reported a cost of £10 million in each of the three years of the contract in your accounts. That's because when the contract ended, and the player was free to walk out of the door, he was no longer worth anything to your club.

Now, player trading tends to involve relatively small financial transactions relative to the total amount you hear reported. When you read a report that club X paid £50 million for player Y, usually club Z who sold the player doesn't get that much money. A lot is usually offset by players being traded in the other direction, or payment is delayed and contingent on all sorts of things that might never end up happening.

Nonetheless, even if no money changed hands, the contract value in the accounts is still £50 million. The paying club will amortize it over the life of the player contract: £10 million a year, if it's a five-year contract. So when a club reports losses because of heavy amortization, it's probable that there was very little real money going out.

And amortization has become a huge item in the financial accounts of big clubs. For example, in 2016 Premier League clubs in total reported revenues of £2.29 billion and pre-tax losses of £140 million. But they also reported amortization charges of £703 million – not much of which is 'real' money that they actually paid out. So in fact they may have had a 'cash' surplus of £563 million (703 minus 140), which sounds a lot healthier. Strip out amortization, and you get a better picture of how rich these clubs really are.

That brings us back to the meaning of 'cash' in modern finance. When finance experts say 'cash', they don't generally mean notes and coins. Rather, they mean the excess of actual revenues over money actually paid out. Amortization isn't money paid out; it's just an adjustment made by the accountant. Of course, if you did pay out real money to finance all your player transfer spending then you would have a big cash deficit, but that rarely happens. In practice, Premier League clubs plus the leading dozen or so continental European clubs have become big cash machines, even though they are not big profit makers.

Cash, in modern finance, means opportunity. A business that generates a lot of cash can borrow a lot of money – as long as the banks think the cash generation is backed up by a solid business, such as charging people big money to watch good football.

There are many ways to exploit this opportunity. Some owners, notably the Glazer family, used the club's own cash to buy the club. The Glazers persuaded banks that Manchester United was a cash machine. The banks then lent them the money to finance the purchase. Finally, the Glazers used the club's cash to repay the banks. Some owners have used the cash opportunity to borrow money to build bigger and better stadiums. Some Premier League owners would like to use the cash to make their league the best in the world.

But if big football keeps generating more cash, then soon many business people are likely to be tempted in because they want to finance some other business altogether. Viewed this way, the big clubs are becoming like banks. They generate far more cash than they need to finance their operations. Theirs is a world of opportunity.

In short, at the top of the game, we are seeing the contours emerge of something new: football still isn't big business, but it is finally becoming midsized. And the next area where we think it can make more money is social media.

SOCIAL MEDIA: HOW MANCHESTER UNITED CAN MONETISE ABDUL IN MALAYSIA

In about 2008, some executives from Facebook urged Cristiano Ronaldo's management team to start a Facebook page for him. 'Listen, you have to be there,' the Facebook people said. 'He has the potential to get to 10 million followers.' Ronaldo's handlers replied: 'We don't believe you. That's the size of Portugal.'

Even so, in 2009 Ronaldo quietly debuted on Facebook. A year later, he used social media to announce the birth of his son by an unnamed mother. As of December 2017, Ronaldo had 123 million Facebook followers, the most for any human. In second place was Shakira, the Colombian singer (and girlfriend of Barcelona's Gerard Piqué).

Today all leading clubs and most leading players are on social media, in multiple languages, adding new followers every minute. Richard Arnold, group managing director of Manchester United, has boasted that his club generates 'more engagement' on Facebook than any celebrity from any field or any other sports team on earth. Big clubs think that social media can, for the first time ever, help them reach their legions of fans worldwide. Facebook, Twitter, Instagram, China's Weibo and other platforms are enabling clubs and players to compile computer databases of their fans. The next step: to turn the fans' love into money at last. After the boom in TV rights, social media should give clubs their next big source of income.

As late as 2011, many football clubs weren't even on Twitter or Facebook. As we've seen, they are classic late adopters of new technology. For years most of them saw social media as a threat: a new platform for gaffes, scandals and hacker attacks. Manchester United was 'very cautious and careful' about Facebook, admits Arnold. The club joined it only in 2010, and Twitter in 2012.

United's fear was in part rational. If its Facebook page were hacked – as has happened to some corporations – it would be global news.

Social media do create scandals. Players are constantly getting into trouble for things they say online. For instance, in 2014 Rio Ferdinand, then playing for QPR, was suspended by the English Football Association after a spat on Twitter in which he referred to a heckler's mum with the obscene slang term 'sket'. From 2011 through October 2014, the FA charged sixty participants in football for inappropriate comments on social media. Wenger said, 'We are concerned about Twitter and things going out of the club that should not go out.' Clubs issue their players with endless rules of what not to say online.

It's partly for fear of scandal that Ronaldo doesn't put up his own posts on Facebook. His page is in English, and his mother tongue is Portuguese, so he will typically send his handlers a message and let them find the right words and post it. Sometimes he sends them a photo from a restaurant dinner, but he doesn't 'share' nearly as much as image-rights manager Polaris Sports would like.

Indirectly, a picture of a player eating pasta can generate money. That's because this kind of material can help clubs get in touch with fans they never knew. Imagine a Manchester United fan in Kuala Lumpur called Abdul. He has never been to Europe, let alone to United's stadium Old Trafford, but he owns a pirated United shirt, scours the internet for United news and watches their games on TV in a local restaurant. However, the club's total income from Abdul is zero. In fact, until very recently United didn't know he existed. The club wasn't able to appropriate – make money out of – his love.

Social media changes that. Once Abdul follows United online, the club can start tapping him for money. Of the 1.3 billion-plus people on Facebook in 2014, 500 million were hardcore football fans, the Facebook executive Glenn Miller told the International Football Arena (IFA) conference in Berlin. Football's caution irritates Miller. He thinks clubs worry too much about media scandals. Most young people are used to wild spontaneous exchanges on social media, and often haven't even heard of the newspaper that breaks a scandal.

Meanwhile, young people consider social media an essential element of sports fandom. Many of them watch games while bantering with other fans on their mobile phones – the so-called 'second screen', though it's rapidly becoming the first screen as it's often more entertaining than the game itself. In 2012, sport accounted for just 1.3 per cent of TV programming but 41 per cent of TV-related tweets, said the measurement company Nielsen.

Slowly, clubs have learned to see social media as a business opportunity. In 2013 Borussia Dortmund tweeted a photograph of its then coach, Jürgen Klopp, renewing his contract. The focus of the picture was the pen with which he signed. Quite by chance – it had presumably been the nearest thing to hand – it was a Stabilo pen. Fans on social media noticed. The Schwan-Stabilo company was delighted.

A club that exploits social media is worth more to sponsors. It's no accident that in 2012, soon after United plunged into social media, the club signed a deal for shirt sponsorship with Chevrolet for £47 million a year, a world record.

But the endgame for clubs like United goes way beyond sponsorship. If United can use social media to register people like Abdul, the club could become a de facto database company. Then its value would lie chiefly in its knowledge of the identities and consumption habits of its supporters.

Of course, businesses in many sectors want to become 'identity companies'. Facebook and Google, famously, are exactly that. They offer free services, and in return the user gives them his identity. But football clubs' databases could be particularly valuable, says German branding expert Oliver Kaiser of the Ledavi agency. For a start, big clubs have more social-media followers than regular companies: Manchester United have more than either Nike or McDonald's. Second, clubs – unlike most corporations – command love and loyalty. 'A fan is the most emotional thing in the world. He will do everything,' says Kaiser. If you can reach the fan through his phone while he's watching a game, you catch him at a moment of maximum emotion.

Soon a club's database will allow it to tailor offers to each individual fan. Then the club can sell him a team shirt, or a TV subscription, but it can also help bigger companies sell to him. Imagine, for instance, if a club could give an automobile company a list of twenty-something American male fans who earn over $5,000 a month and need a new car. Kaiser says: 'The intelligent club in the future will say, "Well, company, you want to have my 25 million fans. I don't give it to you. It's mine."' The company will have to fork out. A database of 25 million fans could be worth billions, says Kaiser.

Clubs want to find out exactly who each fan is. It's not enough to know that 'Abdul in KL' follows you on Twitter. Is Abdul twelve years old, or forty-two? What does he earn? What sort of stuff does he buy? Have you got his credit card details? One trick that some clubs use: build a club app, and make every fan who downloads it register with you.

Kaiser is sceptical that football clubs – as we've seen, not always the cleverest businesses – will win the battle to build serious identity databases. Google and Facebook are nifty competitors.

Still, big clubs are starting to regard social media as part of their core business. Creating a Facebook page, an Instagram account, even a Twitter account in Indonesian is just the start of it. Fans will only use these platforms if they find exciting material there. A club trying to recruit online followers must use social media to give fans apparently intimate glimpses inside the club. Juventus, for instance, once posted a video of its then playmaker Andrea Pirlo sitting opposite the Sydney Opera House witnessing all sorts of bizarre scenes while never changing his characteristic impassive gaze. Under the hashtag '#Pirloisnotimpressed', the video quickly racked up nearly a million YouTube views.

Big clubs are now hiring teams of video film-makers, web editors and multilingual journalists. 'This is quite a big cultural change in the organization,' notes Francesco Calvo, chief revenue officer of Juventus, and a veteran of the tobacco company Philip Morris. Most of Juve's new employees come from sectors outside football. Many are Anglophones.

Bayern Munich's social-media team travel with the players and stay in the same hotels, so they can give fans a club-approved inside view. It's similar at Manchester United. 'We are a mobile-first media organisation,' says Arnold. 'We operate in eighteen languages – a huge volume of work for us.'

One side effect of all this work: clubs now compete with traditional media. As recently as 2010, if you wanted news about Arsenal, you might go to a newspaper website, or even, if you were getting on in years, buy an actual newspaper. Today you can go straight to Arsenal's Facebook page, where the club posts a video of the line-up before each match and an exclusive player interview after it. No outside journalist can get this kind of access. Consequently, many clubs and players have built larger audiences than traditional media. As of January 2018 Ronaldo had 68.1 million Twitter followers, or fourteen times as many as Spain's leading sports daily, *Marca*.

Players increasingly cut out journalists by speaking directly to fans. Ferdinand has complained that journalists 'paint that picture and you see a caricature of you evolve. And you sit there thinking, "Woah, you don't know me".' Twitter, he said, had been 'the biggest thing in my armoury' in changing his image. And Twitter makes him money. In 2012 he posted four 'teaser' tweets about knitting, to arouse fans' curiosity. What was this all about? Nothing to do with knitting, it turned out. The fifth tweet: a picture of himself opening a Snickers bar.

However, the Snickers money didn't come free. Ferdinand was reported to the Advertising Standards Authority for covert advertising. The ASA rejected the complaint. Nonetheless, greedy shilling of this sort – like Cristiano Ronaldo advertising the nutritional company Herbalife when it was a suspected pyramid scheme – can hurt the image of players and clubs. Fans don't like it when clubs and players behave like rapaciously commercial, privacy-invading offshoots of the US National Security Agency. Football needs to tread carefully in social media. Bayern's fans 'are not a cash cow', warned Stefan Mennerich, the club's director of digital media. 'They want to be respected for their love of the club.'

Fans have been complaining for twenty years that football has become too commercialized. On the other hand, not many of them seem to have been put off. In the era of social media, the long-time cliché that football is 'big business' might finally come true.

BIG CLUBS BECOME BUSINESSES: WHY WE SAY YAH BOO SUCKS

So clubs are generating untold amounts of cash, and aren't going bust the way many people have long feared, while sugar daddies are being pushed out of the European game. That might sound like an appealing scenario to many fans. However, we think it's all bad news. We preferred the loss-making, sugar-daddy-funded football of the early 2000s.

If sugar daddies continue to drift out of European football, there is a danger that investment in the continent's clubs will dry up. Already, rich Chinese have begun channelling big sums of money into their domestic league. As we write, the best-paid player on earth is Carlos Tevez, who earns a reported £32 million a year (or £650,000 a week) at Shanghai Shenhua. If the Chinese keep up that kind of pace, they could eat into Europe's dominance.

It's hard to think of any other activity in which organizations actively seek to stop rich people from investing. Not many universities, opera houses or aid agencies say no to sugar daddies. We think European football needs these people.

The sugar daddies are often depicted as a curse on the game. It's easy to see why a Manchester United fan would dislike Manchester City. Setting aside local rivalry, it's the age-old disdain of the aristocracy for the nouveaux riches. City are upstarts who have used wallets full of foreign currency to barge their way onto the top table. When City won the Premier League in 2012, it did so with several players bought from Arsenal, and at United's expense. Of course United fans oppose sugar daddies.

But why should fans of smaller clubs be so bothered by sugar daddies? In most walks of life we welcome the outsider who comes in and shakes up the existing order. Taking the aristocrats down a notch is the plot of endless feel-good movies (not to mention the French Revolution, Brexit and Donald Trump's election). Why should it be different for football? It certainly seems that when a club's fans learn that a sugar daddy is in the offing, they perk up. Finding a sugar daddy is like winning the lottery.

Some argue that the 'excessive' spending of sugar daddies drives smaller clubs into bankruptcy. In fact, if anything, the opposite is true. Sugar daddies buy players and then pay them very high wages. The usual argument is that this forces other clubs to pay their players higher salaries to stay. However, a) this will only apply to a small number of players, and b) no club can be forced to pay more than it can afford. Certainly if clubs without a sugar daddy try to match the ambitions of sugar daddies that will end in tears, but then that's also the case for clubs that try to compete with aristocrats. Whether you want to be a Manchester United or an oil-funded Manchester City, if you have no sugar daddy you will fail.

The problem for small clubs is that they just don't have the resources to compete in Europe with the dominant clubs, and have not had them for decades. This has very little to do with sugar daddies.

But sugar daddies are good for the football economy for one big reason: the cash they inject supports other clubs. Think of the hundreds of millions that Abu Dhabi-owned Manchester City has spent in transfer fees. Some of that money ended up with agents, but by far the biggest chunk has gone to other clubs. Those clubs spent some of that money on players, and some on improving training facilities or building better stadiums.

We lament the seizing of so much of the world's wealth by a small number of billionaires – many of them heirs, criminals or tax-dodgers – but it has been good news for football. To understand how sugar daddies help the game, it's instructive to study the Glazers, because they are the opposite of sugar daddies. The Glazers make sure United makes a profit. That might sound 'healthy' and 'sustainable'. However, that profit represents money that the owners can then take out of football. The Glazers sucked somewhere between £500 million and £700 million out of United from 2005 to 2015. That's precisely why most United fans resent them.

United's profits would have been welcome had they been reinvested in buying players, or building a bigger stadium, or even funding a cut in ticket prices – but then of course they would have ceased to be profits. So if sucking money out of clubs is a bad thing, then putting money into clubs is surely a good thing. We have always been happy to see rich owners blow fortunes on building teams. We don't want them to start making profits. We would rather they put the money back into football.

Quite probably, more owners of big European clubs will now follow the Glazers' profit-seeking lead. Several Premier League clubs are already owned by Americans. These people come from a country where many sports franchises actually make money. Most of them didn't buy into football because they love the game, but as a business proposition. They think football has the power to capture foreign markets in a way that American sports don't. They see the ceaseless rise in the Premier League's broadcast income. They see FFP curbing clubs' spending. In the end, these owners hope to take money out of football.

The advent of profit-making clubs might sound like a new 'healthy', 'sustainable' era in football. But we don't think it is. We preferred the old days when clubs spent every penny they had, and often more. We do not see the point of enriching the owners. However, as things stand it looks as if they might become very enriched in the next few years.

To imagine what European football's future might look like, think of Arsenal. Wenger, the club's manager, doesn't like spending money. His austerity hasn't won him any league titles lately, but it does please Arsenal's American majority owner, Stan Kroenke. From 2002 to early 2013, Arsenal's share price jumped nearly 1,200 per cent, compared with a rise of just 60 per cent for British shares in general.

Arsenal isn't a great football club any more, but it is a good business. This is what a football club run as a business looks like: high ticket prices, little desire to win trophies and big profits. If cost controls continue to restrain football's spending, and other big clubs end up being run like Arsenal rather than like Manchester City, then we predict:

⚽ slower rises in players' wages;
⚽ a rise in club profits, which would mean more money being taken out of the game by people like the Glazers.

It's a classic example of the law of unintended consequences: Platini, a self-professed football romantic, wanted to ban debts and foreign sugar daddies. Instead his rules risk turning the sport into an industry run by hard-nosed businessmen.

We don't think clubs should be profit-oriented businesses. A club has a different purpose from a company like Apple or Shell. Companies exist to turn profits. By contrast, most of a club's customers (its fans) and employees (its players and coaches) and usually even its owners would say that the club exists to play well and win things, not to make its owners rich. That's why a 1974 report by the British Commission on Industrial Relations quoted an anonymous club chairman as saying, 'Any club management which allows the club to make a profit is behaving foolishly.'

Traditionally football clubs have behaved more like charitable trusts than like for-profit businesses. In the not-so-distant past the FA used to forbid club owners from profiting from their investment. Directors couldn't get paid, and dividends were capped. The aim was to ensure that clubs were run by 'the right class of men who love football for its own sake'. These rules were abolished in the early 1980s. If they still existed, they might have stopped the businessmen Tom Hicks and George Gillett at Liverpool and the Glazers at Manchester United from burdening these clubs with a combined debt of nearly £1 billion simply to finance their takeovers.

The business of football is football. Clubs shouldn't chase profits. Instead they should invest every cent they have in the game. But that doesn't mean they should continue to be badly run. The weight of money that now washes through football demands a more business-like approach to managing cash. Bungs might have been no big deal when transfer fees were measured in the hundreds of thousands of pounds, but they become a problem when they run into the tens of millions.

Football clubs need to know what they are. They shouldn't even aspire to be big profit-making companies like BBA Aviation. Rather, they are like museums: public-spirited organizations that aim to serve the community while remaining reasonably solvent. If football becomes profitable, fans may end up pining for the days when it was the worst business in the world.

NEED NOT APPLY: DOES FOOTBALL DISCRIMINATE AGAINST BLACK PEOPLE?

In 1991 Ron Noades, chairman of Crystal Palace, popped up on British TV talking about black people. 'The problem with black players,' explained Noades, whose heavily black team had just finished third in England, 'is they've great pace, great athletes, love to play with the ball in front of them. . . . When it's behind them it's chaos. I don't think too many of them can read the game. When you're getting into the midwinter you need a few of the hard white men to carry the athletic black players through.'

Noades's interview was one of the last flourishes of unashamed racism in British football. Through the 1980s racism had been more or less taken for granted in the game. Fans threw bananas at black players. Pundits like Emlyn Hughes explained the curious absence of black players at Liverpool and Everton by saying, 'They haven't got the bottle.' The writer

Dave Hill summed up the stereotypes: '"No bottle" is a particular favourite, lack of concentration another. "You don't want too many of them in your defence," one backroom bod told me, "they cave in under pressure." Then there is the curious conviction that blacks are susceptible to the cold and won't go out when it rains.'

It's clear that English football in those days was shot through with racism: prejudice based on skin colour. But what we want to know is whether that racism translated into discrimination: unfair *treatment* of people. People like Noades may have been prejudiced against black players, but did they make it harder for these players to get jobs in football? The eighties black striker Garth Crooks thought they did: 'I always felt I had to be 15 per cent better than the white person to get the same chance,' he said.

Yet the notion of discrimination against black people clashes with something we think we know about football: that on the field at least, the game is ruthlessly fair. In football good players of whatever colour perform better than bad ones. Fans and chairmen and managers may walk around with Noadesian fantasies in their heads, but when a black player plays well, everyone can see it. Nick Hornby writes in *Fever Pitch,* in his famous riff on Gus Caesar, 'One of the great things about sport is its cruel clarity; there is no such thing, for example, as a bad one-hundred-metre runner, or a hopeless centre-half who got lucky; in sport, you get found out. Nor is there such a thing as an unknown genius striker starving in a garret somewhere.'

In short, it would seem that in football there is no room for ideologies. You have to be right, and results on the field will tell you very quickly whether you are. So would clubs really discriminate against black players at the cost of winning matches? After all, even Ron Noades employed black players. (He seems to have known something about football, too: after leaving Palace he bought Brentford, appointed himself manager, won promotion, and was voted manager of the year in the Second Division.) In fact, the very success of black players might be taken as evidence that the opportunities were there.

It's also often hard to prove objectively that discrimination exists. How can you show that you failed to get the job because of prejudice rather than just because you weren't good enough? Liverpool and Everton might argue that they employed white players in the 1980s simply because the whites were better.

Luckily, there is no need to get into a 'he said, she said' argument. We have data to prove that English football discriminated against black players. We can show when this particular kind of discrimination ended. And we can predict that the new forms of discrimination that pervade English football today will be harder to shift.

* * *

The first black person to set foot in the British Isles was probably a soldier in Julius Caesar's invading army, in 55 BCE. The 'indigenous' English themselves arrived only about four hundred years later, during the collapse of the Roman Empire.

Much later, under Victoria, Britain's own empire ruled a large share of the world's black people. A few of the better-educated or entrepreneurial ones made their way from the British Raj in India, the Caribbean or Africa to Britain. Arthur Wharton, born in 1865 in the Gold Coast (now Ghana), became the world's first black professional footballer. As well as keeping goal for Preston, he set the world record of ten seconds for the one hundred-yard sprint.

But until the 1950s most Britons had probably never seen a black person. Unlike Americans, they never developed any kind of relationship with black people, whether positive or negative. Then, after the Second World War, hundreds of thousands of colonial immigrants began arriving. The influx was small enough – less than 5 per cent of Britain's total population, spread over a quarter of a century – to pose little threat to the concepts of Englishness, Scottishness or Welshness. Nonetheless, the signs went up in the windows of apartment houses:

No Coloureds

One of the authors of this book, Stefan Szymanski, is the son of an immigrant from Poland who had escaped to London in 1940 and joined the British army to fight the Nazis. Stefan remembers his father telling him about looking for lodging in London in the early 1950s and finding signs in the windows saying

Rooms to let – no Poles, no Hungarians

Not only was this kind of discrimination legal, but Stefan's father accepted it. In his mind, he was the immigrant, and it was his job to fit in. Luckily for him (and for Stefan), he was an educated man, able to find a reasonable job and make a reasonable living. He was also a racist. This might sound harsh, but by today's standards most British adults seemed to be racist in the 1970s, when Stefan was growing up. In the popular comedy series of the time *Till Death Us Do Part,* the hero, Alf Garnett, was a ludicrously prejudiced Londoner who favoured labels like 'coon', 'nig-nog', 'darky', 'Paki' and 'the Jews up at Spurs' (Garnett supported West Ham). Not only were these words used on the BBC, but they were accompanied by canned laughter (the series was such a success that a US version followed, giving birth to Archie Bunker). Admittedly the joke of the series was ultimately on Garnett, who was regularly exposed to the falsity of his own prejudices. But Stefan used to argue that these labels were offensive. His father took this as evidence of his son's lack of a sense of humour.

It was against this 1970s background of instinctive racism that black players began arriving in English football. Most were the British-born children of immigrants. That didn't stop them from being treated to monkey noises and bananas. (As Hornby notes in *Fever Pitch,* 'There may well be attractive, articulate and elegant racists, but they certainly never come to football matches.') For a while, neo-Nazi parties even imagined that they could lead a revolution from the football terraces.

Given the abuse the early black players received, it would have been easy for them to give up on football. It was thinkable that they would be driven out of the game. Instead they stayed, played and triumphed. In 1978, when Viv Anderson became the first black man to play for England, it became apparent that children of Caribbean immigrants might have something of a role to play in English football. Still, even after the black winger John Barnes scored his solo goal to beat Brazil in Rio in 1984, the Football Association's chairman was harangued by England fans on the flight back home: 'You fucking wanker, you prefer sambos to us.'

As late as 1993 you could still witness the following scene: a crowd of people in a pub in London's business district, the 'City', is watching England versus Holland on TV. Every time Barnes gets the ball, one man – in shirtsleeves and a tie, just out of his City office – makes monkey noises. Every time, his co-workers laugh. If anyone had complained, let alone gone off to find a policeman and asked him to arrest the man, the response would have been: 'Where's your sense of humour?' (Hornby's line on this sort of problem: 'I wish I were enormous and of a violent disposition, so that I could deal with any problem that arises near me in a fashion commensurate with the anger I feel.')

Whenever people reminisce about the good old days, when ordinary working people could afford to go to football matches, it's worth scanning the photographs of the cloth-capped masses standing on the terraces for the faces you *don't* see: black, Asian or female. It's true that today's all-seaters in the Premier League exclude poor people. However, the terraces before the 1990s probably excluded rather more varieties of people. In the 1970s and 1980s, when football grew scary, the violence forced out even many older white men.

* * *

In the late 1980s Stefan began thinking about the economics of football. He was then working for the Centre for Business Strategy at London Business School. Everyone in the centre was an economist, and therefore tempted to think that markets more or less 'worked'. The theory was that any businessperson who came up with a brilliant innovation – inventing the telephone, say – would not keep his advantage for long, because others would imitate him and compete.

But the economists were interested in the few companies that stayed successful despite competition. Clearly there must be something to learn from them. Stefan suggested looking for these paragons in football. It was obviously a highly competitive industry, yet some clubs succeeded in dominating for years on end. How did they manage to stay ahead for so long?

Stefan enlisted the support of Ron Smith, who had taught him when he was writing his PhD. Smith, as well as being an expert on Marxist economics and the economics of defence, is a well-known econometrician. Econometrics is essentially the art of finding statistical methods to extract information from data – or, as a lawyer friend of Stefan's likes to put it, taking the data down into the basement and torturing them until they confess. Studying the accounts of football clubs, Stefan and Ron could see how much each club spent on salaries. The two discovered that this spending alone explained almost all the variation in positions in the English Football League. When Stefan analysed the accounts of forty clubs from 1978 to 1997, he found that their wage spending accounted for 92 per cent of the variation in their league positions.

Clearly the market in players' pay was highly efficient: the better a player, the more he earned. And this made sense, because football is one of the few markets that indisputably meets the conditions in which competition can work efficiently: there are large numbers of buyers and sellers, all of whom have plenty of information about the quality of the players being bought and sold. If a player got paid less than he was worth, he could move to another club. If he got paid more, he would soon find himself being sold off again.

But what about the variation in league position that remained unexplained after adjusting for players' pay? If buying talent was generally enough to win titles – as rich club chairmen like Jack Walker at Blackburn Rovers and Roman Abramovich at Chelsea would soon demonstrate – what else accounted for a team's success? If it was something that was easy to copy – a new tactic, for instance – then other teams would copy it, and the advantage would disappear. That got Stefan thinking about discrimination. What if owners were simply not willing to copy the secret of others' success, because they didn't want to hire the kinds of players who brought that success? He began to search for discrimination against black players.

In most industries, there is a way to demonstrate that discrimination exists. Suppose you could construct a sample of all applicants for a job, and also of all their relevant qualifications. If you then found that a much larger proportion of relevantly qualified white applicants received job offers than relevantly qualified black applicants, you could reasonably infer the presence of discrimination. For example, if 50 per cent of whites with doctorates in philosophy got job offers from university philosophy departments but only 10 per cent of their black equivalents did, then you should suspect discrimination.

This is essentially how economists have tried to identify job discrimination. The method also works for wage discrimination. If equivalently qualified black people (or women, or left-handers, or whoever) get lower wages for equivalent jobs, then there is probably discrimination going on. Researchers have put together databases of thousands of workers, each identified by dozens of relevant qualifications, to test whether discrimination exists. When it comes to ethnic minorities and women, the evidence usually shows that it does.

The problem is that there are few measurable qualifications that make someone a great footballer. When a company is accused of racism, it often says that while the black (or purple, or female) candidates may possess some of the relevant characteristics, there are other, less quantifiable characteristics that they don't have. Intellectually, this point is hard to overturn. Hundreds of cases of racial discrimination have been fought in American courts, and evidence based on the kinds of studies we have mentioned has often run into trouble.

Happily, there is another way to test for discrimination in football. Once again, it relies on evidence from the market. As a general rule, the best way to find out what people are up to is to see how they behave when faced with a price. Don't know whether you prefer Coke to Pepsi? Well, let's see what you choose when they both cost the same. (Most people choose Coke.) Do managers prefer white players to black ones? Well, let's see how they spend their clubs' money.

If clubs discriminate, then they will prefer to hire a white player to an equivalently talented black player. If they do that, then black players will find it harder to get jobs as professional footballers. The blacks will then be willing to accept lower wages than equivalently talented whites. After all, when demand for what we sell is lower, we tend to lower our asking price. So black players become cheaper than white players. If there is discrimination, we would expect to find black players earning less than equally talented whites.

If black players are being discriminated against, that creates an economic opportunity for unprejudiced clubs. By hiring

black players they can do just as well in the league as an equivalently talented (but more expensive) team of whites. That
means that a simple experiment will reveal whether discrimination exists: *if teams with more black players achieve higher
average league positions for a given sum of wage spending,
then the teams with fewer black players must have been discriminating.* Otherwise, the whiter teams would have seen that
black players were good value for the money and would have
tried to hire them. Then black players' wages would have risen
due to increased competition for their services, and the relative advantage of hiring black players would have disappeared.

Note that the argument is not that some teams hire more
black players than others. That could happen for many reasons. Rather, we can infer discrimination if a) some teams
have more black players than others and b) those same teams
consistently outperform their competitors for a given level of
wage spending.

After Stefan figured this out, he had the luck of running into
just the right person. Around that time he was also research-
ing the relationship between the pay of senior executives in
the biggest British companies and the performance of their
companies. (Very unlike footballers' wages, there turned out to
be almost no correlation between the pay of senior executives
and the performance of a company's share price, until share
options became common in the 1990s.) Stefan was inter-
viewed for a BBC programme by the political journalist Michael
Crick. Over time he and Crick got to talking about football.

Crick is a famously thorough researcher. Book reviewers
delight in finding errors, no matter how trivial, but they never
succeed with Crick's political biographies. And as it happens, Crick supports Manchester United. In 1989 he wrote
a fascinating history of the club with David Smith, describing
how United packaged its legend for commercial gain. About
this time Crick became interested in whether football clubs

discriminated in their hiring. Everyone knew of the suspicious cases of the day, chiefly Liverpool and Everton.

Crick began collecting data from the 1970s onward to see which clubs had hired black players. This was no easy task. How do you decide who is 'black'? Crick took a common-sense approach. He started with the old *Rothmans Football Year-books*, which published a photograph of every English league team. From this he made a judgement as to which players 'looked black'. He then followed up by asking clubs and supporters' clubs to fill in any gaps. It took him months to come up with a list of players who, to most fans, would have appeared to be black. This sounds arbitrary, but it is precisely what was required. Prejudice is based on appearance. For example, several years after Crick did his research, it emerged that the Manchester United winger Ryan Giggs had a black father. Giggs even spoke publicly about his pride in his Caribbean ancestry. However, until that point, most people would not have considered Giggs a black player. He didn't *look* black, and for that reason he would have been unlikely to face discrimination. So Crick was right not to count Giggs as black.

When Crick told Stefan about his list of black players, it was a cinch to create a test for discrimination. All that was necessary was to count how many times each black player had played for his club in a given season. It would then be clear which teams employed a larger proportion of black players.

Stefan then matched these data with figures on each team's league position and its spending on wages. If there were no discrimination in the market, then wages alone would almost entirely explain league performance. Everything else would just be random noise – 'luck'. But if black players were systematically being paid less than equally talented white players, then logically the teams that hired an above-average proportion of black players would do systematically better than their wage bill alone would predict.

Back in the 1970s, there were very few black players in English football. Combining our data on wages with Crick's database had given us a sample of thirty-nine out of the ninety-two professional league teams. In the 1973–1974 season only two of these clubs had fielded any black players at all. By 1983–1984 there were still twenty teams in our sample that did not field a black player all season. However, at this point there seems to have been a major breakthrough. By 1989 every team in the sample had fielded at least one black player at some point. By 1992, when the Premier League was founded, only five teams in the sample did not field a black player that season. This implied that about 90 per cent of clubs were putting black players in the first team. Attitudes were changing. Bananas left the game. When Noades voiced his theories on black players in 1991, he was widely mocked.

It is interesting to look at the characteristics of the black players in the English game in these years. For purposes of comparison, Stefan constructed a random sample of an equal number of white players with similar age profiles. Almost all the black players (89 per cent) were born in Britain, not very different from the white players (95 per cent). Most of the black players were strikers (58 per cent), compared with only 33 per cent of white players. There were no black goalkeepers at the time. Noades would have noted the fact that black players seemed underrepresented in defence. But then strikers always carry a premium to defenders in the market: it takes more talent to score than to stop other people from scoring.

Certain facts about the sample stood out: the careers of the black players averaged more than six years, compared to less than four for the whites. Few footballers last long in the pro game. And 36 per cent of the blacks had played for their countries, compared with only 23 per cent of the whites. On this evidence, it looked suspiciously as if the black players were better than the whites.

The proof came when Stefan deployed the economist's favourite tool, regression analysis. He used it to isolate the distinct effects of wages and the share of black players on each club's league performance. What he found was discrimination. The data showed that clubs with more black players really did have a better record in the league than clubs with fewer blacks, after allowing for wage spending. If two teams had identical annual wage budgets, the team with more blacks would finish higher in the league. The test implied that black players were systematically better value for money than whites. Certain teams of the 1980s like Arsenal, Noades's Palace and Ron Atkinson's West Bromwich Albion (this was years before Atkinson called Marcel Desailly 'a fucking lazy thick nigger' on air) benefited from fielding black players.

The clubs with fewer blacks were not suffering from a lack of information. Anyone who knew football could judge fairly easily how good most players were just by watching them play. So the only credible reason clubs would deny themselves the opportunity to hire these players was prejudice. Clubs didn't like the look of black players, or they thought their fans wouldn't, either simply because of skin hue or because they perceived weaknesses that just were not there. By testing the behaviour of managers against the market, it proved possible to uncover evidence of discrimination.

In football you can judge someone's performance only against other competitors. This means that I lose nothing by being inefficient if my competitors are inefficient in the same way as I am. I can go on hiring mediocre players as long as other clubs do, too. As long as all clubs refused to hire talented black players, the cost of discriminating was low. What the data showed was that by the beginning of the 1980s, so many teams were hiring talented black players that the cost of discriminating had become quite high. Teams that refused to field black players were overpaying for white players and losing more matches as a consequence. Yet some level of discrimination persisted. Even by the end of the 1980s, an all-white team like Everton would cost around 5 per cent more than an equally good team that fielded merely an average proportion of black players. As Dave Hill wrote in the fanzine *When Saturday Comes* in 1989, 'Half a century after Jesse Owens, a quarter of a century after Martin Luther King, and 21 years after two American sprinters gave the Black Power salute from the Olympic medal rostrum, some of these dickheads don't even know what a black person is.' But by the time Hill wrote that, precisely because football is so competitive, more and more clubs had begun to hire black players. In 1995 even Everton signed the Nigerian Daniel Amokachi. The economic forces of competition drove white men to ditch their prejudices.

Quite soon, enough clubs were hiring blacks that black players came to be statistically overrepresented in English football. Only about 1.6 per cent of people in the 1991 British census described themselves as black. Yet in the early 1990s about 10 per cent of all players in English professional football were black. By the end of the decade, after the influx of foreign players, the share was nearer 20 per cent.

So did clubs learn to overcome their prejudices? A few years after Stefan ran his first test for discrimination, he badgered some students who were looking for undergraduate projects into compiling a list of black players for another six seasons. That took the data set up to the 1998–1999 season. Once again Stefan merged the data with figures on wages and league performances. Now he could run the regression to the end of the 1990s. For these six additional years, there was no evidence that the share of black players in a team had any effect on team performance, after allowing for the team's wage bill. In other words, by then black players were on average paid what they were worth to a team.

Perhaps the best witness to football's acceptance of black players is Lilian Thuram. A black man born on the Caribbean island of Guadeloupe and raised in a town just outside Paris, Thuram played professionally from 1991 to 2008 and became France's most capped player. He won the World Cup of 1998 with that famous multi-coloured French team. He is also a French intellectual, possibly the only footballer ever to have spoken the words, 'There's an interesting young ethnographer at the Musée de l'Homme . . .'

Thuram is acutely sensitive to racism. He now runs an anti-racism foundation. Nonetheless, in 2008, in the final months of his long playing career, he insisted to us that football was innocent of the sin. Over late-night pasta in an Italian restaurant in Barcelona, he explained, 'In football it's harder to have discrimination, because we are judged on very specific performances. There are not really subjective criteria. Sincerely, I've never met a racist person in football. Maybe they were there, but I didn't see it.' In fact, he added, 'In sport, prejudices favour the blacks. In the popular imagination, the black is in his place in sport. For example, recently in Barcelona, the fitness coach said about Abidal [the black French defender], "He's an athlete of the black race." It's not because he stays behind after training to run. No, it's because he's black.'

So by the 1990s discrimination against black players had disappeared. Gradually they came to feel at home in the industry. Here is a scene from inside the marble halls of the old Arsenal stadium, after a game in 1995: Arsenal's black Dutch winger Glenn Helder is introducing his black teammate Ian Wright (one of Ron Noades's former players) to some Dutch people. Then Helder says, 'Ian, show these guys what I taught you.' A look of intense concentration appears on Wright's face, and he begins jumping up and down and shouting in Dutch, 'Buzz off! Dirty ape! Dirty ape!' He and Helder then collapse laughing. There was still racism in football, but by then blacks could mock it from the inner sanctums of the game's establishment.

The story of racism in American sports followed much the same arc. Right through the Second World War, baseball and basketball had segregated blacks into Negro Leagues. In 1947 Branch Rickey of the Brooklyn Dodgers broke an unspoken rule among baseball owners and hired black infielder Jackie Robinson to play for his team. Robinson eventually became an American hero. However, the co-star of his story was economics. The Dodgers had less money than their crosstown rivals, the New York Yankees. If Rickey wanted a winning team, he had to tap talent that the other owners overlooked. Racism gave him an opportunity.

Of course, discrimination against black players persisted in American sports long after Robinson. Lawrence Kahn, an economist at Cornell University, surveyed the data and found little evidence that before the 1990s baseball teams were withholding jobs or pay from blacks. But he did think they were giving black players unduly short careers, and using them only in certain positions. In basketball, Kahn did find wage discrimination. When he repeated his study in 2000, he discovered, like Stefan the second time around, that discrimination was fading. British and American sports were becoming fair to black athletes.

Only one category of players still suffers routine discrimination in European male football: women. It's true that on average, top-class female athletes are less quick and physically strong than top-class male athletes. Yet the superstars of women's football – think Carli Lloyd of the US or Germany's Alexandra Popp – are so skilful and tactically gifted that they are surely better players than most male professionals. Given the lack of money in the women's game, they might be willing to join even a second-tier men's team. A clever club would try to recruit them. Some female players already make a living as 'ringers' in unofficial semi-professional men's football in the US.

In the past, official male professional clubs who tried to sign female players were banned from doing so. 'There must be a clear separation between men's and women's football,' ruled FIFA's executive committee in 2004, when stopping Mexican second-division club Celaya from signing the female international Maribel 'Marigoal' Dominguez. But why? 'Custom,' FIFA told us. 'Custom has been that men and women compete in different competitions. And if you allow women to compete in the men's game, you would then have men applying for the same rights in women's competitions.' You could have Cristiano Ronaldo starring for Portugal in the next women's World Cup.

But 'custom' isn't a brilliant argument. Eleanor Sharpston QC, a barrister specializing in European law, who once rowed competitively in a men's boat, once told us that FIFA's ban on female players might not stand up if it came before the European Court of Justice. 'There is a strong trend within the European legislation to uphold equal treatment,' she said. 'What we're talking about is somebody making a living. The way I would argue it on behalf of the woman is to say, "It's a job like any job," just as if the issue were being somebody who mends mobile phones. It's not so special as to justify derogating from the normal principle of equal treatment.' Now that women occupy combat roles in most Western armed forces, it's hard to see why they need to be protected from the dangers of playing men's football. And the men's game could benefit from their presence. Whether that would be good for women's football is a separate argument.

* * *

We suspect that racial discrimination still exists in some national football leagues. In Russia in 2012 for instance, fans from Zenit St Petersburg's largest supporters' group, Landscrona, wrote to their club demanding that black and gay players be excluded from the team. They said that black players were 'forced down Zenit's throat', while gay players were 'unworthy of our great city'. These views seem to be pretty common in Russian football, and in Eastern Europe more generally. In that kind of atmosphere, a club brave enough not to practise racial discrimination can still expect to pick up good players cheaply.

We had thought that in Western Europe, at least, racial discrimination had died out. But there is a strange postscript to our story. In April 2011, the French website Médiapart leaked the minutes of a secret meeting at France's football federation.

The meeting, held in November 2010, had begun fairly innocuously. At first the officials had mused about admitting fewer youngsters of double nationality (often French plus African) into the federation's academies. It bothered the officials that some of these youngsters eventually chose to play for Algeria, say, rather than for France. However, the discussion quickly spread to scarier territory: complaints about black players per se.

France's coach, Laurent 'Le Président' Blanc (who had played alongside Thuram in the black–white–Arab French team of '98), was quoted as telling the meeting, 'You have the feeling that we are producing really only one prototype of player: big, strong, fast . . . and who are the big, strong, fast players? The blacks. That's the way it is. That's the way things are today.'

According to the leaked minutes, Blanc continued, 'I think we need to refocus, above all for boys of thirteen–fourteen, twelve–thirteen – introduce other parameters, adjusted to our own culture. . . . The Spanish say to me: "We don't have this problem. We don't have any blacks."' Blanc did add that he was talking about football qualities, not colour. He wouldn't mind if the whole French team was black, he said, as long as there was a balance of size and skill.

Even so, it's difficult to know where to start with a critique of his position. Most obviously, Blanc seemed to be conflating the

dull uncreative physical French style of the time with the presence of black players. Second, the issue of double nationality
scarcely mattered: a player of African origin good enough to play
for France, like the Senegalese-born Patrick Vieira, will choose
France. It's generally only French-raised players overlooked by
France, such as Marouane Chamakh (Morocco) or Riyad Mahrez
(Algeria), who will represent another country.

Yet some inside the French federation seemed to want to let
fewer boys of African origin into the academies. Blocking the
pipeline to professional football would mean job discrimination
against blacks. It would be a return to the practices of English
football of the 1980s. Nobody – we had previously thought –
was barred from top-class football in Western Europe anymore
because of his skin colour. Whereas ordinary Arab and black
people in France struggled to find jobs, we had imagined that
Arab and black footballers in France did not.

But even before the federation's secret meeting, many
French football fans had started to call for discrimination.
There had long been popular grumbling about the number of
non-white players in the national team. Every year France's
National Consultative Commission on Human Rights publishes
a big survey on racist attitudes. In 1999 a new question was
inserted into the survey: Were there 'too many players of foreign origin in the French football team?' You would not have
imagined anyone thought so. The players of foreign origin had
just made *les Bleus* world champions. Yet in 1999, 31 per cent
of respondents either totally or mostly agreed with this statement. In 2000, 36 per cent agreed. More than a third of French
people did not want this team even when it was the best on
earth. Jean-Marie Le Pen, then leader of France's racist Front
National party, knew exactly what he was doing when he led
the grumbles about France's black players.

As the team began playing worse after 2000 and became
blacker, public disquiet only grew. The philosopher Alain

Finkielkraut (and in France, philosophers are heard) voiced the thoughts of many French people when he complained that the 'black–black–black' team had become an international joke.

In 2010 France's then coach, Raymond Domenech, omitted three gifted young men of North African origin from his squad for the World Cup: Samir Nasri, Karim Benzema and Hatem Ben Arfa. We are sure that Domenech made his choices without any racist intention. There were football-based arguments against each of the trio. Nevertheless, says the French sociologist Stéphane Beaud, author of *Traîtres à la Nation?* ('Traitors to the Nation?'), a book on *les Bleus* and ethnicity, Domenech seemed unable to deal with a new, more assertive generation of North African youth.

The *Bleus* of 2010 were different from those of 1998, explains Beaud. The '98 team had come mostly from stable, fairly comfortably off working-class families not all that far from the French mainstream. Thuram, for instance, had grown up playing for an ethnically Portuguese team in the far-from-deprived Parisian suburb of Fontainebleu. But the 2010 team reflected the later wave of immigration to France: many players were from poorer and broken immigrant families who lived in the ghettos outside France's big cities. These men had grown up at a distance from the French mainstream. And whereas most of the heroes of '98 had spent many years earning relatively modest salaries in the French league, getting married and raising children, the new lot tended to have moved abroad very young, had spent their whole careers playing for top-level teams amid huge stress, and often had chaotic private lives, says Beaud.

The new generation can be harder to deal with for an older white Frenchman like Domenech (himself of Spanish descent). He was furious when Benzema (of Algerian descent) said he didn't want to come on as a sub in a game against Romania. In the minds of many white Frenchmen, the image of *les Bleus* became that of spoiled young globalized multimillionaires slouched on the team bus wearing massive headphones, ignoring fans who had waited hours to see them. And of course, these *Bleus* weren't white.

Popular anger erupted one Sunday night during the World Cup of 2010. French TV showed live how the players, angry with Domenech at their training ground in the South African tourist town of Knysna, reached for an authentically French remedy: they went on strike. They got onto their bus refusing to train. Nicolas Anelka swore at Domenech. The phrase 'the bus of shame' entered the French language. Knysna was 'a national affair, a political affair,' says Beaud. These mostly black and brown players were perceived as rejecting France. Worse than losing to Mexico and South Africa, they had (briefly) refused to play for the shirt. France's national anger against the young black players echoed the national anger of 2005 against the young black rioters in the ethnic ghettos. 'Scum', then interior minister Nicolas Sarkozy had called the rioters. In 2010 President Sarkozy instituted an inquiry into the football team.

A few months later came the federation's meeting in Paris. In a horrible way it made sense that officials of a national federation should be tempted by discrimination. Clubs are all about winning. National teams, however, have an additional function: to incarnate the nation. Many white French people – and of course the federation's officials were overwhelmingly white – seemed to feel that their nation could not be incarnated by a non-white team. If the officials had complained about black players publicly rather than in secret, a lot of French people would have been delighted.

After Médiapart leaked the minutes of the meeting, Thuram broke the unwritten social code of football to attack his old teammate Blanc. Three years earlier Thuram had told us that discrimination in football was impossible. Now he argued that Blanc had been guilty at least of 'unconscious racism' and promoting 'racial stereotypes'. If you say that blacks are stronger and faster than whites, Thuram argued, you open the door to saying that whites are more intelligent than blacks. Vieira, another black hero of 1998, complained, too. 'I know Laurent Blanc and I don't think he is racist,' he said. 'But I don't understand how any of the officials present at that meeting can stay in their job.'

In the end, Blanc and the others did stay in their jobs, cleared by a government inquiry, to the joy of most French fans. 'I think a similar affair at the federation is still imaginable,' Thuram told us in 2016. The French quotas scandal had changed nothing. Even the black players stayed on the team. They were the best, and that is still (almost always) what matters in football.

DO COACHES MATTER? THE CULT OF THE WHITE MANAGER

Trevor Phillips points a finger at his own shaven black head: 'Excuse me, here I am: bull's-eye!' The son of an early Caribbean immigrant to Britain, Phillips was raised in London and has supported Chelsea for over fifty years. But in the 1970s, when throwing darts was the favourite sport of Chelsea's Shed End, he didn't go to matches. His head felt like an obvious target. Hardly any black people went to Chelsea then. 'Now I can take my daughters,' he marvels.

Yet the long-time head of Britain's Equality and Human Rights Commission (he held the post until 2012) doesn't think football has slain discrimination yet. Over breakfast one snowy morning years ago, Phillips identified an enduring type of discrimination in European football: 'Loads of black players on the field and none in the dugout.'

You might think this form of discrimination would eventually disappear, that just as competition pushed clubs into buying black players, it will push them into hiring black managers.

But in fact, the prejudice against black managers has proved harder to shift. Long after our conversation with Phillips, it's still in place, almost unchanged. As soon as you get to thinking about what it will take to get more black people into coaching jobs, you are brought face to face with the great question about the football coach: Does he really matter? It turns out that the vast majority of coaches or managers (call them what you like) simply don't make that much difference. Consequently, the market in football managers is much less efficient than the market in players. That means blacks will continue to have a hard time finding coaching jobs.

Like discrimination against black players, discrimination against black managers first became visible in American sports. As early as 1969 the first black man to play in baseball's major league, Jackie Robinson, who had become quite rebellious as he grew older, refused to attend Old Timers' Day at Yankee Stadium, in protest at baseball's shunning of black coaches and managers.

The issue hit Britain only when the pioneering generation of black players began to retire (it being a longstanding article of faith in football that only ex-players had what it took to become managers). The former England international Luther Blissett, who as a player had made that ill-fated transfer to Milan, applied for twenty-two jobs as a manager in the 1990s. He did not get a single interview. Stella Orakwue, who recounts his story in her 1998 book *Pitch Invaders*, concludes, 'I feel a British black managing a Premiership team could be a very long way off.' Indeed, only in 2008, ten years after she wrote this, did Blackburn give Paul Ince a chance. After Ince's appointment, John Barnes, who himself had struggled to get work as a manager in Britain, still maintained, 'I believe the situation for black managers is like it was for black players back in the 1970s.' Ince lasted less than six months at Blackburn. As of January 2018, he hasn't managed a club for four years.

Not even good results with Newcastle could save the black manager Chris Hughton in 2010: he had won the club promotion to the Premier League the season before, but four months into the new season, with Newcastle safely in eleventh place in the top division, he was sacked. 'Regrettably the board now feels that an individual with more managerial experience is needed to take the club forward,' the club explained. Newcastle finished the season in twelfth place. Hughton went on to do well at Birmingham, stayed in the Premier League with Norwich (but was sacked regardless) and took Brighton into the top flight in 2017. It's hard to avoid the impression that he would be more highly regarded as a manager if he were white.

True, the black managers Ruud Gullit and Jean Tigana did get longer stints in the Premier League. But as Orakwue notes, the crucial point is that they were foreigners. They were perceived in Britain first of all as Dutch or French, and only secondarily as black. Gullit was cast as a typical sophisticated Dutch manager, not as an untried 'black' one.

In the 2016–2017 season there wasn't a single black manager in the Premier League. Only 4 per cent of senior coaches in England that year were non-white, compared with 25 per cent of players.

The 'Rooney Rule' in the American NFL – which requires teams to interview at least one minority candidate when recruiting a head coach or other senior officials – has made quite a difference there. Ten English clubs agreed to try it in the 2016–2017 season, but results were disappointing: these clubs had committed themselves to interview an ethnic-minority candidate for managerial jobs, even if no such candidate applied, yet they met that promise on only two out of eight occasions that season. Still, as of January 2018, all 72 English professional clubs below the Premier League agreed to expand the rule for an 18-month trial period. They committed to interview a suitably qualified minority candidate for all coaching jobs right up to the first-team manager. The FA itself pledged to do the same for all coaching positions including England manager. Let's see if this changes anything.

Almost all other football leagues have been equally unwelcoming towards black coaches. The MLS, for example, had just two in its first twenty-one seasons to 2017, according to Ben Lyttleton. He quotes Lilian Thuram as saying, 'Sometimes black players ask themselves, "Should I become a manager?" But then they think, "Even if I get my qualifications, who's going to hire me?" I think that in the collective unconscious, we have trouble imagining a black manager.' Nelson Rodriguez, general manager of the Chicago Fire, has said, 'I refuse to believe that the best people and best professionals are mostly white males. I would find that an incredible set of coincidences.' Yet that is the basic principle of coaching recruitment in football. In Europe, the issue mostly goes undiscussed. Even as sophisticated a club president as Andrea Agnelli of Juventus, who has fought against racism in the stands, shrugged when we asked him why there were so few black coaches: 'I haven't got a clue. I don't think it's to do with discrimination. I have never really thought about the issue.'

You would think that given the existing job discrimination, unprejudiced clubs could clean up by hiring the best black (or female) managers at low salaries. A small club like Tranmere Rovers, say, could probably take its pick of the world's black managers. It could get the best female manager in history. Yet it probably won't. That's because the market in football managers is so different from the market in players. Markets tend to work when they are transparent – when you can see who is doing what and place a value on it. That is pre-eminently true of footballers, who do their work in public. When you can't see what people do, it's very hard to assign a value to their work. Efficient markets punish discrimination in plain view of everyone, and so discrimination tends to get rooted out. Inefficient markets can maintain discrimination almost indefinitely.

Black footballers became accepted because the market in players is transparent. It is pretty obvious who can play and who can't, who's 'got bottle' and who hasn't. The market for players, as we have seen, is so efficient that salaries can explain about 90 per cent of the variation in clubs' league positions in the long run. If a player is underpaid relative to his contribution to the team, another club will probably sign him on a higher salary. That's why the club with the best-paid players typically finishes at the top, and the one with the worst-paid at the bottom. However, the market in managers doesn't work nearly as well. If players' salaries determine results almost by themselves, then it follows that the vast majority of managers are not very relevant – much less so than most media and fans imagine. Thomas Tuchel, one of the most thoughtful and successful German coaches of recent times, calls football 'a players' game' not 'a coaches' game'.

Because there is so much data in football, it's actually possible to demonstrate statistically how inefficient the market for managers is. For the last few years Stefan has been working with Thomas Peeters and Marko Terviö on this issue. Thomas is now an assistant professor at Erasmus University in Rotterdam. He graduated from the University of Antwerp (with a staggeringly high score in the university exams) under the tutelage of Professor Stefan Késenne, a pioneer of sports economics in Europe. Stefan K. asked Stefan S. to sit on Thomas's PhD committee, and so a collaboration was born. Together they used game-by-game data on English football between 1973–1974 and 2009–2010 to generate estimates of managerial ability. To account for differences in wage spending they were able to obtain the figures from the financial accounts of English clubs. This is not as hard as it sounds. All clubs except one were limited companies during this period, and therefore obliged by law to file annual accounts with Companies House. You can obtain copies online (they used to charge a small fee, but since 2015 you can download them for free).

As they worked on it Thomas realized that this was the perfect opportunity to test a theory developed by the Finnish economist Marko Terviö. The theory had to do with markets for very talented individuals. The problem, Terviö argued, is that firms often have limited incentives to invest in finding these people if their ability is only revealed on the job, because once it is revealed they will sell themselves to the highest bidder – in economic jargon, the employer gets a small share of the rents and so has little incentive to go prospecting for talent. The outcome, Terviö concluded, would be underinvestment in finding talent and overinvestment in 'mediocrities' – employees who are not terrible, but very probably not as good as an untried market entrant.

To Stefan and Thomas this sounded just like the market for football managers. Experienced mediocrities keep their jobs, and even get hired after they lose their jobs, because clubs are afraid of experimenting with inexperienced entrants. In fact, there's additional fear of experiment in the market for football managers: if an entrant turns out to be very poor, and gets his club relegated, then the club might be bankrupted. That encourages clubs to go with tried and trusted mediocrities.

Using a sample of one thousand managers covering seventy-five thousand games over thirty-seven seasons, Stefan and Thomas generated estimates of managerial ability on a month-by-month basis. Put more simply, they updated their estimates after every month (typically four or five games) to produce a profile of changing ability. And, just as Terviö predicted, they found that a significant number of managers were mediocre – in the sense that their estimated ability at a point in time was lower than the ability of the average entrant (based on the performance of entrants over the previous five years). Fully one-third of managers fitted into this category. We think that most football fans will recognize this pattern: some managers seem able to find job after job in which they are okay but not great. This is because it is an inefficient market.

Just look at the career of Claudio Ranieri. In 2015, fresh from a disastrous spell with Greece, which had ended with defeat at home to the minuscule Faroe Islands, he joined Leicester City. At that point he had been a manager for twenty-nine years without any outstanding successes. 'He was the perfect loser, with a capital L,' says the Italian football writer Tommaso Pellizzari. 'Everyone in Italy thought he was very nice, polite, kind, but please never call him to my team.' Then in Ranieri's first season at Leicester, the club won an utterly unexpected English title. Ranieri himself said there was no explanation for the team's success. He claimed no credit for it. But many people looking for a narrative and a main character attributed the triumph to him, as if at age sixty-four he had suddenly become a genius. *Harvard Business Review* published an article extolling his management skills.

The next season, after just five victories in twenty-five games, Leicester sacked him. If you looked at one club over one season, you might think that Ranieri was a magical motivator. But if you studied his whole career, or indeed looked at hundreds of managers over decades, as we have, it becomes very hard to believe that these people are the secret to winning trophies.

So maybe it's not just that the market for managers is inefficient. Maybe they just don't matter very much. Think of the contribution of the personnel manager of any large company. Did that person cause the success of Apple, Shell or Toyota? Well, all big companies need personnel managers, and in theory these people could have a big impact, but on the list of explanations for corporate success the personnel manager would not typically figure very high.

There is an important caveat: players' wages don't explain everything about league position – merely almost everything at most clubs. That leaves some room for a few good managers to make a difference. The question then is: Which elite managers finish consistently higher with their teams than their wage bills would predict, not just over one season, like Ranieri, but for most of their careers? In other words, to borrow a phrase from José Mourinho: Who are the special ones?

For an earlier edition of *Soccernomics*, Stefan made some rudimentary calculations to try to identify the best coaches. That database included about 700 managers. However, nearly 400 of them hadn't even managed thirty professional games – far too short a run on which to evaluate them. Even judging a manager on a couple of seasons isn't entirely fair, because that's still a short enough period for luck to play a big role. So he ranked only managers who had worked in the game for five or more full seasons: 251 men. Allowing for wage spending, he produced a statistical estimate of the ability (measured by contribution to winning) of these managers, which could then be used to generate a ranking. It must be said that few of the managers who had worked under five seasons looked like overachievers. Indeed, most of them had drifted out of the game early because of their poor records. Some of the worst performers exited the profession fastest – but a few survivors seem capable of producing sustained underperformance.

Malcolm Allison (a fêted assistant manager with Manchester City in the late 1960s, but a failure as a go-it-alone manager afterwards) made our list of shame, as did Alan Mullery, Harry Gregg and a few lesser-known names it would be kindest not to mention. However, even this handful of failures didn't seem to be terrible managers. Their underachievement was not what statisticians call 'statistically significant'. In simple English: it could have just been chance.

The analysis didn't treat all divisions equally. There are ninety-two professional teams in England, spread over the four divisions. A manager in the bottom tier, League Two, who has the ninetieth-highest budget in England but manages to finish eightieth in the country is doing well. However, a manager with the third-highest budget in England who succeeds in winning the Premier League is probably doing even better. At the top of football, competition is fiercer, the amount of money typically required to jump a place is much higher, and so the model gave more credit to overachieving managers in the Premier League than to overachievers lower down. Still, the model does allow some lower-division managers to make it to the top of our rankings.

All in all, somewhere between forty and seventy of the managers in the sample made a positive difference: that is, they usually overachieved with their teams. Note that this is almost 28 per cent of the 251 survivors in the database – and these survivors would themselves tend to be the elite, because underachieving managers rarely last five years in the game. In other words, of the 700 managers whom we observed for more than thirty games from 1973 through 2010, at most about 10 per cent look like overachievers. These managers tend to have stayed in their posts relatively long, which makes sense.

We ended up with two lists of overachievers. For our first list, we put all English clubs together and ranked each club's wage spending relative to the other ninety-one. The second list separated the clubs into four divisions, and measured each club's spending relative to the other clubs in its division. We mention this because each method produced a slightly different list of overachieving managers. Here are our two lists:

OVERACHIEVING MANAGERS IN ENGLAND, 1973–2010

'Total wage' method		'Divisional wage' method	
Rank	Manager	Rank	Manager
1	Bob Paisley	1	Bob Paisley
2	Alex Ferguson	2	Bobby Robson
3	Kenny Dalglish	3	Alex Ferguson
4	Arsène Wenger	4	Arsène Wenger
5	Rafael Benitez	5	David Moyes
6	Bobby Robson	6	Kenny Dalglish
7	Gérard Houllier	7	John Beck
8	Steve Parkin	8	Dave Mackay
9	Dave Mackay	9	Howard Kendall
10	Roy Evans	10	Steve Tilson
11	Howard Kendall	11	Rafael Benitez
12	Steve Tilson	12	Ronnie Moore
13	George Graham	13	Lou Macari
14	Martin Allen	14	Paul Sturrock
15	Martin Ling	15	Steve Coppell
16	Paul Simpson	16	George Graham
17	Ronnie Moore	17	Martin Allen
18	David Hodgson	18	Ray Mathias
19	Steve Wignal	19	Dave Stringer
20	Ian Atkins	20	Sam Allardyce
21	John Beck	21	Martin O'Neill
22	Sean O'Driscoll	22	Mel Machin
23	Leroy Rosenior	23	Jimmy Sirrel
24	Brian Clough	24	Keith Peacock
25	David Moyes	25	Tony Pulis
26	Russell Slade	26	Dave Smith
27	Steve Cotterill	27	Jack Charlton
28	Gary Peters	28	Paul Simpson

29	Micky Adams	29	Bobby Gould
30	Brian Laws	30	Gary Megson
31	Kevin Keegan	31	Terry Venables
32	Ron Atkinson	32	Danny Wilson
33	Dave Stringer	33	David O'Leary
34	David O'Leary	34	Trevor Francis
35	Paul Sturrock	35	Joe Kinnear
36	Keith Alexander	36	Graham Taylor
37	Gary Johnson	37	John Neal
38	Terry Neill	38	Steve Parkin
39	Barry Fry	39	Mike Buxton
40	Roy McFarland	40	Dave Bassett

It should be noted that the great Brian Clough, who appears on one of our lists, undoubtedly would have ranked somewhere in the top on both if only we'd had financial data for his glory years with Nottingham Forest in the 1970s. Uniquely within the (then) Football League, Forest was not a limited company at the time. It was a members' club, and therefore didn't lodge annual accounts at Companies House. Our list shows that even in his declining alcoholic years from 1982 onward, Clough was among the elite.

Here's our final ranking of managers who made both lists:

THE SPECIAL ONES

Manager	Rank ('divisional wage' method)	Rank ('total wage' method)
Bob Paisley	1	1
Alex Ferguson	3	2
Bobby Robson	2	6
Arsène Wenger	4	4
Kenny Dalglish	6	3

Rafael Benitez	11	5
Dave Mackay	8	9
Howard Kendall	9	11
Steve Tilson	10	12
John Beck	7	21
Ronnie Moore	12	17
George Graham	16	13
David Moyes	5	25
Martin Allen	17	14
Paul Simpson	28	16
Steve Parkin	38	8
Paul Sturrock	14	35
Dave Stringer	19	33
David O'Leary	33	34

This list of nineteen names must stand as our best stab at identifying the best managers in England in these years. Paisley won six league titles and three European Cups with Liverpool from 1974 to 1983.

Of course, there are all sorts of caveats to attach. First, our valuations are by no means precise. Wenger ranks a touch higher than Dalglish in our table, but please don't read that as saying that Wenger is the better manager. Our list cannot be that exact. Working at Arsenal from 1996 is a different experience from working at Liverpool, Blackburn and Newcastle in the 1980s and 1990s. Many other factors besides the manager might have caused each club's overachievement. It's notable that Paisley and Benitez also overachieved with Liverpool relative to wages, and George Graham with Arsenal. Perhaps it was easier to overachieve at Arsenal and Liverpool than at other clubs because these two used to produce many excellent youth players, allowing managers to do well without spending a fortune on wages. Perhaps Liverpool's famous 'boot room' of the 1970s and 1980s – the gang of old-time coaches and scouts who would sit around drinking whisky and dreaming up plans together – gave Paisley and Dalglish the wisdom of crowds. Quite likely Paisley, Dalglish, Wenger and Graham landed in helpful settings. Yet they do seem to have been good managers, too.

There's another caveat to make. Our table measures only spending on wages, not on transfers. We saw in Chapter 2 that Wenger and Ferguson had relatively low net spending on transfers, which makes their high rankings in our list even more impressive. But we also saw that Benitez (likewise high on our list) blew fortunes on transfers at Liverpool. So even though he economized on wages, he didn't get his league positions cheaply.

In fact, every manager in this table requires closer analysis. Just as you cannot sign a player simply on the basis of his match data, you cannot simply hire a manager from our list and sit back and wait for the trophies to roll in (although it would certainly be a much better method than hiring a guy because he was a good player). Some managers on our list succeeded in circumstances that might not be repeatable elsewhere. For instance, we suspect Bobby Robson did so well for Ipswich in the 1970s because he was one of the few managers of the time to strive for passing football and to scout on the Continent. Today he'd have had to find new tricks.

A STUDY IN OVERACHIEVEMENT: FERGUSON AND WENGER

Critics will ask why such a high proportion of our highest-ranked managers work for giant clubs. Well, for a start, the best managers tend to end up at the best clubs. Arsenal hired Wenger after he'd excelled at Monaco; Manchester United signed Ferguson after he'd broken the Celtic–Rangers duopoly with Aberdeen in

Scotland. In fact, Ferguson might have ranked even higher in our table had we been able to include his brilliant Aberdeen years. Unfortunately, we had to omit Scottish clubs because the financial data wasn't detailed enough. A second reason that managers of giant clubs dominate our list: by definition, more overachieving clubs will end up at the top of the league than at the bottom. And third, as we've said, the top of football is more competitive than the bottom, and so we have given extra credit to managers who overachieve at the summit.

Some may wonder whether a manager of Manchester United and Arsenal can overachieve by much. After all, United has the highest revenues in English football, and Arsenal isn't far behind. Surely clubs that rich ought to be winning league titles? (Indeed, we must admit that we used to think so ourselves. Simon now blushes with shame to think that he once wrote that if he managed United, with all its money, he would probably do about as well as Ferguson did.) But Ferguson and Wenger do seem to have added value. Once you look at the numbers, it turns out that for many years Ferguson's United and Wenger's Arsenal usually spent more on wages than most of their frustrated rivals, but performed even better than this high spending predicted.

Since there are twenty clubs in the Premier League it follows that the average club accounts for 5 per cent of the division's total wage bill. Manchester United is always above that 5 per cent line, but especially in the 1990s it wasn't above it by very much. In 1995–1996, for instance, the club spent just 5.8 per cent of the Premier League's total wages yet won the title. From 1991 through 2000, United's average league position was 1.8 (i.e. somewhere between first and second place) and yet in that decade the club spent only 6.8 per cent of the Premier League's average on wages. Ferguson was getting immense bang for his buck. In part, he owed this to the Beckham generation. David Beckham, the Neville brothers, Paul

Scholes, Nicky Butt and Ryan Giggs were excellent players who were performing with great maturity, but given their youth they would have been earning less than established stars. Furthermore, because Ferguson was at Old Trafford from 1986 until 2013, he had chosen every player at the club himself. He wasn't paying the unwanted signings of his predecessors large sums to rot in the stands. That helped keep United's wages down.

Ferguson continued to overachieve in the 2000s, even after the Beckham generation had become big names earning top dollar. Admittedly his overperformance was less striking than in the 1990s. From 2001 through 2010 United's average league position was again 1.8, but in this decade he spent nearly 9 per cent of the Premier League's total on wages. Another way of putting it: in the 1990s he spent only 35 per cent more than the division average, whereas in the 2000s he spent 80 per cent more than the average to achieve the same result. No wonder, because life had become ever more competitive at the top, with Chelsea and Manchester City getting shots of oil money and Arsenal and Liverpool receiving ever more income from the Champions League. None of that had happened in the 1990s.

The amount of money Ferguson required to dominate seemed to keep rising. In 2010, the last year in our database, United's share of the Premier League's wage spending peaked at just over 10 per cent. Yet even that wasn't outsize. Manchester City that year spent about the same proportion, and Chelsea accounted for 14 per cent of the Premier League's total outlay on wages from 2004 to 2010 – the largest share for any top-division club in the thirty-seven years of our database. Other clubs, too, have exceeded 10 per cent of the division's total spending in the past, notably Leeds United, which was at nearly 12 per cent when Clough spent his infamous forty-four days there in 1974. In short, Ferguson was a phenomenon for most of his time at Old Trafford. From 2003 through 2013 he consistently had to compete against clubs with higher wages. Mostly, he won. Even so, it's hard to work out exactly what he was doing right. If it were obvious, other managers would simply have copied him.

Indeed, since Ferguson's departure first David Moyes and then Louis van Gaal and Mourinho have demonstrated that not everyone can win the league (or even get close) with United. Their failures help us understand some of Ferguson's strengths – but also his failings.

Ferguson retired from United in May 2013 saying he was leaving behind 'an organisation in the strongest possible shape. . . . The quality of this league-winning squad, and the balance of ages within it, bodes well for continued success.' That proved false.

For decades Ferguson had planned ahead, renewing United's teams even when they were at their zenith. However, in his final years he focused less on rebuilding. Consciously or not, he seems to have constructed a team to peak in his last season. Even by August 2012, when he bought Robin van Persie for £24 million from Arsenal, he must have had some inkling that he himself would be retiring before long. The Dutchman's transfer fee paid off in the short run: Van Persie's brilliant first six months at United sealed Ferguson's last title. But then the ageing injury-prone striker got injured again. Ferguson's best player missed most of Moyes's tenure.

Several other starting players whom Moyes inherited in 2013 – Patrice Evra, Rio Ferdinand, Michael Carrick, Ryan Giggs and Nemanja Vidic – were well past thirty. Moyes should have cleared most of them out as soon as he arrived. Then, their standing was still high, and some would have fetched decent transfer fees. Furthermore, by shedding their hefty salaries, he would have freed funds to build a new team.

But his failure to do so points to a major disadvantage he had compared with Ferguson: Moyes had little status. And if you are managing United, your perceived status is very important.

No other British company in any sector receives more press coverage than United. Managing the club is therefore in large part a public relations job. Moyes's lowly status hampered him throughout his unhappy ten-month reign. Arriving from smaller Everton without a big name, he lacked the standing to dismantle United's revered team. He probably didn't dare confront the veterans in any PR battle. Their reputations exceeded his; his eleven years of diligent, impressive work managing Everton (he appeared on both our lists of managerial overachievers) hadn't earned him legendary status. At United, he may also have feared getting blamed for a new young team's teething troubles. Fatally, he allowed the old men one more season.

Then, when they faltered, leaving United seventh in the Premier League, his own PR failed him.

The ageing of United's squad, coupled with the loss of Van Persie for much of the season, were surely the main explanations for Moyes's disastrous reign. Yet most media pointed instead to the loss of Ferguson's motivational skills. The widespread fascination with motivation in football is exaggerated. Almost any player who has risen high enough to play for Manchester United can motivate himself. Most players play for their own careers, rather than for a club or manager. Judged every match by millions of knowledgeable observers, they have strong incentives to perform, under any manager.

Moreover, it's often players rather than the manager who shape team tactics. Peter Schmeichel later said of Eric Cantona's first training session under Ferguson in 1992: 'From that day, Manchester United's style of play changed. The arrival of Cantona suddenly made it clear to the coaching staff exactly how the team should play to be successful.'

Talk of Moyes 'losing the dressing room' at United was surely overplayed too. Of course players were dissatisfied with him. That's because they were losing. In top-class football, results usually determine mood, rather than vice versa.

In PR terms, Moyes's response to bad results was dreadful. His long, baffled, unhappy face – shown on TV whenever United conceded a goal – became the symbol of his team's malaise. Ferguson, a master of PR, usually responded to defeats with anger. That displaced blame – onto the referee, or, implicitly, onto his players. Moyes's sad expression looked like an admission of guilt.

Nor did he ever construct a narrative of hope. Had he fielded a new young team that lost matches, he could have said, 'Rebuilding takes time, but we're gradually creating another great United team.' Instead, at press conferences he seemed glum and defensive. He also treaded on United's own values. The club stands for attacking football and self-assurance. Moyes's team began playing defensively, and he came to sound defeatist – proclaiming Liverpool favourites, for instance, before United's old rivals visited Old Trafford. After Liverpool won 0–3, their manager Brendan Rodgers commented: 'I would never say that at Liverpool – even if we were bottom of the league.'

One aspect of Moyes's image problem was probably beyond any PR agency's control: succeeding Ferguson. Sir Alex didn't merely win trophies, but also incarnated United's history and values. By comparison, Moyes inevitably looked like a hired hand.

United had given Moyes a six-year contract. But in this media-driven era, the club could allow him only ten months of failure. Part of the manager's job is to act as scapegoat, shielding his club's owners from blame. United's owners, the Glazers of Florida, didn't want the media's focus to shift from Moyes to the £500 million-plus they had taken out of United since their £790 million leveraged buyout in 2005. If Moyes and Ferguson had had £500 million more to spend, United's team would have been younger and stronger.

In any case, the failure of Ferguson's successors leaves the Scot alone on his pedestal. Wenger's record was possibly even more awesome in his early years. In his first seven seasons at Arsenal, from 1996–1997 onward, the Frenchman achieved an average league position of 1.6 while accounting for 7.5 per cent of the Premier League's wages. That was a bigger share than Ferguson was spending then, but hardly plutocratic. Admittedly Wenger's performance declined somewhat after 2004. In the six seasons to 2009–2010, Arsenal had an average league position of 3.3 while spending 8.8 per cent of the Premier League's wages. That's still overachievement, but less striking than before. It should also be said that Arsenal's relatively low wage spend was a choice made by Wenger. The club could have afforded to spend more. If it had done so, Arsenal's average league position would probably have been higher.

Since 2010 Wenger's results have been less awesome than before. We can explain why he might have declined over the years. When he arrived in insular England in 1996, he brought knowledge that nobody else in England possessed at that point. 'I felt like I was opening the door to the rest of the world,' he said later. English football then still offered many gaping knowledge gaps to exploit. Arsenal's pre-Wenger diet, for instance, was suboptimal. Michael Cox writes in *The Mixer*:

> They'd enjoy a full English breakfast before training, and their pre-match options included fish and chips, steak, scrambled eggs and beans on toast. Post-match, things became even worse: on the long coach journey back from Newcastle, for example, some players held an eating competition, with no one capable of matching the impressive nine dinners consumed by centre-back Steve Bould.

Wenger introduced dieticians at Arsenal, and when the team stayed in a hotel, he had the minibars in the players' rooms emptied. But he was a pioneer in many other fields besides. For instance, he encouraged the use of supplements such as Creatine; he was one of the only managers already using statistics to analyse players' performance; and above all, he knew foreign transfer markets. Hardly any other manager in England in the mid-1990s scouted abroad, notes Cox. Middlesbrough had spotted the Brazilian Juninho in 1995 only after he had shone for Brazil in a tournament in England, under the eyes of England's assistant manager Bryan Robson, who happened to be Boro's player-manager. That same summer, Manchester City bought Georgi Kinkladze after he had impressed in two games for Georgia against Wales.

In short, Wenger back then had almost the whole world to himself. He seems to have been the only manager in England to realize that Milan's reserve Patrick Vieira and Juventus's reserve Thierry Henry were great players. Spotting that didn't require mystical insight – Vieira convinced the Highbury crowd of the same fact inside forty-five minutes on his debut against Sheffield Wednesday – but none of Wenger's British rivals appeared even to know who Vieira was. And so Wenger over-achieved magnificently.

His problem was that he was too successful for his own good. Other managers began to study what he was doing. They copied his innovations in diet, scouting and statistics. Meanwhile, like many brilliant pioneers, Wenger seems to have fallen into the trap of becoming more like himself – less willing to learn new tricks or listen to intelligent criticism – as he got older.

Eventually, when English football caught up with the world, and everyone had more or less the same knowledge, Arsenal was overtaken by clubs with bigger wage bills. That is what happens to knowledge gaps inside a league: they close fast. This would explain why from 2005 to 2017, Wenger's haul of trophies amounted to three victories in the FA Cup, the consolation prize of modern English football.

Yet during his worst moments, such as after the 8–2 thumping at Old Trafford in 2011 or the 10–2 aggregate defeat to Bayern Munich in 2017, his critics were too harsh on him. Given that he was up against several richer clubs, and against another great overachieving manager in Ferguson, it would have been astonishing had Arsenal continued to win titles. It was particularly unfair to castigate Wenger for fielding teams that kept getting outmuscled by Chelsea. There is a common belief that Wenger actively doesn't want players who are both brilliant and strong, such as Didier Drogba or Cristiano Ronaldo. In fact, Wenger built his first Arsenal team around Vieira, and privately regrets that he never managed to sign Drogba and Ronaldo when he could afford them. It's just that he knows that nowadays Arsenal cannot afford players who have it all. The club has to economize on one quality or another, and, forced to choose, Wenger has tended to prefer players who are skilful and quick but not strong. Chelsea hasn't had to make that choice.

Arsenal's board cannot very well tell the fans, 'Forget it. We can't stay ahead of Chelsea, City and United over a whole season.' But the board knows that this is true. It doesn't expect Wenger to win titles anymore. That's why he was allowed to continue through so many disappointments.

As we've seen, since Abramovich took over Chelsea in 2003, he has thrown money at the problem. In the 1970s Chelsea was still spending a touch less than the average in the top division. Only from the mid-1990s did the club's spending start to rise, and at the end of the 1990s it hit 8 per cent of the Premier League's total. By about 2000 Chelsea's Italian manager Gianluca Vialli was spending more than 10 per cent of the Premier League's wage bill, yet Ferguson repeatedly won the league on less.

When Abramovich bought Chelsea, he gave his manager Claudio Ranieri a mammoth 16 per cent of the Premier League's wage spending for 2003–2004. The club's payroll that year was £115 million, which was 65 per cent higher than Arsenal's. Of course, Ranieri ought to have won the league that season. However, we shouldn't be too harsh on him. Even with the highest wage bill, it's tricky to finish on top, because you are competing against both bad luck and the well-funded overachievers Wenger and Ferguson. Though Mourinho's Chelsea outspent its rivals, he deserves credit for winning two straight titles. But Mourinho spent only three full seasons in England before his return in 2013, and therefore doesn't yet figure in our rankings.

Chelsea were the country's biggest-spending club for six or seven years until the rise of Manchester City, and Abramovich's money bought him three league titles. By 2013, City almost certainly had the highest wage bill in England. Yet Ferguson kept his Mancunian neighbours from the title that season, confounding the odds one last time.

TINY GIANTS: GREAT MANAGERS WHOM NOBODY NOTICED

So far we've discussed only overperforming managers of giant clubs. However, several of our best managers of the 1974–2010 period – men such as Paul Sturrock, Steve Parkin, Ronnie Moore and John Beck – have spent their careers in the lower reaches of the game. As we write, in January 2018, none of them is managing a club. Beck left semi-professional Kettering Town in 2012, escorted from the stadium just before a game; Sturrock was sacked by the fourth-tier club Yeovil in 2015, and has since officially retired; Moore left fifth-tier Eastleigh in 2016; while Parkin as we write is assistant manager of Bolton Wanderers. These men were titans of the lower divisions, but hardly anybody higher up pays any attention to titans of the lower divisions. It seems that the market in managers does not work very efficiently: many of the best do not seem to get rewarded, while hundreds of managers who add no value continue to muddle on and get jobs, often good ones.

Admittedly some of our lower-division titans succeeded by playing a long-ball game that might not work higher up. 'I think my style of play has been successful in the lower leagues,' Sturrock told us cautiously in his bare little office at Southend one winter's night in 2011. Yet most good managers could surely adjust their methods to better players. We suspect these men were undervalued because they didn't physically look the part, or lacked charisma, or have had their reputations unfairly tarnished somewhere along the way. Sturrock thought this happened to him during his only, brief stint in the Premier League: his thirteen matches with Southampton in 2004. He complained, 'Everybody to this day thinks that I was fired. I walked out of the football club. It was an agreement between me and the chairman. It was the best for both of us. So maybe people tagged me that I'd failed in that environment. But if you look at my games ratio to any of the other managers that were round about me at that time, I probably had the most successful thirteen games any manager's had there.' Indeed, Sturrock won five of those games – pretty good at a small club – but fell out with Southampton's chairman, Rupert Lowe. He never got a chance at the top level again. In his Southend office, he reflected, '"I've been to the show," as the Americans would say. The one thing I'll say is that I enjoyed every minute of it.'

We're not telling Manchester City or Newcastle to go and hire one of the lower-league titans on our list sight unseen. But it couldn't hurt to take a look.

Still, the message from our data is that great managers are rare. Most managers seem to add so little value that it is tempting to think that they could be replaced by their secretaries, or their chairmen, or by stuffed teddy bears, without the club's league position changing. In typical football talk, the importance of managers is vastly overestimated. As Sturrock says, 'Money talks and money decides where you finish up in the leagues.' All in all, Jamie Carragher gets the significance of managers about right in his autobiography:

> The bottom line is this: if you assemble a squad of play-ers with talent and the right attitude and character, you'll win more football matches than you lose, no matter how inventive your training sessions, what system you play or what team-talks you give. But anything that can give you the extra 10 per cent, whether that's through diet, your general fitness or the correct word in your ear, also has merit.

QPR's chairman Tony Fernandes insists: 'I think managers do play a big part.' But he adds: 'Ultimately, if you have rubbish players, there's nothing a manager can do.' Perhaps the main service a manager can perform for his club is to avoid spend-ing much money on transfers. After all, transfers usually fail, and they waste funds that could have been spent on boosting the all-determining players' wages. Wenger is a better manager than Benitez in part because he blows less of his budget on transfer fees. But there isn't much else most club managers can do to push their teams up the table. After all, players mat-ter much more. As Johan Cruyff said when he was coaching Barcelona, 'If your players are better than your opponents, 90 per cent of the time you will win.'

There cannot be many businesses where a manager would make such an extravagant claim. The chairman of General Motors does not say that the art of good management is sim-ply hiring the best designers or the best production managers. Instead he talks about organization, motivation or building a team. We typically think of businesses as complex organisms. Yet when it comes to football, someone as insightful as Cruyff described management as little more than assembling the best players. Seldom has a prescription for successful management been so simple.

As we'll argue later in the book, we think that managers of national teams have a better chance of making a difference. A manager can outperform when he brings his team foreign knowledge that it didn't previously have. Fabio Capello arguably did that for England, and Guus Hiddink for South Korea, Australia and Russia. These men passed on to their players some of the latest Western European football know-how. However, it's very rare for such knowledge gaps to exist in a league like England's. All serious English clubs are now stuffed with people from all over the world and have access to current best practice. The Premier League is like a market with almost perfect information. Consequently, very few club managers can make much difference.

One counterargument to ours would be that the clubs that pay their players the most also tend to pay their managers the most. So the clubs with the best players would also be the clubs with the best managers.

We believe this argument is false in most cases. First, if some managers are good and others are bad, why does the performance of managers over time vary so much more than the performance of players? Eden Hazard and Neymar are always good players. They will have the odd bad match, but over the years nobody ever thinks they are terrible and in need of sacking. The history of management, by contrast, is littered with blokes appointed as the Messiah and sacked as a loser a few months later. Most managers' careers seem to follow a random walk: some good seasons, some bad ones. Just look at Ranieri. And anyway, how can managers make much difference when most of them last so briefly in each job? In 1992 the average manager's tenure in English football was 3.5 years. But the fifty-eight managers sacked in the 2015–2016 season – a record high – had been in their posts for an average of just 1.29 years. Of the ninety-two managers of English clubs in January 2018, only Wenger and Paul Tisdale at Exeter City had held their jobs for over seven years.

Tenure is even shorter in other major football countries. The median survival time for head coaches in the top two professional tiers in Germany, France, Spain and Italy from 2001 to 2015 was just 350 days, found the economists Alex Bryson, Babatunde Buraimo and Rob Simmons. The coaches most likely to be sacked were the older ones, and those who hadn't played professional football. Italian clubs were the most ruthless, and German clubs the least.

Chris Anderson and David Sally take on our argument about managers in their book *The Numbers Game*. They argue that managers matter rather more than we say, and they point to studies of chief executives making a difference in other industries. However, football isn't like most other industries. For a start, CEOs in other industries tend to stay in their jobs for much longer. In 2011, the average tenure of chief executives of companies ranked in the S&P 500 (the stock-market index of 500 big companies in the US economy) was 8.4 years. These people have more time to make a difference than a manager of a football club. Second, although CEOs in all industries like to make speeches about 'the talent of our people', individual talent of staff members probably counts for more in football than it does at, say, Tesco. For a big retailer, having the right processes and technology is probably what matters most, and these things are largely under the CEO's control. But if you want to beat Chelsea, you need eleven excellent players. That might help explain why footballers tend to get paid a lot more than workers in other industries.

Furthermore, the individual football manager has probably become even less important in recent years. It's typically the chief executive who now negotiates player contracts. Managers at big clubs today tend to work with dozens of staffers, ranging from physios to defensive coaches to data analysts. Jürgen Klopp at Liverpool has outsourced much (perhaps most) of his training and match tactics to his assistant, Željko Buvač, whom he has called him the 'brain' of his coaching team.

Wenger told Arsenal's website in an unusually revealing interview in 2015:

> I just compare now to when I started, when I was on my own with my players. Today I have a team of about 20 people around me who take care of the players but also give me information: statistics, the analysis of the game, the quantification of the players' work rate and their performances.
>
> Modern managers have so much information available to them . . . the modern manager is a guy who selects what is important and leaves what is less important . . . the manager isn't a lonely man anymore.

At many clubs the staffers have been appointed by the club chairman or the technical director, and will stay in their jobs long after the manager leaves. The manager still appears at the post-match press conference, and gets public credit for victory and blame for defeat. Day to day, though, his staffers may have a bigger impact on results. Fernandes says coaching staff are 'underrated . . . I think coaching staff make a big difference.'

Most people in the media love to focus on great men, but today it probably makes more sense to talk of management teams rather than individual managers. Indeed, you could argue that the main point of the 'top job' now is as a focus of competition for the other staffers, who can aspire to become manager one day. Brendan Rodgers, André Villas-Boas and Steve Clarke, for instance, all made it from Mourinho's staff at Chelsea to managing big clubs of their own. Clubs themselves increasingly seem to understand the importance of staffers. After Leicester won the title in 2016, several of the club's staffers got lucrative offers from other clubs. The scout Ben Wrigglesworth, for instance, jumped to Arsenal, while chief scout Steve Walsh became director of football at Everton. On the other hand, no big club tried to poach the supposed miracle-maker, Ranieri himself.

It's doubtful anyway whether many clubs or countries choose a manager chiefly because they think he will maximize performance. Often the manager is chosen more for his suitability as a symbolic figurehead than for his perceived competence. In other words, he's more of a king, or head of public relations, than an executive.

When a club or country appoints as manager a former iconic player like Maradona or Bryan Robson, it is not simply betting that he will garner more points than some upstart like Thomas Tuchel. Performance is only one of the criteria used for hiring a manager. That's because a club or country exists only partly to win matches. Its other job is to incarnate the club or country's eternal spirit. So a national team has to be the nation made flesh. Nobody could incarnate Argentina better than Maradona, and so he was made manager. Winning football matches had little to do with it. Whereas players are almost always employed because the club thinks they help win matches, that doesn't go for managers. Popular ex-players often get the job because they are easily accepted by fans, media, players and sponsors. They are hired as much for who they were as for what they can do.

The other criterion in hiring a manager is typically his gift for PR. Image has become all the more important for managers as football has become omnipresent on television since the 1990s. Managerial press conferences now attract rooms full of journalists, even though these events are generally streamed online. A manager might not affect his team's result, but after the game he's the person who explains the result at the press conference. He is the club's face and voice. That means he has to look good – which is why so many of them have glossy, wavy hair – and say the right things in public. This aspect has become increasingly important as football has received ever more media coverage. The late Helenio Herrera, Inter Milan's legendary manager in the 1960s, once told us that before his time, managers were unpaid men of low status. 'In those days it was the players who ran the teams,' he said. 'You had the team of Di Stefano, the team of Mazzola, the team of Sivori, and the trainer was the man who carried the bags,' and he mimicked an overburdened porter.

Televised press conferences have probably done more than anything else to create the modern myth of the omnipotent manager. No wonder that the thing Tony Blair seemed to like best about football (according to his former right-hand man, Alastair Campbell) was the post-match press conference. When Blair was British prime minister, he'd often spend time at the weekend slumped on the sofa watching football on TV. He took a mild interest in Burnley, the club Campbell supported. But Campbell tells us that Blair grew fascinated with the then Burnley manager Stan Ternent, a character with a thick Geordie accent and a gift for exuding gloom. After games Blair, a born actor, liked to put on his best Burnley accent and ring Campbell: 'Reet, Ally, 'ow did Burnley get on today, then?'

The forte of most managers is not winning matches – something over which they have little control – but keeping all the interest groups in and around the club (players, board, fans, media, sponsors) united behind them. That's why so many managers are charismatic. Their charisma may not help their teams win matches, but it does help the managers keep support.

The general obsession with managers is a version of the Great Man Theory of History, the idea that prominent individuals – Genghis Khan, or Napoleon, or even Stan

Ternent – cause historical change. Academic historians, incidentally, binned this theory decades ago.

The myth of managerial omnipotence has been both good
and bad for managers. When the manager became the face of
the club, his salary and fame rose. On the other hand, he also
became more vulnerable. If the team was losing matches, the
obvious thing to do was to get rid of its symbolic figurehead.
Indeed, British club directors in the early twentieth century
upgraded club secretaries to the position of manager partly
so that when a team's results were bad, the directors would
be able to deflect blame from themselves onto a lower-class
scapegoat. Barney Ronay writes in *The Manager: The Absurd
Ascent of the Most Important Man in Football*, 'The manager
was born to be sacked, and sacked with some sense of cathartic public ceremony.'

Sacking the manager is now an ancient ritual, football's version of the Aztecan human sacrifice. English clubs spent an
estimated £99 million sacrificing their managers in the 2010–
2011 season, if you add up the cost of compensation, legal
fees and 'double contracts' (paying the old and new manager
at the same time), according to the League Managers Association. All this money could have been more usefully spent on
players' wage bills or on improving stadiums.

As it happens, after the manager is sacrificed, a team's
performance does tend to improve briefly. Sue Bridgewater,
professor at Warwick Business School in the UK, analysed
sackings in the Premier League from 1992 to 2008 and found
that 'there is a boost for a short honeymoon period.' For
instance, after Manchester City sacked Mark Hughes at Christmas 2009, it won its first four games under Roberto Mancini.
However, that's not because Mancini or any other new manager can work magic. The short honeymoon is easy to explain.
Typically the average club earns 1.3 points a match. Typically,
Bridgewater found, an English club sacks its manager when it

averages only 1 point a match – that is, at a low point in the cycle. Any statistician can predict what should happen after a low point: whether or not the club sacks its manager, or changes its brand of teacakes, its performance will probably 'regress to the mean'. Simply put, from a low point you are always likely to improve. The club may have hit the low due to bad luck, or injuries, or a tough run of fixtures, or – as perhaps in Manchester City's case – the time it takes for a largely new team to gel.

Whatever the reason for hitting a low, things will almost inevitably improve afterward. The new manager rarely causes the pendulum to swing. He's just the beneficiary of the swing. Perhaps some players do briefly work harder to impress him, though on that logic clubs should sack managers even more often.

Eventually results regress to the mean. Bridgewater found that three months after a sacking, the typical club averaged the standard 1.3 points a game. 'Most studies find that coach dismissals do not improve team performance,' say the Dutch economists Jan van Ours and Martin van Tuijl in a study that found the same thing.

Sheikh Mansour, City's billionaire owner, should probably have just stuck with Hughes and waited for results to rebound, but in business doing nothing is often the hardest thing. (And not just in business. Harold Macmillan, British prime minister during the Cuban missile crisis of 1962, mused then 'on the frightful desire to do something, with the knowledge that not to do anything . . . was prob. the right answer'.)

Inevitably Mancini was credited with City's short honeymoon. 'Mancini really is magic,' proclaimed *The Sun* newspaper, and people began to whisper that the Italian might win that season's Premier League. No wonder, because the wavy-glossy-haired Italian looks like a manager and boasts a glittering résumé as a player. Those facts reassure fans, media, social media, players and sponsors, even if they don't help City win matches. Mancini's salary – like any manager's – therefore reflected his iconic status and his gift for PR as much as his expected contribution to performance. So it's probably not the case that the best-paid managers are the best performers.

It's different for players. They are judged almost solely on results. Very occasionally a player does get bought because he is an icon, or good at PR. However, those qualities in themselves won't sustain him in the team. Any player who doesn't play well will be out the door swiftly, no matter how wavy his hair or how white his skin. As we've just shown, being a player is all about performance. Being a manager isn't. Although clubs pay players only for their contribution to performance, that's not true of how they pay managers.

Perhaps one day clubs will dispense with managers altogether and let a large sample of their fans pick the team instead. In 2007 the semi-professional side Ebbsfleet United gave its 30,000 fan-owners – who had each paid £35 for the privilege – a vote in player selection. Coincidence or not (and the money the fan-owners put in probably made the biggest difference), Ebbsfleet almost immediately experienced its greatest triumph, victory in the FA Trophy Final at Wembley in 2008. Afterward the club's performance declined, as many of the fans stopped paying, and most of the players had to be let go. Still, it was interesting to see a club select its team using the wisdom of crowds. It would be even more interesting to see what happened if more clubs did this – if they stopped hiring managers and allowed an online survey of registered fans to pick the team. We suspect the club would perform decently, perhaps even better than most of its rivals, because it would be harnessing the wisdom of crowds. And it could use the money it saved on managers to up those crucial players' wages.

None of this is good news for black managers. Because it is so hard to measure a manager's performance without complex grinding of stats over many seasons, it will probably never become painfully obvious that clubs are undervaluing black managers. That means clubs can continue to choose their managers based on appearance. Any club appointing someone who is not a white male ex-player with a conservative haircut must worry about looking foolish if its choice fails. Hiring a black manager feels risky, because as John Barnes says, 'Black guys haven't proved themselves as managers.' White guys have – or at least some of them appear to have.

Footballers get more or less the jobs they deserve. If only other professions were as fair.

THE SECRET OF CLAUDE MAKELELE: HOW 'MATCH DATA' ARE CHANGING THE GAME ON THE PITCH

Early in 2011, Simon visited Manchester City's tranquil training ground in the village of Carrington. (City have since moved to a spiffier training ground just across the road from the Etihad Stadium.)

It was a glorious sunny winter's morning, and outside the gates hired hands were washing footballers' SUVs and sports cars. The defender Kolo Touré coasted past in a giant black contraption straight out of *The Godfather*.

'Abu Dhabi Travellers Welcome,' said the message on the facade of City's sky-blue training centre. Abu Dhabi's ruling family owns Manchester City, and one thing it did after buying the club in 2008 was hire a large team of data analysts. Inside the building was Gavin Fleig, City's head of performance analysis, a polite, sandy-haired man in a neat black City sweater. Hardly anyone outside Manchester City has heard of him, and yet Fleig has been a prime mover in English football's data revolution. Largely unseen by public and media, data on players had begun driving clubs' decisions – particularly decisions about whom to buy and sell. At many clubs, obscure statisticians in back rooms are helping shape transfers.

Fleig gave me the sort of professional presentation you'd expect from a 'quant' in an investment bank. Not long before, to his excitement, City had acquired stats on every player in the Premier League. Imagine, said Fleig, that you were thinking of signing an attacking midfielder. You wanted someone with a pass completion rate of 80 per cent, who had played a good number of games. Fleig typed the two criteria into his laptop. Portraits of the handful of men in the Premier League who met them flashed up on a screen. A couple were obvious: Cesc Fàbregas and Steven Gerrard. You didn't need data to know they were good. But beside them was a more surprising face: Kevin Nolan, then with Newcastle. The numbers wouldn't immediately spur you to sign him. But they might prompt you to take a closer look.

After many false starts, the number crunchers at big clubs had begun to unearth some stats that matter. For instance, said Fleig, 'The top four teams consistently have a higher percentage of pass completion in the final third of the pitch. Since the recruitment of Carlos Tevez, David Silva, Adam Johnson and Yaya Touré to our team, in six months, our ability to keep the ball in the final third has grown by 7.7 per cent.'

That stat had not necessarily driven their recruitment, Fleig cautioned. Indeed, some English clubs lean far more on stats than Manchester City does. Most of them rarely talk about it, though, for fear of sharing their secrets or getting ridiculed for relying on numbers. Few outsiders understand just how far football's data revolution has progressed. 'We've somewhere around 32 million data points over 12,000, 13,000 games now,' said Mike Forde, Chelsea's then director of football

operations, one morning in the empty stands of Stamford
Bridge in 2011. Since then the data revolution has continued,
albeit with many stumbles and still a fair bit of resistance.
Football on the field is gradually becoming cleverer.

*   *   *

Charles Reep, a wing commander in Britain's Royal Air Force,
made possibly the first recorded attempt to log match data at a
football game. Reep had become interested in the topic in the
1930s, recounts Jonathan Wilson in *Inverting the Pyramid*. He
began collecting stats during the second half of a Swindon Town
game in 1950. In that one half, he recorded 147 attacks by
Swindon. Extrapolating from this small sample, Reep calculated
that 99.29 per cent of attacks in football failed.

He kept logging matches, and over time he developed a
theory – based on extremely dubious numbers – that too much
passing was a risky waste of time. Most goals came from very
short moves, he said. The way to win, he concluded, was long
balls forward.

Reep advised the strong Wolves team of the 1950s, and in
the early 1980s influenced Graham Taylor, the future England
manager, and Charles Hughes, the English Football Association's future director of education and coaching. Using his
dodgy stats, Reep encouraged both men to develop the long-
ball thinking that would eventually culminate in England's failure to qualify for the World Cup of 1994.

Reep's crude models probably did more to discredit the
project of match data than to further it. However, one of his
associates did put data to good use in the lower reaches of
English football. Neil Lanham, a tidy-moustached auctioneer,
had gotten to know Reep in the Suffolk village where both men
lived. In the 1960s Lanham began logging games, but with
rather more rigour than the wing commander. 'The findings that

I talk of,' Lanham wrote in a paper for *Football Journal* in 2008, 'are based on hand-recording every possession for every team in more than 4,000 games. . . . When you sit in the stands and write down every possession by hand, you see and virtually kick every ball.'

His methods led him to some startlingly exact findings. For instance, Lanham reckoned that teams scored on average once every 180 possessions, a figure that he said was 'near constant' for any division of English football and for the World Cup. This finding, he added, was based on '328,018 hand-noted possessions'.

Lanham came to the same conclusion as Reep: the secret of football was putting the ball near the other team's goal fast. 'Two-thirds of goals come from possessions won in the final third of the field,' he lectured. The great sin, to him, was losing the ball near your own goal.

Sometime in the 1980s Lanham wrote to clubs offering his analysis. Many ignored him, but Wimbledon's manager, Dave Bassett, replied at once. Advised by Lanham, Wimbledon won two promotions and the FA Cup of 1988. Generally, long-ball football seemed to work better at lower levels than it would in the early 1990s for Taylor's England. Lanham, billing himself with the startling twenty-first-century title 'football performance analyst', went on to advise Sheffield United, Crystal Palace and Cambridge United as they used long-ball tactics to climb the divisions. 'Eight promotions', read the stat on Lanham's letterhead. He also did 'various works for international managers', he told us in a letter in 2011.

Though Lanham was determinedly artisanal, in 1985 he began feeding his shorthand codes into what he called 'a database computer system'. Computers were about to revolutionize match data. In the late 1980s, the young French manager of Monaco, Arsène Wenger, a keen mathematician, began using a computer program called Top Score, developed by a friend, which gave marks for every act performed during a game. 'Most players who had very high scores went on to have successful careers,' Wenger said later.

A less likely pioneer of match data was the late, great vodka-sodden Ukrainian manager Valeri Lobanovsky. When Simon visited Kiev in 1992, Lobanovsky's pet scientist, Professor Anatoly Zelentsov, had him play the computer games that Dynamo Kiev had developed to test players. When Lobanovsky said things like, 'A team that commits errors in no more than 15 to 18 per cent of its actions is unbeatable,' he wasn't guessing. Zelentsov's team had run the numbers.

Meanwhile up in Norway, one of Reep's disciples was making great strides. The Marxist Egil Olsen and Wing Commander Reep had become unlikely allies. They shared a love of stats that went far beyond football. Olsen knows (and will sometimes name) the highest mountain of every country in the world. As manager of Norway, he used to gather his players before games to show them their latest individual stats on a big screen. It got to the point that when the midfielder Lars Bohinen mishit a pass at the World Cup of 1994, he'd instantly think, 'Oh no – I've got an "M"' – Olsen's code for a misplaced pass. Still, the methods seemed to work. Norway briefly rose to second place in FIFA's rankings. When Olsen became Wimbledon's manager in 1999, the ninety-five-year-old Reep – still billing himself as 'wing commander' – offered his services as an analyst, writes Wilson. But Olsen, Wenger and Lobanovsky were years ahead of their time. The broader breakthrough for stats came in 1996, when Opta Consulting in London began to collect match data for the English Premier League. The management consultancy's main aim was to build its own brand by creating football rankings. The Premier League's sponsor, Carling, paid for the so-called Opta Index. Clubs and media got the data for free. Each club received an Excel report with some basic statistics. By today's standards, it was primitive. But in football then, it was revolutionary.

Within just a few years, the game moved from a paucity of data to a state of too much information. Pretty soon Opta and its rivals were sending out thousands of new data points each week. Clubs learned facts they had never contemplated before: how many kilometres each player ran per match, and how many tackles and passes he made.

Collecting these numbers took – and still takes – meticulous work. Most people know the impact of computers on our lives, but the work of the grunts is often forgotten. They are like the farm labourers of the pre-industrial age who were required to bring in the harvest. Opta's tenth-floor offices next to London's Waterloo Station provide a spectacular view of the city, but the dozens of 'analysts' barely notice.

Simon visited Opta's offices the day after Manchester City won 1–6 at Old Trafford in October 2011. Two young men were sitting side by side, each in front of a computer, both watching the same images from the game on a screen. One logged all of City's actions, and the other all of United's. Two other people had logged the game live the day before, with a third person watching for quality control, but Opta liked to repeat the process the next day 'with a different set of eyes', said John Coulson, head of professional football services at the company.

Opta's analysts type in the minutiae of every televised game they can find, from the Premier League to the MLS or the Montenegrin First League. All the ones we saw were men, generally in their twenties, kitted out in regulation grunge and looking wan. Most were college graduates who hadn't been able to resist the temptation of earning pitiful amounts of money to watch football. 'We take on one person of the twenty or thirty who apply for these jobs,' said Coulson. Not that the analysts can really watch the games, as they sit there logging every single event in endless detail (long pass, weight on the ball, origin of the ball, where the ball lands). In all, Opta now collects several hundred categories of data. Doing the analysis looks like a harder job than playing football. Most of the grunts are burned out after a couple of years, but then there are plenty more people willing to give it a go.

Gradually managers started to pay attention to these stats. In 2001 Alex Ferguson of Manchester United suddenly sold his defender Jaap Stam to Lazio. The move surprised everyone. Some thought Ferguson was punishing the Dutchman for a silly autobiography he had just published. In truth, although Ferguson didn't say this publicly, the sale was prompted partly by match data. Studying the numbers, Ferguson had spotted that Stam was tackling less often than before. He presumed the defender, then twenty-nine, was declining. So he sold him. It was a milestone in football's history: a major transfer driven largely by stats.

As Ferguson later admitted, it was also a mistake. Like many football men in the early days of match data, the Scot had studied the wrong numbers. Stam wasn't in decline at all: he would go on to have several excellent years in Italy. The American statistician Nate Silver points out in his book *The Signal and the Noise* that as more data becomes available, we become more likely to use them to make mistaken decisions. Often, the masses of data seem to form a pattern that just isn't there. That's why you often see false positives for breast cancer in mammograms, or false assessments of footballers.

Despite the dangers, Ferguson's rival Wenger embraced the new match data. He once said that the morning after the game he's like a junkie who needs his fix: he reaches for the spreadsheets. 'Wenger always used to love the averages, the trends,' Opta's chief executive, Aidan Cooney, told us. One day around the millennium, in a period when Arsenal's rivals Manchester United were piling up English titles, Wenger handed his new young French scout Damien Comolli a piece of paper covered in stats. As recounted by the French journalist Aurélien

Delfosse in 'La data révolution', Wenger asked Comolli: 'Do you know why we always finish second in the league? Look at these numbers – in every sector of the game we're second behind United. Second in shots, second in passes, second in tackles won . . .'

Wenger was then already using stats to make counterintuitive team selections. Dennis Bergkamp, in his book *Stillness and Speed*, describes how the manager 'used statistics on me' during the Dutchman's declining years as a player at Arsenal. Their conversations would go something like this:

BERGKAMP: Where in your statistics does it say that I changed the game with a killer pass?
WENGER: You run less in the last thirty minutes and you're more at risk of getting injured, and your pace is dropping.

Few would suspect it of the former England manager (albeit for just one match), Sam Allardyce, but his somewhat Neolithic appearance also conceals a professorial mind. As a player Allardyce spent a year with Tampa Bay, where he grew fascinated with the way American sports used science and data. In 1999 he became manager of little Bolton. Unable to afford the best players, he hired good statisticians instead. The analysts fixed upon one particular number that enchanted Allardyce. 'The average game, the ball changes hands four hundred times,' recited Chelsea's Forde, who got his start in football under Allardyce. Big Sam loved the figure and would drum it into his players. To him, it summed up the importance of switching instantly to defensive positions the moment the ball was lost.

More concretely, stats led Allardyce to a source of cheap goals: corners, throw-ins and free kicks. Fleig, another Allardyce alumnus, recalled that Bolton used to score 45 to 50 per cent of their goals from such 'set pieces', compared with a league average of about a third. Fleig said, 'We would be looking at, "If a defender cleared the ball from a long throw, where would the ball land? Well, this is the area it most commonly lands. Right, well, that's where we'll put our man."'

By the early 2000s Allardyce's then club Bolton was valuing players in much the way financial investors value cattle futures. Take Bolton's purchase of the thirty-four-year-old central mid-fielder Gary Speed in 2004. On paper, Speed looked too old. But Bolton, said Fleig, 'was able to look at his physical data, to compare it against young players in his position at the time who were at the top of the game, the Steven Gerrards, the Frank Lampards. For a thirty-four-year-old to be consistently having the same levels of physical output as those players, and showing no decline over the previous two seasons, was a contributing factor to say: "You know what, this isn't going to be a huge concern."' Speed played for Bolton till he was thirty-eight (and, tragically, committed suicide at forty-two).

Just when Bolton was buying Speed, Wenger was search-ing for an heir to Arsenal's all-action midfielder Patrick Vieira. As Christoph Biermann recounts in his book *Die Fussball-Matrix*, Wenger wanted a player who could cover lots of ground. The manager is a great believer in running around. He argues that if you run 11 kilometres and your opposite number covers 12, the difference will probably manifest itself in the last fif-teen minutes, often in the shape of the opponent popping up unmarked in front of your keeper.

Wenger scanned the data from different European leagues, and spotted an unknown teenager at Olympique Marseille named Mathieu Flamini who was running 14 kilometres a game. Alone, that stat wasn't enough. Did Flamini run in the right direction? Could he play football? Wenger went to look, established that he could, and signed him for peanuts. Flamini prospered at Arsenal, and after a few years with Milan returned to Arsenal and prospered there again. As Wenger once defined his recruitment strategy: 'With every player there is a moment when his value is higher than the price. The key is to get that timing right.' Long before other managers had cottoned on, stats were helping him do that. Wenger, said Beane, 'is undoubtedly the sports executive I admire most.'

Conversely, the clubs that stuck with 'gut' rather than numbers began to suffer. In 2003, Real Madrid sold Claude Makelele to Chelsea for £17 million. It seemed a big fee for an unobtrusive thirty-year-old defensive midfielder. 'We will not miss Makelele,' said Madrid's president Florentino Pérez. 'His technique is average, he lacks the speed and skill to take the ball past opponents, and 90 per cent of his distribution either goes backwards or sideways. He wasn't a header of the ball and he rarely passed the ball more than three metres. Younger players will cause Makelele to be forgotten.'

Pérez's critique wasn't totally wrong, and yet Madrid had made a terrible error. Makelele would have five excellent years at Chelsea. There's now even a position in football named after him: the 'Makelele role'. If only Madrid had studied the numbers, it might have spotted what made him unique. Forde explained: 'Most players are very active when they're aimed towards the opposition's goal, in terms of high-intensity activity. Very few players are very strong going the other way. If you look at Claude, 84 per cent of the time he did high-intensity work, it was when the opposition had the ball, which was twice as much as anyone else on the team.'

If you watched the game, you could miss Makelele. If you looked at the data, there he was. Similarly, if you looked at Manchester City's Yaya Touré, with his languid running style, you might think he was slow. If you looked at the numbers, you'd see that he wasn't. Beane said, 'What stats allow you to do is not take things at face value. The idea that I trust my eyes more than the stats, I don't buy that because I've seen magicians pull rabbits out of hats and I just know that the rabbit's not in there.'

Yet by the mid-2000s, the numbers men in football were becoming uneasily aware that many of the stats they had been trusting for years were useless. In any industry, people use the data they have. The data companies had initially calculated passes, tackles and kilometres per player, and so the clubs had used these numbers to judge players. However, it was becoming clear that these raw stats – which still sometimes get beamed up on TV during games – mean little.

Forde remembered the early hunt for meaning in the data on kilometres. 'Can we find a correlation between total distance covered and winning? And the answer was invariably no.' You might know how many passes a player had given, but that didn't tell you whether they were splitting through-balls or sideways shoves into a teammate's feet.

Tackles seemed a poor indicator too. There was the awkward case of the great Italian defender Paolo Maldini. 'He made one tackle every two games,' Forde noted ruefully. Maldini positioned himself so well that he didn't need to tackle. That rather argued against judging defenders on their number of tackles, the way Ferguson had when he sold Stam. Fleig said, 'Tackles to me are a measure of being under pressure.' To this day, how to value a defender remains one of the great mysteries of football. For the moment, stats can still tell us much more about the quality of an attacker, a creative midfielder, or a keeper.

Forde reflected, 'I sat in many meetings at Bolton, and I look back now and think, "Wow, we hammered the team over something that now we think is not relevant."' Looking back at the early years of data, Fleig concluded, 'We should be looking at something far more important.'

In 2003 football's data revolution had got a new impetus when Michael Lewis published *Moneyball*. 'I bought twenty copies and sent them out to all the Premier League managers,' recalled Cooney. He pauses and chuckles. 'Didn't get one response.' Nonetheless, a few people in English football read the book and sat up. They began thinking about doing 'a *Moneyball* of football': using stats to find new ways of valuing players.

It so happened that just as football executives were getting interested in *Moneyball*'s hero, Billy Beane, Beane was getting interested in football. On a London vacation with his wife, he'd encountered the game and fallen hard for it. Forde, who had studied in Beane's home town of San Diego and followed American sports, made the pilgrimage to Oakland to quiz Beane about the uses of data. That proved tricky: Beane spent the first few hours of the conversation quizzing Forde about football. 'In the last half an hour I managed to turn it around to talk about his role in baseball,' Forde told us, laughing.

In 2011 Simon visited Beane in the Oakland Coliseum. We spoke in what looked like the junk room but in fact is the clubhouse. Beane can often be found sprawled on a dilapidated sofa here watching European football matches while sceptical baseball players watch him. When Beane watches football, he sees a game full of emotion, and where there is emotion, he knows people will be making emotional decisions.

Football will follow baseball in turning into 'more of a science', Beane predicted. 'I always say, in a casino there's a reason guys who count cards get kicked out and guys who bet on gut feel don't.' Beane agreed that data probably wouldn't transform football as they had baseball, but then they didn't need to, he said. If using statistics in football gives you an edge, then all clubs will end up having to use statistics. He explained, 'If somebody's right 30 per cent of the time using gut feel, and you can find a way to be right 35 per cent, you create a 5 per cent arbitrage, and in sports that can make the difference between winning and losing.' (In 2015 Beane took his first official post in football, as part-time adviser to the Dutch club AZ Alkmaar, and then took part in the takeover of

Barnsley by an international consortium in 2017. So far he has kept his day job with the A's.)

Beane's closest friend in football was Comolli. The Frenchman had lived in Northern California for a year as a teenager. He became a baseball fan, and an A's fan, and the ideal reader of *Moneyball*. When he took over as director of football at Tottenham in 2005, he began using data to inform the club's decisions on transfers.

The surprise is not that this happened but that it happened so late. London had long since been taken over by highly educated professionals. Every other serious company in town uses data and computers. It just took London's football clubs a while to catch up.

Comolli unearthed some excellent players for Tottenham: Luka Modric, Dimitar Berbatov and a seventeen-year-old left-back from Southampton named Gareth Bale. He identified Bale and Modric the old-fashioned way, not with stats but just by watching them play. 'I'm not an ayatollah of stats,' Comolli told Delfosse. However, data did lead him to Berbatov, then playing for Bayer Leverkusen. 'His statistics were remarkable,' Comolli recalled. 'His number of shots, shots on target, assists.' Above all, Berbatov performed as well in away games as at home. Even though the Bulgarian was scoring twenty goals a season, other clubs were undervaluing him (possibly because of his unfashionable nationality).

Yet Comolli's three years at Spurs encapsulated many of the struggles of football's data revolution. British football had always been suspicious of educated people. The typical manager was an ex-player who had left school at sixteen and ruled his club like an autocrat. He relied on gut, not numbers. He would have noticed that in many other industries, lesser-educated working-class men like himself had been replaced by people with degrees or by computers. In American banks, for instance, says Michael Lewis, fat mortgage traders 'who had high-school degrees from New Jersey and traded by their gut . . . are replaced by hairless wonders from MIT'. The losers from the American data revolution would eventually help put Donald Trump in the White House.

In football, gnarled old ex-players had no wish to be replaced by hairless wonders with laptops. Naturally, then, the manager wasn't about to obey some French whippersnapper who wasn't even an ex-pro.

The manager's suspicion might sound perverse: after all, Comolli's numbers might have helped the club win games. However, many people in football are less bothered about winning than about hanging on to their own job and power base. A manager, in particular, lives with massive job insecurity. Every day, he wants to look like an expert (or even a Messiah), a man without weaknesses, so if he isn't well versed in data, he will be tempted simply to reject it. And to be fair to managers, not all of football's data analysts know what they are doing. Precisely because the people running the clubs are often statistically illiterate, they don't always hire the cleverest geeks. (See also football's tendency to employ insiders and their pals, as detailed in Chapter 3.)

But even clever geeks often get ignored. Chris Anderson remarked after his experience trying to introduce more informed decision-making at Coventry City that a manager will often smack down his video analyst with the words, 'I know exactly what happened.' The problem, says Anderson, is that managers tend to remember the most memorable events of a match rather than the most important ones. Nobody can force the manager to listen: he is the 'Boss', at least until the day he is sacked. In any case, the manager often has no time to take on board his data analysts' insights: the next game is always around the corner.

Beneath the quarrels about data lurks a bigger issue. When it comes to knowledge, the world divides into progressives and conservatives. Conservatives tend to believe that we have reached the limits of what we can know and that delving further is not only futile but immoral – some things are better left unknown. Progressives, on the other hand, tend to believe that even if we don't know how something works, patient analysis will eventually reduce the problem to a manageable set of proven relationships. Ever since Renaissance scholars began figuring out where a cannonball would land, the conservatives have been on the retreat. So many things we once thought were beyond analysis are now well understood, from the aerodynamics of flight to the mechanisms of disease. Now neuroscientists are starting to find answers to questions about how we know what we like, how we fall in love and what we achieve in life.

The conservative's ultimate fear is that one day we may know so much about what happens next that there are no choices left to be made; the universe will seem so predetermined that no one will bother to get out of bed. It's probably true that football's data revolution has reduced creativity. It has increased the tendency of players to spend the match following the coaching staff's instructions. Though the game on the field will never become fully automated, it is certainly less freewheeling now than even a decade ago. In particular, we are getting used to the idea that defensive players tend to move around in patterns dictated by their coaches, almost like in American gridiron football. Perhaps that's inevitable, given the speed at which players today have to act. Oliver Bierhoff, general manager of the German national team, says the average time of contact with the ball for Germany's players has dropped from 2.6 seconds in 2004 to 1.1 seconds in 2015. With so little reaction time, it helps to have analysts tell you in advance where to go and where to pass.

In football the conservatives fought back. There was one question the nerds kept having to answer. Yes, the conservatives would say, stats may well be useful in a stop-start game like baseball. The pitcher pitches, the batter hits, and that event provides oodles of clear data for nerds to crunch. But surely football is too fluid a game to measure?

Forde responded, 'Well, I think it's a really genuine question. It's one that we ask ourselves all the time.' However, the nerds can answer it. For a start, good mathematicians can handle complex systems. At Chelsea, for instance, Forde employed a statistician who had a past in insurance modelling. Football – a game of twenty-two people played on a limited field with set rules – is not of unparalleled complexity. Marcus du Sautoy, maths professor at Oxford University and football nut, says that players tend to move in fairly predictable patterns rather than randomly. It is simply not the case that data is useful in every single industry on earth except football. Second, the fluid game of basketball has already found excellent uses for data. Beane said, 'If it can be done there, it can be done on the football field.' And third, a third of all goals in football don't come from fluid situations at all. They come from corners, free kicks, penalties and throw-ins – stop-start set pieces that you can analyse much like a pitch in baseball.

Data-resistant managers haven't died out yet, but they are less common among the younger generation of football coaches, says Ted Knutson, who as owner of the consultancy StatsBomb Services has consulted many clubs on using data. Bill James, the pioneering sports statistician in baseball, has a piece of advice for football statisticians who still have to fight traditionalists: 'The number one strategy is never argue with anybody. Just simply ignore those people who disagree with you, who criticize you, who explain why you're wrong. The people you can reach are the people who are listening. I guarantee you in football there are an awful lot of people who are listening now, who are just being very quiet about it.'

MONEYBALL IN FOOTBALL: A TALE OF ONE CLUB AND TWO CITIES

Soon after Comolli was ousted from Spurs in 2008, he got a second chance. In 2010 Boston Red Sox owner John Henry bought Liverpool. Henry, who made his money trading commodities, believes in numbers. In 2002 he had tried to bring Billy Beane to Boston. Beane said no, but the Red Sox subsequently won two World Series using *Moneyball* methods. Bill James, who works as a data consultant for the club, told us: 'John could have had my job. I mean, if John had not had an ability to make an extremely good living from financial instruments, he could very well have been the person who made a living by analysing baseball and explaining it to others.'

Henry wanted to do 'a *Moneyball* of football' at Anfield. The only problem was that he knew nothing about football. He called Beane to ask for advice. Beane told him to hire Comolli. The Frenchman was made Liverpool's director of football. Often, during his time at Anfield, he'd exchange ideas with the father of *Moneyball* 5,000 miles away. Beane told us, 'You can call him anytime. I'll email him and it will be two in the morning there and he'll be up, and he'll email me and say, "Hey, I'm watching the A's game," because he watches a lot of A's games on the computer. The guy never sleeps.'

Comolli became the poster-boy for the '*Moneyball* of football'. When Liverpool sacked him in April 2012, the experiment accordingly appeared discredited. But meanwhile, almost unnoticed, just across town, Liverpool's rivals Everton had been playing *Moneyball* quite successfully for years. The story of Liverpool and Everton illustrates both the scope and the shortcomings of *Moneyball* in football.

At Liverpool, Comolli had a lot of power to use data to shape club policy. In January 2011 he bought Andy Carroll and Luis Suarez for a combined £58 million, and sold Fernando Torres to

Chelsea for £50 million. 'When you find yourself handling three of the biggest transfers in English football history in the last days of the market,' Comolli said at the time, 'precise figures allow you not to do that blind.' He didn't say much more than that, but before selling Torres, he undoubtedly would have tracked the player's rate of decline. With older players – and at twenty-six a pacy striker is getting old – the key question is, 'How fast is he fading?' You can measure that by comparing the player's key outputs from year to year. If, for instance, his top sprinting pace, number of shots on goal and number of completed passes in the final third are gradually declining, you can probably see his future. (Comolli presumably knew that Steven Gerrard's number of shots on target – a key stat – had been falling since he was twenty-six. A canny unsentimental Liverpool might have sold Gerrard at twenty-eight, before others noticed his decline.)

After a rudimentary analysis of Suarez's stats, Comolli was willing to pay more for the Uruguayan than he had initially intended. What struck him in particular, he told Delfosse, was that Suarez was decisive for Ajax Amsterdam. Very often, Suarez scored the important first or second goal of the game, he scored in the closing minutes, he scored against the best teams and he scored away as well as at home. Still, there was a statistical problem: Suarez was scoring these goals in the easy Dutch league. What formula do you use to translate Dutch goals, shots or assists into their equivalents in tougher England? Luckily, Suarez's Dutch numbers spoke loudly. Beane says, 'He was so dominant there that even though he was jumping into a bigger league, I think they felt like they were going to have at least a certain calibre of player no matter what.' By now there are so many years of statistical analysis on players from every big foreign league that English clubs are much better able to predict how well a newcomer from a particular league will make the jump. One finding: the Dutch league is so weak and slow that success there says nothing about how a player will fare in England, as Memphis Depay would demonstrate when flopping at Manchester United. It just so happened that Suarez did succeed in England.

In summer 2011, numbers guided Comolli again. Few followers of football had identified Stewart Downing as a great talent, but the data showed that he was one of the most prolific dribblers and creators of chances in the Premier League. According to rankings produced by Opta with the CIES Football Observatory in Switzerland, the midfielder was responsible for 17 per cent of Aston Villa's 'overall club production' in the 2010–2011 season, a greater share than any other player at any other club in the Premier League. Comolli bought him and Jordan Henderson, who, aged just twenty, was already Sunderland's link man, responsible for 13.6 per cent of the team's passing. The 'expected goal' index showed that Henderson was an excellent creator of chances. Both players also had very good stats for regaining possession in and around the opponents' penalty area. Together, they were supposed to provide the crosses for Carroll to head home.

It didn't work out. Just as previous Liverpool managers Gérard Houllier and Rafael Benitez had relied on experience and gut feel to make bad transfers (as discussed in Chapter 2), Comolli's data-driven purchase of the Carroll–Henderson–Downing trio went wrong. The Frenchman had inadvertently demonstrated that stats can't guarantee success on the transfer market. They can only improve your hit rate. 'Player recruitment is simply a game of risk management,' says Rory Campbell, head of technical analysis at West Ham. However, Comolli's failure at Liverpool had many people asking the question: can *Moneyball* thinking work in football? Even John Henry has said football is 'too dynamic' to allow stats to guide recruitment.

Yet the Comolli experience needs to be examined more carefully.

What it showed was that the *Moneyball* of football was still in its infancy. Comolli had assembled the best possible players for a crossing strategy. The problem is that as we learn more about match data, we discover that crosses from open play are a poor way to score goals. Much of the best work on match data is done not in football clubs but by amateurs on the sofa. Many of these amateurs have day jobs in statistics – working in insurance, doing maths PhDs and the like. One excellent blogger, who identifies himself merely as 'a Liverpool support-ing atmospheric scientist who spends far too much time look-ing at numbers', analysed Liverpool's play in the 2011–2012 season. He found that Liverpool had hit more crosses than any other team in the Premier League. However, he wrote: 'Their conversion from crosses was simply atrocious. They required a staggering 421 open-play crosses to score a single goal in open-play on average last season. This was the worst rate in the whole league.'

It turns out that crossing is not the way to victory. Comolli had bet the company on a bad strategy. A cross from a free kick makes sense, because the player hitting it has time and space to achieve precision. But to send a man sprinting down the wing with a defender in his face, and then count on his cross being nodded in, is usually hopeless. Much more effec-tive is for a player to reach the byline near the goal, and then roll the ball back along the ground into the path of an incoming teammate

Another problem for football's *Moneyball*ers has to do with the game theory that we discussed in the last chapter. It's one thing to plan a strategy – for instance, heading in crosses – and to show statistically that this strategy produced goals using historic data. It's quite another to declare that this strategy will keep working in the future. Once you have signed a good crosser and a tall striker, it is perfectly obvious to your opponents what you are going to do and therefore how they should set about defending against your strategy. In some extreme cases (Messi and Cristiano Ronaldo spring to mind) defending may be impossible even if you know what your opponents are planning, but generally this is not the case. Telegraphing your strategy is a pitfall when using big data in football.

At least the Liverpool experiment taught us more about which data matter: crosses rarely work. That knowledge is progress of sorts. It's also wrong to write Comolli off as a failure: even at Liverpool, he recruited Suarez while also selling the declining Torres for what was then the largest fee ever paid by an English club. In part, Comolli got scapegoated because he's exactly the type of person whom media, fans and ex-players-turned-pundits are quick to scapegoat: a bespectacled Frenchman who has never played professionally and isn't very easy-going or clubbable. His habit of claiming credit for good decisions also bit him in the leg when there were bad decisions looking for an owner.

But there's more to *Moneyball* in football than Comolli. Everton is the smaller and poorer of Liverpool's two clubs, yet in both 2012 and 2013, it finished above Liverpool in the table. In part, at least, this was thanks to data analysis. One day in 2013, Simon visited the club's training ground at Finch Farm, on the city's semi-rural outskirts. It was a Monday morning, two days after Everton had beaten super-rich Manchester City, yet there weren't hordes of fans waiting outside Finch Farm. In fact there was nobody waiting there at all.

In the dining room a few players in shorts were eating lunch. At the other end of the room was a table with four members of manager David Moyes's support staff. One of the men, David Weir, a quiet Scotsman in a cardigan, had played for Everton for years before becoming a coach there; but the other three were unknown outside Finch Farm. Steve Brown, James Smith and Dan Hargreaves, in their blue elephant-adorned training kit, were Everton's unheralded assets, who earned dozens of times less than the players they worked with.

These men had been picking brains inside and outside football to improve their use of data. They were painfully aware that no one in their group had so much as a maths degree. They shouldn't have been embarrassed. In the typical corporation, very few human-resources staff have college degrees involving numbers, says Rob Symes, who made the documentary *Outside View* on sports and data.

In the film, Daniel Kahneman, the psychologist who won the Nobel Prize for Economics in 2002, says that a key to good decision-making is to let statistics 'not humans make the final decision'. That is what Everton's data team were trying to do. Moyes clearly took them seriously. Smith and Brown, the club's main performance analysts, weren't hidden away in some backroom where nobody could hear them scream. Instead their offices were on the corridor directly opposite the manager's.

Often Moyes would march into their rooms firing out questions: how efficient was next Saturday's opponent at scoring from crosses or throw-ins? What types of passes did their midfielders make? When Everton faced Gareth Bale at Tottenham, Moyes wanted 'an assessment of where Bale is actually picking up the ball compared to the areas where you think he is working', said Brown. Smith added: 'He [Moyes] is quite demanding in terms of data. In terms of managers, he is probably as into it as any.' (A measure of the staff's awe for Moyes is that they rarely referred to him by name – what to call him? 'Moyes'? 'Mr Moyes'? 'David'?)

Moyes had no particular ideology of how he wanted his team to play. Instead he worked out what the opposition did, and then tried to stop it. Before facing Manchester City, for instance, he identified the positions where City's playmaker Silva usually received the ball, and put men there. (This, incidentally, is excellent game theory.)

The insights that Moyes and his staff gleaned from video and statistics were constantly transmitted to Everton's players. Brown said, 'There is a post-match data sheet that goes up in the changing room. Some players will actually sit down and look at the Prozone data with us; they will look at pass-maps and their "receive positions", their crossing data. We have one central midfielder who comes in every week and looks at his pass completion.' The analysts cautioned that you always need to understand the context of any piece of data. For instance, what was a player's role in a particular game? Who was he playing alongside? Match data without context is meaningless.

Weren't some players sceptical of numbers? 'There is a bit of that,' agreed Brown. But mostly, the analysts said, Everton's players appreciated the help. Many players considered stats (about themselves and about opponents) a survival tool that could give them as many high-earning years as possible at the top of the game. Smith said: 'Going out to play in the Premier League is a daunting thing. They want David Moyes to tell them what to do. That's reassuring. One player once said to me, "They might complain about a meeting, but if it wasn't there they would be the first to say, 'Where is the meeting?'"'

The staffers noted that most fans and media seem unaware of all the analysis that goes into preparing games. Often, in pubs and TV studios, a game is discussed as if it were a mix of bursts of inspiration, individual blunders and a manager's motivational powers. Hargreaves said: 'What the public sees isn't necessarily what's happening. The level of ex-player punditry doesn't lend itself to what's happening behind the scenes.' In part, that's because managers like Moyes won't reveal their tactical secrets. So journalists end up writing about how a winning manager 'psyched out' his opponent with 'mind games'.

It's not that Moyes at Everton based his every decision on data. Rather, they were one of the things he considered. They made signing a player, for instance, a little less of a leap in the dark. 'Watching players is actually a very subjective thing, an inexact science,' said Smith. 'There are all kinds of inputs: live player reports, extensive video analysis, speaking to people who have worked with them, and data is one of those layers. Data plays a role – not a massive role at the moment.'

One occasion when data did matter was in 2008, when Everton was trying to replace its midfielder Lee Carsley. Smith said, 'We needed someone to replace things that he had been doing: possession regains, winning tackles and headers, protecting the back four.' The club's eye fell on a twenty-year-old Belgian, obscure but for his enormous mane of hair, named Marouane Fellaini. 'We'd followed him at the 2008 Olympics but he didn't have a great tournament, and actually he got sent off quite early on,' Smith recalled. There were few match stats for Fellaini, because at the time there was no data available for Belgian league matches. And so Everton watched videos of him to compile their own set of stats, using key performance indicators that seemed relevant. Smith said: 'Fellaini was one of those where everything said, "Yes, do it": the data, the subjective reports, the age, the fact that he was already playing for Belgium, his size.' And so Everton gambled £15 million on him – then the club's record transfer fee. It paid off. In 2013, after Moyes had moved to Manchester United, he bought Fellaini for £27.5 million.

WHERE ARE WE HEADING?

Every season, football gets a little cleverer. Quietly, behind the scenes, some big clubs have arrived at statistical insights that are incrementally changing the game. Especially in England and Germany, where clubs have tended to look more at match data than in Spain or Italy, the 'quants' can now isolate numbers that matter. 'A lot of that is proprietary,' Forde told us at Chelsea.

'The club has been very supportive of this particular space, so we want to keep some of it back.' But the quants will discuss certain findings that are becoming common knowledge in football. For instance, rather than looking at kilometres covered, clubs now prefer to look at distances run at top speed.

Sprinters have been gaining respect inside football. When the then Spurs manager Harry Redknapp was tempted to sell his disappointing young left-back Gareth Bale in 2009, Tottenham's performance director Michael Edwards managed to dissuade him partly by pointing to the kid's physical stats: Bale could make repeated sprints at an astonishing pace. His passing in the final third of the pitch was pretty mean too. The problem, Edwards explained, was that Bale wasn't really a full-back. He'd do much better as a winger. For once, writes Delfosse, the old traditionalist Redknapp listened to stats and kept Bale.

Similarly, Fleig at Manchester City cares about 'a player's high-intensity output'. Different data companies measured this quality differently, he told us, 'but ultimately it's a player's ability to reach a speed threshold of seven metres per second.' If you valued this quality, you probably would never have made the mistake Juventus did in 1999 of selling Thierry Henry to Arsenal. 'For Henry to reach seven metres per second, it's a relative coast,' said Fleig admiringly. The Frenchman got there almost whenever he ran.

Equally crucial is the ability to make repeated sprints. Tevez, Manchester City's star player for years, was a bit like a windup doll: he'd sprint, briefly collapse, then very soon afterwards be sprinting again. Fleig said, 'If we want to press from the front, then we can look at Carlos's physical output and know that he's capable of doing that for ninety minutes plus.' Fleig didn't mention it, but the data show that Tevez's successor, Sergio Agüero, does much less defensive running. The whole team needs to work harder to allow Agüero to score his goals.

The quants have also gotten better at valuing goalkeepers. They used to rank keepers by what percentage of shots each one stopped. However, that technique tended to favour keepers from big clubs, who play behind tight defences and therefore see a higher proportion of easy shots from outside the penalty area. The key metric now is 'expected save value': the chance of a certain keeper making a save from a certain shot, taking into account the difficulty of the shot. That makes the rankings more telling. Before Comolli left Spurs, he used numbers to identify a young keeper whom the club ended up signing several years later. Based on a stat called 'goal difference contribution', Comolli calculated that the Frenchman Hugo Lloris would earn Spurs eighteen more points a season than the club's incumbent goalkeeper Paul Robinson. Comolli had found only one other keeper who scored as high on the index as Lloris: a youngster at Schalke 04 named Manuel Neuer.

Of course, different clubs care about different stats. Some managers request custom-made numbers from the data companies: how many players each team puts by each post at corner kicks, for instance. Favoured stats differ by country, too. Italian clubs, said Cooney of Opta, don't use the concept 'tackle'. German clubs love what they call 'duels' – broadly, contests between two players for the ball. The Germans even track duels when there is no ball nearby. Jos Luhukay, coach of Hertha Berlin from 2012 till 2015, used these stats to pick his team. Naturally Hertha's players followed their own numbers obsessively, recalled the team's Dutch winger Roy Beerens. 'After the match, the guys sit in the changing room looking at their phones: "How much did I run? How many duels did I win?" Bizarre.'

This exemplifies a trend in football: players are learning to be de facto data analysts. This has good consequences, and bad ones. On the one hand, giving them insight into data may help them do more useful things on the field. It also discourages laziness. On the other hand, if you tell a player you will judge him largely on how many kilometres he runs, then you can be sure he will run a lot of kilometres, whether those runs help your team win or not.

Data providers have made it ever easier for players and clubs to use the stats. For instance, you can now crunch data in umpteen categories to identify the right-back in the German Second Bundesliga who best meets your specifications, and then click on a button and watch video of every through-ball he has hit in the past month. Or, if you are Real Madrid and looking for the next Sergio Ramos, you can ask the computer to find the central defenders in Europe under age twenty-three whose attributes most closely resemble his. No set of human scouts could ever carry out such a wide search.

* * *

There are always a handful of innovative clubs that drive the data revolution forward. For a while, two of the pioneers were Brentford in England and FC Midtjylland in Denmark. Both were majority-owned by Matthew Benham, a British former hedge-fund manager who claims to have got rich beating the bookmakers by making stats-driven bets on sports.

Midtjylland was quite radical in scouting potential signings only using data. One of the club's mantras was 'Distrust your eyes.' Rasmus Ankersen, Midtjylland's thirty-something chairman, believed that sending a scout to watch a player could be a dangerous mistake. 'If you base your opinion of a player on a few games you've attended, it will blur your vision,' he told the Dutch journalist Michiel de Hoog. 'It's a small sample. We believe it is more effective to see lots of matches on video.'

Midtjylland became Danish champions in 2015. One year later Brentford was promoted to the English Championship. Yet since then, both clubs have discarded their analysts and reverted to a more conventional approach. For now, when you ask insiders which English clubs are pioneering in analytics, they often say that Manchester City still has possibly the industry-leading in-house data department. City's data team may have more long-term power over club strategy than which-ever temp happens to be the manager of the moment. The club's policy of performance-related pay (which often accounts for as much as 40 per cent of a City player's income) is driven by data. That's pretty unusual in football. For now, agents are more likely than clubs to bring match data into pay talks.

Yet it's not clear how much influence City's data department has on the club's signings or tactics. If you had to identify an English club where the man in charge is guided by data, it's Arsenal.

Wenger is probably the manager who has thought about stats hardest as well as longest. At this point it's customary to scoff, 'If he's so clever, why does he never win the league?' but as we said in Chapter 6, he has consistently overachieved rel-ative to Arsenal's wage bill. (Of course, the fact that the club's wage bill has remained below those of its rivals is partly down to Wenger's own stinginess.)

Like Beane, Wenger never entirely trusts the evidence of his own eyes. For instance, he told Arsenal.com in 2015: 'Mesut Özil's work rate is very high, but people don't always think that. Because people can sometimes have a style – fluent, not as aggressive – that can cheat the eye.'

So Wenger tries to supplement his eyes with data. He says, 'Sometimes numbers highlight what I have not seen, so I have to be humble enough to see that maybe there's something there and I have to analyse it deeper.'

In 2012, Arsenal's then head of business development, Hendrik Almstadt, persuaded Wenger to buy StatDNA, a sports analytics company based in Chicago that had been consult-ing the club. Almstadt argued that better data analytics could

have helped Arsenal avoid bad signings such as Marouane
Chamakh and South Korean Park Chu-Young, reported the *New
York Times*. Wenger paid £2.165 million for StatDNA. As he
once told Arsenal.com: 'I think football today is ahead of other
sports [in the use of data] because we have more money and
it's easier for us to improve the way we analyse things.'

StatDNA staff members spend a lot of time at Arsenal's training ground. The company produces stats tailored especially for
the club, including some quite exotic data: for instance, the
number of times a defender fails to spot an attacker running
past him; the value of certain combinations of players; and
each player's level of tiredness, measured by how long his foot
is planted in the ground when he runs, according to the *New
York Times*.

Above all, StatDNA uses the new gold standard of football
analytics, 'expected goals', which predicts the chance of a
given player generating a goal for or against his team in a given
situation. It's a stat that insiders now use almost as often
as they do actual goals. However, most outsiders (and even
many people in football) have still never heard of 'expected
goals' – which is why it was a milestone when Wenger once
casually name-checked it in a press conference.

StatDNA doesn't get everything right. On the upside, it
encouraged Wenger to try to sign Gonzalo Higuain before the
striker joined Napoli, but on the other hand it suggested that
Real Sociedad's young French winger Antoine Griezmann didn't
have brilliant metrics.

So even Wenger doesn't blindly trust stats. They will never
tell the whole story of football on the field. As Bill James says
about data: 'What we don't know is always a million times bigger than what we do.' Wenger told Arsenal's website in 2015,
'Usually what you feel from the game has a truth as well and
you have to respect that. The raw impression you get from the
game has to have a weight, especially when you've managed

2,000 games.' If stats point him towards a certain signing, he says, 'Before I buy I want to see!'

He'll make sure to gather verbal intelligence about the player's attitude and physique. Here's where old-fashioned scouts can still come in useful. As Michael Lewis says about baseball, 'I never thought scouts were totally pointless, I thought they were just looking for the wrong things. I told Billy [Beane]: "If I were you I'd hire a bunch of female journalists who go and find out about the lives of these players. Find out if they're alcoholics, that stuff."' To some degree, this has happened in baseball. Today a laptop evaluates a player's quality, and the scouts evaluate his personality. That is probably a way forward for football, too.

Arsenal's use of stats is unusually sophisticated. Yet even quite primitive methods can be better than no stats at all. Leicester won the Premier League in part by taking stats seriously. It built a specialist analysis room directly connected with the home changing room at the King Power Stadium, allowing the players and coaches to see data at half-time. And because the club knew it couldn't buy expensive stars, it used stats to try to find undervalued players. When N'Golo Kanté was an obscure little midfielder with mid-table Caen in 2014–2015, a glance at his stats suggested something out of the ordinary. He ran a lot more than anyone else. He led the French league in interceptions. And his forward passing was excellent. These straightforward numbers drew Leicester's attention.

The club certainly wouldn't have found Riyad Mahrez without data. It signed him after compiling its own stats on him, because so few numbers were available for the French second division, where he was playing at the time. The season Leicester won the title, Mahrez was voted England's Players' Player of the Year. Leicester, more aggressively than most clubs, had broken with football's tradition of making new signings based on intuition, tips from friendly agents and random past experiences of a player.

But taking leagues as a whole, the Bundesliga probably leads the field in data and video analysis. Recently Stefan and Christian Deutscher of the University of Bielefeld in Germany stumbled on a case in point. They had been gathering data on player ratings published by Germany's *Kicker* magazine. At every match, *Kicker*'s assessors rate players on a scale of 1 (best) to 6 (worst), the grading system used in German schools, where 1 is the best. The *Kicker* ratings have turned out to be highly correlated with quantities that predict winning the game, performing better than the pre-match betting odds, and so on.

Kicker has been rating players forever, but Christian organized some students to collect the data for the last decade. This amounted to almost seventy thousand individual ratings over more than three thousand Bundesliga games. First, Stefan and Christian tested something very simple. Out of the 1,300 or so players in the data, nearly 300 had moved between Bundesliga teams during the sample period. The simple question was this: What rating did players *who would later move* obtain against teams that *they would one day play for* compared with their ratings against other teams? In a rational market there should be no statistical difference in rating. Any team should want to hire good players, but there's no advantage from hiring a player who happened to have played better against your team than against others. Of course, randomly, some players would have better ratings against future employers than against others, but equally some would have worse ratings. The average should be near zero.

Unless, that is, there is cognitive bias. One well-known form of bias is that people tend to place more weight on the evidence of their own eyes than on other forms of evidence. Research on 'visual dominance' showed this in the 1970s.

A manager who decides on transfers has to weigh two kinds of evidence: 1) reports from scouts on players whom the manager himself has not watched; 2) performances of players whom the manager has seen playing against his club.

And indeed, it turned out managers were putting most faith in the evidence of their own eyes. Christian and Stefan found that players moving to a club had on average a statistically better *Kicker* rating against that club than against other clubs.

But they also noticed something else. The statistical support for this finding was very strong for the first half of the period analysed (2005/06–2009/10), but in the second half (2010/11–2014/15) the effect all but disappeared. To solve this puzzle, the German football author Christoph Biermann recommended that Christian speak to Jörg Jakobs, an experienced coach and scout at FC Cologne. Jorg explained that internet-based companies that provided in-depth video material of player performance had revolutionized scouting in recent years. All Bundesliga clubs had shifted to using video analysis of players provided by Wyscout and Scout7. So scouts no longer had to rely on their own words to persuade managers to buy players. They could show the managers more persuasive visual evidence instead. And when did the change happen? Wyscout had a major launch of their platform in 2010 – just where the break in the data appeared. So in this case at least, technology had actually eliminated a cognitive bias, even though at the time no one had even realized that it was there.

STILL NOT CLEVER ENOUGH: TIPS FOR THE ROUTE AHEAD

The most telling statistics in the world aren't much use if you ignore them. Many football clubs still do. Often the 'chief data analyst' is still just a guy who has branched out from making videos. He tends to find the flood of data that arrives each week overwhelming. He is drowning in information. Opta has video of some games from Liechtenstein, Lesotho and Nicaragua. Who has time to watch that? Ignacio Palacios-Huerta, the penalty expert who does some data analysis and talent identification for his beloved Athletic Bilbao, laments, 'Clubs have amazing datasets but they don't know what to do with them.'

Baseball has the same problem, Bill James told us in 2014 that the sport's data providers 'are generating so much computerized information so rapidly that frankly we have no idea what it means. Where we are right now is in a long process of digging out from under these huge mountains of information so that we have an idea what they look like from the outside.'

Anyway, knowledge is no use if people in power won't use it. Manchester United under Ferguson was an example of a club with only limited use for statistics. Ferguson did employ a large data department, but then he was constantly vacuuming up information from all sources: from ex-managers he spoke to on the phone all day as well as from mathematics graduates. And he couldn't do what Wenger does and crunch numbers himself. 'If you showed him a laptop,' growled an employee of Ferguson's, 'he'd think it was a place mat.' Even after Ferguson, United still does relatively little with statistics.

It's worse at some other clubs, where analysts get locked in computer-filled back rooms and never meet the manager. Some managers and club chairmen still dismiss the data revolution as a bit silly and overblown. Often they use stats to justify a transfer they wanted to make anyway, rather than letting numbers drive the decision. A key question in any company is, 'Who controls the budget?' In English football, typically the manager does. Quants almost never make the final decision on who gets bought or sold. As we described in Chapter 2, not all clubs have entirely perfected their transfer policies.

Twenty-plus years after Opta first started supplying data to English clubs, *Moneyball* has made a lot less headway in football than in baseball or basketball. Massive problems still remain. For instance, Carlo Ancelotti told us, stats still can't reveal much of interest about what a player does in the eighty-nine minutes that he doesn't have the ball. One implication of that: the data still say more about attack than about defence, because it's hard to measure things that never happened, such as a goal the striker didn't score because the defender was marking him too tightly to be passed to. For now, says Ancelotti, stats are most useful in assessing and improving the physical condition of players. That's the area in which football has made the greatest progress in the last decade.

But it's possible to identify areas of progress to come. For instance, players still constantly shoot at goal from outside the penalty area. Yet Opta's data show that in the Premier League, only 2 per cent of shots from just outside the area produce goals. Presumably the players have in their minds images of crackers flying into the top corner: these are the beautiful goals that stick in the memory long after all the balls that disappear into the crowd have been forgotten. Statisticians have a lobbying job to do here.

There's a particular problem with free kicks. Whenever a team gets one anywhere near the penalty area, the team's biggest name generally grabs the ball, makes a great show of placing it – probably the most exciting thing about free kicks is the choreography – then steps back, pauses momentously, and then whams it into the crowd. Taking free kicks is a superstar's perk, rather like the film star's trailer with his name on it in Hollywood. In the 2010–2011 season, write Anderson and Sally in *The Numbers Game*, the average team in the Premier League scored from just one of every thirty-five direct free kicks. Yet a free kick should be the perfect opportunity to pass. Your opponents have to retreat ten yards, and they need to put two or three people in the wall in case you shoot. That leaves large spaces to pass to runners in the penalty area. Almost inevitably, teams will start to do that instead of shooting from free kicks. It's notable that in 2015 Midtjylland had a phase of scoring nearly a goal a game from free kicks, the highest average in Europe.

The nerds can still point to so many obvious irrationalities in football, especially in the transfer market – so many areas where clever clubs could clean up. Market failures still abound. For instance, goalkeepers have longer careers than forwards, yet earn less and command much lower transfer fees. Clubs often sign large players but actually tend to use the smaller ones, having belatedly realized that they have overvalued size. And few clubs have asked themselves even basic questions, such as whether they earn more points when certain players are on the field.

Since you can hire perhaps fifty statisticians for the £2 million-plus that the average player in the Premier League earns, you'd think it might be worth paying nerds to study these questions.

But those nerds need to learn to communicate with old-style football types. 'Letting even a top-level statistician loose with a more traditional football manager is not really the right combination,' says Forde. One simple tip for number-crunching: football people, like most people, are better at absorbing visual than verbal information (let alone mathematical information).

The German national team's data department – possibly the most sophisticated outfit in the sport – understands this. Months before the World Cup in Brazil began, every man in the German squad was given access to an app on which analysts posted useful videos. Before the France–Germany quarter-final, the analysts emphasized one video in particular: an apparently unremarkable scene of the Dutchman Daley Blind tracking his opponent in a Holland–Germany under-21s match in 2013.

You watch the video and forget it almost instantly: the German attack peters out, with the Dutch keeper easily picking up a low pass. But that's because Blind was doing something crucial: after two German players attempted a one–two pass, he didn't follow the ball. Instead he kept running with the German who had started the move, staying with him until the attack was dead.

It was exactly the right thing to do. The German analysts expected Blind's defensive ploy to be especially important against the French, whose football culture favours one–twos. The German players studied Blind, and tried to do as he did. Before the semi-final against Brazil and the final against Argentina – two other countries that like one–twos – the players watched the video again. Seeing Blind's example was much more effective than listening to a lecture about one–twos. When the German football federation's chief data analyst Chris Clemens told this story to De Hoog, he even suggested a headline for the Dutchman's article: 'How Daley Blind saved Germany's World Cup'. This is a story about the pre-planned, analytics-driven nature of modern defending.

In general, if you want to know what's next in football, the thing to do might be to steal a laptop from a German data analyst. Clemens told Christoph Biermann that the quest now is for 'positional data that describe the constellations in which players and ball move around the field'. The key question, says Clemens, is 'which constellations of people on the field produce goals'. Already analysts have figured out one basic truth: having more players than the opposition near the ball is an advantage.

And as we get better at tracking players around the field, we will get better at valuing defensive contributions. The STATS company in Chicago suggests one measure: good defences force opponents to try more difficult passes (and then good defenders intercept those passes). Once we know more about which defensive players are best, expect their transfer fees to rise, much as happened in the NBA thanks to better data. In

2016, Chelsea was still able to buy Kanté for about £30 million, the price of a middling Premier League striker. The next Kanté could be a lot more expensive.

German analysts are also asking other big new questions, such as: Given that most goals come from robbing the opposition rather than from a patiently constructed attack, might it make sense to pass the ball to a weak opposing player, and then win it back? Slowly the data revolution progresses, but it's moving fastest in the land of the world champions.

THE ECONOMIST'S FEAR OF THE PENALTY KICK: ARE PENALTIES COSMICALLY UNFAIR, OR ONLY IF YOU ARE NICOLAS ANELKA?

A famous football manager stands up from the table. He's going to pretend he is Chelsea's captain, John Terry, about to take the crucial penalty against Manchester United in the Champions League final in Moscow in 2008.

The manager performs the part with Schadenfreude; he is no friend of Chelsea. He adjusts his face into a mask of tension. He tells us what Terry is thinking: 'If I score, we win the Champions League.' And then, terrifyingly, 'But first I have to score.'

The manager begins pulling at the arm of his suit jacket: he is mimicking Terry pulling at his captain's armband. Terry is telling himself (the manager explains), 'I am captain, I am strong, I will score.'

Still pulling rhythmically at his suit, the manager looks up. He is eyeing an imaginary, grotesquely large Edwin van der Sar, who is guarding a goal a very long twelve yards away. Terry intends to hit the ball to Van der Sar's left. We now know that a Basque economist told Chelsea that the Dutch keeper tended to dive right against right-footed kickers. Terry runs up – and here the manager, cackling, falls on his backside.

Van der Sar did indeed dive right, as the Basque economist had foreseen, but Terry slipped on the wet grass, and his shot into the left-hand corner missed by inches.

'This really is football,' the manager concludes. A player hits the post, the ball goes out, and Chelsea's coach, Avram Grant, is sacked even though he is exactly the same manager as if the ball had gone in.

The penalty is probably the single thing in football about which economists have most to say. The penalty feels cosmically unfair; economists say otherwise. Penalties are often dismissed as a lottery; economists tell both kicker and goalkeeper exactly what to do. (Indeed, if only Nicolas Anelka had followed the economist's advice, Chelsea would have won the final.) And best of all, penalties may be the best way in the known world of understanding game theory.

DIABOLICAL: ARE PENALTIES REALLY UNFAIR?

At first sight, the penalty looks like the most unfair device in all of sports. First of all, it may be impossible for a referee to judge most penalty appeals correctly, given the pace of modern football, the tangle of legs and ball, and the levels of deception by players. When the American writer Adam Gopnik watched the World Cup of 1998 on TV for the *New Yorker* magazine, he as an outsider to football immediately focused on this problem. The 'more customary method of getting a penalty,' he wrote, '. . . is to walk into the "area" with the ball, get breathed on hard, and then immediately collapse . . . arms and legs splayed out, while you twist in agony and beg for morphine, and your teammates smite their foreheads at the tragic waste of a young life. The referee buys this more often than you might think. Afterward the post-game did-he-fall-or-was-he-pushed argument can go on for hours.' Or decades. The fan at home is often unsure whether it really should have been a penalty even after watching several replays.

And the referee's misjudgements matter, because the penalty probably has more impact than any other refereeing decision in sports. Umpires in baseball and tennis often fluff calls, but there are fifty-four outs in a baseball game, and countless points in a tennis match, and so no individual decision tends to make all that much difference. Referees in rugby and American gridiron football blunder, too, but because these games are higher scoring than football, individual calls rarely change outcomes here, either. In any case, officials in all these sports can now consult instant replays.

But football referees cannot. And since important football matches usually hinge on one goal, the penalty usually decides the match. As Gopnik says, the penalty 'creates an enormous disproportion between the foul and the reward'.

No wonder the penalty drives managers crazy. As Arsène Wenger lamented at the end of the 2007–2008 season, 'Every big game I've seen this year has been decided, offside or not offside, penalty or not penalty.' Indeed, it's now a standard tactic for managers in England, after their teams have lost, to devote the post-match press conference to a penalty given or not given. It's a ritual song of lament, which goes like this: The penalty completely changed the outcome of the game. We were clearly winning/drawing but lost/drew because of the (diabolical, unjust) penalty.

The manager knows that most media prefer covering personality clashes to tactics, and so the 'match' reports will be devoted to the press conference rather than his team's losing performance. Meanwhile, the winning manager, when asked about the penalty, recites, It made no difference whatever to the outcome of the game. We were clearly winning and would inevitably have done so without the (entirely just) penalty.

These two ritual managerial chants amount to two different hypotheses about how penalties affect football matches. The first manager is claiming that randomly awarded penalties distort results. The second manager is saying penalties make no difference. On occasion, either manager might be right. But over the long term, one of them must be more right than the other. So which is it – do penalties change results, or don't they? We have the data to answer this question.

Our guru is Dr Tunde Buraimo. One of the growing band of sports econometricians – the British equivalent of baseball's sabermetricians – Tunde works, appropriately, in the ancient heartland of professional football at the University of Central Lancashire in Preston. As the saying goes, the plural of 'anecdote' is 'data', and Tunde prefers to work with tens of thousands of pieces of evidence rather than a few random recollections. To help us with our book, he examined 1,520 Premier League games played over four years, from the 2002–2003 season until 2005–2006. For each game he knew the pattern of scoring and, crucially, which team was expected to win given the pre-match betting odds.

Our test of the two rival hypotheses about penalties is simple. We asked Tunde to divide the games into two groups:

1. games in which penalties were awarded;
2. games in which they were not.

We then asked him to compare how often the home team won when there was a penalty, and how often when there wasn't. This is what he found:

PENALTY AWARDED IN MATCH?

Result	No penalty	Penalty	Total
Home win	577	142	719
	46.76%	49.65%	47.30%
Away win	336	80	416
	27.23%	27.97%	27.37%
Draw	321	64	385
	26.01%	22.38%	25.33%
Total	1,234	286	1,520
	100.00%	100.00%	100.00%

Look at the last column first. Taking all games in the database, 47.30 per cent ended in home wins, 27.37 per cent in away wins and 25.33 per cent in draws. These frequencies reflect the intrinsic advantage of home teams. Now imagine that the first manager is right: penalties change the outcome of the game. How will they do that? It might be that penalties always favour home teams (because referees are cowards), in which case we would expect the percentage of home wins to be greater when penalties are given. Alternatively, it might be that penalties favour away teams (perhaps enabling a team that has its back against the wall to make an escape). If so, the proportion of away wins (or draws) would rise with penalties.

But in fact, as the first two columns show, the percentages for all results barely change whether a penalty is given or not. The percentage of home wins is about three points higher when there is a penalty (up from 46.76 per cent to 49.65 per cent), and the percentage of draws is commensurately lower (down to 22.38 per cent from 26.01 per cent). The percentage of away wins remains almost identical (27.97 per cent against 27.23 per cent) with or without penalties. So in games with penalties, there are slightly more home wins and slightly fewer draws.

It's tempting to read significance into this: to think that the rise in home wins when there is a penalty is big enough to show that penalties favour the home team. However, statisticians warn against this kind of intuitive analysis. The absolute number of home wins when there were penalties in the game was 142. Had the frequency of home wins been the same as in games when there was no penalty, the number of home wins would have been 134. The difference (eight extra home wins) is too small to be considered statistically significant and the difference is probably due to chance. It would have been a different matter had the number of home wins when there was a penalty exceeded 150 (or 52 per cent of the games concerned). Then the increase would have met the standard generally used by statisticians for confidence that there was a statistically reliable difference in outcomes depending on the award of a penalty. As it is, though, the data suggest that awarding a penalty does not affect home wins, away wins or draws.

But perhaps penalties have a different effect on match results. Perhaps they help favourites (if refs favour the big team). Or maybe they help underdogs (if penalties truly are given randomly, they should help the worse team more than the better one). Tunde tested these hypotheses, too.

It's obvious even to the naked eye that penalties have no impact at all on whether the favourite wins: favourites win 51.3 per cent of games without a penalty, and 51.4 per cent with a penalty. It's true that underdogs win nearly 3 per cent more often when there is a penalty than when there is not, but once again the tests demonstrate that this fact has no statistical significance. We can put the increase down to chance. Match results appear to be the same with or without penalties. Penalties do not matter.

Now, this is a statistical statement that requires a very precise interpretation. Penalties do matter in that they often change the outcome of individual games. Clearly a team that scores from a penalty is more likely to win, and so, whatever a manager says, a converted penalty will affect the evolution of almost any game.

However, on average, taken over a large sample of games, a penalty does not make it any more likely that home teams or away teams or favourites or underdogs win. If penalties were abolished tomorrow, the pattern of football results would be exactly the same.

This sounds counterintuitive. After all, we argued that penalties look like the most unfair device in sport. They are often wrongly awarded, they cause a lot of goals and many of these goals decide matches. So surely penalties should make results less fair?

To explain why penalties don't change the pattern of match results, we need to consult the late Graham Taylor. The manager is now remembered as the 'turnip' whose long-ball game cost England qualification for the World Cup of 1994. However, the long-ball game had previously served Taylor very well at his clubs Watford and Aston Villa. No wonder, because it rested on one crucial insight into football: you will score goals only if you get possession in the opposition's final third of the field.

Much the same insight applies to penalties: in practice you will get them only if you have possession (or at least a decent chance of winning possession) in the opponent's penalty area. A penalty is often wrongly given. But it is almost always a reward for deep territorial penetration. That makes it, on average, a marker of the balance of power in the game. That's why good teams get proportionately more penalties than bad teams, and why home teams get more than away teams. On average, a penalty is given with the grain of a game.

RIGHT, LEFT, OR LET VAN DER SAR DECIDE FOR YOU? GAME THEORY IN BERLIN AND MOSCOW

The next question is how to take them. Economists may have no idea when housing prices will crash, but they do know something about this one.

A surprising number of economists have thought hard about the humble penalty kick. Even Steve Levitt, author of *Freakonomics* and winner of perhaps the most important prize in economics (the Clark Medal, which some insiders think outranks the Nobel), once co-wrote a little-known paper on penalties. Probably only a trio of economists would have watched videos of 459 penalties taken in the French and Italian leagues. 'Testing Mixed-Strategy Equilibria When Players Are Heterogeneous: The Case of Penalty Kicks in Football' is one of those you might have missed, but it always won Levitt handshakes from European economists. Here's an American who gets it, they must have thought. Levitt, P.-A. Chiappori and T. Groseclose explain that they wrote the paper because 'testing game theory in the real world may provide unique insights.' Economists revere the penalty as a real-life example of game theory.

Game theory was developed in the 1940s by the likes of John von Neumann, a brilliant mathematician who also helped create the architecture of the modern computer. It is the study of what happens when people find themselves in situations exactly like a penalty-taker facing a goalkeeper: when what I should do depends on what you do, and what you should do depends on what I do.

The American government used game theory extensively during the Cold War to plan its interactions with the Soviet Union and to try to predict Soviet moves. (It has been said that game-theoretic advice was given during the Cuban Missile Crisis to consider questions like, 'If we bomb Cuba, then the Russians will seize West Berlin, and then we'll have to attack Russian troops,

and then they'll use nuclear bombs, and then . . .') Today economists use game theory all the time, particularly to plan government policies or analyse business strategy. Game theory even
plays a big role in research on biology.

The key to game theory is the analysis of how the strategies of
different actors interact. In a penalty kick, for instance, the kicker
and the keeper must each choose a strategy: where to kick the
ball and where to dive. But each person's strategy depends on
what he thinks the other person will do.

Sometimes in game theory, what's best for the actors is if
they both do the same thing – going to the same restaurant
to meet for dinner, for instance. These kinds of situations are
known as coordination or cooperative games. But the penalty
kick is a non-cooperative game: the actors succeed by achiev-
ing their objectives independently of others. In fact, the penalty
is a 'zero-sum game': any gain for one player is exactly offset
by the loss to the other side (plus one goal for me is minus
one goal for you).

The issue of game theory behind the penalty was best put in
'The Longest Penalty Ever', a short story by the Argentine writer
Osvaldo Soriano. A match in the Argentine provinces has to
be abandoned seconds before time when a bent referee, who
has just awarded a penalty, is knocked out by an irate player.
The league court decides that the last twenty seconds of the
game – the penalty kick, in effect – will be played the next
Sunday. That gives everyone a week to prepare for the penalty.

At dinner a few nights before the penalty, Gato Díaz, the
keeper who has to stop it, muses about the kicker:

'Constante kicks to the right.'
'Always,' said the president of the club.
'But he knows that I know.'
'Then we're fucked.'
'Yeah, but I know that he knows,' said el Gato.

'Then dive to the left and be ready,' said someone at the table.

'No. He knows that I know that he knows,' said Gato Díaz, and he got up to go to bed.

Game theorists try to work out strategies for players in different types of games, and try to predict which strategy each player will pursue. Sometimes the prediction is easy. Consider the game in which each player has only two choices: either 'develop a nuclear bomb' or 'don't develop a nuclear bomb'. To make a prediction, you have to know what the pay-off is to each player depending on the game's outcome. Imagine the players are India and Pakistan (but it could be Israel and Iran, or any other pair of hostile nations). Initially Pakistan does not know if India will or won't develop a bomb, so it figures:

IF INDIA HAS NO BOMB, THEN:

(a) We don't get a bomb: we can live alongside each other, but there will always be incidents.

(b) We get a bomb: India will have to treat us with respect.

IF INDIA HAS A BOMB:

(c) We don't get a bomb: we can't resist anything India does.

(d) We get a bomb: India will have to treat us with respect.

Plainly, if you are Pakistan, you will end up developing the bomb, whether India has the bomb or not. Likewise, India will choose the same strategy, and will develop the bomb whether Pakistan does or doesn't. So the equilibrium of this game is for both nations to acquire a bomb. This is the gloomy logic of an arms race. The logic of football is much the same, and there are many examples of arms races in the sport, from inflation of players' wages to illegal doping.

PIECES OF PAPER IN STUTTGART, JOHANNESBURG AND MILAN

The problem for experienced penalty-takers and goalkeepers is that, over time, they build up track records. People come to spot any habits they might have – always shooting left, or always diving right, for instance. Levitt and his colleagues observed 'one goalie in the sample who jumps left on all eight kicks that he faces (only two of eight kicks against him go to the left, suggesting that his proclivity for jumping left is not lost on the kickers)'.

There have probably always been people in the game tracking the past behaviour of kickers and keepers. Back in the 1970s, a Dutch manager named Jan Reker began to build up an archive of index cards on thousands of players. One thing he noted was where the player hit his penalties – or at least the penalties that Reker happened to know about. The Dutch keeper Hans van Breukelen would often call Reker before an international match for a briefing.

Nobody paid much attention to this relationship until 1988. That May, Van Breukelen's PSV Eindhoven reached the European Cup final against Benfica. Before the match in Stuttgart, the keeper phoned Reker. Inevitably the game went to a penalty shoot-out. At first Reker's index cards didn't seem to be helping much – Benfica's first five penalties all went in – but Van Breukelen saved the sixth kick from Veloso, and PSV were the European champions. A month later, so were Holland. They were leading the USSR 2–0 in the final in Munich when a silly charge by Van Breukelen conceded a penalty. But using Reker's database, he saved Igor Belanov's weak kick.

In Berlin in 2006, the World Cup quarter-final between Germany and Argentina also went to penalties. Jens Lehmann, the German keeper, emerged with a crib sheet tucked into his sock. On a little page of hotel notepaper ('Schlosshotel, Grunewald', it said), the German keeper's trainer, Andreas

Köpke, had jotted down the proclivities of some potential Argentine penalty-takers:

1. Riquelme	left
2. Crespo	long run-up/right, short run-up/left
3. Heinze	6 [his shirt number, presumably given for fear that Lehmann would not recognize him], left low
4. Ayala	2 [shirt number], waits long time, long run-up right
5. Messi	left
6. Aimar	16, waits a long time, left
7. Rodriguez	18, left

Apparently the Germans had a database of 13,000 kicks. The crib sheet might just have tipped the balance. Of the seven Argentines on the list, only Ayala and Maxi Rodríguez actually took penalties. However, Ayala stuck exactly to Lehmann's plan: he took a long run-up, the keeper waited a long time, and when Ayala dutifully shot to Lehmann's right, the keeper saved. Rodríguez also did his best to oblige. He put the ball in Lehmann's left-hand corner as predicted, but hit it so well that the keeper couldn't reach it.

By the time of Argentina's fourth penalty, Germany were leading 4–2. If Lehmann could save Esteban Cambiasso's kick, the Germans would maintain their record of never losing a penalty shoot-out in a World Cup. Lehmann consulted his crib sheet. Sönke Wortmann, the German film director, who was following the German team for a fly-on-the-wall documentary, reports what happened next: 'Lehmann could find no indication on his note of how Cambiasso would shoot. And yet the piece of paper did its job, because Lehmann stood looking at it for a long time. Köpke had written it in pencil, the note was crumpled and the writing almost illegible.'

Wortmann says that as Cambiasso prepared to take his kick, he must have been thinking, 'What do they know?' The Germans knew nothing. But Cambiasso was psyched out nonetheless. Lehmann saved his shot, and afterwards there was a massive brawl on the field.

Both Van Breukelen's and Lehmann's stories have been told before. What is not publicly known is that Chelsea received an excellent crib sheet before the Champions League final in Moscow in 2008.

In 1995 the Basque economist Ignacio Palacios-Huerta, who was then a graduate student at the University of Chicago, began recording the way penalties were taken. In the early years this was quite an artisanal labour: his wife and mother would send him videotapes of Spanish football TV programmes. His paper 'Professionals Play Minimax' was published in 2003.

One friend of Ignacio's who knew about his research was a professor of economics and mathematics at an Israeli university. It so happened that this man was also a friend of Avram Grant. When Grant's Chelsea reached the final in Moscow in 2008, the professor realized that Ignacio's research might help Grant. He put the two men in touch. Ignacio then sent Grant a report that made four points about Manchester United and penalties:

1. Van der Sar tended to dive to the kicker's 'natural side' more often than most keepers did. This meant that when facing a right-footed kicker, Van der Sar would usually dive to his own right, and when facing a left-footed kicker, to his own left. So Chelsea's right-footed penalty-takers would have a better chance if they shot to their 'unnatural side', Van der Sar's left.

2. Ignacio emphasized in his report that 'the vast majority of the penalties that Van der Sar stops are those kicked to a mid-height (say, between 1 and 1.5 metres), and hence

    that penalties against him should be kicked just on the ground or high up'.

3. Cristiano Ronaldo was another special case. Ignacio wrote in the report, 'Ronaldo often stops in the run-up to the ball. If he stops, he is likely (85%) to kick to the right-hand side of the goalkeeper.' Ignacio added that Ronaldo seemed able to change his mind about where to put the ball at the very last instant. That meant it was crucial for the opposing keeper not to move early. When a keeper moved early, Ronaldo always scored.

4. The team that wins the toss before the shoot-out gets to choose whether to go first. But this is a no-brainer: it should always go first. Teams going first win on average 60 per cent of the time, presumably because there is too much pressure on the team going second, which is always having to score to save the game. Many players – especially those who normally never take penalties – succumb to the stress. Ignacio explains: 'Yes they are hyper-professionals, but they are not professionals in shoot-outs. Shoot-outs happen very infrequently.' Lots of players go their entire careers without ever taking a penalty in a shoot-out.

You find exactly the same pattern in chess. A chess match is typically played over six or ten games, but by two players who alternate the colour of pieces from game to game. However, the player who has white in game one has a 60:40 chance of winning the entire match.

In football, few pundits even seem to be aware of the advantage of kicking first. When a game goes to a penalty shoot-out, many TV channels switch to a commercial break during the coin toss. The commentators rarely bother to mention who won it. Bookmakers don't shift their odds immediately after the toss is done – a mistake from which gamblers could benefit.

Usually the team that wins the toss is intelligent enough to kick first, but not always. A month after Chelsea–Manchester United in Moscow, Italy's captain Gianluigi Buffon may have decided the outcome of Euro 2008 when he won the toss for a shoot-out against Spain but let the Spaniards shoot first. They won, and then won the tournament. (This didn't necessarily gladden the heart of the Basque Ignacio.)

Ignacio didn't know whether his research would be used by Chelsea in Moscow, but watching the shoot-out on TV, he was certain it was being used. Indeed, once you know the content of Ignacio's note, it's fascinating to study the shoot-out on You-Tube. The Chelsea players followed his advice almost to the letter, as Grant confirmed to him years later – except for poor Anelka.

United's captain, Rio Ferdinand, won the toss, and turned to the bench to ask what to do. Terry tried to influence him by offering to go first. Unsurprisingly, Ferdinand ignored him. United went first, meaning that they were now likely to win. Carlos Tevez scored from the first kick.

Michael Ballack hit Chelsea's first penalty high into the net to Van der Sar's left. Juliano Belletti scored low to Van der Sar's left. Ignacio had recommended that Chelsea's right-footed kickers choose that side. But at this early stage, he still couldn't be sure that Chelsea was being guided by his report. He told us later, 'Interestingly, my wife had been quite sceptical about the whole thing as I was preparing the report for coach Grant, not even interested in looking at it. But then the game went into extra time, and then into a penalty shoot-out. Well, still sceptical.'

At this point Cristiano Ronaldo stepped up to take his kick for United. Watching on TV, Ignacio told his wife the precise advice he had given Chelsea in his report: Chelsea's keeper shouldn't move early, and if Cristiano paused in his run-up, he would most probably hit the ball to the keeper's right. Cristiano did indeed pause in his run-up.

To Ignacio's delight, Chelsea's keeper, Petr Cech, stayed motionless – 'not even blinking', in the Spanish football phrase. Then, when Cristiano duly shot to Cech's right as predicted, the keeper saved. Ignacio recalled later, 'After that, I started to believe that they were following the advice quite closely.' As for his wife, 'I think she was a bit shocked.'

What's astonishing – though it seems to have passed unnoticed at the time – is what happened after that. Chelsea's next four penalty-takers, Frank Lampard, Ashley Cole, John Terry and Salomon Kalou, all hit the ball to Van der Sar's left, just as Ballack and Belletti had done. In other words, the first six Chelsea kicks went to the same corner.

Ashley Cole was the only one of the six who partly disregarded Ignacio's advice. Cole was left-footed, so when he hit the ball to Van der Sar's left, he was shooting to his own 'natural side' – the side that Ignacio had said Van der Sar tended to choose. Indeed, the Dutchman chose correctly on Cole's kick, and very nearly saved the shot, but it was well struck, low (as Ignacio had recommended), and just wriggled out of the keeper's grip. But all Chelsea's right-footed penalty-takers had obeyed Ignacio to the letter and kicked the ball to their 'unnatural side', Van der Sar's left.

So far, Ignacio's advice had worked very well. Much as the economist had predicted, Van der Sar had dived to his natural side four times out of six. He hadn't saved a single penalty. Five of Chelsea's six kicks had gone in, while Terry's, as the whole world knows, flew out off the post with Van der Sar in the wrong corner.

It was Anelka's turn to kick. On United's bench, Alex Ferguson was growing frustrated with his keeper. 'As Anelka jogged to the penalty spot,' Ferguson later recalled, 'I was thinking – dive to your left. Edwin kept diving to the right.'

But after six kicks, Van der Sar, or someone else at Manchester United, had figured out that Chelsea was pursuing a strategy. The Dutchman had noticed that the team was putting all its kicks to his left.

As Anelka prepared to take Chelsea's seventh penalty, the gangling keeper, standing on the goal line, extended his arms to either side of him. Then, in what must have been a chilling moment for Anelka, the Dutchman pointed with his left hand to the left corner. 'That's where you're all putting it, isn't it?' he seemed to be saying. (This is where books fall short as a medium. We urge you to watch the shoot-out on YouTube.)

Now Anelka had a terrible dilemma. This was game theory in its rawest form. United had come pretty close to divining Chelsea's strategy: Ignacio had indeed advised right-footed kickers like Anelka to put the ball to Van der Sar's left side.

So Anelka knew that Van der Sar knew that Anelka knew that Van der Sar tended to dive right against right-footers. What was Anelka to do? He decided to avoid the left corner, where he had presumably planned to put the ball. Instead he kicked to Van der Sar's right. That might have been fine, except that he hit the ball at mid-height – exactly the level that Ignacio had warned against. Watching the kick on TV, Ignacio was 'very upset'. Perhaps Anelka was at sea because Van der Sar had pressured him to change his plans at the last moment. Van der Sar saved the shot. Ferguson said afterward, 'That wasn't an accident, his penalty save. We knew exactly where certain players were putting the ball.' Anelka's decision to ignore Ignacio's advice probably cost Chelsea the Champions League.

RANDOMIZATION: HOW FRANCK RIBÉRY CRACKED GAME THEORY

Crib sheets like Lehmann's might just work on penalty shoot-outs. Many of the players who take kicks in a shoot-out aren't regular penalty-takers. (After Gareth Southgate missed England's crucial kick in the semi-final against Germany at Euro

'96, his mother said that the last time he'd taken a penalty was three years before, and he'd missed that one, too.) These inferior penalty-takers are not skilled or steady-headed enough to be able to vary their strategy. Quite likely, they will just aim for their favourite corner, hoping that their lack of a track record means the other side won't know their preference.

However, that is not how a good penalty-taker – his team's regular man – thinks.

Suppose the good kicker always chose the same corner for his penalty (game theorists call this a 'pure strategy'). It would be easy to oppose: if the kicker always kicks left, then the goalkeeper knows what to do. Pure strategies don't work for penalty-taking. As Levitt and company found, 'There are no kickers in our sample with at least four kicks who always kick in one direction.' Take that, Jens Lehmann. According to the goalkeeper's crib sheet, Messi's penalties tended to go left. In fact, the mini-Argentine randomizes his spot kicks almost perfectly. 'He can also change his mind at the very last instant,' adds Ignacio. Sometimes Messi waits for the keeper to shift his weight very slightly to one side, then shoots to the other corner.

Even a more complicated pure strategy than always choosing the same corner does not work. For example, suppose the kicker always shoots in the opposite corner to the one he chose last time. (Diego Forlán tended to do this.) Then a future opponent studying this player might discover the sequence – left, right, left, right, left, right – and with a bit of thought guess what comes next. The essence of good penalty-taking is unpredictability: a good penalty-taker will be one whose next penalty cannot be predicted with confidence from his history of penalty-taking.

This is a particular kind of unpredictability. It does not mean that the kicker should go left half of the time and right half of the time. After all, most kickers have a natural side, and favouring that side gives them a higher chance of scoring. But even if you naturally shoot to the keeper's right, as most right-footed kickers do, sometimes you have to shoot to his left, just to keep him guessing. In fact, if a kicker knows his chances of scoring for either corner of the net (depending also on which way the goalkeeper dives), he can choose the proportion of kicks to his natural side that maximizes the probability of scoring. A right-footed kicker won't put 100 per cent of his kicks to his natural right side, because that would give the goalkeeper certainty. Even a small change, like kicking right only 99 per cent of the time, would raise the chances of scoring considerably by creating uncertainty in the goalkeeper's mind.

Kicking to the left 50 per cent of the time would leave the keeper very uncertain. However, it would also entail the kicker hitting many poor shots to his unnatural side. So the kicker does best by hitting somewhere over half his kicks to his natural right side.

Likewise, we can calculate the proportion of times a goalkeeper should dive left or right. (Note that we are assuming the goalkeeper cannot know which way the ball is going before he decides which way to dive.) Kickers and keepers who mix it up like this are pursuing what game theorists call 'mixed strategies'.

Mixed strategies are peculiar because they require the actor to incorporate randomness into decision-making. Should I go to the pub or the cinema? A mixed strategy requires me to toss a coin, which sounds odd, since one might expect that I prefer one to the other. With a mixed strategy, you let the coin make the decision for you.

Game theorists have wondered for years whether people in the real world follow mixed strategies. They have found in tests that people tend not to use mixed strategies even when it is profitable for them to do so. In fact, our behaviour seems to fall short of mixed play in a very specific way: in most cases our sequence of choices is predictable, because people tend to do the opposite of what they have done in the past. For instance, they choose first left, then right, then left, then right, left, right, left, right, confusing change with randomness. These guinea pigs would not make good penalty-takers.

Eventually game theorists began to test mixed strategies in the natural laboratory of penalty-taking. Years before Ignacio Palacios-Huerta advised Chelsea, he collected a database of 1,417 penalties taken between 1995 and 2000. First he calculated the proportion of successful kicks based on whether the kicker went to his natural side (left or right). The success rate was 95 per cent if the kicker went to his natural side and the goalkeeper went to the opposite side (the remaining 5 per cent of kicks missed the goal). The success rate was 92 per cent if the kicker went to his 'unnatural' side and the goalkeeper went to his own natural side. Obviously the kicker's success rates were lower if the keeper chose correctly: a scoring rate of 70 per cent if both keeper and kicker went to the kicker's natural side, and 58 per cent if both went to the other side.

Using these figures, Ignacio calculated the optimal mixed-strategy choices for each player. To maximize the chance of scoring, an imaginary penalty-taker would have to hit 61.5 per cent of his kicks to his natural side and 38.5 per cent to the other side. In reality, the penalty-takers Ignacio observed got pretty close to this: they hit 60 per cent to their natural side and 40 per cent the other way.

A keeper's best strategy (if he insists on diving rather than standing still) is to dive to the kicker's natural side 58 per cent of the time and to the other side 42 per cent of the time. The actual figures, Ignacio found, were scarily close: 57.7 per cent and 42.3 per cent. Levitt's team, using a different database of penalties, found that keepers went to the right 57 per cent of the time. So, it looks as if keepers as well as penalty-takers really do follow mixed strategies.

But what we most want to know are the choices of individual kickers and goalkeepers, not the overall averages. Ignacio studied twenty-two kickers and twenty goalkeepers, each of whom was involved in more than thirty penalties in his database. Again, Ignacio calculated the success rates depending on the side the kicker and goalkeeper chose, and calculated the frequencies in each direction that would maximize the chances of success for kickers and keepers.

In real life, the actual frequencies the players observed were indistinguishable from the best mixed-strategy choices in more than 95 per cent of cases. We can say with a high degree of confidence that penalty-takers and goalkeepers really do use mixed strategies. Levitt's paper found the same thing: except for the bizarre keeper who always dived left, almost all the other kickers and keepers played mixed strategies.

Finally Ignacio tested the most important question of all: Are footballers capable of constructing a truly random sequence in their penalty-taking decisions, as the mixed-strategy theory requires? Careful statistical testing showed that indeed they are. In other words, it is impossible to predict which way a regular penalty-taker will kick based on his history of kicks. Each time he chooses his corner without any reference to what he did the last time.

Randomization of penalties is a completely logical theory that against all odds turns out to be true in practice. As long as the penalty-taker is a pro, rather than some terrified Southgateian innocent roped in for a job that he doesn't understand, simple lists like Lehmann's are not much use.

All this shows the extraordinary amount of subconscious thought that goes into playing top-level football. Previous studies in game theory had shown that people could construct random sequences if the problem was first explained to them in some detail. Nobody is suggesting that footballers have sat at home coming up with mixed-strategy equilibria. Rather, the best players intuitively grasp the truth of the theory and are able to execute it. That is what makes them good players.

For years, Franck Ribéry took penalties for Bayern Munich and France. Needless to say, the scar-faced little playmaker placed his kicks according to a randomized mixed strategy. But more than that, one of his former managers explained, even once Ribéry had embarked on his jagged hither-and-thither run-up, he himself did not know which corner he would choose. When the born economist Arsène Wenger was told this, he gushed with admiration.

As good a player as Ribéry was, he might have done even better as a game theorist.

THE ECONOMIST IN THE WORLD CUP FINAL

Ignacio Palacios-Huerta watched the World Cup of 2010 from his home in Spain's Basque country, in between bouts of child care. It baffled him, he told Simon over the phone during the tournament, that he probably knew more about the penalty-takers there than did any team in South Africa. 'I have nothing at stake,' he reflected. 'They have lots: the whole nation.'

Four years on from 2006, some teams did have crib sheets more sophisticated than Lehmann's. One team in the quarter-finals told us it had an hour's film of penalties taken by players of the country it was due to face, plus a penalty database. That's why it was silly of England's coach Fabio Capello to announce his designated penalty-takers before playing Germany. He potentially gave the opposition time to study their habits.

Still, Ignacio reckoned that even the cleverest teams in South Africa probably just counted who shot how often to which corner. 'I would be super-surprised if they do any kind of statistical test,' he said. He himself runs two. The first: Does a particular kicker follow a truly random strategy? If the kicker does randomize, then the direction he chooses for his next kick – right of the keeper, through the middle or left – cannot be predicted from his previous kicks.

But Ignacio had detected patterns in several of the penalty-takers at the World Cup. Argentina's Gonzalo Higuain, for instance, before the World Cup had been kicking too often to the keeper's right. Germany's keeper Manuel Neuer had also been failing to randomize: too often in club games, Neuer had dived to the opposite corner from his previous dive, going first right, then left, then right, etc.

Next, Ignacio tested the kicker's success rate with each strategy. The kicker should have an equally high scoring rate whether he shoots right, middle or left. But going into the World Cup both Argentina's Sergio Agüero and Germany's Miroslav Klose were scoring more often when shooting right of the keeper. That would logically encourage them to aim right if they had to take a kick in South Africa.

Only rarely does Ignacio find a kicker with a very skewed strategy, but England's Frank Lampard was such a man. For years Lampard had randomized his kicks beautifully. But in the 2009–2010 season, Ignacio noted, 'he kicked thirteen out of fifteen times to the right of the goalkeeper – and the two lefts were in the same game when he had to retake the same penalty three times.'

No wonder Lampard had developed a habit of missing penalties. Keepers had figured him out. Portsmouth's David James, for instance, had chosen the correct corner for Lampard's penalty for Chelsea in the FA Cup final held a month before the World Cup – perhaps with help from Ignacio, who had sent Portsmouth a briefing note before the game. As it happened, Lampard's shot went wide. Admittedly Kevin-Prince Boateng missed his penalty for Portsmouth in the match, but then he had ignored Ignacio's advice to kick left of Petr Cech. It is probably harder for penalty-takers than for goalkeepers to follow someone else's advice.

On the phone Ignacio told Simon, 'I don't think serious analysis of the data has arrived yet in football, but it's coming. I think the world will be a different place in a decade or so.'

That phone call got Simon thinking. When Holland and Spain made the World Cup final, Simon, a lifelong fan of the

Dutch, emailed an official he knew in Holland's camp. Would the Dutch be interested in a penalty analysis of the Spaniards provided by a specialist? The official said they would. And so Ignacio began pulling all-nighters to draw up a report on his fellow countrymen ready for 11 July 2010. On the Sunday morning of the final, he emailed a PDF of his report to the Dutch camp. (True, Ignacio has a Spanish passport, but as a Basque he was perfectly happy to see Spain lose.) Soon we got an email back from the Dutch goalkeeping coach Ruud Hesp: 'It's a report that we can use perfectly.'

That chilly Johannesburg evening, we proponents of *Soccernomics* genuinely thought we might be within five minutes of deciding the World Cup final. In extra time at Football City, Holland and Spain were still tied 0–0. A penalty shoot-out loomed. Simon, sitting in the media stand, was barely watching the game anymore. Instead he was rereading on his laptop Ignacio's PDF file. In the circumstances, it made compelling reading. For instance, Ignacio had predicted that Xavi and Andres Iniesta, as right-footed players who didn't usually take penalties, would probably hit their kicks to the right of the Dutch keeper Maarten Stekelenburg. And Fernando Torres almost always kicked low. Against him, Stekelenburg would need to dive to the ground fast. It looked as if we might be about to help the Dutch win the World Cup. Alternatively, if our advice was wrong, we might be about to help them lose it. 'I was super, super nervous,' recalled Ignacio.

Just then, down on the field, Cesc Fàbregas found Andres Iniesta unmarked, as if in some childhood training session on the sunny fields of Barcelona's academy, the Masía. Iniesta fired home. Simon closed the PDF and began writing his match report.

Soccernomics hadn't won the World Cup, but football was changing. Over the last few years, penalty reports have become standard. Keepers at the most advanced big clubs now face penalties not as freewheeling gamblers, but with pretty precise instructions for what to do. In January 2017, for instance, when Chelsea's penalty-taker Diego Costa stepped up to take his spot-kick, Liverpool's keeper Simon Mignolet had a plan. Liverpool's analysts – who always talk him through all the opposition's set-pieces – had told him that Costa usually kicks to the keeper's right, writes Murad Ahmed in the *Financial Times*. But it was impossible to predict whether Costa would kick high or low. Liverpool's analysts had advised Mignolet to dive 'in between', which would give him a chance whatever the height of the shot. Costa kicked low to Mignolet's right, and the keeper saved it. Analyses like these, never discussed at post-match press conferences, increasingly decide football matches.

And that's especially true of Champions League finals, which often go to shoot-outs. In 2012 Chelsea played Bayern in the final. By then the Londoners had enough in-house penalty knowledge not to need to call someone like Ignacio. Their keeper Petr Cech prepped for the match by watching a two-hour DVD containing every Bayern penalty since 2007, and received an elaborate briefing from his club's sophisticated data team. On the night, Cech chose the correct corner for all six of Bayern's penalties (one during the game and five in the shoot-out). Chelsea won its first ever Champions League.

But the spread of best practice was uneven. In 2016 the Champions League final in Milan's San Siro stadium between Real Madrid and its city rivals Atlético went to a penalty shoot-out. Atlético won the toss, but then made a kindergarten error: they chose to shoot second. Why? Because in an earlier match in the tournament against PSV Eindhoven, Atlético had shot second and won. Ignacio emailed us: 'Incredible to see this at this level!!!!!' Atléti had gambled their European title on a single event (victory over PSV) whereas Ignacio by then had 11,000 events (penalties) in his database.

When Real Madrid's captain Sergio Ramos told his team-mates that although he had lost the toss they would get to shoot first, they were incredulous. Real had the penalty intelligence that Atlético so sadly lacked. Just like in the 2008 final in Moscow, almost none of the millions of people around the world watching the shoot-out spotted what was happening, but a couple of days later the Dutch football analyst Pieter Zwart posted a remarkable video on Facebook, titled 'Did Real Madrid know what Jan Oblak was going to do?'* The video reveals that Atlético's keeper Oblak had a crucial tell, a giveaway: just before each penalty was taken, he stepped towards the side where he was going to dive. The step helped him get to his chosen corner faster. The problem comes when the opposition know what he is doing – and Real clearly did. The players seemed to be working off a sophisticated penalty report. Four out of the five Real players run up slowly, wait for Oblak to take his step, and then slot the ball gently in the other corner. Data analysis won the Champions League. Football is becoming clever.

And that's becoming true even of some football officials. Ever since Ignacio discovered that the team shooting first has a 60 per cent chance of winning, he has dreamed of reforming the shoot-out to make it fairer. In 2010 we of *Soccernomics* connected him with a senior UEFA official to explain his ideas. Ignacio proposed scrapping the current system in which team A shoots one penalty, then team B, then A, then B, and so on. Instead he suggested using the same sequence as in the tiebreak in tennis:

A B B A – A B B A – A B B A – A B B A

In other words, team A takes one penalty, then team B takes two, then A takes two, etc. In 2010 Ignacio sent this suggestion to

---

* You can watch it at www.facebook.com/Catenaccio.nl/videos/ 1159047960806155.

all the members of the International Football Association Board committee, which determines the laws of football. He never heard anything back. But in October 2016 he again contacted the IFAB committee members, who by then were a different set of people from six years earlier. In March 2017 IFAB announced that it was going to trial the 'ABBA' system for penalty shoot-outs, explaining that research had shown that under the traditional ABAB system, the team shooting first won on average 60 per cent of the time. 'We believe that the ABBA approach could remove that statistical bias,' explained the Scottish FA's chief executive Stewart Regan. In May 2017, after the Germany–Norway semi-final at the women's under-17 European Championship went to a shoot-out, the ABBA system got its first run-out. The rules were new, but the outcome was the same as it had always been: Germany won.

Ignacio had waiting years to watch an ABBA shootout. 'To change a rule to improve football is really a dream of any scientist,' he once mused. 'If I ever manage to do that, I retire. That's it.' We think he was joking.

THE SUBURBAN NEWSAGENT'S: CITY SIZES AND FOOTBALL PRIZES

The scene: the VIP room at the Athens Olympic Stadium, a couple of hours before the 2007 Champions League final between Milan and Liverpool kicks off. Michel Platini and Franz Beckenbauer are being buttonholed every couple of yards by other middle-aged men in expensive suits. There is a crush at the buffet, and another across the room, where a familiar silver cup with 'big ears' stands on a dais. You line up, assume a conquering pose beside the Champions League trophy and grin. Nice young ladies from UEFA slip the picture into a frame for you.

An Englishman watching the scene, a football official, confides that he first got this close to the cup thirty years ago. Where? In Bramcote, a suburb of Nottingham. One of Brian Clough's brothers ran the local post office-cum-newsagents, and Clough himself would sometimes pop in and serve customers, or just stand behind the counter reading the papers. One Sunday morning when the future official went in with his grandfather, there was the European Cup freshly won by Forest, plunked on top of a pile of *Nottingham Evening Posts*. Behind it stood Brian Clough, holding an open newspaper in front of his face. He neither moved nor spoke, but he knew the boy would remember the scene for ever. The official remembers, 'I was too young and shy to speak to the man, which I regret to this day.'

It's odd to think of the game's biggest club trophy ending up in a place like Bramcote (population 7,318). Yet it's not that exceptional. The provincial cities Nottingham, Glasgow, Dortmund, Birmingham and Rotterdam have all won European Cups, while London, Paris, Rome, Berlin, Istanbul and Moscow never had until Chelsea finally got one in 2012. Nottingham still has more than all those first-rank metropoles put together. This points to an odd connection between city size, capital cities and football success. Here's why London took so long to win the Champions League – and why Europe's biggest cities might now start adding some trophies.

GENERAL FRANCO'S TRANSISTOR RADIO: THE ERA OF TOTALITARIAN FOOTBALL

The best measure of success in club football is a simple list: the names of the clubs that have won the European Cup since the competition began in 1956. Study this list, and you'll see that the history of the European Cup breaks down into three periods.

The first, from 1956 through the late 1960s, is dominated by the capital cities of fascist regimes. Of the first eleven European Cups, eight were won by either Real Madrid (favourite club of General Francisco Franco) or Benfica (from the capital of the Portuguese dictator Salazar). Seven of the losing teams in the first sixteen finals also came from fascist capitals: Real, Benfica and, in 1971, Panathinaikos from the Athens of the colonels' regime.

But by the start of the 1970s, the dominance of fascist capitals was eroding. Fascist governments seldom outlast their leaders, and Portugal's had entered a twilight after Salazar died in 1970. Meanwhile, everyone was waiting for Franco to go, too.

Yet even after fascism disappeared, teams from Europe's remaining dictatorial capitals continued to thrive. Steaua Bucharest, run by a son of the Romanian dictator Nicolae Ceauşescu, won the cup in 1986. Red Star Belgrade triumphed in 1991 just as Yugoslavia was breaking into pieces. The same phenomenon was at work in the communist countries as in the fascist capitals before them. Dictators send resources to the capital because that is where they and their senior bureaucrats and soldiers and secret policemen live. So the dictators do up the main buildings, boost the local economy and help the football club. That's totalitarian football.

A communist takeover of Britain could have done wonders for a capital team like Arsenal. Just look at the triumphs of Dynamo Berlin, founded in the former East Germany with the express purpose of keeping the league title in the capital. The club president until the Berlin Wall fell was Erich Mielke, feared octogenarian chief of the East German secret police, the Stasi. Mielke loved Dynamo. He made all the best East German players play for it. He also talked to referees, and Dynamo won a lot of matches with penalties in the ninety-fifth minute. Dynamo was popularly known as the Elf Schweine, the eleven pigs, but it did win the East German league title every year from 1979 to 1988. This was possibly Europe's most extreme case of politicians rigging the football market.

Dynamo never got far in the European Cup, but General Franco's local team did. The general made a point of catching Real Madrid's games on the radio, taking a transistor along with him if he was out partridge shooting, writes Jimmy Burns in *When Beckham Went to Spain*. It wasn't so much that Franco fixed referees or gave Real money. Rather, he helped the club indirectly, by centralizing Spain's power and resources. And he believed that Real's European Cups helped him. Fernando María Castiella, foreign minister under Franco, called Real Madrid 'the best embassy we have ever had'.

DOWN AND OUT, PARIS AND LONDON: THE FAILURE OF DEMOCRATIC CAPITALS

Totalitarian capitals got off to a great start in the European Cup. But for the first forty-two years of the trophy's life, the democratic capitals of Europe never won it.

There is only one caveat: Amsterdam is nominally the Dutch capital, and Ajax of that city won the European Cup four times. However, Amsterdam really is only nominally the capital. The government, parliament, the king's palace, and the embassies are all in The Hague, a city that has often gone years at a stretch without having a team in the Dutch premier division. The Hague's only professional club, ADO, traditionally plays its games in front of a few thousand people, a large proportion of whom are nuts. Little happens on the field beyond the occasional smoke bomb or plague of rabbits. Only in the last few seasons has ADO even established itself as a regular in the top Dutch division. This is the curse of the democratic capital.

Instead of Western capitals, provincial Western European cities have dominated the European Cup and Champions League. The rule of the provinces holds true even in the most obsessively centralized countries. Teams from five provincial British cities won the European Cup before London finally got one. Olympique Marseille won the cup in 1993, but Paris Saint-Germain never has. Porto has won it twice since Portugal went democratic, while the Lisbon clubs have been winless since 1962. Clubs from Milan and Turin have won a combined total of twelve trophies; Roman clubs, zero. The cup has gone to Munich and Hamburg, but never to Bonn or Berlin. For many years, in fact, neither of those cities even had a team in the Bundesliga. Hertha Berlin, the only big club in the current capital, have not been champions of Germany since the Weimar Republic.

Capitals – especially London, Paris and Moscow – tend to have the greatest concentrations of national resources. It's therefore striking how badly their clubs seem to perform. We can speculate about why this is. But perhaps the main reason teams from democratic capital cities are not up to much is psychological. In capital cities, no football club can matter all that much. There was an instructive sight, sometime in the late 1990s, of a group of visiting fans from an English provincial town wandering down London's Baker Street yelling their club songs at passers-by. In their minds, they were shaming the Londoners, invading the city for a day, making all the noise. But the Londoners they were shouting at – many of them foreigners anyway – didn't care, or even understand the point they were making.

Capitals simply have less to prove than provincial cities. They have bigger sources of pride than their football teams. Londoners don't go around singing songs about their city, and they don't believe that a prize for Arsenal or Chelsea would enhance London's status. Roman Abramovich and David Dein helped bring trophies to Chelsea and Arsenal, but neither ever could have been voted mayor of London. Football matters even less in Paris, where it's possible to spend a lifetime without ever knowing that football exists. Paris Saint-Germain, whose ground is only just inside the city's Péripherique ring road, is hardly going to become the main focus of Parisian pride.

London, Paris and Moscow don't need to win the Champions League. It is a different type of city where a football club can mean everything: the provincial industrial town. These are the places that have ousted the fascist capitals as rulers of European football.

DARK SATANIC MILLS: WHY FACTORY TOWNS BECAME FOOTBALL TOWNS

In 1878 a football club started up just by the newish railway line in Manchester. Because the players worked at the Newton Heath carriage works of the Lancashire and Yorkshire Railway Company, their team was called Newton Heath. They played in work clogs against other work teams.

Famously, Newton Heath became Manchester United. But what matters here are the club's origins, well recounted in Jim White's *Manchester United: The Biography*. White describes the L&YR's workers, 'sucked in from all over the country to service the growing need for locomotives and carriages'. Life in Manchester then was neither fun nor healthy, he writes. 'In the middle of the nineteenth century the average male life expectancy in Little Ireland, the notorious part of Manchester . . . was as low as seventeen.' This was still the same brutal Manchester where a few decades before, Karl Marx's pal Friedrich Engels had run his father's factory, the industrial city so awful it inspired communism.

Industrial Manchester had grown like no other city on earth. In 1800 it had been a tranquil little place of 84,000 inhabitants, so insignificant that as late as 1832 it did not even have a Member of Parliament. It was the Industrial Revolution that changed everything. Workers poured in from English villages, from Ireland, from feeble economies everywhere. For instance, the great-grandparents of Simon, one of this book's authors, came to Manchester from Lithuania.

By 1900 all these newcomers had made Manchester the sixth-biggest city in Europe, with 1.25 million inhabitants, more than Moscow at the time. It was still a hard city. In the early twentieth century Simon's great-grandparents emigrated on to much healthier southern Africa, after two of their children had died in Manchester of scarlet fever.

Inevitably, most of the early 'Mancunians' were rootless migrants. Unmoored in their new home, many of them embraced the local football clubs. Football must have given them something of the sense of the community that they had previously known in their villages.

The same thing happened in Britain's other new industrial cities: the migrants attached themselves to football clubs with a fervour unknown in more established towns. When the English Football League was founded in 1888, six of the twelve founding members came from industrial Lancashire, while the other six were from the industrial Midlands. Montague Shearman wrote that year, 'No words of ours can adequately describe the present popularity [of football] which, though great in the metropolis, is infinitely greater in the large provincial towns. . . . It is no rare thing in the north and midlands for 10,000 people to pay money to watch an ordinary club match, or for half as many again to assemble for a "Cup Tie".' It helped that workers in the textile industry in the north-west began to get Saturdays off in the 1890s, a luxury that workers elsewhere in Britain did not enjoy.

By 1892, all twenty-eight English professional clubs were from the north or the Midlands. Football was as northern a game as rugby league. The champions in the Victorian era came from northern industrial towns such as Preston, Sheffield or Sunderland, then still among the richest spots on earth. When these places became too poor and small to support successful clubs, the league title merely migrated to larger northern cities.

The legacy of the Industrial Revolution still shapes English fandom. Today the combined population of Greater Merseyside, Greater Manchester and the county of Lancashire is less than 5.5 million, or a little over 10 per cent of the English population. Nonetheless, at the end of the 2016–2017 season, four of the top seven clubs in the Premier League table – the two Manchester teams, Liverpool and Everton – were based in this region. Their advantage: more than a century of brand building. Manchester United became arguably the most popular club on earth largely because Manchester had been the first industrial city on earth. The club is only the biggest local football relic of that era. The forty-three professional clubs within ninety miles of Manchester probably represent the greatest football density in the world.

Almost all of Europe's best football cities have a profile like Manchester's. They were once new industrial centres that sucked in hapless villagers. The newcomers cast around for something to belong to, and settled on football. Supporting a local club helped them make a place for themselves in the city. So clubs mattered more here, and grew bigger, than in capital cities or ancient cathedral towns with old-established hierarchies.

The best way to gauge a club's support nowadays (given that most fans don't come to the stadium on Saturday) is to tot up its social-media followers. *Forbes* magazine and Hookit (a company that tracks sponsorship value across media) ran the numbers for the world's biggest sports clubs from June 2015 through June 2016. Top was Barcelona with 145 million followers across Facebook, Twitter and Instagram combined – slightly more than all thirty-two American NFL teams put together. The top English club was Manchester United, with 88.4 million. Bayern Munich (46.8 million) led in Germany, Paris Saint-Germain (32.7 million) in France and Juventus (30.3 million) in Italy.

These obviously aren't the total numbers of each club's fans. Many people follow multiple teams online, and lots change their allegiances depending on who just won the league or where Paul Pogba happens to be playing. However, *Forbes*' ranking does tell us something. Few would dispute that these five clubs are (at the moment, at least) the best-supported in their respective countries. And there is something remarkable about this list: the biggest clubs are not in the biggest cities. They are in the formerly industrial ones. In only one of the five big European leagues – France, very much the fifth of the big five – does the most-followed club come from a capital city. That probably wasn't even true for most of the period before 2011, when a wing of the Qatari state took over PSG and stuffed the team with superstars. We saw that when the research company Sport+Markt surveyed European fandom in 2006, it found that France's most popular club was provincial Lyon.

Real Madrid is the king of European football, with twelve European Cups (to 2017), but it's the exception. All the other major powers are provincial industrial cities. If you take Barcelona, Manchester, Turin and Munich, and add on Milan and Hamburg, then large provincial cities won a combined twenty-six out of fifty-five European Cups from 1963 to 2017. The smaller industrial or port cities Liverpool, Glasgow, Nottingham, Birmingham, Marseille, Porto, Dortmund, Eindhoven and Rotterdam have won an additional fifteen between them. And all these industrial cities have a story much like Manchester's, although their growth spurts happened later. Peasants arrived from the countryside, leaving all their roots behind. Needing something to belong to in their new cities, they chose football. That's why in all these places, the football clubs arose soon after the factories.

In most of these cities, the industrial migrants arrived in a whoosh in the late nineteenth century. Munich had 100,000 inhabitants in 1852, and five times as many by 1901. Barcelona's population trebled in the same period to 533,000. Turin, for centuries a quiet Piedmontese town, began acquiring factories in the 1870s. Milan surged with the new railways that followed Italian reunification.

Once the local merchants had grown wealthy and discovered English ways, they founded football clubs: Juventus in

1897, Barcelona and AC Milan two years later, Bayern in 1900. The clubs then grew with their cities. Newly industrial Milan, for instance, sucked in so many migrants that it could eventually support two of the three most popular teams in the country.

The second stage of the football boom in the continent's industrial cities happened after the war. The 1950s and 1960s were the years of Italy's 'economic miracle', when flocks of poor southern Italian peasants took the 'train of the sun' north. Many of these people ended up in Turin, making cars for Fiat. The historian Paul Ginsborg writes, 'So great and persistent was the flow from the South, that by the end of the sixties Turin had become the third largest "southern" city in Italy, after Naples and Palermo.' The migrants found jobs, but not enough schools or hospitals or apartments. Often there was so little space that roommates had to take turns sleeping. Amid such dislocation, football mattered all the more. Goffredo Fofi, author of a study of southern immigration to Turin in the 1960s, said that 'during a Juventus–Palermo match, there were many enthusiastic immigrant Sicilian fans whose sons, by now, like every respectable FIAT worker, backed the home team.'

It's one of the flukes of history that this mass migration to Turin began soon after the Superga air disaster of 1949 had decimated the city's previous most popular team, Torino. The migrants arrived soon after Juve had established itself as the local top dog, and they helped make it a global top dog. For starters, they transmitted the passion to their relatives down south.

Barcelona experienced the same sort of growth spurt at about the same time as Turin. In the 1950s and 1960s perhaps 1.5 million Spaniards moved to the Barcelona area. Entire villages in the country's interior were left almost empty. On wastelands outside Barcelona, self-built shantytowns sprang up – the sort of thing you might now see on the outskirts of Jakarta – packed with peasants who had left behind everything they knew. Many were illiterate. Hardly any spoke the local language, Catalan. A lot of them attached themselves to Barça. In Spain's new Manchester, it was the quickest way to belong.

The link between industry and football is almost universal across Europe. The largest crowds in Europe in the 2015–2016 season were at Borussia Dortmund (average: 81,178), one of many clubs in the industrial German Ruhr region. In France, too, it is the industrial cities that have historically loved their clubs best. The country's few traditional hotbeds of football, besides the port of Marseille, are the mining towns of Lens and Saint-Étienne.

All these industrial cities were products of a particular era. In all of them the Industrial Revolution ended, often painfully. But besides the empty docks and factory buildings, the other legacy of industrialization was beloved football clubs. The quirk of a particular era gave Manchester United, Barcelona, Juventus, Bayern Munich and the Milan clubs enough fans to dominate first their own countries, and then Europe.

The universal principle holds in Turkey, too. The country's capital of football is not the capital city Ankara, but the industrial powerhouse Istanbul, which is home to all three of Turkey's most popular clubs: Galatasaray, Fenerbahce and Besiktas.

It's true that Istanbul, like Saint Petersburg, was once the seat of government, but both cities lost that role more than ninety years ago, long before football amounted to anything in their countries. Even as late as 1950, Istanbul was a sleepy place with barely a million inhabitants. Then it became possibly the last big European city to experience an industrial revolution. Migrants were sucked in from all over Anatolia. Between 1980 and 1985 alone, Istanbul's population doubled. Today it is the largest metropolitan area in Europe, with 14 million inhabitants. The rootless peasants needed somehow to find belonging in their new home, and so they attached themselves to one or other of the city's great clubs. Often, football provided their strongest loyalties in Istanbul.

Admittedly, almost all cities in Europe have some experience of industrialization. But very few have had as much as Manchester, Turin, Milan, Istanbul or Barcelona. These were the European cities with the most flux, the fewest long-standing hierarchies, the weakest ties between people and place. Here, there were emotional gaps to fill. This becomes obvious when we contrast the industrial cities with old towns that have a traditional upper-class streak. In England, Oxford, Cambridge, Cheltenham, Canterbury, York and Bath (including its rural outskirts) are all decent-sized places, with somewhere between 100,000 and 175,000 inhabitants each. Many industrial towns of that size or even smaller – Middlesbrough, Reading, Ipswich, Blackburn, Watford, Burnley – have serious football traditions. Yet by the 2016–2017 season, Oxford, Cambridge, Bath, Canterbury, York and Cheltenham between them had just three small teams in the English Football League: Cheltenham Town, which joined it only in 1999, Oxford United, which re-entered the league after a spell in the semi-professional 'non-league' in 2010, and Cambridge United, which came back in 2014. Cambridge and Cheltenham played in the fourth (or bottom) tier of the English league, and Oxford in the third tier. In towns like these, with age-old hierarchies and few incoming peasants, people simply didn't need football clubs to root themselves.

Oxford's face to the world is the university. In industrial cities it is the football club. Barcelona, Marseille and Newcastle are the pride of their cities, a symbolic two fingers up at the capital. When Barcelona wins something, the president of Catalonia traditionally hoists himself up on the balcony of his palace on the Plaça Sant Jaume and shouts at the crowds below, 'Barça wins, Catalonia wins!'

These provincial clubs have armies of fans, players who will bleed for the club, and backing from local plutocrats. Bernard Tapie put money into Olympique Marseille, the Agnelli family into Juventus and Sir John Hall into Newcastle because they wanted to be kings of their towns. Local fans and sponsors invest in these clubs partly because they feel civic pride is at stake. In the Middle Ages they would have built a cathedral instead.

Usually, provincial cities such as these have only one major club, which often becomes the only thing many outsiders know about the place. For instance, there must be many Manchester United fans around the world who don't know that Manchester is a city in England. True, most provincial cities have two teams that compete for top-dog status: United and City in Manchester, Inter and Milan in Milan, Torino and Juventus in Turin, United and Wednesday in Sheffield, Celtic and Rangers in Glasgow, Forest and County in Nottingham, Everton and Liverpool FC in Liverpool, Bayern and 1860 in Munich, Barça and Espanyol in Barcelona. Many of these rivalries have something to do with religion or politics or both. But usually one team struggles. Manchester City, Torino and 1860 Munich have all spent long phases in the lower divisions. City only reached the top thanks to the arrival of a billionaire Arab sheikh in 2008. Everton last won the league in 1987. FC Amsterdam went bust. Midsize provincial cities are simply not big enough to sustain two big clubs for long. Almost always, one club pulls ahead.

'THEY MOVED THE HIGHWAY': THE RISE AND FALL OF SMALL TOWNS

Provincial industrial towns and cities began to dominate the European Cup in the late 1960s. But their rule breaks down into two main periods. The first, from 1970 to 1981, is the small-town/city era, when clubs from some very modest places won the European Cup. Here they are, with the populations not just of the cities

themselves but of their entire metropolitan areas, including people in all the local suburbs:

Club	Year(s) they won it	Metropolitan area
Feyenoord Rotterdam	1970	1 million
Ajax Amsterdam	1971–1973	1 million
Bayern Munich	1974–1976	2.9 million
Liverpool	1977, 1978, 1981	1.4 million
Nottingham Forest	1979, 1980	470,000

Note that we are estimating the size of these places very generously, going way beyond the city borders. The figure for Liverpool, for instance, includes all of the local Merseyside region.

The rule of the small is even more striking when you consider some of the losing teams in European Cup finals in this
era. In a remarkable four-year period from 1976 to 1979, the
towns of Saint-Étienne, Mönchengladbach, Bruges and Malmö
all had teams in the final.

Club	Size of town	Size of total metropolitan area
Saint-Étienne	175,000	320,000
Mönchengladbach	260,000	260,000
Bruges	115,000	270,000
Malmö	240,000	600,000

Perhaps the emblematic small-town team of the seventies is
Borussia Mönchengladbach, whose rise and fall encapsulates
that of all these towns.

In the 1970s Gladbach won five German titles and reached
four European finals. The Bökelberg stadium, perched on a hill
among the gardens of smart houses, saw the best years of
Günter Netzer, Rainer Bonhof and Allan Simonsen. Fans drove
in from neighbouring Holland and Belgium, as well as from
the town's British army barracks. Decades later, a German

marketing company showed that the knee-jerk response of the country's fans to the word 'counterattack' was still Gladbach.

It was a cosy little club: Berti Vogts spent his whole career here, and when Netzer later played in Zurich he often used to drive up, sometimes to scout players for Spanish clubs, but often just to eat sausages in the canteen.

Like David Cassidy, Gladbach would have done well to combust spontaneously at the end of the seventies. In 1980 the club lost its last UEFA Cup final to Eintracht Frankfurt, and the decades since have been disappointing. There was the spell in 1998, for instance, when it just couldn't stop getting thrashed. 'We can only get better,' announced Gladbach's coach, Friedel Rausch, just before his team lost 8–2 to Bayer Leverkusen. 'I feel I can solve our problems,' he said afterwards. When Gladbach lost its next match 7–1 to Wolfsburg, Rausch was sacked. Gladbach spent time in Germany's second division, and has never regained its former heights.

This upsets leftist, educated fifty-somethings all over Germany, who still dislike Bayern, revere the socialist Netzer, and on Saturday afternoons check the Gladbach result first. But there is nothing to be done. The glory days cannot come back, because what did in Gladbach was the modern era.

In the words of Norman Bates in Hitchcock's *Psycho*: 'They moved the highway.' In the seventies Gladbach's coach, Hennes Weisweiler, was able to build a team of boys from the local towns. The part-Dutch Bonhof came from nearby Emmerich, Vogts was an orphan from Neuss-Buttgen and Hacki Wimmer, who did Netzer's dirty work, spent decades after his playing career running his parents' stationery shop just down the road in Aachen.

These stars stayed at Gladbach for years because there was little more money to be earned anywhere else in football, because most rich clubs were allowed only a couple of foreign players at most, and because their own club could generally stop them from leaving. In short, there were market restraints. That's why

Gladbach, Nottingham Forest, Bruges and Saint-Étienne could thrive in the 1970s. Even then, big cities had more resources, but they had limited freedom, or limited desire, to use them.

The beginning of the end for small towns was the day in February 1979 when Trevor Francis became football's first 'million-pound man'. In fact, Clough agreed to a fee of only £999,999 to bring him from Birmingham to Forest, but there were taxes on top. Three months later Francis headed the goal (against Malmö) that gave Forest the European Cup. But the swelling of the football economy that he embodied would eventually do in small clubs like Forest.

In the 1980s TV contracts grew, and Italy opened its borders to foreign players. Later, teams around Europe began renovating their stadiums, which allowed the ones with a lot of fans to make more money. After the European Court of Justice's 'Bosman ruling' in 1995, big clubs could easily sign the best players from any country in the European Union. Around the same time, the clubs with the most fans began earning much more from their television rights. Big clubs everywhere got bigger. Bayern Munich, previously Gladbach's main rival, mushroomed into 'FC Hollywood'.

After that, clubs like Gladbach could no longer keep their best players. Lothar Matthäus made his debut for 'Die Fohlen' at the end of the golden era, but when he was only twenty-three he graduated to Bayern. The club's next great prospect, the local lad Sebastian Deisler, left Gladbach for Hertha at age nineteen in 1999, as soon as he distantly began to resemble Netzer. Small towns couldn't afford the new football.

'THAT'S NOT COCAINE, IT'S SAFFRON': THE DEMISE OF THE CATHEDRAL CITIES

Wandering around Florence, you can still imagine it as the centre of the universe. It is the effect of the great cathedral, the endless Michelangelos and all the tourists paying £7 for an orange juice.

A Medici ruler returning from the dead, as in one of Florence's umpteen paintings of the Day of Judgement, might feel his city had won the battle of prestige among European city-states.

But he would be wrong. These days a midsize city in Europe derives its status less from its cathedral than from its football club. Here, towns the size of Florence (600,000 people in its metropolitan area) have slipped up.

Fiorentina's last flurry came in 1999, when it beat Arsenal in a Champions League match at Wembley thanks to a goal by Gabriel Batistuta, with Giovanni Trapattoni sitting on the bench. In those days 'Trap's' biggest problems were his players' insistence on busing the 150 yards from the locker room to the training ground and Brazilian Edmundo's ritual late return from the Rio Carnival. But those days will never return. In the Champions League, the midsize cities are now finished.

Fiorentina's demise can be dated to the day in July 2001 that the Italian police raided the home of the team's owner, the Italian film baron Vittorio Cecchi Gori. What happened was exactly what should happen when police raid a film baron's home, as if Cecchi Gori had read up on Jackie Collins beforehand.

The police broke into his apartment in the Palazzo Borghese in Rome, but then took ninety minutes to find him. This was because his bedroom door was concealed inside a mirrored wall. Only after the Filipina maid had pointed this out did they enter the bedroom to find Cecchi Gori asleep with his girlfriend, Valeria Marini, a sort of early prototype of Kim Kardashian, who calls herself a singer-actress but in fact can do neither.

The police told Cecchi Gori to open his safe. Donning his silk dressing gown, he did so. When the police remarked on the stash of cocaine stored inside, Cecchi Gori replied nonchalantly, 'Cocaine? That's not cocaine, it's saffron!'

Meanwhile, his business empire was unravelling. It should be said that he acquired the empire only by inheritance from his father, Mario, who before dying in 1993 had warned his old business partner, Silvio Berlusconi, 'Take care of Vittorio, he is so impulsive and naive.'

Vittorio's problem was that he wanted to be Berlusconi. He bought commercial TV channels (a failure), pumped fortunes into his football team (no titles) and dabbled in politics (getting no further than senator), but might have been okay had he not gotten caught in a divorce expected to be so expensive that it alone could have funded Fiorentina for years. Cecchi Gori remained admirably upbeat even after all this, leaning out of the window of his Mercedes limousine on Rome's Via Veneto to shout 'La dolce vita!' to friends. However, he ruined Fiorentina.

It was hard to work out which bit of Cecchi Gori's empire owed what to which, but it was clear that he had borrowed tens of millions of dollars from the club. After everything went wrong, he tried the traditional Italian remedy, putting his eighty-two-year-old mother in charge, but even she could not save Fiorentina. A fax from a Colombian bank offering to pay off the club's entire debt proved, amazingly, to be a forgery.

In 2002 Fiorentina went bankrupt, slipping into Italy's fourth division, where it had to visit Tuscan village teams whose players were mostly Fiorentina fans. Now it is back in Serie A, but the days of Trap, Batistuta and 'The Animal' Edmundo won't return. Florence is just too small now.

Florence is typical. Midsize European cities (between 150,000 and 1 million inhabitants) have all but dropped off the map of European football. They can no longer afford to compete with clubs from bigger places. In early 2004 it was the turn of Parma, whose owners, the dairy company Parmalat, turned out to have mislaid 10 billion euros. Leeds United is the great English example. In Spain Deportivo La Coruña, pride of a midsize Galician city, suddenly discovered that its debt had hit the strictly notional figure of 178 million euros. Valencia followed a few years later. These clubs fell short because they had hardly any supporters outside their own city walls. Other midsize cities – Glasgow, Amsterdam, Nottingham – have retreated with less fanfare, but they too must know they will never again produce European champions. Even Newcastle is slowly emerging from denial.

The third period of the European Cup began in 1982 and hasn't ended yet: rule by sturdy provincial city. There were still a few undersize winners: Porto and Liverpool twice each, and Eindhoven, Marseille and Dortmund. However, these cities are not exactly midgets. Four of the five are agglomerations of 1.2 million inhabitants or more. Only Eindhoven has just 210,000 people and a metropolitan area – if you draw it very generously – of 750,000. In general, European champions are getting bigger. In modern times, the race has usually gone to the rich. Even historic champions like Liverpool no longer seem to be in the running. With an urban population of under 500,000, and only about 1.5 million people in the wider metropolitan area, it has won just one Champions League since 1984.

The swelling of the football economy – the bigger TV contracts, the new stadiums, the freer movement of players, and so on – favoured the most popular clubs. For historical reasons, these tended to be the ones in big provincial cities. Their teams came to dominate the Champions League in a sort of endless loop. Every club that won the trophy from 1998 to 2011 had won it at least once before. Most had won it several times before. Are their fans growing blasé? When you have won the thing ten times, the buzz probably starts to fade.

The dominant clubs until now haven't been from the megacities of Moscow, London, Paris or Istanbul but from urban areas with about 2 million to 5 million inhabitants: Milan, Manchester, Munich, Madrid and Barcelona. These cities are big enough to produce the required fan base yet provincial enough to generate a yearning for global recognition.

Strangely, one of these cities, Madrid, is a democratic capital. How could Real break the golden rule of the Champions

League and win the trophy in 1998, 2000, 2002, 2014, 2016 and 2017? Because it had built its mammoth stadium, brand and support in the days when Madrid was the capital of a dictatorship. Spain may have gone democratic, but Real's players still enter the Santiago Bernabeu in those white 'meringue' shirts as if it were 1955. The club's global standing is a relic of the fascist era.

GEORGE ZIPF COMES TO LONDON: THE DAWNING METROPOLITAN ERA

George Kingsley Zipf is an almost forgotten Harvard linguist. Born in 1902, and dying in 1950 just as he was starting to make a name, Zipf is now known only for having formulated a law that explains almost everything. Among other things, Zipf's law tells us that London or Paris should start winning Champions Leagues soon.

Consider the following: if you rank every American city by the size of its population, the difference in population between two consecutive cities is simply the ratio of their ranks. So if you compare cities number 1 and 2, city 2 has half (or 1/2) the population of city 1. If you compare cities number 2 and 3, city 3 has two-thirds (2/3) the population of city 2. City 100 has 99/100ths the population of city 99 and so on down the list. Statistically speaking, the fit of this relationship is almost as perfect as it is possible to be.

This is a particularly elegant example of a more general relationship known as Zipf's law, and it applies to a lot more than city sizes. For instance, it is also true of the frequency with which words are used in English. 'The' is the most commonly used word in the language, 'of' is second, and so 'of' is used about half (1/2) as often as 'the'. All in all, Zipf's law has been called possibly 'the most accurate regularity in economics'. (The Nobel Prize-winning economist Paul Krugman says,

'Anyone who spends too much time thinking about Zipf's law goes mad,' but we hope that is a joke.)

Zipf's law works for European cities, too, though not quite as neatly as for American ones. City sizes in most European countries are more closely bunched, and so the second city is closer to the first city's size than in the United States, the third closer to the second, and so on.

Why might this be? Zipf's law must have something to do with migration. People will always try to migrate to where the money is. In the United States, with its open markets and very high mobility of labour, they generally do. But in Europe, political and cultural barriers have curbed migration. That might explain why city sizes are more compressed there. Nonetheless, the academics Matthieu Cristelli, Michael Batty and Luciano Pietronero showed in an article in the prestigious journal *Nature* in 2012 that 'Zipf's Law holds approximately for the city sizes of each European country (France, Italy, Germany, Spain, etc).' They add that the law 'completely falls apart' if you rank them as cities within a single state, i.e. the European Union, but then that is no surprise – these cities grew big in their nation-states long before the EU was ever thought of.

For a long time, nobody could understand why Zipf's law should hold for so many different phenomena. Now, though, economists and scientists are starting to generate models of growth in which the natural outcome of a process is distribution obeying Zipf's law. Recently the economist Xavier Gabaix of New York University came up with an explanation for why Zipf's law applies to city sizes. He said Zipf's law emerges when all cities grow at the same rate, regardless of their size and their history, but subject to random variation. This implies that common factors drive the growth of cities within a country, while the differences in growth are due to a series of random events ('shocks', in the economic jargon), such as bombing during the war, which in principle could occur anywhere. A story this simple is enough to explain the city sizes that Zipf's law predicts.

Two consequences of Zipf's law are crucial to football. First, giants – whether giant cities, giant football clubs or giants of any other kind – are rare. That is because becoming a giant requires a long sequence of positive shocks, like tossing a coin fifty times and coming up 'heads' every time. It can happen, but it is rare. Second, once a city becomes a giant, it is unlikely to shrink into the middle ranks unless it experiences a long series of repeated misfortunes (fifty 'tails' in a row). By contrast, small cities are unlikely ever to become giants. In other words, the hierarchy of cities, which has established itself over centuries, probably won't change much in the foreseeable future.

This 'law of proportionate growth' has some other consequences. What's true for cities is also true for many other social phenomena. For example, if your kid is behind at school, don't worry: he or she will almost certainly catch up, since all children tend to learn at the same rate, plus or minus a few shocks. Likewise, if you think your brilliant six-year-old footballer is going to become another Messi or Ronaldo, don't. More likely the boy had a few positive shocks in his early years, which will cancel out. Messi's and Ronaldo's almost never happen. The distribution of talent is thus a bit like the distribution of city sizes: a few great talents stand out at the top, but as you go down the list, the differences become smaller and smaller.

This brings us back to European cities: there are only a few giants, chiefly Moscow, Istanbul, Paris and London. You would expect these giant cities to produce the biggest clubs, yet they have won just one single Champions League between them.

But soon they might win more. Football is changing. It is becoming more of a free market, as fascist dictators no longer interfere and the best players can move between clubs almost at will. Inevitably, the best players are starting to move to the biggest markets, as happens in major league baseball. These biggest markets – the capital cities – have generally been doing better economically than the provinces. And so you would expect dominance in European football to move, too: after rule by dictatorial capitals, midsize provincial towns and big provincial cities, now London and possibly Paris should get in on the action at last, while Madrid is already expanding its dominance.

Paris might, because it has nearly 12 million inhabitants and only one top-division football club, Paris Saint-Germain, which was appallingly run for years before being taken over by Qataris who have converted oil into footballers. And London is now showing signs, for the first time ever, of becoming the football capital of England.

For the first few decades of English professional football, the north dominated. Only in 1931 did a club from the south of the country – Arsenal – first win the league. But the long decline of manufacturing hit the north's economy. That hit its football clubs, and from the early 1970s onwards there were often more southern clubs than northern ones in England's top two divisions. Yet throughout the twentieth century, the title generally went north.

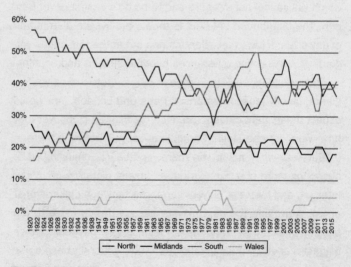

Top Two Divisions

When Arsenal and Chelsea finished in the top two spots in the Premier League in 2004, it was the first time in history that two London teams had achieved that feat. In 2005 they did it again. No London team had ever reached the Champions League final before 2006. From 2006 through 2012, Arsenal got there once and Chelsea twice, notching London's first trophy by beating Bayern on penalties in 2012. (This is one prediction we got right in the first edition of *Soccernomics* in 2009: we wrote then that 'soon' Arsenal or Chelsea 'could become the first London team to be champions of Europe'.)

In 2017, London (this time in the shape of Chelsea and Spurs) again hogged the top two places in the Premier League. The city's advance is unsurprising. It has the largest local economy in Europe. It already supports two of Europe's biggest football teams and could probably cope with more. This represents quite a change. In the early 1990s London rather resembled Moscow circa 1973. Tired people in grey clothes waited on packed platforms for 1950s Tube trains. Coffee was an exotic drink that barely existed. Eating a meal outside was forbidden. The city centre was almost uninhabited, and closed at 11 p.m. anyway. There was a sense of permanent decline.

But in the 1990s London transformed. Cheap flights from five airports took Londoners around Europe. Trains began running to Paris and Brussels. Today it is quicker to get there than to the shrinking northern cities of Liverpool and Manchester, and less of a culture shock when you arrive. London became a European city, detached from the rest of Britain – and is desperate to remain so even after Brexit. The geographer Daniel Dorling has said that Britain is starting to look like a city-state. Moreover, the city has begun to grow again. Greater London had been losing inhabitants from the Second World War until the 1980s, but boom-time London changed that. From 1989 to 2016 its population grew by nearly 2 million to hit an all-time record of 8.8 million.

It remains to be seen, of course, whether the city can maintain its growth after Brexit. But certainly from the late 1990s until today, London has offered a technicolour vista of raucous young people from all over the world dressed in weird youth-culture outfits chucking cash at each other. The Tube trains have ceased to be antique curios. The place smells of money. All this has raised London's status in football.

At the same time as the city became fully international, so did the market in footballers. The best ones can now work wherever they want. Many of them – like many investment bankers and actors – have chosen London.

Black and foreign players like living in a city where 95 per cent of the inhabitants agree with the statement, 'It is a good thing that Britain is a multicultural society.' When Thierry Henry was spending his best years at Arsenal, he said, 'I love this open, cosmopolitan city. Whatever your race, you never feel people's gaze on you.' In a virtuous cycle, foreigners attract foreigners. The Frenchman Jacques Santini, Tottenham's manager for about five minutes, wanted to come to London because his son Sebastien already lived there – a classic example of chain migration.

Equally to the point, a footballer can still earn a living in London. The capital's clubs have been coining it. First, their customers can afford to pay the highest ticket prices in global football. Chelsea can charge such high prices that in 2014–2015 it earned more than six times as much per match day as poor northern Sunderland despite having smaller crowds. In 2014–2015 Arsenal charged £1,014 for its cheapest season ticket, which was the highest rate in English and probably in global football (and almost ten times more than Barcelona or Bayern charged for their cheapest tickets).

So many Londoners are happy to fork out this kind of money that Arsenal has been able to build a new stadium with 60,000 seats and sell it out. No club in London's history has drawn such a large regular crowd, but Arsenal's city rivals are all now plotting to match it. West Ham moved into the converted Olympic Stadium in 2016, sold out the 57,000 seats and intends to expand to 66,000. Spurs wants to open its new 61,559-seat stadium in 2018, and Chelsea's new 60,000-seat ground should follow by 2021. Already, over the 2016–2017 season, the business advisory firm Deloitte ranked Arsenal, Chelsea and Spurs among Europe's eleven richest clubs; PSG, another capital club, was in seventh place. Imagine how that ranking might look by, say, 2022.

No other European city has more investors than London. When Roman Abramovich decided to buy a football club, it was always likely that he would end up owning Chelsea rather than, say, Bolton. The word is that he chose it because it was the nearest club to his house on Eaton Square. Even Queens Park Rangers are owned by the Malaysian Tony Fernandes and Indian Lakshmi Mittal, the world's eighty-second-richest man according to *Forbes*, who of course lives around the corner from the club in Kensington. Yes, other rich foreigners have bought Liverpool, Manchester City, Blackburn and Aston Villa, but London is still a touch more appealing to billionaires. Also, as the north's factories have closed, the region no longer produces many home-grown magnates like Sir John Hall at Newcastle or Jack Walker at Blackburn, who in the 1990s bankrolled their clubs to success. It says a lot about the north-east's troubles that Newcastle's shirt sponsor until 2017 was the payday lender Wonga, which is often accused of exploiting poor people.

The handful of the biggest provincial clubs – notably Manchester United, Liverpool, Bayern and Barcelona – have built up such strong brands that they will remain at the top of European football, chasing Madrid. However, the old elite's new challengers probably will not be other provincial clubs but teams from London and Paris, as well as Madrid's historical second team Atlético, which should gain a boost from its big new chic Wanda Metropolitano stadium. Even before the new ground opened, Atlético reached the Champions League final in 2014 and 2016. This means that in the six finals from 2012 to 2017, four of the winners and two runners-up came from democratic capitals.

At last, being in a capital is becoming a strategic asset to a football club. Sport used to be practically the only bit of French and British life in which the provinces could humiliate the capital. Now even that last pleasure has gone.

UNFAIR AND UNBALANCED: DO WE NEED MORE LEICESTERS?

Everyone loved it when Leicester won the Premier League.
If only, many people said, it weren't such a one-off – if only small clubs won the title more than once every twenty-five years. A common moan in modern football is that the game has got boring because the big clubs almost always win. It's become a truism to say that we need a more level playing field.

However, this truism is not true. Fans may say that they wish football were fairer – the Champions League as well as the Premier League – but the truth is that most of them don't really wish it. The majority of supporters prefer unequal leagues. In fact, if football were even less fair, if teams like Leicester had even less chance of winning, it might become even more popular.

Football stole the idea for a league from baseball. Professional American baseball players had come up with the concept in 1871. The format worked because fans turned out to want a championship in which the winner had played all the other teams. Early championships had involved either irregular schedules, in which some teams may not have faced all the others, or the knockout cups beloved of English public schoolboys. The all-play-all format of a league has nothing romantic about it, but the winner can justly claim to be the best over a sustained period. No underdog who wins the FA Cup can say the same. Even some world champions can't.

William McGregor proposed the format for his new Football League in 1888, prompted by the musings of several journalists and inspired, according to some contemporaries, by league baseball. His public-school detractors pointed out the idea's American origins as a way of implying that he was only doing it for the money. Yet leagues spread around the world almost as quickly as football did. If cups are high drama, then a league is a soap opera in dozens of episodes with endless crises and some sort of suspense until the very last day. In sports where leagues have traditionally been weak, like rugby union or cricket, fans tend to focus on the national team, and don't follow the sport day-to-day.

The English league has always had strong and weak teams. However, for decades the differences between them had little to do with money. Football was not a free market. Players used to have little freedom to join rich clubs, which is why a small club like Stoke City could hang on to Stanley Matthews for so long. Little clubs were sometimes able to keep a set of good players together for a while. Though Liverpool won the English league from 1982 to 1984, the runners-up were first Ipswich, then Watford, then Southampton. This is no accident. Any rigid labour market will keep talent locked in place.

But we have seen that from the 1980s rich clubs got richer, mostly thanks to new stadiums and TV contracts. As players became freer to change teams, the best went where the money was. In 1995 the Bosman ruling became football's Big Bang: suddenly a European player could join any club in the European

Union once his contract had ended. Rich clubs started to gain a monopoly on good players.

In 1992 all the teams in the English top division combined had a total income of £166 million. Over the next twenty-five years that figure grew by 14 per cent annually to reach £3.7 billion in 2016. This is more than twice as fast as the growth of the British housing bubble in the same period (6 per cent a year; even in Greater London, where price increases were fastest, they only grew at an average of 8 per cent per year). And with the Premier League's latest TV contracts, revenues have kept on soaring since 2016.

Meanwhile, in that 1992–2016 period the teams in the second tier of English football raised their revenues by a mere 10 per cent a year. Their total income went from £62 million to about £556 million.

Thanks to those four extra percentage points of growth a year, the biggest clubs ran away from the rest. In 1991, remarkably, the English club with the highest income was Tottenham, with £19 million. Hull City, with £1 million, had the lowest income in the Second Division. By 2016 the highest revenue of any club in English football was £515 million (Manchester United), and the lowest in the second tier was Preston North End, with £11 million. In other words, the ratio of biggest to smallest in these divisions had jumped from 19:1 to 47:1.

The rich put their money to use. Since the creation of the Premier League in 1992, only very rich clubs have won the title – usually Manchester United, but sometimes Arsenal or a sugar-daddy club.

Perhaps the main critic of dominance by big clubs was UEFA's president, Michel Platini, until he was banned from football in 2015. The Premier League's lobbyists needed to portray the Frenchman as a dangerous enemy, given that nobody with any power in Britain opposed their product, and the old romantic did his best to oblige. Platini was always talking about helping the smaller clubs. Though a former superstar, he even manages to look like a friend of the little man. He is a touch chubby, his suit trousers are too long and he has the friendly grin of a local grocer.

During an interview in UEFA's headquarters on Lake Geneva in 2008, Platini kept grumbling about big money in football. Abu Dhabi's takeover of Manchester City had upset him. Manchester City ought to be a local club, he said. 'Otherwise why should the club call itself Manchester? They should call themselves, I don't know, Coca-Cola.'

Platini spent a lot of energy trying to limit the disproportionate buying power of English clubs. However, he had almost no success. 'The English TV rights are very, very, very, very, very significant,' he mused to us. 'So the English league is the richest, so players go to the English league. How to even that out?'

Perhaps it's impossible to even out?

He paused, then admitted: 'Legally it's impossible. You can't stop the foreigners from coming. Financially it's impossible.'

Searching for a way to even things out, in the spring of 2009 Platini put a team of UEFA officials on a plane to the US. Like many others in European football, he had been impressed by the equality in American sports. Perhaps this was something that football could copy? Even Emilio Butragueño, when he was sporting director of plucky little Real Madrid, told the BBC: 'You need uncertainty at the core of every competition . . . We may eventually have something similar to the [salary cap] system in the US, to give a chance to all the clubs.'

Andy Burnham, Britain's then culture secretary, warned in 2008 that while the Premier League was 'the world's most successful domestic sporting competition', it risked becoming 'too predictable'. He told the Guardian: 'I keep referring to the NFL, which has equal sharing . . . In the US, the most free-market country in the world, they understand that equal distribution of money creates genuine competition.'

Indeed, the NFL of American football has been called 'the socialist league'. Its clubs share TV income equally. Moreover, 40 per cent of each game's gate receipts goes to the visiting team. In the famous slogan promoted by the league, 'On any given Sunday any team can beat any other team.' Baseball, basketball and the US's Major League Soccer also share far more of their income than European football does. Take the New York Yankees baseball cap, one of the most popular pieces of merchandise in all of sport. Outside of New York, the Yankees receive only one thirtieth of the profit on each cap sold, the same as every other team in baseball. It is as if each Premier League club got one twentieth of the profit every time Manchester United sold a shirt. That's the sort of thing Platini and Burnham seemed to dream of.

Yet their premise was wrong. There is almost no evidence to support their arguments for balance. The data show that, overall, football fans prefer unbalanced leagues.

If predictable results bored fans, then more of them would go to matches where the outcome was very uncertain. How to test whether fans really behave like that? Researchers have tried to gauge expected outcomes of games by using either pre-match betting odds, or the form of both teams over the previous half-dozen games. Studies of football, mostly in England, show mixed results. Some find that more balanced games attract more fans. Others find the reverse.

A moment's thought suggests why some unbalanced games might be very attractive. Often they involve strong home teams playing weak away teams (Manchester United v Burnley, say), in which case the home team typically has lots of fans who enjoy watching their heroes score lots of goals; or they are games between weak home teams and strong away teams (Burnley v Manchester United), in which local fans come to see the visiting stars or in the hope of seeing an upset.

The economists David Forrest of Salford Business School and Robert Simmons of Lancaster University have done some of the best work in this field. They found that a balanced game could sometimes increase attendance. However, they also carried out a simulation to show that if the English leagues became more balanced, they would attract fewer fans. That is because a balanced league, in which all teams were equally good, would turn into an almost interminable procession of home wins and away losses. By contrast, in real existing football, some of the most balanced games occur when a weak team plays at home against a strong team (again, Burnley v Manchester United).

Forrest and Simmons found that the people who care most about competitive balance are television viewers. Most fans at the ground are the hard core: they simply want to see their team. But TV viewers tend to be 'floating voters'. When the outcome of a game seems too predictable, they switch off. The two economists found that the closer a televised match was expected to be (measured by the form of both teams going into the game), the higher the viewing figures on Sky TV. Yet the size of this effect was modest. Forrest and Simmons said that even if the Premier League were perfectly balanced (in the sense that each team had an equal probability of winning each game), TV audiences would rise by only 6 per cent. That would be a small effect for such a revolutionary change.

Perhaps the Premier League is just balanced enough. In Spain, Real Madrid and Barcelona win most of their games easily. So do Bayern Munich in the Bundesliga. But the Premier League doesn't have quite so dominant a team. On the downside, from 2009 to 2017 English clubs won just one Champions League (Chelsea, in 2012). On the upside, to adapt the NFL's slogan, on any given day any English team can beat any other English team. In short, the very lack of a brilliant team makes the Premier League more competitive and intense.

By contrast, the best continental teams rarely play very intense league matches, because they usually win at a canter. 'Barcelona could play 50 per cent of its games with its B team,' the current Liverpool manager Jürgen Klopp remarked a couple of years ago. 'There are games in which Messi runs only 4.3 kilometres but scores five goals. There's nothing like that in any English match.' Klopp is exaggerating slightly, but goal stats back up his general point. In the 2015–2016 season Barcelona averaged 2.95 goals per league game, Real Madrid 2.89 and Bayern 2.35. The most prolific team in the Premier League, Manchester City, managed only 1.87.

The Premier League is more even than its continental rivals, and games tend to be more box-to-box. Mid-ranking and bottom English teams make lots of mistakes, lose the ball often and play many long passes, Dustin Böttger of the statistical database Global Soccer Network told the German newspaper *Die Welt*. That results in more tackles to win 50–50 balls. And players in the Premier League can go in hard, because English referees rarely blow for fouls.

Lately the Premier League seems to be becoming more equal than before. Leicester was not the only outlier in the 2015–2016 season. Several other clubs also defied expectations, but in a bad way. Chelsea had a disastrous early season despite having the third-highest payroll, sacked José Mourinho and finished tenth. In general, the big teams struggled that season. That may have something to do with a more equal distribution of resources.

Inequality in the Premier League peaked around 2007, when the team with the highest wage bill paid out nearly eight times more than the team with the lowest. The gap was so wide then because the rich clubs were making such a big chunk of their money in the Champions League, from which the small clubs were excluded. That's why the 2000s were a decade of unprecedented dominance. The big four of the time – Manchester

United, Arsenal, Chelsea and Liverpool – took the top four slots most seasons.

But the divide between rich and poor clubs' wages has been falling since 2011. In 2015–2016, the ratio between highest and lowest wage bill fell to just 4:2.

The big change in favour of the small clubs was the jump in TV rights in the Premier League. That, rather than the Champions League, is the big cash cow for English clubs. In recent years the value of the Premier League's overseas broadcast rights has grown faster than the domestic rights. That matters because overseas revenues are split equally, while the domestic split is structured to favour the big clubs.

And the smaller clubs now have the world as their transfer market. They can spend more than even foreign giants: Bournemouth, say, can now sometimes out-pay Inter Milan. A small English club that unearths the next N'Golo Kanté or Riyad Mahrez could go far. So the Premier League has become more competitive – for whatever that's worth.

* * *

Another way of looking at competitive balance is to view the league as a whole, rather than match by match. Do more spectators come when the title race is exciting than when one side runs away with it?

It turns out that a thrilling title race does little to improve attendances. Fans will watch their teams play in the league even when they haven't a hope of winning it (or else dozens of English clubs would not exist).

It is true that a game has to be significant to draw fans, but that significance need not have anything to do with winning the title. A study by Stephen Dobson and John Goddard showed that when a match matters more either for winning the league or for avoiding relegation then attendance tends to rise. Trying to qualify for Europe also gives meaning to matches. Most matches in the Premier League are significant for something or other. Given that they can be significant in many different ways, it is unclear why a more balanced league would create more significance. As the Premier League's chief executive Richard Scudamore has said: 'There are a lot of different tussles that go on in the Premier League, depending on whether you're at the top, in the middle or at the bottom, that make it interesting.'

There is a third way of looking at balance: the long term. Does the dominance of the same teams year in, year out turn fans off? Let's compare a long period with dominance to a long period without dominance: the fairly 'equal' era in English football that ran from 1949 to 1968, and the 'unfair' era of the Premier League from 1993 to 2012. In the first twenty-year period, eleven different teams won the English league. The most frequent winner, Manchester United, won five titles in the period. The second period was far more predictable: only five teams won the title, with United taking it thirteen times. And yet during the first, 'equal' period, total annual attendance in the first division fell from an all-time high of 18 million in 1949 to only 15 million in 1968 (and even that figure got a temporary boost from England winning the World Cup). During the second, 'unequal' period, total attendance rose from below 10 million to over 13 million, even though tickets became much more expensive and people had many more choices of how to spend their free time.

Anyone who says that the Premier League has become 'one of the most boring leagues in the world', a closed shop that shuts out smaller clubs from the lower divisions, has to explain why so many people now go to watch all levels of English league football. In the 2016–2017 season almost 32 million spectators saw professional games in England, a figure that has been steady for the last decade, notwithstanding the biggest recession since the 1930s. Twenty-five years ago the figure was around 20 million. You have to go back to 1950s, when fans paid a couple of shillings to stand on dilapidated terraces, to find a time when attendance was as high as it is today. The Premier League draws vast crowds despite its intense predictability. But more than half of those 30 million-plus watched the Football League, the three divisions below the Premier League. All the clubs in the Championship have supposedly been doomed to irrelevance by the super-rich clubs, and can only dream of clinging on at the bottom of the Premier League, yet their division in 2016–2017 was Europe's third-best attended league, if you rank it by total number of spectators. Of all Europe's elite leagues, only the Bundesliga generated a higher total than England's second tier. The Championship's annual attendance has now been higher than Italy's Serie A, the fifth-ranked league by attendance, in every season since 2006.

Some of English football's critics have not digested these figures. When we pointed out to Platini that English stadiums are full nowadays, he replied: 'Not all. They're full at the teams that win.' Indeed, whenever rows of empty seats appear at struggling teams near the bottom of the table, it is back-page news, and regarded as ominous for the Premier League as a whole.

Yet it's natural that some fans should desert disappointing teams, while others flock to exciting ones. Sunderland, Arsenal, Manchester United and other clubs have built bigger stadiums, and filled them. Not every English team has gained spectators since 1992, but the vast majority have. All twenty clubs in the Premier League in 2016–2017 had a higher average attendance than in 1990–1991. If the team had been in the Premier League in 1991, the average increase was 63 per cent; if it had risen from a lower division, the average increase was an even more handsome 124 per cent. Even teams that were in the Premier League in 1990–1991 but not in 2016–2017 usually had higher attendance. Only Coventry (now third tier) and Luton (fourth tier) lost spectators. The rising English tide had lifted almost every boat.

Admittedly today's large crowds don't in themselves prove that dominance attracts fans. After all, many other things have changed since the more equal 1949–1968 period. Crucially, the stadiums have improved. However, the rising attendances do make it hard to believe that dominance in itself significantly undermines interest. Indeed, pretty much every football league in Europe exhibits more dominance than the American major leagues, and yet fans still go.

There are good reasons why fans generally prefer inequality to balance. First, most fans in the stadium are fans of the home team, and so they do not really want a balanced outcome. Second, big teams have more fans than small ones, and so if Manchester United beat Burnley more people are happy than if Burnley win. Third, fans are surprisingly good at losing. Psychological studies show that they are skilled at transferring blame: 'We played well, but the referee was rubbish.' This means that fans will often stick with a team even if it always loses. Burnley or Sunderland fans are used to losing, it's what they usually do, and they can cope. In fact, losing is something that most football fans do well. This also explains why, the morning after England get knocked out of a World Cup, people don't collapse into depression but get on with their lives.

Fourth, dominant teams create a special interest of their own. In the 1990s, millions of people supported Manchester United, and millions of others despised them. In a way, both groups were following the club. United were the star of football's soap opera. Every other team's fans dreamt of beating them. Much of the meaning of supporting West Ham, for instance, derives from disliking Manchester United. Kevin Keegan, as manager of Newcastle United, thrillingly captured that national sentiment with his famous 'I will love it if we beat them! Love it!' monologue in 1996. Big bad United made the league more fun.

Strangely, it was the fanzine *When Saturday Comes* that put this best. *WSC* is, in large part, the journal of small clubs. It publishes moving and funny pieces by fans of Crewe or Swansea. Few of its readers have much sympathy with Manchester United (though some, inevitably, are United fans). Many have argued for a fairer league. One of the magazine's regular writers, Ian Plenderleith, is fairly typical in being a Lincoln City supporter. Yet in 2008 Plenderleith, who lived outside Washington, DC, argued in *WSC* that American major league soccer, in which 'all teams started equal, with the same squad size, and the same amount of money to spread among its players' wages', was boring. The reason: 'No truly memorable teams have the space to develop.'

'MLS is crying out for a couple of big, successful teams,' Plenderleith admitted. 'Teams you can hate. Dynasties you really, really want to beat. Right now, as LA Galaxy coach Bruce Arena once memorably said: "It's a crapshoot."'

In short, the MLS lacks one of the joys of an unbalanced league: the David v Goliath match. And one reason why fans enjoy those encounters is that surprisingly often, given their respective budgets, David wins.

The economist Jack Hirshleifer called this phenomenon 'the paradox of power'. Imagine, he said, that there were two tribes, one large, one small. Each can devote its efforts to just two activities: farming and fighting. Each tribe produces its own food through farming, and steals the other tribe's food through fighting. Which tribe will devote a larger share of its efforts to fighting?

The answer is the small tribe. The best way to understand this is to imagine that the small tribe is very small indeed. It would then have to devote almost all its limited resources to either fighting or farming. If it chose farming, it would be vulner-able to attack. Everything it produced could be stolen. On the other hand, if the tribe devoted all its resources to fighting, it would have at least a chance of stealing some resources. So Hirshleifer concludes – and proves with a mathematical model – that smaller competitors will tend to devote a greater share of resources to competitive activities.

He found many real-world examples of the paradox of power. He liked citing North Vietnam's defeat of the US, but one might also add the Afghan resistance to the Soviet Union in the 1980s, the Dutch resistance to the Spanish in the sixteenth century or the American resistance to the British in the War of Independence. In these cases the little guy actually defeated the big guy. In many other cases, the little guy was eventu-ally defeated, but at much greater cost than might have been expected on the basis of their physical resources (the Spar-tans at Thermopylae, the Afrikaners in the Boer War, the Texans at the Alamo). More recently, little ISIS managed to defy the Western powers for years.

In football, as in war, the underdog tends to try harder. Big teams fight more big battles, and so each contest weighs a little less heavily than it does with their smaller rivals. Little teams understand that they may have few opportunities to compete at the highest level, and so they give it everything. They therefore probably win more often than you would predict on the basis of ability alone.

Fans enjoy unbalanced modern football. Yet the complaints about its imbalance continue. The curious thing is that these complaints are relatively new, a product of the last twenty years or so. Contrary to popular opinion, football was unbalanced in the past too, but before the 1990s fewer people complained.

It is a fantasy that in the past every team had a chance to win, just as it's a fantasy that football used to be more popu-lar. (It is possible that more people are interested today than at any time in the past.) Europe as a whole has never been a very balanced footballing continent. In smaller countries, clubs from the capital tended to rule. Serie A was always dominated by Juventus, Milan and Inter, and the Spanish league by Barcelona and Real Madrid. By the 1980s Bayern dominated in Germany, and in the post-war era English football has been dominated by Manchester United, Arsenal and Liverpool. United's thirteen titles in twenty-one seasons to 2013 may sound boring, but Liverpool won ten in twenty between 1969 and 1988. A handful of sides have dominated for most of English football's history. Even a club as large as Newcastle have not won the title since 1927 – and yet big crowds still go to watch them. The imbalance in England as in all European leagues was reinforced by European competition, which handed the dominant teams more money. The old European Cup was seldom much fairer than the Champions League is now. We saw in the previous chapter that only between 1970 and 1981 did teams from modestly sized cities regularly win the trophy. Usually the cup went to the biggest provincial cities, or to Madrid. Even Platini admitted to us: 'For forty years it's been the biggest clubs that won the Champions League; when I played, too. With or without home-grown players, it was Real Madrid, Liverpool, Manchester, Juventus who won. English clubs won the cup ten times in a row, I think. No? In the 1980s.'

Oh dear. Platini is not going to win any pub quizzes any time soon. In fact English clubs won six European Cups from 1977 through 1982. But his point stands: inequality in the European Cup is nothing new.

He smiles, thinking again of that English dominance in the 1980s: 'It's funny. There were no great debates then, saying, "We have to change everything." Today it's the money that makes the difference.'

That is precisely the point. Today's inequality bothers people not because it is unprecedented, but because it is more driven by money than it used to be. In the old days, a middling team could suddenly enjoy years of dominance if it happened to hire an excellent manager who signed excellent players. That's what happened to Liverpool under Bill Shankly, and to Forest under Brian Clough. Today, a middling team can suddenly enjoy years of dominance if it happens to be bought by a billionaire who hires an excellent manager who signs excellent players. That is what happened to Chelsea under Roman Abramovich. In short, inequality in football, as well as not being boring, is not even new. The one thing that is new is the money.

Many people tend to feel that inequality becomes unfair when it is bought with money. It disgusts them that Chelsea can sign the best players simply because they are a rich club. This is a moral argument. It's a form of idealistic egalitarianism, which says that all teams should have more or less equal resources. This stance may be morally right (we cannot judge), but it is not a practical political agenda, and it probably doesn't reflect what most football fans want. Spectators vote with their feet. It's certainly not the case that millions of them are abandoning the Premier League because the money offends them. The evidence of what they go to watch suggests that they want to see the best players competing against each other. It was nice that Leicester won, but the Premier League would have been just fine had the fairy tale never happened.

PART II

THE FANS

Loyalty, Suicides and Happiness

ARE FOOTBALL FANS POLYGAMISTS? A CRITIQUE OF THE NICK HORNBY MODEL OF FANDOM

Just this one afternoon started the whole thing off – there was no prolonged courtship. . . . In a desperate and percipient attempt to stop the inevitable, Dad quickly took me to Spurs to see Jimmy Greaves score four against Sunderland in a 5–1 win, but the damage had been done, and the six goals and all the great players left me cold: I'd already fallen for the team that beat Stoke 1–0 from a penalty rebound.

Nick Hornby in *Fever Pitch* (1992),
on the origin of his lifelong love of Arsenal

Fever Pitch is a wonderful memoir, the most influential football book ever written, and an important source for our image of the football fan. The 'Fan', as most Britons in particular have come to think of him, is a creature tied for life to the club he first 'fell for' as a child. Hornby says his love of

Arsenal has lasted 'longer than any relationship I have made of my own free will'. But is Hornby's 'Fan' found much in real life? Or are most British football supporters much less loyal than the world imagines them to be?

Let's start with Hornby's version, because it is the accepted story of the British Fan (and a story that is told to a greater or lesser degree in most countries with a long football tradition). As far as life allows, the Hornbyesque Fan sees all his club's home games. (It's accepted even in the rhetoric of fandom that travelling to away games is best left to unmarried men under the age of twenty-five.) No matter how bad his team gets, the Fan cannot abandon it. When Hornby watched the Arsenal of the late 1960s with his dad, the team's incompetence shamed him but he could not leave: 'I was chained to Arsenal and my dad was chained to me, and there was no way out for any of us.'

'Chained' is a very Hornbyesque word for a Fan's feelings for his club. Often the Fan uses metaphors from drugs ('hooked') or romantic love ('relationship', 'fell for'). Indeed, some adult Englishmen who would hardly dare tell their wives that they love them will happily appear in public singing of their love for a club, or for a player who would snub them in a nightclub if they ever managed to sneak past his entourage.

No wonder the Fan's loyalty to his club is sometimes described as a bond stronger than marriage. Rick Parry, as chief executive of the Premier League in the 1990s, recited the then dominant cliché about fandom: 'You can change your job, you can change your wife, but you can't change your football team. . . . You can move from one end of the country to another, but you never, ever lose your allegiance to your first team. That's what English football is all about. It's about fierce loyalty, about dedication.' (The Argentine variant: 'You can change your wife – but your club and your mother, never.') Recently, in more metrosexual times, football officials trying to emphasize the strength of club brands have extended the cliché by one more attachment: you can even change your gender, the officials say, but not your club.

Ideally, the Hornbyesque Fan supports his local team (even if Hornby did not). This gives the Fan roots, a sense of belonging. In a wonderful essay on fandom in the highbrow journal *Prospect*, Gideon Rachman quotes an archetypal declaration of faith from a Carlisle Fan named Charles Burgess, who wrote in the *Guardian*, 'There never was any choice. My dad . . . took me down to Brunton Park to watch the derby match against Workington Town just after Christmas 41 years ago – I was hooked and have been ever since. . . . My support has been about who we are and where we are from.'

In real life Rachman is a commentator on international politics in the *Financial Times*, but his essay in *Prospect* is a key text in the British debate about fandom. It is the anti-*Fever Pitch*. In it, Rachman outs himself as a 'fair-weather fan, an allegiance-switcher', who at different times in his life has supported Chelsea, QPR and Spurs. So casual are his allegiances that he registered with FIFA for the World Cup of 2006 as an Ivory Coast supporter, figuring that he wouldn't face as much competition for tickets. He got into every round including the final. He went to the World Cup in South Africa as a registered Paraguay fan.

Rachman treats the passions of Hornbyesque Fans as slightly bizarre. After all, in England a Fan's choice of team is largely random. Few clubs have particular religious or class affiliations, and few English people have an attachment dating back generations to any particular location. Some children become fans of their local team, however terrible it might be, but if you live in a rural part of England like Cornwall you may have no local team, while if you live in London or around Manchester you will have many. As Rachman asks, 'Why devote a huge amount of emotion to favouring one part of west London over another?'

Nonetheless, the Hornbyesque Fan is a widely admired figure in Britain, at least among men. Whereas fanatic is usually a pejorative word, a Fan is someone who has roots somewhere. As we will argue later, this respect is connected to the quirks of British history: in Britain, roots of any kind are in short supply.

However, our first question is: How true is the Hornby model of fandom? Does it really describe the way most British fans feel about their clubs?

THE CHINESE SERIAL FAN

Very little is known about sports fans who are not hooligans. The academics D. L. Wann and M. A. Hamlet estimated in 1995 that only 4 per cent of research on sports concentrated on the spectator.

So we start our quest into the nature of fandom with only one or two fairly safe premises. One is that foreign fans of English clubs, at least, are not all monogamous in their devotion. Rowan Simons explains in *Bamboo Goalposts*, his book about Chinese football, that many Chinese fans support 'a number of rival teams at the same time' and are always changing their favourite club. Simons adds, 'So dominant is the serial supporter in China that it is quite rare to find a fan with a real unflinching loyalty to one team.'

The market researchers Sport+Markt found polling data to back up Simons's claim. Sport+Markt noted that since the late 1990s hordes of new fans around the world – including many women – have come to football without long-standing loyalties. A lot of these people appear to be 'serial supporters' who probably support Manchester United and Liverpool, or Real Madrid and Barcelona, simultaneously. No wonder that clubs like United or Real keep changing their guesses as to how many fans they have worldwide. The following table presents a few of United's estimates of the past few years:

Figure 12.1 Fan estimates for Manchester United

Year	Estimated fans	Source
2003	75 million	Mori
2007	About 90 million	Manchester United
2008	333 million (including 139 million 'core fans')	TNS Sport
2012	659 million	Kantar

None of these estimates is necessarily wrong. There may well be 659 million people on earth who have feelings for Manchester United. However, few of these 'fans' are likely to be lifelong Hornbyesque devotees. Jose Angel Sanchez, now director general of Real Madrid, a club with its own share of foreign serial supporters, thought many of these serial fans might eventually evolve into Hornbys. He told us in 2003, 'We used to say that the chances of changing your team is less than changing your partner or even your sex. But the way that people enter football in Asia is different: they enter through the stars. But this will not stay this way, in my opinion.' Well, perhaps.

Still, surely British fans are a lot more loyal than those fickle Chinese, right? Unfortunately, polling suggests otherwise. In 2008 Sport+Markt found that Chelsea had 2.4 million 'fans' in Britain. Again according to Sport+Markt, that represented a rise of 523 per cent in the five years since Roman Abramovich had bought the club. Yet even that figure of 2.4 million represented a swift decline: in 2006, when, no doubt coincidentally, Chelsea had just won the league twice running, Sport+Markt credited the club with a mammoth 3.8 million British fans.

Again, we are not saying that Sport+Markt's figures were wrong. Rather, its premise was. To serial supporters, the question 'Which is your preferred football club?' does not make sense. It presumes that everyone who likes football is a one-club Hornbyesque Fan. Instead, researchers should be asking,

'Which are your preferred football clubs?' After all, a very large proportion of people who like football are polygamous consumers. One of the authors of this book, Stefan, as a Saturday-morning coach of grade-school children saw the colour of the shirts switch from red to blue and back again depending on who last won the league. It's likely that fantasy football leagues encourage this behaviour: you can end up becoming attached to the players in your fantasy team, no matter which clubs they play for.

Newly rising clubs (such as Chelsea in the early 2000s) are particularly prone to attracting short-term fans, a Sport+Markt executive told us. Clubs like Liverpool or Manchester United with more longstanding brands tend to have more loyal long-term supporters, he added. In fact, the likes of Manchester United are likely to have both far more Hornbys and far more casual fans than other clubs. But detractors of United tend to seize upon the hordes of casual fans and don't mention the Hornbys.

Hornby himself recognized the prevalence of casual fans in football. Many of the people who pop up briefly in the pages of *Fever Pitch* enjoy the game but are not wedded to a particular club. Hornby calls this type the 'sod-that-for-a-lark floating punter', and speaks of it with admiration: 'I would like to be one of those people who treat their local team like their local restaurant, and thus withdraw their patronage if they are being served up noxious rubbish.'

SPECTATORS: THE HARD CORE

We know there are, broadly speaking, two types of football fan: the Hornbys and the sod-that-for-a-lark floating punters. We know that the sod-that-for-a-lark people are heavily represented among foreign fans of clubs like United, and even seem to be pretty common in Britain. By 2006, if we can believe Sport+Markt's figures, about 90 per cent of Chelsea's British fans were people who had not supported them in 2003. No doubt clubs like Hartlepool have a higher percentage of devoted Hornbys among its fans, but then clubs like Hartlepool don't have many fans full stop.

One might carp that the sod-that-for-a-lark lot are mostly just armchair fans, and that 'real' fans tend to be Hornbys. However, it would be wrong to dismiss armchair fans as irrelevant. The overwhelming majority of football fans in Britain are armchair fans, in the sense that they hardly ever go to games. According to a survey by the market researchers Kantar Media in 2016, about 36 per cent of Britons describe themselves as football fans. Yet average weekly attendance figures of all professional clubs in England and Scotland equal only about 3 per cent of the population. In other words, most of the country's football fans rarely or never enter football stadiums.

Fletcher Research, in one of the first serious market analyses of English football in 1997, found that only about 5 per cent of supporters of Premier League clubs attend even one match in an average season. If only a small minority of football fans get to the stadium at all, even fewer see every single home game for years on end, as Hornby did.

Most football fans are armchair supporters. If we want to unearth the Hornbys, we need to concentrate on the elite of fans who actually go to games: the spectators.

We know that in the Premier League at least, most spectators now watch every home game their club plays. Often they have to: at the most successful clubs, only season-ticket holders can get seats. Many of these regular spectators may be sod-that-for-a-lark punters at heart, who have been enticed by ticketing policies to show up every week. However, it's among this group of week-in and week-out spectators that we must look for the small hard core of lifelong Hornbys in English football. At moments of high emotion, the TV cameras like to zoom in on spectators in the stands – heads in hands, or hugging their friends – as if these people incarnated the feelings of the club's millions of supporters. They don't. Rather, they are the exceptions, the fanatical few who bother to go to games. Some of these spectators presumably support their club 'through thick and thin', watching them unto eternity like Hornby does.

At least, that is the theory. But we studied attendance numbers in English football over the past sixty years and found that even among the actual spectators, a startlingly high proportion appeared to be sod-that-for-a-lark types.

* * *

Nobody seems to have tried before to calculate how many British fans are Hornbys. Yet the figures required to make some sort of estimate do exist. That marvellous website, www.european-football-statistics.co.uk, has statistics on attendance rates and league performance for all clubs in the top four divisions of English football since 1947. Using these data we can find out (a) the annual mortality rate of football spectators – that is, how many of the people who watched last season don't come back the next; and (b) the sensitivity of new spectators to the success of teams. Do most newcomers flock to Chelsea when Chelsea wins the league?

Our model is based on some fundamental truths of football fandom. Generally speaking, teams cannot have very loyal Hornbyesque Fans (that is, a low mortality rate) and at the same time be capable of attracting large numbers of new spectators when they are successful. If most of the crowd consisted of Hornbys who never gave up their seats, then when a team did well, there would be no room in the stadium for all the new fans who wanted to watch them. So floating supporters can get tickets only if the mortality rate of the existing spectators is high enough.

Previous studies have shown that a club's attendance tends to rise and fall with its league position. (The rare exceptions include Newcastle, Sunderland and the Manchester City of the late 1990s, when bad results failed to deter spectators.) In our data for the sixty-one-year period from 1947 to 2008, there were 4,454 changes in clubs' final league position. The average club moves six or seven league positions a year. In 64 per cent of the cases where the club rose in the league, its home crowd increased, too. In 74 per cent of the 'down' years, home attendance fell. This means that 69 per cent of all cases confirmed the simple hypothesis that fans respond to performance. Simply put: there is a market in football spectators. The few academics who study fandom – most of them in the US – explain the fans' motives through the psychological phenomenon of 'BIRGing', or 'basking in reflected glory'.

To account for the ebb and flow of English football fans, we have constructed a very simple model. It consists of two elements that are logically connected to one another. First, there are the 'new fans' coming into the game. New fans are estimated as the difference between the total attendance for the season and the number of loyal fans left over from the previous season. We divide new fans into two groups: the BIRGers, who come to watch the team depending on its success, and those who come for reasons we can't explain. We will treat these reasons as random factors, although each person probably had a good reason to come to the game at the time – a friend invited him, a girlfriend left him, or some such.

The second element of our model is the 'loyal fans': those who came back from the previous season. Loyal fans are estimated as the difference between the total attendance for the season and the new fans entering the game. Of course, the difference between the loyal fans plus the new fans and last season's attendance is the 'lost fans'. We can think of these lost fans as falling into two groups as well: the BIRGers who were lost to the club because its performance declined, and those who were lost for other reasons that we cannot measure (got back together with girlfriend, took up DIY, or whatever).

So,

$$\text{Total fans} = \text{loyal fans from last year}$$
$$+ \text{ fans sensitive to winning}$$
$$+ \text{ random fans}$$

In our model we estimate the shares of loyal fans and fans sensitive to winning by minimizing the number of random fans. We minimize random fans precisely because we think most fans go for a reason: either loyalty or BIRGing. Randomness surely plays a relatively small role.

Now, we are not claiming that we can identify new fans, loyal fans and lost fans individually. However, we can identify these categories in a statistical sense, as groups. We know how many people are in each group, even if we do not know their names.

Our model produces two results. First, it gives us an estimate of the BIRGers: the fraction of new fans that a team can expect to attract as a result of the position it achieves in the league. Looking at the annual changes in attendance figures, we found that spectators are only mildly sensitive to a team's performance. Our estimates implied that the club that won the Premier League would attract 2.5 per cent of all new spectators entering the league the next season (presuming there was space in the club's stadium). However, a team that finished at the bottom of the Premier League, or at the top of the Championship (English football's second tier), does almost as well: it attracts 2 per cent of all the league's new spectators. Teams in the middle of the four divisions (that is, those ranked around forty-sixth in England) would attract 1 per cent of all new spectators, while teams at the very bottom of the fourth tier would attract almost nobody. In short, while new spectators do like success, the vast majority of them are not simple BIRGers, glory hunters. Judging by the ebb and flow of crowds over the sixty-one years to 2008, most people seem to go to a plausible club playing near their home.

That is the profile of the newcomers. But how many of last year's crowd do they replace? What is the mortality rate of the existing spectators?

We know how many spectators each club lost or gained, season by season for sixty-one years. We also know how many spectators the league as a whole lost or gained. That means that for every club we can calculate the average percentage of spectators at a given game one season who would not attend that same fixture the next season. And the percentage that fits the data best: 50. Yes: on average in the post-war era, half of all spectators in English football did not take their seats again for the equivalent match the next season.

Let's be clear about what exactly we are saying. Imagine that Bristol City plays Preston one season, in front of 15,000 spectators. The next season, for the same fixture, even if there are again 15,000 spectators, half of them would typically be people who had not seen the previous year's match; 7,500 of last year's crowd would be gone. Now, many of those 7,500 people might well see other games in the new season. Many of the 'newcomers' might be people who had seen Bristol City–Preston two years before, or ten years before, but had then gone missing at that fixture for a while. However, the point still stands: at any given match in England, half the spectators would be new compared with the same match the season before.

Here's an example of how the model works (for the sake of simplicity, we have rounded up all numbers):

Bristol City finished the 2006–2007 season in second place in League One, the English third tier. The team's total attendance that season was 295,000. Note that that doesn't mean 295,000 different people. Rather, 295,000 tickets were sold for all City's matches combined. Most fans would have attended multiple matches. The total attendance for all four divisions was 29.5 million.

The next season,

(a) The total attendance for all four divisions rose by 400,000, to 29.9 million.

(b) Bristol City came in fourth in the Championship – a rise of twenty-two places.

So to calculate Bristol City's expected attendance in 2007–2008, we estimate its number of loyal 'returning' fans and of new fans:

(c) Loyal fans are 50 per cent of the previous season's total: 148,000.

(d) New fans are calculated by estimating Bristol City's share (based on league performance) of new fans of the entire league.

(e) We predict 15.1 million new spectators for English football as a whole. That equals this year's total attendance (29.9 million) minus loyal fans from last year (50 per cent of 29.5 million = 14.8 million) = 15.1 million.

(f) Given that Bristol City finished twenty-fourth out of ninety-two clubs, we estimate its share of all new fans in the country at 1.7 per cent. Its number of new fans should therefore equal 0.017 x 15.1 million = 257,000.

(g) So Bristol City's loyal + new spectators = 148,000 + 257,000 = 405,000.

(h) Bristol City's actual number for 2007–2008 was 374,000, so our model overestimated their support by 31,000, or 8 per cent.

Obviously the model does not work perfectly for every club. At big clubs, such as Arsenal or Manchester United, there is very little flux in the stands. Their stadiums are pretty much always full, and total attendance therefore always the same. Most of their spectators are season-ticket holders who see every game. These people generally renew their season tickets each year, because they know that if they don't their seats will be snapped up by others and they might never get back into the stadium again.

However, taking all ninety-two clubs together, the estimate that fits the data best is that 50 per cent of the fans who saw a game last season do not see it again the next season. To quote one analysis of the English game, 'One Third Division club in the London area, for example, has an estimated "hard core" support of about 10,000; this rises to 20,000 according to the team's success and the standing of the visiting team.' These words were written in 1951 in an economic study of football published by the London-based Political and Economic Planning think tank. They remain a good summary of English fandom as a whole since the war.

The discovery that half of all spectators – supposedly the hardest of hard-core Fans – are not there when the same fixture rolls around the next season conflicts with the Hornby version of loyal one-club fandom. Yet it has to be true, to explain the churn we see in attendance numbers. Even a club like Leeds, noted for its devoted fans – while stuck in League One it drew significantly larger crowds than Juventus – saw attendance fall from a peak of 755,000 in the 2001–2002 season to only 479,000 in 2006–2007.

Nor is this high mortality rate a new phenomenon. Our sixty-one years of attendance data suggest that habits of English spectators have changed little over the years. While there has always been a hard core of Hornbys, it seems it has also always been the case that the majority of people who go to

English football matches go only once in a while, and are often quite fluid about whom they choose to watch. And given that spectators are the fans who commit the most time and money to the game, their devotion is in most cases really rather limited. The long-term devoted spectator of the kind that Hornby described in *Fever Pitch*, far from being typical, is a rare species. Committed one-club lifelong fandom is a beautiful theory – or as Gandhi supposedly said of Western civilization, 'It would be a good idea.' The reality is that in English football, the loyal Hornbys are a small shoal in an ocean of casual Rachmans. England may be a nation of fans, but it's scarcely a nation of Hornbys.

CALL YOURSELVES 'LOYAL SUPPORTERS'

In 1996 Alan Tapp, a professor of marketing at Bristol Business School, started to develop a relationship with a struggling club in the Premier League. Over the next four years he met the club's executives, got to see the data they had on their supporters and assembled a team of researchers who conducted hundreds of interviews with the club's fans. Tapp eventually published two papers about his work in academic marketing journals. Together they add up to a rare, marvellous study of how the spectators of one club actually behave. Tapp titled his second paper, published in 2004, 'The Loyalty of Football Fans – We'll Support You Evermore?' with a very pregnant question mark. What he found was that fans talk loyal but don't always act it.

The club Tapp and his colleague Jeff Clowes studied – based in a Midlands town that is quite easy to identify – was not very good. It wasn't the sort of outfit to attract many BIRGing glory hunters. Most of the club's spectators lived locally. In a survey in 1998, a massive 87 per cent of them agreed slightly or strongly with the phrase, 'I would describe myself as a loyal supporter.'

Well, they would say that, wouldn't they? Tapp cautions that many of those 87 per cent might have been engaging in 'socially desirable responding'. After all, almost nobody in English football calls himself a 'sod-that-for-a-lark floating punter'. That would be socially taboo. Most fans told Tapp and Clowes that they regarded sod-that-for-a-lark types as 'pariahs'. As Rick Parry said, English fans pride themselves on their loyalty.

Yet when Tapp studied how these spectators behaved, he found a remarkable lack of loyalty. To start with the most basic fact: the club's average crowd during the four-year period of study slipped from about 24,000 to just 16,000.

The average across the period was about 21,000, which broke down as follows:

- ⚽ about 8,000 season-ticket holders;
- ⚽ another 8,000 places typically filled from a group of 15,000 or so regular attendees;
- ⚽ 5,000 spectators who came from 'a "revolving door" of perhaps 20,000 "casual fans"'.

Tapp came up with three labels for the different groups: 'fanatics', 'committed casuals' and 'carefree casuals'.

The 'fanatics', or Hornbys, were mostly season-ticket holders. Tapp said some of these people were veritable '"football extremists" who had commitment to the sport and the club that is arguably unparalleled in other business or leisure sectors'. There was the man who, when asked by Tapp's team what he would save if there were a fire in his house, replied, 'Oh my [match] programmes and tapes. No question. And my wife and kids of course.' Many of the fanatics came from the local area and had supported the club since childhood.

But even some of the fanatics were less fanatical than they claimed to be. Tapp found that each season, on average, 1,000 of the 8,000 season-ticket holders did not renew their seats and were replaced by new people. 'Even at the fanatic end, the loyalty bucket had significant leaks,' he remarked.

The team were playing badly. In one season, a mere 2 per cent of fans proclaimed themselves 'very satisfied' with performances. However, it was not the bad football that was driving them away. When Tapp's team asked people why they were letting their season tickets lapse, the lapsers usually talked about their lives away from the stadium. Fans were much more likely to give up their season tickets if they had children under age five, or if they described their lives as 'complicated'.

So it wasn't that the lapsers felt less loyal to the team than the people who kept going year in, year out. They were simply at different stages in life. Some regular fans admitted that at one point in life 'they had simply lost interest, often in their late teens and early 20s'. Others had been 'triggered' by a son or daughter to return to the stadium. Older people, whose lives were presumably more stable, were the most likely to renew their season tickets. Tapp surmises that they 'have simply settled into some form of auto-repurchase'. In other words, showing up to the stadium year in, year out is not a good marker of loyalty. Rather, it is a good marker of age.

At the far end of the scale from the 'fanatics' were the 'carefree casuals'. Few of the carefree casuals claimed to be 'loyal supporters'. They were 'football fans' rather than 'club fans', they preferred to see a good game rather than a victory for their team, and they treated football as just one of several possible activities on a Saturday. Tapp noted, 'Being club supporters is not part of their self-image.'

Many of the 'carefree casuals' sometimes went to watch other teams. Tapp reckons that it is probable that some regulars at Derby County, for instance, also occasionally show up at Derby's rival Nottingham Forest, even if this flies in the face of everything we are always told about English football fans.

Tapp adds that these people are mostly not 'brand switchers', who switch from supporting one club to supporting another. Very few people love Derby one year, Forest the next and Carlisle the year after. Rather, these adulterous spectators are engaging in what marketing experts call 'repertoire buying': they purchase different brands at different times. In normal consumer markets in almost every country, 'repertoire buyers' are thought to outnumber both 'brand-loyal' and 'price buyers'. In football, too, repertoire buyers seem to be fairly common. Tapp says, 'Repertoire fans took a lot of pleasure from a multiplicity of aspects of the game itself, while single club fanatics were less interested in football, more devoted to the club as an entity.'

Tapp's middle group of spectators at the Midlands club was made up of 'committed casuals'. These people didn't go to every match, but they did tend to describe themselves as 'loyal supporters'. They rarely watched other clubs and were more interested than the 'carefree casuals' in seeing their team win. However, they too treated football as just one option for their Saturday. Tapp said they 'perhaps have their football support in perspective with the rest of their lives'.

In short, through close-up study very rare in English football, he had gotten past the cliché of 'We'll support you evermore.' Instead he found the same thing that we did: there are some Hornbys in British football, but even among the self-proclaimed 'loyal supporters' of an inglorious club they are outnumbered by casual fans who can take it or leave it. Tapp ends by cautioning sports marketers that for all the rhetoric of undying love pervading English football, fans' 'loyalty cannot be relied upon'. He urges marketers to 'look under the surface of supporter loyalty', where they will find 'loyalty patterns quite similar to, say, supermarket goods sectors'.

HORNBYS, CLIENTS, SPECTATORS AND OTHERS

It turns out that few British football fans are either Hornbys or BIRGing glory hunters. Rather, most have a shifting relationship with the club or clubs they support. Of the 50 per cent of spectators who do not show up for the same fixture from one season to the next, the largest group may well continue to be monogamous fans of that club. They just don't watch every game, or can't afford to go anymore, or are busy raising children, or have moved to another part of the country, or simply care less than they used to. The object of their love might not have changed, but the intensity has. Many of them may once have been Hornbys who fell for a team as eight-year-olds when their fathers took them to their first game. However, by the time they are twenty-eight or eighty-eight they are no longer the same fans. For many people, fandom is not a static condition but a process.

Alex Ferguson understood this. In the mid-1970s he managed the Scottish club St Mirren, which played in Paisley, a town that by Ferguson's account had displayed 'years of apathy towards football'. He began campaigning to engage people who were only mildly interested in the club:

> An electrician at the ground, Freddie Douglas, had the idea that he and I should go round the town in his van and address the potential supporters through a loudspeaker. I was gaining a reputation for innovative management but to me it was simply a case of being willing to try anything that might make the club more successful ... I have to confess that Freddie did most of the hailing, but I was good at waving.

Some lapsed fans will have lost interest in football altogether. Others still might be shifting their allegiances to another club or clubs, either because they have moved to a new town, started to follow the team their kids support, or simply fallen for better football elsewhere. Rachman, for example, explains in his *Prospect* essay that he stopped supporting Chelsea 'because they were a terrible team, followed by violent cretins'.

Instead he made a two-and-a-half-mile journey within West London and became a QPR fan. In the rhetoric of English football, the choice facing the supporter is often presented as stark: either he sticks with his local team, or he becomes a BIR-Ging glory hunter. However, reality is more nuanced. England is so densely stuffed with professional football clubs – forty-three within ninety miles of Manchester, as we saw – that many people can find a new local side without going to the trouble of moving house. Today Rachman follows Fulham.

Then there is a dirty secret of football: many fans support more than one team. If you live in Plymouth, say, you might support Plymouth Argyle, Chelsea and Barcelona, and have a fondness for a half-dozen other clubs, even though if Plymouth ever makes the FA Cup final, you will travel to Wembley decked out as a 'lifelong Plymouth fan'. Hornby himself, in *Fever Pitch*, supports Cambridge United as well as Arsenal. In fact, whereas the usual analogy for football fandom is idealized monogamous marriage, a better one might be music fandom. People are fans of the Beatles, or the Cure, or the Pixies, but they generally like more than one band at the same time, and are capable of moving on when their heroes fade.

As so often, it was Arsène Wenger who put this best. In 2009 he gave Arsenal's website an untraditional account of how he thought fandom worked:

Football has different types of people coming to the game. You have the client, who is the guy who pays one time to go to a big game and wants to be entertained. Then you have the spectator, who is the guy who comes to watch football. These two categories are between 40 and 60 [years old]. Then you have two other categories. The first is the supporter of the club. He supports his club and goes to as many games as he can. Then you have the fan. The fan is a guy between 15 and 25 years old who gives all his money to his club.

Obviously Wenger's four categories are not exact. Here and there they even conflict with those of Tapp and Clowes, who found that many fans lose interest between fifteen and twenty-five. But Wenger agrees with the other observers that there are several different categories of spectator, of varying emotional intensity, and that people move between these categories depending largely on their stage in life.

Ties in football fandom are much looser than the rhetoric of 'We'll support you evermore' suggests. In that regard, they resemble ties of real existing marriage in Britain today. People still get married promising 'till death do us part', but in 2016 there were 107,071 divorces in England and Wales (including 112 same-sex couples). That was nearly five times as many as in 1960, even though the number of marriages has plummeted. In 2014 only just over half of all adults in England and Wales (51.5 per cent) were either married or in a civil partnership. A lifelong monogamous marriage has become almost as rare as a lifelong monogamous love of a football club.

THE INAUTHENTIC NATION

Against all evidence, the stereotype persists that the typical British football fan is a full-on Hornby. No wonder it does, because the tiny percentage of fans who are Hornbys dominate the national conversation about fandom. Of course they do: they are the people who are most motivated to join the conversation. For them, following football is not just a hobby but an identity. Also, they make up a disproportionately large share of the football economy – 'the most valuable customers', Tapp calls them – and so clubs and media listen to them more than to the sod-that-for-a-lark punters. And the Hornbys have a compelling story to tell. Most of the best stories are about love, and these are people who proclaim their love in public every week.

Yet there is a deeper reason the Hornby account of fandom has been so easily accepted in Britain. That is because it tells a story of roots, of belonging – a lifelong love of the club your father or grandfather supported before you – in a country that is unusually rootless. In transient Britain, the story of the rooted Fan is especially seductive.

Britain was the first country on earth where peasants left their native villages to go to work in rootless industrial cities. It was among the first countries where the churches began to empty; a tie that helps root people all over the world has long been extraordinarily weak among native Britons.

Even after the Industrial Revolution, the British never settled down much. The average Briton changed his residence about once every seven years, more often than all other Europeans except the Nordics and the Dutch, according to a Eurobarometer survey for the European Commission in 2005. There are particularly strong flows in and out of London: typically people move to the capital to start their careers, and then start leaving it from about age thirty-two.

Many Britons leave the country altogether. About 4.9 million of them live outside Britain, a larger number than for any other country in the European Union, estimated the United Nations in 2015. (This may surprise some of the people who voted for Brexit because they were fed up with immigration.) Probably only India and China have produced diasporas that are as large and as widely spread, says the British government.

It is hard for people this transitory to build up deep ties of any kind, even to football clubs. Admittedly, Tapp and Clowes found that many of the 'fanatical' supporters of the club they studied had spent their lives in the local town. But it was the club's 'casual' fans, who 'had often moved to the area as adults', who were more typical of British migratory patterns. For instance, Tapp and Clowes identified one group whom they called 'professional wanderers': 'people (mainly managers/ professionals) who have held jobs in a number of different places who tended to strike up (weakly held) allegiances with local teams, which they retain when they next move'. Like most Britons, the professional wanderers were too rootless to become Hornbyesque Fans. None of the casual fans inter-viewed by Tapp and Clowes 'felt a close part of the local com-munity, in contrast to the fanatics'.

And Britons have suffered yet another uprooting: as well as leaving their place of birth, many of them have left their class of birth, too. This upheaval began on a large scale in the 1960s. As the economy grew, and more Britons stayed on at school and went to university, a mostly working-class nation turned into a mostly middle-class one. For many people this was a traumatic change. Their fathers had been factory workers, and now they were managers/professionals, with the different set of experiences and attitudes that entails. They lost touch with their roots. Natu-rally, many of them began to worry about their authenticity deficits.

In the 1990s, British football went upscale. The price of tickets jumped. In the food stands outside the stadiums, the proverbial middle-class quiches replaced the proverbial working-class pies. All these changes prompted endless laments for a lost cloth-capped proletarian culture from people who themselves somewhere along the way had ceased to be cloth-capped proletarians. They yearned to be authentic.

All this makes the true Fan a particularly appealing charac-ter to Britons. He is the British version of a blood-and-soil myth.

Unlike so many actual Britons, the Fan has roots. Generations may pass, and blue collars turn to white, but he still supports his 'local' team in what is supposed to be the 'workingman's game'. Lots of Britons who aren't Hornbyesque Fans would like to be. The Fan is more than just a compelling character. He is a British national fantasy.

FANS' SUICIDE NOTES: DO PEOPLE JUMP OFF BUILDINGS WHEN THEIR TEAMS LOSE?

It is one of the eternal stories that are told about football: when Brazil gets knocked out of a World Cup, Brazilians jump off apartment blocks. It can happen even when Brazil wins. One writer at the World Cup in Sweden in 1958 claims to have seen a Brazilian fan kill himself out of 'sheer joy' after his team's victory in the final. Janet Lever tells that story in *Football Madness*, her eye-opening study of Brazilian football culture published way back in 1983, when nobody (and certainly not female American social scientists) wrote books about football. Lever continues:

Of course, Brazilians are not the only fans to kill themselves for their teams. In the 1966 World Cup a West German fatally shot himself when his television set broke down during the final game between his country and England. Nor have Americans escaped some bizarre ends. An often cited case is the Denver man who wrote a suicide note – 'I have been a Broncos fan since the Broncos were first organized and I can't stand their fumbling anymore' – and then shot himself.

Even worse was the suicide of Amelia Bolaños. In June 1969 she was an eighteen-year-old El Salvadorean watching the Honduras–El Salvador game at home on TV. When Honduras scored the winner in the last minute, wrote the great Polish reporter Ryszard Kapuscinski, Bolaños 'got up and ran to the desk which contained her father's pistol in a drawer. She then shot herself in the heart.' Her funeral was televised. El Salvador's president and ministers, and the country's football team walked behind the flag-draped coffin. Within a month, Bolaños's death would help prompt the 'Football War' between El Salvador and Honduras.

Then there was the Bangladeshi woman who reportedly hanged herself after Cameroon lost to England in the World Cup of 1990. 'The elimination of Cameroon also means the end of my life,' said her suicide note. In fact, if *The Hindu* newspaper in India is right, Bangladeshis have a terrible proclivity for football suicides. After Diego Maradona was thrown out of the World Cup of 1994 for using ephedrine, 'about a hundred fans in Bangladesh committed suicide,' said an article in *The Hindu* in 2006. (It would be fascinating to know the newspaper's source.)

By now the notion that football prompts suicide has become a truism. It is often cited to show the grip of the game over its devotees, and as one reason (along with heart attacks on sofas during televised matches) the average World Cup causes more deaths than goals.

We found that there is indeed an intimate connection between suicide and football. However, the connection is the opposite of what is commonly believed. It's not the case that fans jump off buildings when their teams lose. (Indeed, after Brazil's 1–7 defeat to Germany in Belo Horizonte in 2014, the international media could find only one fan of Brazil who was moved to commit suicide: a teenage Nepalese schoolgirl who lived nearly 10,000 miles away.) Working with a crack team of Greek epidemiologists, we have found evidence that rather than prompting suicide, football stops thousands of people from killing themselves. The game seems to be a life-saver.

*   *   *

Measured suicide rates rose by 60 per cent in the forty-five years to 2011, estimates the World Health Organization. More than 800,000 people a year now kill themselves, according to the WHO. That is more than four times as many as died in armed conflicts worldwide in the bloody year of 2014, and about 60 per cent more than die of breast cancer each year. To use Germany as an example: in 2005, 10,260 Germans officially died by suicide, more than were killed by traffic accidents, illegal drugs, HIV, and murder and other violence put together. For Germans under age forty, suicide was the second-most common cause of death. And the reported figures for suicides were understatements, said the University Medical Center Hamburg-Eppendorf, which runs a therapy centre for people at risk of suicide: 'There may be a significant share of unrecognized suicides among the death types labelled "traffic accidents", "drugs" and "causes of death unknown".'

The suicide risk varies depending on who in the world you are. If you are an elderly, alcoholic, clinically depressed, divorced Lithuanian man, be very afraid, but suicide rates are relatively low in Latin America, leaving aside for the moment the issue of World Cups. Globally, women attempt suicide more often than men do, but most 'successful' suicides are males. In the US, for instance, 78 per cent of the 42,773 people who were reported as having taken their own lives in 2014 were male. For reasons that nobody quite understands, suicide peaks in spring when daylight hours are longest. In the Northern Hemisphere, that means May and June.

The question of why people commit suicide has preoccupied sociologists since sociology began. In 1897 Émile Durkheim, descendant of a long line of French rabbis, published his study *Suicide*. It wasn't just the first serious sociological study of suicide. It was one of the first serious sociological studies of almost anything. Drawing on copious statistics, Durkheim showed that when people lost their connection to wider society because of a sudden change – divorce, the death of a partner, a financial crisis – they sometimes killed themselves. He concluded that this particular form of suicide 'results from man's activities lacking regulation and his consequent sufferings'.

A few decades later, sociologists began to wonder whether man's sufferings might possibly include the results of sports matches. The numbers of suicides this caused might be significant: after all, most suicides are men, and sports give meaning to many men's lives. Frank Trovato, a sociology professor at the University of Alberta in Canada, was among the first to investigate the suicide–sports nexus. He found that when the Montreal Canadiens ice-hockey team – once described as the national team of French Canada – got knocked out of the play-offs early between 1951 and 1992, Quebecois males aged fifteen to thirty-four became more likely to kill themselves. Robert Fernquist, a sociologist at the University of Central Missouri, went further. He studied thirty American metropolitan areas with professional sports teams from 1971 to 1990 and showed that fewer suicides occurred in cities whose teams made the play-offs more often. Routinely reaching the play-offs could reduce suicides by about twenty each year in a metropolitan area the size of Boston or Atlanta, said Fernquist. These saved lives were the converse of the mythical Brazilians throwing themselves off apartment blocks.

Later, Fernquist investigated another link between sports and suicide: he looked at the suicide rate in American cities after a local sports team moved to another town. It turned out that some of the fans abandoned by their team killed themselves. This happened in New York in 1957 when the Brooklyn Dodgers and New York Giants baseball teams left, in Cleveland in 1995–1996 when the Browns football team moved to Baltimore and in Houston in 1997–1998 when the Oilers football team departed. In each case the suicide rate was 10 to 14 per cent higher in the two months around the team's departure than in the same months of the previous year. Each move probably helped prompt a handful of suicides. Fernquist wrote, 'The sudden change brought about due to the geographic relocations of pro sports teams does appear to, at least for a short time, make highly identified fans drastically change the way they view the normative order in society.' Clearly none of these people killed themselves just because they lost their team. Rather, they were very troubled individuals for whom this sporting disappointment was too much to bear.

Perhaps the most famous recent case of a man who found he could not live without sports was the Gonzo author Hunter S. Thompson. He shot himself in February 2005, four days after writing a note in black marker with the title 'Football Season Is Over':

No More Games. No More Bombs. No More Walking. No More Fun. No More Swimming. 67. That is 17 years past 50. 17 more than I needed or wanted. Boring . . .

Thompson, an occasional sportswriter, loved gridiron football. One night during the presidential campaign of 1968, he took a limousine journey through New Hampshire with his least favourite person, the Republican candidate Richard Nixon, and they talked football nonstop in the backseat. 'It was a very weird trip,' Thompson wrote later, 'probably one of the weirdest things I've ever done, and especially weird because both Nixon and I enjoyed it.' The reminiscence, in *Fear and Loathing on the Campaign Trail '72*, segues into an ominous musing on suicide, as a Nixon aide snatches away the cigarette Thompson is smoking over the fuel tank of the candidate's plane. Thompson tells the aide, 'You people are lucky I'm a sane, responsible journalist; otherwise I might have hurled my flaming Zippo into the fuel tank.'

'Not you,' the aide replies. 'Egomaniacs don't do that kind of thing. You wouldn't do anything you couldn't live to write about, would you?'

'You're probably right,' says Thompson. As it later turned out he was wrong, and no doubt for reasons that went well beyond football. His ashes were fired from a cannon in Aspen, Colorado.

So much for suicides and North American sports. We know much less about the connection between suicides and European football. In one of the very few European studies done so far, Mark Steels, a psychiatrist at the University Hospital in Nottingham, asked whether Nottingham Forest's worst defeats prompted local suicides. He looked at admissions for deliberate self-poisoning to his hospital's accident and emergency department on two bad days for Forest: after the team's defeats in the FA Cup final of 1991 and the FA Cup quarter-final of 1992. He found that both games were followed by an increase in self-poisonings. After the cup final, the rise was statistically significant, meaning that it was unlikely to have happened by chance. Steels concluded that 'a sudden disappointment experienced through an entire community may prove one stress too many for some vulnerable members of this community.'

* * *

All this is fascinating but inconclusive. For starters, the sample sizes of all these studies are pretty small. How many people are admitted to a Nottingham hospital for self-poisoning after a football match? (Answer: ten in the twelve hours after the 1991 cup final, nine after the 1992 quarter-final.) How many people kill themselves in Cleveland in any given month? The other problem is that almost all these researchers pursued what you might call the Brazilian block-of-flats hypothesis: that when people suffer a sporting disappointment, they kill themselves. Mostly these are studies of the dogs that barked: people who did commit suicide.

But what if the relationship between suicide and sports is deeper than that? If sports give meaning to fans' lives, if they make them feel part of a larger family of fans of their team, if fans really do eat and sleep football like in a Coca-Cola ad, then perhaps sports might stop some of these fans from killing themselves. We wanted to find out whether there were dogs that didn't bark: people who didn't commit suicide because sports kept them going.

It so happens that we have a case study. Frederick Exley was a fan of the New York Giants football team, whose life alternated between incarcerations in mental hospitals and equally unhappy periods spent in the bosom of his family. In 1968 Exley published what he called 'a fictional memoir', *A Fan's Notes*, one of the best books ever written about sports. Nick Hornby gave *Fever Pitch* the subtitle 'A Fan's Life' in part as a tribute to Exley.

The Exley depicted in *A Fan's Notes* is a classic suicide risk. He is an alcoholic loner separated from his wife. He has disastrous relationships with women, alienates his friends, and spends months at a time lying in bed or on a sofa at his mother's or aunt's house. For a while his only friend is his dog, Christie III, whom he dresses in a mini blue sweatshirt like his own and teaches to stand up like a man. 'Like most

Americans,' Exley writes, 'I had led a numbingly chaste and uncommitted existence in which one forms neither sympathies nor antipathies of any enduring consequence.'

Only one thing in life provides him with any community: the New York Giants. While living in New York City he stands on the terrace during every home game with a group of Brooklyn men: 'an Italian bread-truck driver, an Irish patrolman, a fat garage mechanic, two or three burly longshoremen, and some others whose occupations I forget. . . . And they liked me.'

When the Giants are not playing, Exley spends much of his time drinking alone. But when a game is on, he watches – depending on the stage of his life – with his Brooklyn group, or with other people in bars, or with his stepfather at home. Exley is the stepfather's eternal houseguest from hell, but 'things were never better between us than on autumn Sunday afternoons': 'After a time, hardly noticeable at first, he caught something of my enthusiasm for the beauty and permanent character of staying with someone through victory and defeat and came round to the Giants.' Fittingly, the stepfather dies just before a Giants game: 'Seated on the edge of the davenport watching the starting line-ups being introduced, he closed his eyes, slid silently to the floor, and died painlessly of a coronary occlusion.'

Inevitably, at one point in the memoir, Exley contemplates suicide. He has convinced himself he has lung cancer. Determined to avoid the suffering his father went through, he decides to kill himself instead. Drinking with strangers in bars, he gets into the habit of working 'the conversation round to suicide' and soliciting their views on how best to do it. The strangers are happy to oblige: 'Such was the clinical and speculative enthusiasm for the subject – "Now, if I was gonna knock myself off . . ." – that I came to see suicide occupying a greater piece of the American consciousness than I had theretofore imagined.'

Only one thing keeps Exley going. The Giants are 'a life-giving, an exalting force'. He is 'unable to conceive what [his] life would have been without football to cushion the knocks'. When he is drunk, unemployed and loveless in Chicago, he writes: 'Though I had completely disregarded football my first year in that happy city, during the autumn of 1956, after losing my job, I once again found that it was the only thing that gave me comfort.' At some point or other in life, we have all known how that feels.

The real-life Frederick Exley lived to the age of sixty-three, dying in 1992 after suffering a stroke alone in his apartment. He might never have got that old without the Giants.

There may be a great many Exleys around. The viewing figures we saw earlier in this book suggest that sport is the most important communal activity in many people's lives. About a third of Americans watch the Super Bowl. However, European football is even more popular. In the Netherlands, possibly the European country that follows its national team most eagerly, three-quarters of the population have watched Holland's biggest football games. In many European countries, World Cups may now be the greatest shared events of any kind. To cap it all, World Cups mostly take place in June, the peak month for suicides in the Northern Hemisphere. How many Exleys have been saved from jumping off apartment buildings by international football tournaments, the world's biggest sporting events?

This is not just a rhetorical question. A study of football tournaments and suicide would bring together both an incomparably compelling communal event and a sample the size of several countries. So we set about finding the data.

We needed suicide statistics per month over several years for as many European countries as possible. These figures do not seem to be published anywhere. Luckily, we found out that the Greek epidemiologists Eleni Petridou and Fotis Papadopoulos had laboriously got hold of these data by writing to the statistical offices of several countries. A statistician who works with Petridou and Papadopoulos, Nick Dessypris, went through the numbers for us. He found that in almost every country for which he had numbers, fewer people kill themselves while the national team is playing in a World Cup or a European Championship. Dessypris said the declines were 'statistically significant' – unlikely to be due to chance.

Let's take Germany, the biggest country in our study and one that always qualifies for big tournaments. Petridou and Papadopoulos had obtained monthly suicide data for Germany from 1991 to 1997. A horrifying total of 90,000 people in Germany officially killed themselves in this period. The peak months for suicides were March to June.

But when Germany was playing in a football tournament – as it did in the Junes of 1992, 1994 and 1996 – fewer people died. In the average June with football, there were 787 male and 329 female suicides in Germany. But rather more people killed themselves in the Junes of 1991, 1993, 1995 and 1997, when Germany was not playing football. In those football-free Junes, there was an average of 817 male and 343 female suicides, or thirty more dead men and fourteen more dead women than in the average June with a big tournament. For both German men and women, the June with the fewest suicides in our seven-year sample was 1996, the month that Germany won Euro '96.

We found the same trend for ten of the twelve countries we studied. In Junes when the country was playing in a football tournament, there were fewer suicides. These declines are particularly remarkable given how much alcohol is consumed during football tournaments, because drinking would normally be expected to help prompt suicides. Only in the Netherlands and Switzerland did football tournaments not seem to save lives; these two countries saw very slight increases in the suicide rate during tournaments. In the other countries, the life-saving effect of football was sometimes spectacular. Our data for Norway, for instance, run from 1988 to 1995. The football-mad country played in only one tournament in that period, the World Cup of 1994. The average for the seven Junes when Norway was not playing football was fifty-five suicides. But in June 1994 there were only thirty-six Norwegian suicides, by far the lowest figure for all eight Junes in our data set. Or take Denmark, for which we have suicide tallies from 1973 to 1996, the longest period for any country. In June 1992 the Danes won the European Championship. That month there were fifty-four male suicides, the fewest for any June since 1978, and twenty-eight female suicides, the joint lowest (with 1991) since the data set began.

We have tried to make some very rough estimates of how many lives these tournaments saved in each country. 'Lives saved' represents the decline in deaths during the average June when a country's national team is playing in a World Cup or European Championship compared to the average June when the team isn't playing. Here is the tally:

	Male lives saved	Female lives saved
Austria	9	−3
Czech Republic	14	6
Denmark	4	4
France	59	8
Germany	30	14
Greece	0	5
Ireland	2	1
Netherlands	−5	0
Norway*	[19 lives saved spread across both genders]	
Spain	4	1
Sweden	4	15
Switzerland	−1	−2

*The data for Norway were not broken down by gender

The figures are negative for the Netherlands and Switzerland because more people killed themselves when their teams were playing than when there was no football.

The next question is what happens after a team is knocked out. Do all the people who had been saved from suicide by football then fall into a void and jump off apartment buildings? If so, you would expect a rise in suicides in the period after the tournament.

However, we found that in ten of our twelve countries, suicides declined for the entire year when the national team played in a big tournament. Only in the Netherlands did suicides rise in the year when the team played; in Spain the difference was negligible. But in the other ten countries, even after the team got knocked out and the euphoria ended, there was no compensating rise in suicide. On the contrary: it seems that the uniting effect of the tournament lasted for a while afterward, continuing to depress the suicide rate. For each of these ten countries, more lives were saved on average over the entire year than in June alone. Here are our very rough estimates for lives saved over the entire year when the national team plays in a tournament ('lives saved' represents the decline in deaths during a 'football' year compared to the average year):

	Male lives saved	Female lives saved
Austria	46	15
Czech Republic	55	12
Denmark	37	47
France	95	82
Germany	61	39
Greece	9	13
Ireland	19	-10
Netherlands	-10	-1
Norway	[92 lives saved spread across both genders]	
Spain	2	-3
Sweden	44	16
Switzerland	20	2

Very roughly, the typical football tournament in this period appears to have helped save several hundred Europeans from suicide.

We couldn't find any monthly suicide data for any of the British nations. However, the only two previous studies on this topic that we know of in Britain suggest that the life-saving effect works there, too.

'Parasuicide' is a suicidal gesture in which the aim is not death but rather self-harm, or a cry for help. One example of parasuicide is taking a not-quite-lethal overdose. George Masterton, a psychiatrist in Edinburgh, and his co-author J. A. Strachan studied Scottish parasuicides during and immediately after the World Cups of 1974, 1978, 1982 and 1986. Each time, Scotland had qualified for the tournament. Each time, Masterton and Strachan found a fall in parasuicide for both genders during the tournament that 'has been sustained for at least eight weeks after the last game'. The Scottish case is a pretty strong piece of evidence against the apartment-building theory of football suicides, because if there was ever an excuse for football fans to try to kill themselves, it was Scotland's disastrous performance at the World Cup of 1978. (The team's fantasist manager, Ally McLeod, had boasted beforehand that the Scots would leave with a 'medal of some sort'.)

Later Masterton and Anthony J. Mander studied the numbers of people who came to the Royal Edinburgh Hospital with psychiatric emergencies during and after the World Cups of 1978, 1982 and 1986. The researchers found 'reductions in all illness categories during and afterwards (with the exception of alcoholism during)'. The decline in emergencies applied to both genders, and was more marked after each World Cup than during it. For instance, there was a 56 per cent fall in admissions of male neurotics in the weeks after a tournament.

The authors then tried to explain what was going on here:

There are few outlets which permit a wide and acceptable expression of Scottish nationhood – sport is perhaps the most powerful, and [football] is the national game. . . . We would speculate that such a common interest and endeavour, fused with a surge of nationalism, might enhance social cohesion in the manner proposed by Durkheim to explain the decreased suicide rates that accompany times of war.

Social cohesion is the key phrase here. This is the benefit that almost all fans – potential suicides and the rest of us – get from fandom. Winning or losing is not the point. You can get social cohesion even from losing. Very often, a nation will bond over a defeat in a big football game. People sob in public, perform postmortems in the office the next morning, hunt for scapegoats together. For Brazilians, for instance, their 1–7 defeat in 2014 was a shared national moment at least as memorable as victory in Yokohama in 2002. It is not the case that losing matches makes significant numbers of people so unhappy they jump off apartment buildings. In the US, fans of long-time losers like the Chicago Cubs and the Boston Red Sox baseball teams (Boston only became frequent winners again from 2004, while the Cubs won their first World Series in 108 years in 2016) have not killed themselves more than other people, says Thomas Joiner, author of *Why People Die by Suicide*, whose own father died by suicide.

Joiner's article 'On Buckeyes, Gators, Super Bowl Sunday, and the Miracle on Ice' makes a strong case that it's not the winning that counts but the taking part – the shared experience. It is true that he found fewer suicides in Columbus, Ohio, and Gainesville, Florida, in the years when the local college football teams did well. But Joiner argues that this is because fans of winning teams 'pull together' more: they wear the team shirt more often, watch games together in bars, talk about the team, and so on, much as happens in a European country while the national team is playing in a World Cup. The 'pulling together' saves people from suicide, not the winning. Proof of this is that Joiner found fewer suicides in the US on Super Bowl Sundays than on other Sundays at that time of year, even though few of the Americans who watch the Super Bowl are passionate supporters of either team. What they get from the day's parties is a sense of belonging.

That is the life-saver. In Europe today, there may be nothing that brings a society together like a World Cup with your team in it. For once, almost everyone in the country is watching the same TV programmes and talking about them at work the next day, just as Europeans used to do thirty years ago before they got cable TV. Part of the point of watching a World Cup is that almost everyone else is watching, too. Isolated people – the types at most risk of suicide – are suddenly welcomed into the national conversation. They are given social cohesion. All this helps explain why big football tournaments seem to save so many female lives in Europe, even though relatively few women either commit suicide or (before about 2000 at least) watch football. The 'pulling together' during a big football tournament is so universal that it drags many women along in a way that club football does not.

Other than sports, only war and catastrophe can create this sort of national unity. Most strikingly, in the week after John F. Kennedy's murder in 1963 – a time of American sadness but also of 'pulling together' – not one suicide was reported in twenty-nine cities studied. Likewise, in the US in the days after the September 11, 2001, attacks, another phase of national 'pulling together', the number of calls to the 1-800-SUICIDE hotline halved to about three hundred a day, 'an all-time low,' writes Joiner. And in Britain in 1997, suicides declined after Princess Diana died.

Joiner speculates that 'pulling together' through sports may particularly suit 'individuals who have poor interpersonal skills (often characteristic of severely depressed or suicidal persons)'. You don't have to be charming to be a fan among fans.

* * *

The rowdy communal emotion invested in football tournaments helps deter suicide. But precisely the same emotion can also encourage crime. The number of victims of assault (mostly young men) admitted to English hospital emergency departments rose 38 per cent on England's match days during the 2010 World Cup, according to a study by Liverpool John Moores University. World Cups also seem to encourage (mainly) men to beat their partners (both women and men).

Domestic violence accounts for about a fifth of violent crime in the US from 2003 to 2012, according to interviews with crime victims. However, domestic violence is often an invisible crime: carried out behind closed doors, and rarely reported to the police.

World Cups combine several risk factors for women in relationships with men. Sports, alcohol and 'hegemonic masculinity' make up an awful 'holy trinity' for domestic violence, write Damien Williams and Fergus Neville of Scotland's University of St Andrews. Men watching their national teams often drink themselves into a state of aggressive arousal. And this usually happens on hot summer nights, when violent crimes of all kinds tend to increase.

Big club games, too, can cause mayhem in family homes. After Scotland's 'Old Firm' derbies between Celtic and Rangers, domestic violence in Glasgow rises by an average of 36 per cent – comparable to 'the Christmas holiday effect' – report economists Alex Dickson, Colin Jennings and Gary Koop. But a World Cup rolls the effect out globally. We don't have statistics for every participating country (many don't measure and some don't even forbid domestic violence) but there are several recent studies looking at the case of England.

Stuart Kirby, Brian Francis and Rosalie O'Flaherty analysed domestic abuse reported to the police in north west England during the World Cups of 2002, 2006 and 2010. They found that the risk of abuse on match days rose 26 per cent if England won or drew, and by 38 per cent if the team lost. 'The final day of the tournament for the England team in both 2006 and 2010 exhibited the highest level of reported incidents for the entire month,' write the authors. There was a smaller rise the day after the game too, which probably reflects assaults after midnight. Practitioners working to combat domestic violence are well aware of the problem.

So while it's nice to know that football seems to deter some suicides, the evidence on domestic abuse is extremely disturbing. What can be done? Well, knowing about the link between sports and domestic violence helps. Just as sports organizations have accepted that they have a role in combatting racism, they also need to acknowledge their role in promoting the emotions that can provoke abuse. And there are signs that they do know. Super Bowls now routinely feature public service announcements on domestic violence. Women who have been assaulted get a number to call, and their partners may think twice before hitting them.

In England, too, at recent World Cups, police and charities have tried to raise awareness. One video made by the charity Tender showed a woman with two black eyes, staring at the TV in horror after England are eliminated. She knows she is about to be assaulted. But more must be done. To those who argue that sport can't be blamed for society's problems, we say that sport claims a special place in society, and that means it has special responsibilities. Here is a proven relationship between sport and a specific social problem. People who organize sporting events and profit from the extraordinary commitment of fans need to show that these events are a force for good. Sport is like an addiction – and when it comes to addictive and potentially dangerous activities, society has to choose between two positions. Either we encourage socially responsible consumption (e.g. alcohol and cigarettes) or we ban the thing (narcotics). We think sports should go for social responsibility.

HAPPINESS:
WHY HOSTING
A WORLD CUP IS
GOOD FOR YOU

You don't often see people consciously building a white elephant, but that's what was happening in Brasilia in 2012. Smack in downtown, on the main avenue of Brazil's tropical capital, workers were finishing off a stadium for 70,000 people. The Estadio Nacional was one of twelve stadiums built for the World Cup in 2014. And even before the tournament ended, it was redundant. Brasilia's tin-pot clubs seldom draw 1,000 spectators. Nor will Justin Bieber regularly be flying into this city in the middle of nowhere to fill the Nacional. A few months after the tournament it was already being used chiefly as a bus depot, and by 2017 local clubs were allowed to play there rent-free. Brasilia probably ought to have torn down the stadium after the last World Cup game, and saved itself about $200,000 a month in upkeep costs. Other host cities like Manaus, Cuiabá and Natal should have done likewise.

That useless Brasilia stadium cost $900 million, three times more than budgeted, and was at the time the most expensive stadium in football's history after London's new Wembley. It's this kind of waste that brought Brazilians onto the streets in 2013, demonstrating against their country's hosting of the World Cup and the Rio Olympics of 2016. 'We have world-class stadiums – now we need a country to go around them,' read one protestor's banner. 'A teacher is worth more than Neymar,' said another. Worldwide, from Boston to the International Olympic Committee's headquarters in Lausanne, Switzerland, people are reaching the same conclusion: hosting sports events doesn't make you rich. A truth long known to economists is finally sinking in with the general public. That doesn't happen often.

Whenever a country prepares to host a World Cup or an Olympics, its politicians prophesy an 'economic bonanza'. They invoke hordes of shopaholic visitors, the free advertising of host cities to the world's TV viewers, and the long-term benefits of all the roads and stadiums that will get built, meanwhile intoning the holy word 'sustainability'. This is an ancient tradition: Hitler claimed that the 1936 Olympics had brought Berlin half a billion Reichsmarks. No wonder that for decades, countries competed to host these events. The bidding to stage the World Cups of 2018 and 2022 was the most cut-throat ever. If only the bidding countries could grasp the real reason for wanting to be a host: hosting doesn't make you rich, but it does make you happier. Russia will probably benefit from hosting the World Cup 2018, but not financially.

* * *

The 1989 movie *Field of Dreams* is a sentimental redemption story starring Kevin Costner as an Iowa farmer. Growing up the son of a baseball nut, the farmer had dreamed of being a baseball star. As an adult, he hears a voice telling him to build a baseball diamond on his cornfield. 'If you build it, he will come' is the film's catchphrase. The moral: building stadiums where they do not currently exist is uplifting and good for you. This orig-inally American idea later spread to football around the world.

There is in the US a small industry of 'consultants' who exist to provide an economic rationale for 'If you build it, he will come.' In almost any city in the US at almost any time, someone is scheming to build a spanking new sports stadium. The big prize for most American cities is to host a major league team, ideally an NFL franchise, but if that can't be had, then baseball, basketball or, if nothing else is going, ice hockey or even soccer. Hosting an American sports franchise has a lot in common with hosting a World Cup. Both the franchise and the World Cup are mobile beasts. Their owners are generally willing to move to whichever city or country offers them the best deal. In the US, owners of sports teams usually demand that the host city's taxpayers finance a stadium, with lucra-tive parking lots thrown in. All this is then handed over to the franchise owner, who also gets to keep the money he makes from selling tickets. About seventy new major league stadiums and arenas were built in the US in the twenty years before the financial crisis of 2008. The total cost: $20 billion, about half of which came from the public. In New Orleans, for instance, the taxpayer paid for the Superdome but not for better levees.

In one typical case in 1989, seventy investors, including one George W. Bush, son of the then American president, paid $83 million for the Texas Rangers baseball club. The Bush group wanted a bigger stadium. Strangely, for a phalanx of right-wing millionaires, it decided that local taxpayers should finance it. If that didn't happen, the new owners threatened to move the Rangers elsewhere. The people of the local town of Arlington duly voted to increase the local sales tax by half a per cent, raising the $191 million needed for the ballpark.

The president's son George W. became the Rangers' man-aging director. Mostly this just meant being the official face of the club. He would sit in the stands during games handing out baseball cards with pictures of himself. When he ran for governor of Texas in 1994, he constantly cited his experience in baseball. There wasn't much else on his CV. He was duly elected, and decorated his Austin office with 250 signed baseballs.

In 1998 the Bush group sold the Rangers to Tom Hicks (the man who later briefly became co-owner of Liverpool) for $250 million. Most of the value was in the stadium that the taxpayers had built. Bush personally netted $14.9 million. He admitted, 'When it is all said and done, I will have made more money than I ever dreamed I would make.' Meanwhile, he was already beginning to parlay his governorship into a bigger political prize.

So the trick for American club owners is to persuade the taxpayer to cough up for stadiums. This is where economists come in handy. Economists like to say that people respond to incentives. Well, economists certainly respond to incentives. Anyone hoping to persuade taxpayers to pay for a stadium in the US commissioned an economist to write an 'economic impact' study. By a strange coincidence, these studies always showed that the stadium would make taxpayers rich. (One book describing this racket is aptly called *Field of Schemes*.)

The argument typically went as follows: building the stadium would create jobs first for construction workers, and later for people who worked in it. Fans would flock in from all around ('If you build it, he will come'), and they would spend money. New businesses would spring up to serve them. As the area around the stadium became populated, more people would want to live there, and even more businesses (and jobs) would spring up. 'The building of publicly funded stadiums has become a substitute for anything resembling an urban policy,' notes Dave Zirin in his *People's History of Sports in the United States*.

The 'economic impact' study then typically clothed this model with some big numbers. If you put your mind to it, you could think up a total in benefits that ran into the billions, whatever currency you happened to be working in. Best of all, no one would ever be able to prove that number wrong. Suppose you promise that a stadium will bring a city economic benefits of £2 billion over ten years. If the city's income (hard to measure in the first place) rises by only £1 billion over the decade, then, of course, it was something completely different (the world economy, say) that restricted the income growth. You could prove the original estimates wrong only if you could estimate how much economic growth there would have been had the stadium never been built – but this 'counterfactual' figure is unknowable, precisely because it is a counterfactual. The same economists soon branched out into writing studies that justified ever more extravagant spending on the Olympics.

It would have seemed rude to derail this industry with anything so inconvenient as the truth. But then along came Rob Baade. The quiet, courteous academic seemed an unlikely figure to be taking on the stadium lobby. After all, he is a former top-class athlete himself: at college, Baade captained the Wisconsin basketball team. When the white coach seemed antagonistic to the majority of black players, Baade found himself championing players against coach in what he describes as one of the most difficult years of his life.

Afterwards he wanted to do graduate work in public finance, a branch of economics that usually involves many equations and few words. But he also wanted to coach basketball and to apply something of what he had learned while on the Wisconsin team. A colleague told him about a job at Lake Forest College, an idyllic little place just outside Chicago. To the dismay of some of his purist professors, he went to Lake Forest on a temporary appointment and ended up coaching there for eighteen years, while also rising to full professor of economics. He was a good coach, too: the year before he arrived, the team had not won a single game, but within four years they were winning 85 per cent of their games.

When you start out as an academic you try to write papers that will grab your colleagues' attention. Baade used his own background to enter the economics of sports, then still almost virgin terrain. At a seminar in New York he presented a paper titled 'The Sports Tax.' Journalists from the *New York Times* and the *Wall Street Journal* happened to be in the audience, and they zeroed in on what had been almost a throwaway line in his talk: public investment in stadiums does not provide a good return for taxpayers. As a coach himself, Baade might have been expected to join the stadium boosters. Had he done so, he could have earned himself good money in consulting. Instead he went into opposition.

The Heartland Institute, a conservative think tank, asked him to write up his thoughts. There are few issues in American political life where the Right joins with an intellectual liberal like Baade, but the paper he published in 1987 laid out the problem clearly: 'Contrary to the claims of city officials, this study has found that sports and stadiums frequently had no significant positive impact on a city's economy and, in a regional context, may actually contribute to a reduction in a sports-minded city's share of regional income.'

Baade had asked the awkward questions that stadium boosters always ignored. For instance, where would all the construction workers for the new stadium come from? Wouldn't they have jobs already, and therefore wouldn't a shortage arise somewhere else? Worse still, as competition for their skills intensified, wouldn't costs rise?

Once you start thinking of people as having alternatives rather than just standing around waiting for the stadium to arrive, the economics begin to look less appealing. For every dollar going in, there is probably a dollar going out somewhere else. In particular, if a city has to balance its budget, then spending more on stadiums must mean spending less on hospitals and schools. These lost jobs have to be counted against the stadium's benefits. And if the city doesn't balance its budget, isn't it storing up future burdens for taxpayers, who will have to forgo something, someday?

That is bad enough, but what if the stadium doesn't produce the promised benefits? After all, most stadiums are used for only a few hours a week, and barely at all in the off-season. Even allowing for the occasional rock concert (and there is a limit to how many times Justin Timberlake can play in your town), most of the time the neighbourhood around the stadium will be deserted. Not many people want to live in a place like that. The neighbourhoods around the old Yankee Stadium or Shea Stadium never became desirable, for instance.

Nor did Baade believe that a stadium would draw in much spending from outside the city. Most out-of-town fans would buy a hot dog and beer, watch the game, and leave – hardly an economic bonanza. A mall, or a cineplex, or even a hospital would generate more local spending.

Around the end of the 1980s other economists, too, began asking these awkward questions. However, Baade went one better. To show that the boosters' numbers didn't add up, he generated some numbers of his own. Perhaps he couldn't measure the counterfactual, but he could get close by comparing economic growth in cities that had major league teams with those that didn't. After all, he reasoned, if the boosters were right, then over time cities with stadiums must do better than cities without stadiums.

Baade examined data such as income per head and the numbers of new businesses and jobs created in various cities. The more he looked, the less difference he found between the economic profiles of cities with and without stadiums. All this spending was evidently producing no benefit.

Gradually people took notice. Other economists started to replicate Baade's findings, and found new ways to test the proposition that stadiums create wealth. 'Anti-stadium movements' began in many American cities.

In the mid-1990s Baade was asked to testify before Congress. On the day of his testimony, Congress was also holding hearings on the Clinton Whitewater affair and on military inter-vention in Bosnia, but when the stadium hearings started, the other chambers emptied. One of the people in the room was Paul Tagliabue, NFL commissioner and someone all the con-gressmen wanted to be seen with. Powerful people like Tagli-abue were getting quite irritated by Baade's awkward facts.

Academic freedom is a cherished value of American uni-versities, but, as Baade was starting to realize, so is making money. He recalls an old guy coming up to him after one meet-ing and saying, 'You might be right, professor, but if I were you I would watch my back. You're getting in the way of a whole lotta commercial projects.' A university seldom likes seeing its employees upset local politicians and businesspeople. Lake Forest College always supported Baade, but at times it would have been convenient had he thought differently.

He kept on telling the truth regardless. Among economists, often not the sportiest of types, he developed a special credi-bility as a former athlete. This sometimes came in handy, such as when a questioner in a public debate asked, 'No disrespect, professor, but what does an economist like you know about athletics?'

Eventually Baade descended on football. He and Victor Mathe-son conducted a study on the impact of hosting the World Cup of 1994 in the US. They looked for evidence of faster economic growth in the host cities, and as usual they found nothing. Yet by now, the old bogus American arguments for hosting sports had spread to other countries.

The raising and dashing of hopes of an economic bonanza became as integral a part of a modern football tournament as the raising and dashing of hopes that England would win it. A few months after England hosted Euro '96, for instance, a report by a body called Tourism Research & Marketing said that fewer than 100,000 overseas fans had visited England for the tournament, against a forecast – admittedly plucked out of thin air by the English Football Association – of 250,000. Nor had the visitors spent much. Euro '96 generated about £100 million in direct income for Britain. This was peanut dust beside the £12.7 billion spent by all overseas visitors to the country in 1996. Meanwhile, a study by Liverpool University and the city council found that the 30,000 visitors to Liverpool during Euro '96 spent only £1.03 million between them. How many jobs had that created? Thirty, all of them temporary.

A few years later Japanese and Korean government officials were predicting that the World Cup of 2002 could boost their economies by a staggering $26 billion and $9 billion, respectively. Of course, after the event there was little sign of any such boost, and indeed some evidence that tourists had stayed away for fear of football hooligans. Big sports tournaments attract some visitors, and deter many others. Greek tourism officials estimated in late 2004 that there'd been a 10 per cent fall in tourist arrivals during that year's Athens Olympics, as vacationers choosing summer destinations steered clear of the frenzy. Nor did the twenty-two venues built for the Athens Games generate an economic bonanza. Many of them now lie abandoned, sometimes under piles of garbage, while the canoe and kayaking venue has effectively vanished: it has dried up. This is a waste that Greece could not afford.

After a couple of decades, the weight of this research finally began to stack up. It was becoming obvious that even if you build it, he won't necessarily come. The boosters' claims of economic benefits were growing muted. The estimates produced for the World Cup in Germany in 2006 were altogether more sober. Even a study sponsored by the German football federation suggested a mere $2 billion in new benefits. (Similarly in London, estimates of the likely economic benefits from the 2012 Olympics were kept studiously vague.)

Perhaps the best estimate we have of how much visitors to football tournaments actually spend was made at the 2006

World Cup in Germany. This was the biggest media event in history, a month-long party (except for the boring football), yet even here the hosts didn't make much money.

A team of economists, led by Holger Preuss from the University of Mainz, decided to work out how much 'new' money visitors to the World Cup actually spent. In the old days, when boosters estimated economic bonanzas, they simply multiplied the number of seats in stadiums by some imaginary spending number (counting meals, hotels and transportation as well as tickets) to produce an enormous hypothetical sum.

The problem with this method, as serious economists pointed out, is that not every visitor to an event really injects extra spending into the economy. Preuss's team surveyed a large sample of visitors to the World Cup and found that only about one-fifth were foreigners who had travelled to Germany specifically for the football. More than half the 'visitors' were in fact Germans. For the most part these Germans would have been in Germany anyway, and had there been no World Cup they presumably would have spent their money on other forms of entertainment (such as going to movies or restaurants). If they spent money at the World Cup, they spent less elsewhere in the German economy, which largely offset any economic benefit from the football. Of course, some Germans who might otherwise have been spending their money on Spanish vacations stayed home for the football. However, their spending was probably offset by other Germans who went abroad precisely to avoid the madness of the World Cup.

The remaining foreign visitors to the World Cup – about a quarter of all visitors – were either 'time switchers', who would have come to Germany anyway at some point and simply timed their visit to coincide with the World Cup, or foreigners, who would have been in Germany during the World Cup anyway and just decided to go along and see what all the fuss was about. Preuss's team called this last category 'casuals'.

'Time switchers' and 'casuals' would have added little to spending, because even without the World Cup they would have spent their money in Germany. Preuss's team asked respondents detailed questions about their spending plans. They concluded that the World Cup generated spending by visitors of €2.8 billion. That was negligible beside the Kardashianesque €1 trillion plus spent annually by consumers in Germany. It was also much less than the German state spent preparing for the tournament. Remarkably, more than a third of that visitor income came from people who never got inside a stadium but merely watched the games on big screens in public places. In short, even the World Cup was barely a hiccup in the German economy.

Almost all research shows the same thing: hosting sports tournaments doesn't increase the number of tourists, or of full-time jobs, or total economic growth. Added to all this are the host's costs. If the economic benefits of putting on these tournaments are muted, the expenses seldom are. Economists Brad Humphreys and Szymon Prokopowicz made some rough estimates of the costs to Poland of hosting just half of Euro 2012. Poland needed to lay on a lot more than just new stadiums, airports and hotels for fans. UEFA requires, for its own officials and guests, the use of one entire five-star hotel within a forty-five-minute drive of every stadium. The teams need an additional sixteen hotels, most of them five-star. The referees have to be in five-star hotels near the stadiums. The doctors who perform the doping controls need five-stars 'in the countryside'. Much of the cost of these hotels came courtesy of the Polish government. Poland also had to put up surveillance cameras all over its stadiums and towns.

In all, Humphreys and Prokopowicz estimated that the country would have to spend about $10 billion on Euro 2012. With hindsight, this looks like a serious underestimate. True, some of the infrastructure that Poland bought still has its uses after the tournament. However, much of it doesn't, because the things you need for a football tournament – a massive new stadium, roads to that stadium, an airport in a sleepy town – are never quite the same as the things you need for daily life. This has costs. After the tournament, the annual education budget in one Polish host city, Poznan, had to be cut by 20 million Polish zlotys – which just happened to be the cost of the 'fan zone' that Poznan built for Euro 2012, reports local anthropologist Małgorzata Zofia Kowalska.

Almost all the research points in one direction: hosting doesn't create an economic bonanza. And yet South Africa went into its World Cup in 2010 promising its citizens an economic bonanza. In a sense, the country had to. When about a third of your population lives on less than $2 a day, the government can hardly say it's blowing billions on a month of fun. It has to argue that the football will benefit the poor. You then end up with people like Irvin Khoza, who chaired the tournament's local organizing committee, saying things like, 'The 2010 World Cup will change the face of the country. It may prove a pivotal point in our development as a young democracy.'

The South African ruling class put this message across so energetically that when the country was named host in 2004, crowds celebrating in the township of Soweto shouted, 'The money is coming!' Half the people you met in South Africa in the years before the tournament had a scheme for 2010: buying flats just to rent them out during the tournament, selling sausage and maize pudding outside stadiums, corralling peasant women to weave beaded flags in the colours of all the participating teams. Much of South African conversation was about such schemes, and in newspaper profiles, when a celebrity described what he was working on, he would often add, 'The key thing is to be ready for 2010.' The year had become a magic number.

As 2010 approached, the tournament's expected costs inevitably soared. South Africa had initially promised a cheap World Cup. All the stadiums put together, it had said in 2004, would cost only about $170 million. When we spoke to a FIFA official at the time, he seemed to presume that South Africa would stage the tournament in its existing stadiums, though he did worry that some of them didn't have roofs. Sponsors didn't like getting wet, he noted. But in the end, with FIFA pushing for perfection, and every local powerbroker in South Africa wanting his own 'world-class' stadium, the bill for stadiums ended up about ten times that initial estimate. This embarrassing overrun may be why copies of South Africa's original bid book were 'disappeared'.

Some of the South African organizers ended their journey in 2010 feeling rather chastened. For a start, the expected hordes of foreign visitors never showed up. In 2009 the management consultancy Grant Thornton – producer of a stream of upbeat economic forecasts about the World Cup – was predicting 483,000 foreign visitors for the tournament. (Earlier forecasts had been even sunnier.) A retrospective study based on official South African statistics, co-authored by Stefan with Thomas Peeters of the University of Antwerp and Victor Matheson from the College of the Holy Cross, estimates that the number of additional visitors in June and July 2010 was only 220,000, less than half Grant Thornton's prediction. Given that tourist arrivals from countries outside of Africa averaged about 2 million per year, this represented a boost to tourism, but not a big one. Nor did the economy as a whole see much benefit. John Saker, chief operating officer of KPMG Africa, said: 'The big boost didn't happen.'

Predictably, most of the stadiums that South Africa built for the tournament are now white elephants. The country never had any need for them. The larger hosting cities – Cape Town, Johannesburg, Durban and Pretoria – have for decades possessed large, very decent rugby grounds that can serve the modest needs of local football, too. Johannesburg also had the original Football City, a stadium rightly touted as the best in Africa when South Africa was bidding for the World Cup.

Very few domestic games outside the Johannesburg region draw more than about 10,000 spectators. Provincial towns like Nelspruit, Polokwane and Port Elizabeth now have World Cup stadiums, but they do not have clubs in the country's Premier Football League. (If you are wondering how Port Elizabeth became a host city, it just happens to be the home town of Danny Jordaan, the World Cup's chief executive.) Cape Town ought to pull down its stadium and find better uses for that prime piece of land overlooking the Atlantic Ocean.

BRAZIL 2014: THE HYPE NEVER STOPS

You would have thought that people would learn from the shame of the South African World Cup; from the way FIFA forced a developing country to build unnecessary stadiums fancy enough for sponsors, while a few miles away people lived in corrugated-iron shacks. In 2009 a senior European football official mused to us about putting pressure on FIFA to let Brazil host a cheaper World Cup. It could be done, this man said, if a few powerful football federations – Germany, France, the US, England and some others – argued that Brazil needn't build the most expensive stadiums on earth, just some good solid ones that wouldn't turn into white elephants the day the circus left town.

No such luck, however. One morning in Johannesburg during the World Cup of 2010, one of us, Simon, had breakfast with the Brazilian sports minister, Orlando Silva Junior. The minister was a charming man, wearing the sort of casual clothes we wish ministers in our own countries would try. And he was really looking forward to hosting the World Cup. 'I guess that the cup has served as a stimulus for development and infrastructure here in South Africa,' he said, 'and we will follow the same path in Brazil.' He said his country had deliberately chosen 'less developed regions' to host matches, just to give them the chance to develop. Brazil was building airports, ports and stadiums all over. There'd be jobs galore. In short, the World Cup was just what Brazil's economy needed.

Regrettably Silva left office not long afterwards, resigning in 2011 over a corruption scandal, despite maintaining his innocence. However, Brazil 2014 now looks like a rerun of South Africa 2010. In 2010 the respected Brazilian think tank Fundação Getulio Vargas had predicted that public spending on the tournament (or 'investment,' as officials like to call it) would total 12.8 billion Brazilian reals; actual public spending ended up almost exactly double that, at 25.6 billion reals, according to the government's own 'Transparency Portal' in October 2014.

Sports tournaments almost always cost more than forecast. When researchers at the Saïd Business School in Oxford analysed thirty Summer and Winter Olympics in 2016, they found that none came in within their initial budget. The cost overrun isn't simply bad luck. On the contrary, it's intentional, says Christopher Gaffney of Zurich University. If you are a construction company, or a chamber of commerce that has initiated a city's Olympic bid, you want cost estimates to start off low, so as to get taxpayers and the government on board. But once everyone is committed to the bid, you then want costs to soar, because higher spending generally means higher profits for suppliers. And forcing up spending is easy. The construction companies know the stadiums must be ready by the opening ceremony. This means they can charge almost whatever they like to build them; the government will pay.

No wonder the construction of stadiums so often hits delays. That allows the construction companies to tell the government,

'Oops, this is costing more than we thought. Give us more cash or we won't finish on time and you will look stupid in front of the world.'

The Brazilian World Cup was a wonderful thing if you happen to own a construction business; not so wonderful if you pay taxes in Brazil, or if you were hoping the government would do something about all the terrible Brazilian roads that don't lead to football stadiums.

By the time the last party animals had flown home, there was little sign of any economic boost to Brazil. True, the World Cup had attracted an unexpectedly large number of foreign visitors, about 1 million. However, a lot of the visitors had driven up for just a couple of days from Argentina, Chile or Uruguay, and many saved money in comparatively expensive Brazil by bringing their own food, living in their cars and showering on Rio's beaches. According to the Brazilian central bank, tourists spent about $1.6 billion in Brazil during the World Cup, or 60 per cent more than during the equivalent period in 2013. However, in the same period Brazilians themselves spent much more abroad: $4.4 billion. In fact, July 2014 was the most spendthrift month for Brazilians abroad since 1947. In short, many of them seem to have left the country to escape the World Cup.

Indeed, the World Cup coincided with the start of Brazil's longest recession since the 1930s. That rather undermined claims that it would boost the economy. The impoverished country then had to fork out another $4.6 billion (predictably, 51 per cent over budget) to host the Rio Olympics, according to the Oxford study.

You would at least have expected that all those lovely new stadiums built for the World Cup would have boosted league attendances afterwards. After all, when Brazil was named host in 2007, it didn't have a single stadium good enough for a World Cup. Its football fans were watching – or not watching – in the tumbledown arenas of a poorer era. Suddenly, from 2014, they could watch in much greater comfort. You would think that would encourage them to bring children or friends to games. Admittedly six of Brazil's twelve host cities didn't even have teams in the national championship, but at least the other six stadiums (including a marvellous new Maracanã in Rio) looked as if they would come in handy. That was a better ratio than South Africa managed. In short, Brazil seemed set for the boost in league crowds that most hosting countries enjoy. The French economist Bastien Drut and Stefan showed in an academic paper that in the five years after a country hosts a World Cup or European Championship, league attendances typically rise 15 to 25 per cent.

But it didn't happen in Brazil. Here is the average league attendance in Brazil's national championship, according to the Globo Esporte media company:

Year	Average spectators per match
2009	17,807
2010	14,839
2011	14,976
2012	13,013
2013	14,955
2014	16,555
2015	17,044*
2016	15,200

* The 2015 figure is from the Srgoool.com.br website

In short, average crowds in 2016 were only 1.6 per cent higher than in 2013. This was particularly disappointing given that in 2013 crowds were artificially suppressed because some clubs had to travel far for home games, while their usual stadiums were out of action ahead of the World Cup. Moreover, at no point during or after the tournament did attendances reach the level of 2009. As for Brasilia's underused stadium, here's a weird fact: its biggest crowd after the tournament was the 55,000 that packed in to see the Brazil–Argentina five-a-side match on 7 September 2014. In fact, that was the biggest futsal attendance in history.

Even if the new stadiums made Brazilian clubs a tiny bit richer, this didn't make Brazil as a whole richer. Rather, the Brazilian World Cup is best understood as a series of financial transfers: from women to men (who probably had more fun), from Brazilian taxpayers to FIFA and the world's football fans, and from taxpayers to Brazilian football clubs and construction companies. Possibly Brazilian society desired these transfers. Still, we have to be clear that this is what happened: a transfer of wealth from Brazil as a whole to various interest groups inside and outside the country. This is not an economic bonanza. Brazil sacrificed a little bit of its future to host the World Cup.

Ah, say the boosters, but the biggest economic benefits from these events are long term and intangible. Think of all the billions of people seeing the host country on TV every night. Silva told us that the 2014 World Cup would promote Brazil's image in the world. Well, maybe. First of all, as the American sports economist Andrew Zimbalist says, 'Brazil is hardly a secret as an international tourist destination.' Rio was already the most visited city in the Southern Hemisphere before the two tournaments, he notes. And for years in advance of Brazil's World Cup, foreign media coverage highlighted the country's crime and traffic jams. Some of that bad publicity has probably stuck.

People everywhere are cottoning on to the truth that building stadiums doesn't bring wealth. International sporting bodies have grown afraid of angering taxpayers the way FIFA did in Brazil. That's partly why the IOC gave the 2020 Olympics to Tokyo: the megacity could better afford to stage the Games than its poorer rivals Istanbul and Madrid. In football, UEFA went one step further: it didn't choose a host at all for Euro 2020. The burden would have been too great, explained UEFA's then general secretary Gianni Infantino (who is now president of FIFA). Instead several countries will share the hosting.

Several European cities bidding for the 2022 Winter Olympics pulled out before the vote. The Games were awarded to Beijing, which has no snow, but, crucially, has no referenda either. For the 2024 Summer Games, Boston, the original American candidate, dropped its bid after failing to get much local support. In the end, the only two cities that still wanted to host were Paris and Los Angeles. The IOC gave 2024 to Paris, but immediately locked in LA for 2028, perhaps fearful that otherwise nobody would want the event.

FIFA, too, learned from its Brazilian experience. It now knows that to ask a democratic country to fund white elephants is to ask for protests. As FIFA's secretary general Jerôme Valcke (since fired for corruption) lamented about Brazil: 'Sometimes less democracy is better for organising a World Cup.' Much easier to give the tournament to autocracies such as Russia or Qatar, where protestors are discouraged. No wonder the dictatorships Angola, Gabon and Equatorial Guinea (twice) have hosted recent African Nations Cups.

HAPPINESS IS A WORLD CUP

Most people now agree with Rob Baade: hosting a sports tournament doesn't make a place rich. The question then is why countries still bother. Why did so many countries go to such embarrassing lengths to stage the World Cups of 2018 and 2022? The answer has nothing to do with desire for profit. On the contrary: Qatar, which won the bidding for 2022, has so much money that it can afford to waste pots of it on a month of fun. However, the frantic bidding by respectable democracies, such as Australia, the US, England and Spain, does reveal something about the new politics of happiness slowly emerging in the rich world.

In recent years, social scientists have learned a lot about happiness. Their best source in Europe is the Eurobarometer research programme, which is funded by the European Commission. Each year it asks about 1,000 citizens from each European country how happy they are. To quote the exact question: 'On the whole, are you very satisfied, fairly satisfied, not very satisfied, or not at all satisfied with the life you lead?'

The survey has been conducted for over forty years. By now some insights have accumulated. Perhaps the most interesting is that the simple fact of having lots of money doesn't in itself make you happy. 'There is a paradox at the heart of our lives' is how Richard Layard opens his book *Happiness: Lessons from a New Science*, one of a flood of recent works on the subject. 'Most people want more income and strive for it. Yet as Western societies have got richer, their people have become no happier.' Layard says that in the US, Britain and Japan, people have gotten no happier in the past fifty years even as average incomes have more than doubled.

Most theorists of happiness argue that we do become happier during economic recoveries while incomes are rising. 'That's also because growth is full of promise,' says Claudia Senik, professor at the Paris School of Economics. However, it's not clear that high but stagnant incomes boost happiness in developed countries. It seems that we humans adapt quickly to our environment. The things we once thought of as luxuries soon become necessities (although, by the same token, our sense of well-being would quickly adapt to losing half our income). What we care about is not so much our absolute wealth but our rung on the ladder. The richest people in developed countries are on average happier than middling and poorer people – chiefly, it seems, because they compare themselves with the middling and poorer people.

Only in countries where income per capita is below about $15,000 – countries such as Brazil, the Philippines, and India – has more money indisputably brought greater national happiness. Layard writes, 'The reason is clear – extra income is really valuable when it lifts people away from sheer physical poverty.' But that very rarely happens in Western countries anymore.

Some other truths emerge from the European data. Scandinavians are very happy; Eastern Europeans are not. The Irish both north and south of the border are surprisingly happy. Age, sex and social status matter, too. In the European Union at least, according to Eurobarometer's figures, the average person's happiness tends to peak before the age of twenty-five. (This is a controversial issue. Many economic studies find happiness increases with age, while the psychology literature finds no relationship between age and happiness.) Women seem to be happier than men, which might help explain their much lower rates of suicide. The more educated people are, the happier they tend to be. Married people are generally happier than unmarried ones. What happens around you in society also matters: when unemployment or inflation rises, people tend to grow unhappier. Mentally ill people tend to be very unhappy. Spending time with friends and family makes people happy.

And, we discovered, so does hosting football tournaments. Staging a World Cup won't make you rich, but it does tend to cheer you up.

The day before the World Cup final of 2006, one of the authors, Simon, visited the street where he used to live in Berlin. Fifteen years before, the Hohenfriedbergstrasse had been a dull-brown place with toilets on the stairwells and potentially fatal ancient coal ovens in every flat. Nobody ever spoke to anyone else. This time he had to check the street sign to make sure it was the same place. Flags were flying from every house – German flags made in China, but also flags of many other nations – and children were playing everywhere, even though they had supposedly gone extinct in Germany. The World Cup seemed to have made a usually gloomy nation happy.

This is typical. Georgios Kavetsos and Stefan (with a lot of help from Robert McCulloch, guru of happiness research) took the European Commission's happiness data for twelve Western European countries from 1974 to 2004 and checked whether it correlated at all with sports tournaments. The obvious first question was whether people became happier when their national team did well. It turned out that they didn't: there was no visible correlation. Then they looked at hosting and happiness, and here they found a link. After a country hosts a football tournament, its inhabitants report increased happiness.

In their research they replicated existing studies of happiness using all the measures researchers usually consider (income, age, marital status and so on), and then tested whether living in a host country made a difference as well. Their data on happiness covered eight separate hosts of tournaments: Italy and France for the World Cups of 1990 and 1998 and, for the European Championships, Italy (1980), France (1984), West Germany (1988), England (1996), and Belgium and the Netherlands (2000). In all but one of these eight host countries, there was a significant uptick in self-reported happiness just after the tournament. The only exception was the UK, where happiness fell slightly just after Euro '96, but then we all know that the UK is not England.

George and Stefan are pretty sure these results cannot be ascribed to coincidence. For one thing, their analysis controlled for many potentially confounding factors (such as age, gender, employment and marital status). But one piece of evidence that they found particularly convincing had to do with a peculiarity of the study. Generally Eurobarometer reports the results in annual format, but in fact the data is a product of two surveys, one in the spring and one in the autumn, and researchers can separate these observations in the raw data. It was very clear in the data that the jump in happiness in host nations came from people surveyed in the autumn (just after the football tournament) and not in spring (before).

Interestingly, this chimes with what the late British football writer Arthur Hopcraft observed when England hosted the World Cup in 1966. He wrote two years later:

> The competition released in our country a communal exuberance which I think astonished ourselves more than our visitors. It gave us a chance to spruce up a lot, to lighten the leaden character of the grounds where the matches were played, to throw off much of our inhibition of behaviour, particularly in the provinces, so that we became a gay, almost reckless people in our own streets, which is commonly only how we conduct ourselves when we put on our raffia hats in other countries' holiday resorts. Except in the celebrations that greeted the end of the Second World War, I have never seen England look as unashamedly delighted by life as it did during the World Cup.

Because the Eurobarometer also includes data on incomes, it's possible to work out how far the increase in happiness associated with a football tournament compares to an increase in income. The monetary equivalent of the jump in happiness was quite large. Citizens of wealthy countries like the Netherlands or France would need to make hundreds of euros more a month to experience a similar leap. The effect can also be likened to an unexpected increase in income that takes someone from the bottom half of the income distribution to the middle of the top half. It's not quite winning the lottery, but very satisfying nonetheless. If you calculate this for an entire nation, then the leap in happiness from hosting can easily be worth a few billion euros.

In general, older men in host countries gained the most extra happiness, presumably because many of them were sitting in front of their television sets with little else to do. Lesser-educated people gained more happiness than better-educated ones. Of all the subgroups we studied, only one (a significant one) did not get any happier: women.

For World Cups, the gain in happiness was quite persistent: even two and four years after the tournament, every subgroup we looked at was still happier than before the tournament. European Championships, though, lifted happiness only briefly. George and Stefan found no impact on happiness in the host country a year after the tournament.

But if people gain a lot of happiness after hosting a tournament, they seem to lose a little happiness in the run-up. The ritual fuss over whether the stadiums will be ready, whether hooligans or terrorists will invade their country, and whether their team will be made to look ridiculous appears to cause stress. Six years and four years before hosting a tournament, many of the subgroups they studied showed a decline in happiness.

The London Olympics also seem to have boosted British happiness. The UK's Office for National Statistics (ONS) registered a small rise in self-reported 'life satisfaction' from 2011–2012 to 2012–2013, despite the economic crisis. Of the 165,000 British adults polled, 77 per cent rated their life satisfaction at seven or more out of ten – up a touch from 75.9 per cent in 2011–2012. The ONS commented that the Olympics and the Queen's Diamond Jubilee may have 'influenced people's assessment of their . . . well-being'. Stefan participated in a study with seven other researchers using a panel of 26,000 respondents from residents of London, Berlin and Paris in 2011, 2012 and 2013, asking the simple happiness question. They wanted to see not just if Londoners' happiness increased during the Games, but if it increased compared to the same

time in the previous/following year, and if it increased relative
to changes in Berlin and Paris. What they found was remarkable: a clear and significant jump in happiness on the day of
the opening ceremony, sustained throughout the Games until
the closing ceremony, after which happiness fell back to exactly
where it would have been without the Games.

* * *

It turns out that hosting doesn't make you rich, but it does
make you happy. This begs a question. If countries want to host
football tournaments (and American cities want to host major
league teams) as part of their pursuit of happiness, why don't
they just say so? Why bother clothing their arguments in bogus
economics?

The answer is that few politicians try to speak the language
of happiness. Instead they talk mostly about money. Anything
that serves only to make people happy is often derided with the
contemptuous phrase 'feel-good factor', as if politics should
be above such trivialities. Most politicians simply assume that
the real business of government is to make people richer. For
one thing, measuring income is easier than measuring happiness. And so, when politicians argue for hosting tournaments,
they typically use the language of money. It is almost the only
vocabulary they have. The British economist John Kay, looking
back on the London Olympics, remarked: 'A curious puritanism
requires politicians to pretend activities intended to make us
feel good about ourselves are justified by their contribution to
"the economy". The Olympiad was a good party, which cost the
British population about £200 per head.'

But it has become clear that in rich countries, there is much
more to happiness than money alone. Robert F. Kennedy was
one of the first to see this, remarking in March 1968, three
months before he was murdered, that the gross domestic

product 'measures everything . . . except that which makes life worthwhile'. For a few years before the economic crisis hit in 2008, some European politicians did begin talking less about money and more about happiness. In Britain in 2006, for instance, the Conservative leader David Cameron tried to introduce the acronym 'GWB' – 'general well-being' – to counter the decades-old 'GDP' for 'gross domestic product'. He said, 'Improving our society's sense of well-being is, I believe, the central political challenge of our times. . . . Politics in Britain has too often sounded as though it was just about economic growth.' Instead Cameron wanted politics 'to recognize the value of relationships with family, friends and the world around us'.

Like most European politicians, Cameron dropped the happiness talk after the 2008 economic crisis. However, it seems that football tournaments create exactly the sort of relationships he had been talking about: people gathered together in pubs and living rooms, a whole country suddenly caring about the same event. A World Cup is the sort of common project that otherwise barely exists in modern societies. We've seen that the mere fact of following a team in the World Cup deters some very isolated people from committing suicide. If playing in a tournament creates social cohesion, hosting one creates even more. The inhabitants of the host country – and especially the men – come to feel more connected to everyone else around them. Moreover, hosting can boost the nation's self-esteem, and so makes people feel better about themselves.

In the end, the best reason for hosting a World Cup is that it's fun. Brazil's government ought to have been honest and said, 'It'll cost us money, we'll have less left over for schools and roads and poor people, but we all love football and it should be a fun month, so it's worth it.' Then Brazilians could have a clearheaded debate about the true pros and cons of hosting. It's reasonable enough to want to throw the world's biggest party. But you don't throw a party to make money. You do it because it makes you happy.

Hosting makes even politicians happy. Most of their work is frustrating. You try to get money to build, say, roads, but other politicians stop you. Even when you get the money, it's hard to build the roads, because people pop up to object. It's the same with housing or foreign policy or recycling: being a politician is an endless, tedious struggle with your enemies.

But it isn't when you want to host a sports tournament. Suddenly everyone gets on board. While London was bidding for the Olympics, the rower Steve Redgrave pulled an Olympic gold medal out of his pocket during a meeting at the House of Commons, and MPs of all parties began drooling over him. Even going to war doesn't create that sort of unanimous sentiment anymore.

Ken Livingstone wrote when he was mayor of London, 'Crucially, the Olympics will also bring much-needed new facilities: an Olympic-size swimming pool in a city that has just two Olympic pools to Berlin's 19, and a warm-up track that would be turned over to community use.' But plainly, arguments like these are just excuses. If you want to regenerate a poor neighbourhood, regenerate it. Build nice houses and a train line. If you want an Olympic pool and a warm-up track, build them. You could build pools and tracks all across London, and it would still have been cheaper than hosting the Olympics. The only good reason to host an Olympics is that it makes people happy. The politicians behind London's bid did not say so, but they did sense that the voters would reward them for winning the Games. The 8.7 million Londoners, in particular, have the highest incomes in the European Union, and so would need to receive a fortune in tax rebates to buy the happiness the Games seem to have brought them. London's then mayor, Boris Johnson, told athletes at the post-Games parade: 'For the first time in living memory you caused tube train passengers to break into spontaneous conversation with their neighbours.'

Puritans might rightly argue that even a rich country like Britain has better things on which to spend money. However, the likely gain in happiness from the Olympics does mean the politicians are canny to give the people bread and circuses. In wealthy countries such as Britain, the maths of hosting and happiness probably stacks up.

But it's much less probable that Brazil got its money's worth in happiness from hosting the World Cup. This is still very much a sub-$15,000 average annual income country, where putting more money in people's pockets would have made them happier. And like South Africa, it's among the most economically unequal countries on earth. Both countries have a first-world sector of the economy with the money and skills to host a World Cup – but also a third-world sector that desperately needs the fruits of the money and skills. Millions of Brazilians are still stuck in life-diminishing poverty. Some of them were pushed out of their slums to make way for the World Cup. The American satirical magazine *The Onion* got it about right with the headline 'World Cup Stadium's Walls Reinforced with 10,000 Homeless Brazilians'. Many people in Brazil are now asking how many homes with running water could have been built for the cost of their new stadiums.

We already know the World Cup didn't make Brazilians richer. It also probably wasn't an efficient way to make them happier.

PART III

COUNTRIES

Rich and Poor, Tom Thumb, England, Spain,
Palestine and the Champions of the Future

THE CURSE OF POVERTY: WHY POOR COUNTRIES ARE POOR AT SPORT

When Didier Drogba was five, his parents put him on a plane in the Ivory Coast and sent him to live with an uncle in France. The six-hour flight, alone with his favourite toy, passed in a blur of tears and tissues.

About a decade later Drogba's father lost his job at a bank in the Ivory Coast, and the family moved to a suburb of Paris, where they were reunited with their exiled son. Eight Drogbas ended up living in a flat of a bit over 100 square feet. 'A very large wardrobe, really,' Drogba recalled in his autobiography. 'Hard. Very hard. Even enough to drive you crazy.' The flat was cold, and his little brothers were so noisy he couldn't concentrate on his schoolwork. 'Luckily, my father had allowed me to start playing football again.'

There is a myth that poor people are somehow best equipped to make it as sportsmen. A cliché often used about them is that sport is their 'only escape route from poverty'. The poor are supposedly figuratively 'hungrier' than the rich. If they are black, like Drogba, they are sometimes thought to have greater genetic gifts than white people. And the evidence that poor people excel at sports seems to be in front of our eyes. England are not the only national football team dominated by players from less well-off backgrounds. France since the 1990s has generally fielded a majority of non-white players from underprivileged regions, and few Brazilian internationals are sons of corporate lawyers, either.

Most of the world's best football players started life poor: South Americans like Diego Maradona, who as a toddler almost drowned in a local cesspit, Africans like Samuel Eto'o who appear to support hundreds of people back home, or European immigrants like Zlatan Ibrahimovic or Zinedine Zidane, who grew up in some of the toughest neighbourhoods on the Continent. Drogba's childhood was only slightly more Dickensian than most. The origins of American basketball players and football players are mostly lowly, too. The best preparation for sporting greatness seems to be a poor childhood.

Yet it is not. The facts show that the world's poor people and poor countries are worse at sports than rich ones. It is true that poorer immigrants in rich countries often excel at sports, but the reasons for that have nothing to do with skin colour or 'hunger'.

Let's look at poor countries first. The vast majority of countries on earth are excluded from sporting success simply because they are poor. This becomes apparent in a simple exercise to discover which country is the world's best at sports and which country is best for its size.

To find the best countries, we combined the historical results from many major international sporting events: the Summer and Winter Olympics, world cups in several sports, and the most popular individual sports. For some sports the data go back more than a century, for others only a couple of decades. For all sports, we took June 2017 as the end point.

Our methodology is not perfect. We started with the men's world cups in biggish sports that have seldom or never been featured at the Olympics. We ranked the top five countries in these sports, based first on the number of world titles they have won, and in case of draws, on finishes in the final four. We gave the best country in each sport five points, the second four, the third three, the fourth two and the fifth one. There is no need to read the rankings for every sport, but below are the detailed points tallies for those who are interested.

Basketball is an Olympic event. However, as the world's second-most popular team game it deserves additional input in this quest. We therefore added the results of the basketball World Cup:

US	5	Brazil	2
Yugoslavia/Serbia and Montenegro	4	Argentina	1
Spain	3		

Baseball was trickier. Historically the US dominates the sport. However, it traditionally sent amateurs or minor leaguers to the World Cup – now superseded by the World Baseball Classic. The US ranks only second all-time in the two tournaments combined. But we used our judgement to rank it as the world's best country in baseball, producing this ranking:

US	5	Dominican Republic	2
Cuba	4	Colombia	1
Venezuela	3		

Favouring the US in baseball did not affect the outcome of our quest.

The only women's world cup we counted was football. Women's football is an Olympic event, too, but it is far more widely played than most other women's team games, and therefore it seemed to merit more input. The rankings for women's football:

US	5	Japan	2
Germany	4	Sweden	1
Norway	3		

We also assessed popular individual sports that have seldom or never been represented in the Olympics. We rewarded countries for triumphs by their citizens. In tennis we counted men's and women's Grand Slam tournaments – tennis being a rare sport in that it is played about as much by women as by men. We used only results from the 'open era' starting in 1968, when tennis became very competitive.

MEN'S TENNIS:

US	5	Switzerland	2
Sweden	4	Australia	1
Spain	3		

WOMEN'S TENNIS:

US	5	Belgium	2
Germany/West Germany	4	Yugoslavia/Serbia	1
Australia	3		

In golf we used the results of the men's majors:

US	5	South Africa	3
Britain (including all four home countries and Jersey)	4	Australia	2
		Spain	1

In cycling we counted victories by citizens of each country in the Tour de France, a more prestigious event than the World

Championships. We didn't count doped winners such as Lance Armstrong, who were later stripped of their titles:

France	5	Italy	2
Belgium	4	Luxembourg	1
Spain	3		

In motor racing we chose the most prestigious competition, Formula I, thus discriminating against the US, which prefers its own races. Again, we counted world championships by citizenship. The rankings:

Britain	5	Argentina	2
Germany	4	Finland, Australia,	1 each
Brazil	3	Austria, France	

RUGBY UNION:

New Zealand	5	England	2
Australia	4	France	1
South Africa	3		

CRICKET:

Australia	5	Pakistan	2
India	4	Sri Lanka	1
West Indies	3		

We did not include the world cups of popular sports such as volleyball and ice hockey, because these are longstanding Olympic sports, and so we will assess them through their role in the Olympics' all-time medals table. Boxing was too hard to assess, as there are various rival 'world championships'. We also excluded the athletics World Championships. Athletics is copiously represented at the Olympics, and for most of the history of its World Championships, the entrants have been entire continents rather than single countries.

Clearly the Summer and Winter Olympics deserve to carry more weight in our quest than any single world cup. In the Summer Olympics of 2004, medals were awarded in twenty-eight sports. Many of these, such as archery or kayaking, are played by very few people. Still, because of the event's profusion of sports and its prestige, we gave the Summer Games ten times the weighting of world cups in single sports. So we gave the top country in the all-time medals table 50 points rather than 5 points for a single world cup. (We used the most common global method of ranking countries by gold medals, and counting silvers and bronzes only in case of ties.) Because the whole planet competes in the Olympics – unlike, say, in baseball or cricket – we rewarded the top ten rather than the top five countries in the all-time medals table. The ranking:

US	50 points	France	8
USSR/Russia	40	Italy	6
Britain	30	Hungary	4
Germany	20	East Germany	2
China	10	Australia	1

We gave the Winter Olympics three times the weighting of a world cup. Because few countries play winter sports, we rewarded only the top five in the all-time medals table:

USSR/Russia	15 points	Germany (including West Germany)	6
Norway	12		
US	9	Canada	3

Finally, the football World Cup. Football is an Olympic sport, but it is also the planet's most popular game. We gave its World Cup six times the weighting of world cups in other sports, and rewarded the top ten countries in the all-time points table. The ranking:

Brazil	30 points	England	5
Germany	24	France	4
Italy	18	Netherlands	3
Argentina	12	Uruguay	2
Spain	6	Sweden	1

We then totalled up all the points. Here are our top twenty-three sporting countries on earth:

US	89 points	Spain	13
Germany (including West Germany)	62	China	10
USSR/Russia	58	Sweden, Belgium, South Africa	6
Britain (including England)	46	Yugoslavia/Serbia and Montenegro, New Zealand	5
Brazil	35		
Italy	26	Hungary, India, Cuba	4
France	19	Netherlands, Canada, West Indies, Venezuela	3
Australia	17		
Norway	15		
Argentina	15		

The winner, the US, deserves particular praise given that we omitted two of its favourite sports, American gridiron football and NASCAR, because nobody else plays them. Germany, in second place, would have got closer to the American total if we had credited the united country with East Germany's Olympic medals (and forgotten all the male growth hormones that went into winning them).The USSR/Russia in third place can be slightly less pleased with itself, because it won most of its points when it was still a multinational empire.

Australia in eighth place did brilliantly, given that we ignored its prowess at its very own version of football, 'Aussie Rules'. Brazil was the best developing country by a very long way, and not just thanks to football. It has also diversified successfully into basketball and Formula I motor racing. India (1.2 billion inhabitants, 4 points for cricket) and China (1.3 billion, 10 points for the Summer Olympics) were the biggest flops per capita, though at least China is rising – when we first calculated this table in 2006, it didn't score a single point. The Arab world combined is still on zero points.

But which country is world champion per capita? To find out, we worked out how many points each country scored per million inhabitants (taking their population figures for 2017). That produced this top ten of overachievers:

Norway	2.88
Luxembourg	1.75
New Zealand	1.08
United Germany (excluding the GDR's Olympic medals)	0.76
Australia	0.71
Britain (including England)	0.70
Sweden	0.61
Uruguay	0.58
West Indies (or the nations that together supply almost all West Indian cricketers, namely, Jamaica, Trinidad and Tobago, Guyana, Barbados and Antigua)	0.58
Belgium	0.53

Heia, Norge! Norway's lead as the world's best sporting country per capita is so large that it would most probably have won our sporting Tom Thumb trophy even with a different scoring system. This is a country where at a state kindergarten in suburban Oslo in mid-afternoon, among the throng of mothers picking up their toddlers, someone pointed out to us an anonymous mum who happened to be an Olympic gold medallist in cross-country skiing. Norway won more points in our competition than all of Africa, or China and India put together. We could even have omitted the Winter Olympics – almost a Norwegian fiefdom – and the country still would have finished in the top ten of our efficiency table.

But the main thing the top of our rankings demonstrates is the importance of wealth. Our efficiency table for sports bears a curious resemblance to another global ranking: the United Nations' human development index. This measures life expectancy, literacy, education and living standards to rank the countries of the world according to their well-being. We found that a nation's well-being is highly correlated with its success in sports. Guess which country topped the UN's rankings for human development in 2015: *Heia, Norge*, again.

Australia, fifth in our sporting rankings, was second for human development in 2015. Germany, fourth in the world for sports, was fourth for human development. The only poorer nations that sneaked into our sporting top ten were Uruguay and the West Indian nations. However, even these poor cousins were all classified by the UN as 'highly' developed countries except Guyana, whose development was 'medium'. Generally the most developed countries also tend to be best at sports.

The case of Norway shows why. It's Norwegian government policy that every farmer, every fisherman, no matter where he lives in the country, has the right to play sports. And Norway will spend what it takes to achieve that. Just as supermarkets have sprouted all over Britain, there are all-weather sports grounds everywhere in Norway. Even in the unlikeliest corners of the country there's generally one around the corner from your house. Usually the locker rooms are warm, and the coaches have acquired some sort of diploma. A kid can play and train on a proper team for well under £100 a year, really not much for most Norwegians. Almost everyone in the country plays something. Knut Helland, a professor at Bergen University who has written a book on Norwegian sports and media, told us that Norway has the biggest ski race in the world with about 13,000 participants. 'I'm taking part in it myself,' he added. People all over the world might want to play sports, but to make that possible requires money and organization that poor countries don't have. Money buys sporting trophies.

In football, the best example is probably Iceland (ninth in the UNHDI rankings). When the land of fish, volcanoes and endless winters qualified for Euro 2016, its population of 330,000 made it the smallest country ever to qualify for a Euro or a World Cup. Qualification, as it turned out, was only the start of it. Many of us will long remember the Icelandic TV commentator 'Gummi Ben' ascending into hysteria – 'Never, ever, have I felt as good!' – as he narrated his team's last-minute winner against Austria. Next, Iceland beat England to reach the quarter-finals.

Like Norway, Iceland is a social democracy whose government does its best to give all inhabitants the chance to play sport. It's also a cold country, with long winters, which Icelanders tend to spend hunkered down inside, either working hard or drinking hard while they wait for the summer partying season. What to do while hibernating? Vidar Halldórsson, an Icelandic sports sociologist, says: 'We grew up watching English football on TV, from the 1970s. The only TV station in Iceland showed English games once a week, on Saturdays (not live, but a week later). They were the only professional sports we saw.' In a survey of Icelandic men in 2003, Halldórsson found that 88 per cent could name a favourite English football team. Aron Jóhannsson (raised in Iceland but now an American international footballer) recalls boys fighting in the streets of Reykjavik over English football results. 'That passion was very deep,' he says. It's a passion that arguably reached its apogee in 2006 when the billionaire Björgólfur Guðmundsson – then Iceland's second-richest man after his son, Björgólfur Thor – bought West Ham United. After the financial crisis struck Iceland in 2008, *Forbes* magazine revalued Guðmundsson's estimated net worth from $1.1 billion to zero. In 2009 he was declared bankrupt. Still, no doubt the passion remained.

In the twentieth century, Icelanders watched English football but didn't have much opportunity to play or watch their own. Iceland's league runs from May to September – 'the shortest football season in the world', the country's football federation proudly calls it. But around 2000, Iceland began building an all-weather football infrastructure that may be unparalleled on earth. Over 110 Icelandic schools got artificial mini-fields, and there are now seven heated indoor halls with full-sized football grounds, Nowadays Icelanders can play all year round, whether they belong to a club or not.

Playing football is now a part of life in Iceland, especially in the villages. Gender barely matters: nearly a quarter of the country's registered football players are girls aged under 18. Even 6-year-old kids are trained by qualified, paid football coaches. As the Dutch journalist Michiel de Hoog notes, this distinguishes Iceland from pretty much every other country on earth, where most child players are coached (or just yelled at) by somebody's mum or dad. And Icelandic kids usually play other sports besides.

In Iceland, football is something you do very seriously, for fun, while continuing real life on the side. There can't be many countries where the national team's goalkeeper is also a professional filmmaker. Hannes Thor Halldórsson (not the same guy as his namesake Vidas, the sociologist) actually shot the commercial for Icelandair that featured his own team. 'It was weird,' he told Sports Illustrated. 'I had to act in the commercial as well, so I was directing the commercial in the national kit and boots.' Meanwhile Iceland's legendary handball captain, Olafur Stefansson, seemed to regard himself primarily as an existentialist philosopher. When we asked him during the London Olympics what a handball gold would mean for the little country, he replied that he was unable to answer: 'You have so many different realities. The game is – what is it? A simulacrum of life itself, maybe in simplified terms.'

In Beijing in 2008, Stefansson's team had beaten Spain in the Olympic semi-final. During that game, 'there was not a single transaction made on the Icelandic stock exchange,' says the sociologist Vidas Halldórsson. Stefansson's men ended up with silver. No country that small had ever won an Olympic medal in a team sport.

Broad access to sport is much less common in poor, corrupt countries. The money FIFA supposedly spends to build football fields for kids in these places is often wasted. Over the years the corrupt Trinidadian football boss Jack Warner received at least $26 million from FIFA to build a Dr João Havelange Centre of Excellence in his home country, on land that later turned out to belong to him. But the Centre didn't actually host much football, because Warner preferred to put on profitable 'weddings, dinners, shows', writes David Conn in his *Fall of the House of Fifa*. This helps explain why in January 2018 Trinidad and Tobago stood 80th in the FIFA rankings, sixty places below Iceland. China, which has few public sports fields, and where most kids never get the chance to play football at school, ranked 70th.

After we published the first edition of *Soccernomics*, Christopher Anderson, then still a political scientist at Cornell University, and later briefly managing director of Coventry City, riposted that we placed undue weight on wealth. In his paper 'Do Democracies Win More?' Anderson analysed all football World Cups from 1950 to 2006. The key to winning wasn't so much wealth, he argued, as democracy.

That may well be true. Wealth and democracy tend to correlate very closely. Almost all rich countries (leaving aside a few oil states in the Middle East) are democracies. That makes it tricky to separate the effects of wealth from the effects of democracy. Anderson might well be right that democracy contributes more to winning football games (note also that in making our case, we were looking at many sports rather than just football). Perhaps the average quality of schooling in different countries – if you could measure it perfectly – would be an even better predictor of success in football. After all, schooling is a pretty good gauge of how well a country channels resources to all its people. If you're good at providing schools for everyone, as most democracies are, then you are probably also good at providing good football fields and coaches for everyone. It's impossible to say whether Norway is good at sports because it's rich, or because it's a democracy, or because it's highly educated. Rather, being rich and democratic and well educated and good at sports are all part of the same thing.

However you measure it, poor countries are generally poorer at sports. It's no coincidence that China won nothing at sports before its economy took off and that it topped the medals table at the Beijing Olympics afterwards. Most African countries barely even try to compete in any sports other than football and a few running events – the cheapest sports to become good at. And the best place to find out why the world's poor do worse than the world's rich is South Africa, where some very poor and very rich neighbourhoods are almost side by side, separated only by a highway or a golf course.

South Africa is the only African country to score any points at all in our sporting table. Yet it owes almost all those points to an ethnic group that makes up just 8 per cent of the country's inhabitants: white people.

Only about 4.5 million of the 56 million South Africans are white. Nonetheless, whites accounted for fourteen of the fifteen players in the Springbok rugby team that won the World Cup in 1995, thirteen of the fifteen who won it in 2007, as well as all five South African golfers who have won majors and most of the country's best cricketers. If we treated white South Africa as a separate country, then its six sporting points would have put it in third place in the world in our sporting efficiency table. That is entirely predictable. South African whites were nurtured under apartheid on almost all the resources of the country.

The national teams of South African whites remain world-class in their respective sports. Non-white South Africa's national team does less well. At the time of writing, in March 2018, the Bafana Bafana football team, sometimes known at home as the 'Banana Banana', is 77th in FIFA's rankings, well behind little Panama, let alone Iceland and Wales. The Bafana just missed qualifying for the African Nations Cup of 2012, having failed to figure out that the team needed to beat rather than draw with Sierra Leone in the last qualifying game. (The scenes of the Bafana wasting time in the final minutes to preserve the draw would have been hilarious were they not a terrible reflection on the state of maths teaching in South Africa.)

Here are five vignettes to explain why black South Africa and other poor nations fail at sport.

YOU ARE WHAT YOU EAT: JOHANNESBURG

Steven Pienaar, the South African midfielder who had a long career in the English Premier League, has the frame of a pre-pubescent boy. There's hardly a European football player as reedy as he is. But in South African football his body type is common. Frank Eulberg, a German who was once very briefly assistant coach of the Kaizer Chiefs, South Africa's best team, says that when he arrived at the club, sixteen of the players were shorter than five foot nine. 'I sometimes thought, "Frank, you're in the land of the dwarves."'

Most likely, Pienaar is reedy because he grew up malnourished and without much access to doctors. He was born in a poor Coloured township in 1982, at the height of apartheid, when almost all money and health care went to whites. Growing tall is not just a matter of what you eat. When children become ill, their growth is interrupted, and because poor children tend to get ill more often than rich ones, they usually end up shorter.

Most of the players who represented South Africa in 2010 were born in non-white townships in the 1980s. And so the ghost of apartheid bugged the Bafana at their own World Cup. One reason South Africans are so bad at football is that most of them didn't get enough good food. There are big strong black South Africans like Lucas Radebe and Aaron Mokoena, but not very many of them.

Apartheid, based on the bogus ideology that races are different, ended up creating white, black, 'Coloured' and Indian South Africans, who really were like separate peoples. The whites on average tower over the blacks. No wonder the cricket and rugby teams are so much better than the Bafana. 'Well, they have their moments,' laughs Demitri Constantinou.

This descendant of Greek immigrants, an exercise scientist at Wits University in Johannesburg, directs FIFA's first medical centre of excellence in Africa. When we met, he was running a project with the South African Football Association to help develop young football players. Constantinou's team tested the health of all the players selected for SAFA's programme. In a Woolworths tearoom in one of Johannesburg's posh northern suburbs, among white ladies having afternoon tea, he says, 'The biggest issue was nutrition.' Is malnutrition one reason African teams perform poorly at World Cups? 'I think yes. And I think it has been overlooked as a possible cause.'

Hardly any players in the latter stages of the World Cup of 2006 were shorter than about five foot eight, Constantinou notes. 'There is a minimum height.' If a large proportion of your male population was below that height, you were picking your team from a reduced pool. Conversely, though he didn't say it, one reason that Norway and Sweden (two of the three tallest countries in the world) excel at sports is that almost all their male inhabitants are tall enough. They are picking their teams from a full pool.

A BEAST INTO A TOOTHPICK: CAPE TOWN

George Dearnaley is a big, ruddy white man who looks like a rugby player, but in fact he was once the Bafana's promising young centre-forward. Dearnaley never got beyond promising, because when he was in his early twenties his knee went. He didn't mind much. He spoke a bit of Zulu and had studied literature and journalism at college in Toledo, Ohio, and so he joined the football magazine *Kick Off*. He became its publisher as well as the author of an excellent column.

Over an English breakfast in a Cape Town greasy spoon near the *Kick Off* offices, Dearnaley reflected on the Amazulu team in Durban where his career peaked. Seven of his teammates from the Amazulu side of 1992 were now dead, out of a squad of about twenty-four. Dearnaley said, 'One guy died when his house exploded, so that was probably a taxi war or something. But the rest must have been AIDS. One player, a Durban newspaper said he was bewitched. A six-foot-four beast of a man, who was suddenly whittled down to a toothpick.'

Constantinou says it's quite possible that a fifth of the Bafana's potential pool of players for 2010 carried the HIV virus. Not many people now remember Emmanuel 'Scara' Ngobese, once a great South African 'dribbling wizard', who died at age twenty-eight in a Johannesburg hospital on 11 May 2010, a month before the World Cup kicked off. His cause of death was given as 'tuberculosis'. Scara won the league with the Kaizer Chiefs in 2005, and played once for the Bafana. How many South Africans who could have played in 2010 were dead instead? Thankfully most South Africans with HIV now finally get treatment, but still many of them won't be fit enough to maximize their athletic potential.

THE DARK SIDE OF THE MOON: SANDTON, JUST OUTSIDE JOHANNESBURG

It was quite a step for Danny Jordaan to organize a World Cup, because until he was thirty-eight he had never even seen one. The chief executive officer of the FIFA World Cup 2010 grew up a million miles from the world's best football. Being in South Africa under apartheid was not quite like being on the moon, or being in North Korea, but it was almost as isolated. South Africa was the last industrialized country to get television, in 1976, because the white government was afraid of the device. Even after that hardly any blacks had TV sets, and FIFA did not allow its World Cup to be broadcast in the apartheid state. So the first time Jordaan saw a World Cup on television was in 1990.

The country's isolation continued even after that. As far as most South Africans were concerned, international football might still as well have been happening on Mars. Jordaan told us, 'South Africans played on their own. We thought we were so smart. That's why when we played our first competitive match against Zimbabwe [in 1992], every South African knew we were going to hammer Zimbabwe. But Zimbabwe had this little player called Peter Ndlovu. Nobody knew Peter Ndlovu. By half-time it was 3–0 for them. That was the first entry into international football. That really shook this country.'

As late as 1998, when South Africa entered its first World Cup, large swathes of the population assumed that the Bafana would win it. After all, everyone knew that their native style of 'piano and shoeshine' – essentially, doing tricks on the ball while standing around – was just like Brazilian football but better. The Bafana did not win the World Cup.

Black South Africa was isolated twice over: first by sanctions, then by poverty. However, isolation – a distance from the networks of the world's best football – is the fate of most poor countries. Their citizens can't easily travel to Italy or Germany and see how football is played there, let alone talk to the best coaches. Some can't even see foreign football on television, because they don't have a television. And only a couple of the very best players in these countries ever make it to the best leagues in the world.

One reason poor countries do badly in sports – and one reason they are poor – is that they tend to be less 'networked', less connected to other countries, than rich ones. It is hard for them just to find out the latest best practice on how to play a sport.

Playing for national teams in Africa hardly lifts the isolation. Most poor, isolated African countries compete only against other poor, isolated African countries. At best, they might encounter the world's best once every four years at a World Cup. No wonder they have little idea of what top-class football is like.

'THE ORGANIZERS. IT'S THE BIGGEST PROBLEM': LONDON

For mysterious reasons, in 2006 someone decided that the Bafana should play their annual charity match, the Nelson Mandela Challenge, not in the magnificent 78,000-seat FNB Stadium just outside Johannesburg, but more than 5,000 miles away at Brentford's Griffin Park in west London.

On a grey November London afternoon the day before the game, the Bafana were in their grey-coloured three-star hotel on the outskirts of Heathrow Airport. In the lobby were flight crews, travelling salesmen and cheery men in green-and-yellow tracksuits hanging with their entourage: the Bafana Bafana. Their opponents, the Egyptians, who were also staying in the hotel, had congregated in the bar. Apparently Egypt was furious. It had been promised a five-star hotel, and a match fee that had yet to materialize.

Pitso Mosimane, the Bafana's caretaker manager – a big, bald, bullet-headed man – was also hanging around the lobby. Mosimane complained that African coaches never got jobs in Europe. He gestured towards the bar: 'The coach of Egypt, who won the African Cup of Nations. Don't you think he could at least coach a team in the English first division?' Then Mosimane went off for a pre-match practice at Griffin Park.

Minutes later he was back at the table. 'That was quick,' someone remarked. 'No, we didn't train!' Mosimane said. Nobody had bothered telling Brentford the Bafana were coming, and so the field wasn't ready for them. Now they would have to play the African champions without having trained on the field. 'And I'm carrying players who play for Blackburn Rovers and Borussia Dortmund, and you know? We're laughing about it.' Mosimane jerked a thumb towards four men in suits drinking at the next table: 'The organizers. It is the biggest problem. This wouldn't happen with any other national team.'

He was wrong. Organizational mishaps are always happening to national teams from poor countries. On most sub-Saharan African national teams that make it to a World Cup, players and officials have a ritual dispute over pay about a week before the tournament. In 2002 Cameroon's dispute got out of hand, whereupon the squad made a brief airplane odyssey through Ethiopia, India and Thailand before finally landing in Japan four days late. Jet-lagged and confused, the Indomitable Lions were knocked out in the first round. During the 2014 World Cup, quarrels between officials and unpaid players unsettled the Nigerian, Cameroonian and Ghanaian camps. Ghana's president finally sent $3 million to Brazil on a chartered plane – surely a cash transfer would have been easier? – and Brazilian TV showed defender John Boye kissing his pile of notes. Eventually Moses Armah, an official of the country's football federation, confirmed that he had decked Sulley Muntari after the midfielder had slapped him in the face twice. Muntari and Kevin-Prince Boateng were expelled from the squad. And Ghana, remember, is one of Africa's healthiest democracies and possibly the continent's best team, which came within centimetres of the semi-final in 2010. Clearly FIFA needs to move to a system of sidestepping potentially corrupt national officials and paying players directly at World Cups. But that alone wouldn't solve Africa's football problems.

To win at sports, you need to find, develop and nurture talent. Doing that requires money, know-how and some kind of administrative infrastructure. Few African countries have enough of any.

'COLOURED' BEATS 'BLACK': THE CAPE FLATS

If you stand on Table Mountain at night and look down at Cape Town, you will see a city of lights. Next to the lights are the railway tracks. And on the far side of the tracks are 'black spots': Coloured townships without lights. These are the rainy, murderous Cape Flats where most of South Africa's best football players grew up.

Benni McCarthy – South Africa's record goal scorer – comes from the Cape Flats. So does the man just behind him in the scoring charts, Shaun Bartlett. So does Benni's old friend Quinton Fortune, for years a loyal reserve at Manchester United.

The key point is that according to the racial classifications of apartheid, still tacitly used by most South Africans today, none of these players is 'black'. They are 'Coloured': a group of generally lighter-skinned people, mostly derived from the lighter African tribes of the Cape, though some descend from Asian slaves and mixed white–black liaisons. Less than 10 per cent of South Africans are Coloured, while about three-quarters are black. However, Coloureds often make up as much as half of the Bafana team. Pienaar and striker Delron Buckley, for instance, are from Coloured townships in other parts of South Africa. This density of Coloured talent is a legacy of apartheid.

Under apartheid, the Coloureds were slightly better off than the blacks. They had more to eat and more opportunities to organize themselves. In the Coloured Cape Flats, for instance, there were amateur football clubs with proper coaches like you might find in Europe. Not so in black townships, where a boys' team would typically be run by a local gangster or the shebeen owner, who seldom bothered much with training.

To the irritation of many South African blacks, the Bafana have been a largely Coloured team for much of their history since 1992. The blacks are simply too poor to compete within their own country, let alone with Europeans. Even in the simplest game, the poor are excluded by malnutrition, disease and disorganization. Poor people in poor countries do worse at sports.

That leaves one thing unexplained: Why is it that so many of the best European football players of recent times – Zidane, Drogba (officially an Ivorian but raised in France), Ibrahimovic, Rooney, Cristiano Ronaldo – come from the poorest neighbourhoods in Europe?

It cannot be that boys from the ghetto have an unquenchable hunger to succeed. If that were so, they would do better at school and in jobs outside football. There must be something about their childhoods that makes them particularly well suited to football. That reason is practice.

Malcolm Gladwell, in his book *Outliers: The Story of Success*, popularized the '10,000-hour rule'. This is a notion from psychology, which says that to achieve expertise in any field you need at least 10,000 hours of practice. 'In study after study, of composers, basketball players, fiction writers, ice-skaters, concert pianists, chess players, master criminals,' says neurologist Daniel Levitin in *Outliers*, 'this number comes up again and again. Ten thousand hours is equivalent to roughly three

hours a day, or 20 hours a week, of practice over 10 years. . . .
No one has yet found a case in which true world-class expertise was accomplished in less time.'

The 10,000-hour rule has since been questioned by academics in various fields. It may indeed not apply in very physical sports like running or jumping, where somebody with the
perfect genes can become world-class without much training.
However, in a highly skill-based sport like football, Gladwell's
essential point is correct: practice makes perfect. 'Football is a
very technical sport that unfortunately takes a ridiculous time
to become good,' says Tom Byer, an American who advises
China's education ministry on football. 'So how do you get to
10,000 hours?'

In football, it is the poorest European boys who are most likely
to hit that number. They tend to live in small flats, which forces
them to spend time outdoors. There they meet a ready supply of
local boys equally eager to get out of their flats and play football.
Their parents are less likely than middle-class parents to force
them to waste precious time doing homework. (In China, where
most families have just one child, the intense pressure on the
kid to do well at school helps explain the country's underachievement in football, says Byer.)

Poorer children also have less money for other leisure pur-
suits, which pushes them towards kicking a ball. A constant in
players' ghosted autobiographies is the monomaniacal childhood
spent playing non-stop football and, in a classic story, sleeping
with a ball. Here, for instance, is Nourdin Boukhari, a Dutch-
Moroccan football player who grew up in an immigrant neighbourhood of Rotterdam, recalling his childhood for a Dutch magazine:

> I grew up in a family of eight children. . . . There was no
> chance of pocket money. . . . I lived more on the street
> than at home. . . . And look at Robin van Persie, Mounir El
> Hamdaoui and Said Boutahar. And I'm forgetting Youssef

El-Akchaoui. [Like the other players Boukhari mentions, El-Akchaoui became a professional football player.] Those boys and I played on the street in Rotterdam together. We never forget where we came from and that we used to have nothing except for one thing: the ball . . .

What we have in common is that we were on the street every minute playing football, day and night. We were always busy, playing games, juggling, shooting at the crossbar. The ball was everything for me, for us. We'd meet on squares.

By the time these boys were fifteen, they were much better players than suburban kids. That's probably still more true in Latin America, where poor kids have even fewer options than in Europe and therefore play more football. This may help explain why the world's most skilful players tend to be Latin Americans. The importance of practice also helps to explain why blacks raised in American ghettos are overrepresented in basketball and football.

But it would be misleading to say these European football players grew up 'poor'. By global standards, they were rich. Even in Cristiano Ronaldo's Madeira, Ibrahimovic's Rosengård or Zidane's La Castellane, children generally got enough to eat and decent medical care. It is true that Cristiano Ronaldo grew up in a house so small that they kept the washing machine on the roof, but in black South Africa that washing machine would have marked the family as rich. Besides the 10,000-hour rule, there is another rule that explains sporting success: the $15,000 rule. That's the minimum average income per person that a country needs to win anything. There is only one way around this: be Brazil.

WHY ENGLAND LOSE AND OTHER EUROPEANS WIN

BEATEN BY A DISHWASHER

Here is what we wrote in the first edition of *Soccernomics*, which appeared nine months before the World Cup of 2010:

When the England team flies to South Africa for the World Cup, an ancient ritual will start to unfold. Perfected over England's fourteen previous failures to win the competition away from home, it follows this pattern:

⚽ **Phase 1: Pre-tournament – Certainty that England Will Win the World Cup**

Alf Ramsey, the only English manager to win the trophy, predicted the victory of 1966. However, his prescience becomes less impressive when you realize that almost every England manager thinks he will win the trophy, including Ramsey in the two campaigns he didn't. When his team were knocked out in 1970 he was stunned and said, 'We must now look ahead to the next world cup in Munich where our chances of winning I would say are very good indeed.' England didn't qualify for that one.

Glenn Hoddle, England's manager in 1998, revealed only after his team had been knocked out 'my innermost thought, which was that England would win the World Cup'. Another manager who went home early, Ron Greenwood, confessed, 'I honestly thought we could have won the World Cup in 1982.' A month before the World Cup of 2006, Sven-Göran Eriksson said, 'I think we will win it.'

The deluded manager is never alone. As the England player Johnny Haynes remarked after elimination in 1958, 'Everyone in England thinks we have a God-given right to win the World Cup.' This belief in the face of all evidence was a hangover from empire: England is football's mother country and should therefore be the best today. The sociologist Stephen Wagg notes, 'In reality, England is a country like many others and the England football team is a football team like many others.' This truth is only slowly sinking in.

⚽ Phase 2: During the Tournament – England Meet a Former Wartime Enemy

In five of their last seven World Cups, England were knocked out by either Germany or Argentina. The matches fit seamlessly into the British tabloid view of history, except for the outcome. As Alan Ball summed up the mood in England's dressing room after the defeat to West Germany in 1970, 'It was disbelief.'

Even Joe Gaetjens, who scored the winning goal for the US against England in 1950, turns out to have been of German-Haitian origin, not Belgian-Haitian as is always said. And in any case, the US is another former wartime enemy.

⚽ Phase 3: The English Conclude that the Game Turned on One Freakish Piece of Bad Luck that Could Happen Only to Them

Gaetjens, the accounting student and dishwasher in a Manhattan restaurant who didn't even have an American passport, scored his goal by accident. 'Gaetjens went for the ball, but at the last moment, decided to duck,' England's captain Billy Wright wrote later. 'The ball bounced on the top of his head and slipped past the bewildered Williams.'

In 1970 England's goalkeeper Gordon Banks got an upset stomach before the quarter-final against West Germany. He was okay on the morning of the game and was picked to play, but a little later was discovered on the toilet with everything 'coming out both ends'. His understudy, Peter Bonetti, let in three soft German goals.

There was more bad luck in 1973, when England failed to qualify for the next year's World Cup because Poland's 'clown' of a goalkeeper, Jan Tomaszewski, unaccountably had a brilliant night at Wembley. 'The simple truth is that on a normal day we would have beaten Poland 6–0,' England's midfielder Martin Peters says in Niall Edworthy's book on England managers, *The Second Most Important Job in the Country*. Poland went on to reach the semi-finals of the '74 World Cup.

In 1990 and 1998 England lost in what everyone knows is the lottery of the penalty shoot-out. In 2002 everyone knew that the obscure, bucktoothed Brazilian kid Ronaldinho must have lucked out with the free kick that sailed into England's net, because he couldn't have been good enough to place it deliberately. In 2006 Wayne Rooney would never have been sent off for stomping on Ricardo Carvalho's genitals if Cristiano Ronaldo hadn't tattled on him. These things just don't happen to other countries.

✪ Phase 4: Moreover, Everyone Else Cheated

The Brazilian crowd in 1950 and the Mexican crowd in 1970 deliberately wasted time while England were losing by keeping the ball in the stands. The CIA (some say) drugged Banks. Diego Maradona's 'hand of God' single-handedly defeated England in

1986. Diego Simeone playacted in 1998 to get David Beckham sent off, and Carvalho and Ronaldo connived to do the same for Rooney in 2006.

Every referee opposes England. Those of his decisions that support this thesis are analysed darkly. Typically, the referee's nationality is mentioned to blacken him further. Billy Wright, England's captain in 1950, later recalled 'Mr Dattilo of Italy, who seemed determined to let nothing so negligible as the laws of the game come between America and victory'. The referee who didn't give England a penalty against West Germany in 1970 was, inevitably, an Argentine. The Tunisian referee of 1986 who, like most people watching the game, failed to spot the 'hand of God' has become legendary.

⚽ Phase 5: England Is Knocked Out Without Getting Anywhere Near Lifting the Cup

The only exception was 1990, when the team reached the semi-final. Otherwise, England have always been eliminated when still needing to defeat at least three excellent teams. Since 1970, Bulgaria, Sweden and Poland have got as close to winning a World Cup as England have.

Perhaps England should be relieved that they don't finish second. As Jerry Seinfeld once said, who wants to be the greatest loser? The science writer Stefan Klein points out that winning bronze at the Olympics is not so bad, because that is a great achievement by any standards, but winning silver is awful, as you will always be tortured by the thought of what might have been.

England have never been at much risk of that. The team won only five of their eighteen matches at World Cups abroad from 1950 to 1970, and didn't qualify for the next two tournaments in 1974 and 1978, so at least they have improved since. The general belief in decline from a golden age is mistaken.

⚽ Phase 6: The Day After Elimination, Normal Life Resumes

The one exception is 1970, when England's elimination may have caused the ruling Labour Party's surprise defeat in the British general election four days later. But otherwise the elimination does not bring on a nationwide hangover. On the contrary, England's eliminations are celebrated, turned into national myths, or songs, or commercials for pizza chains.

⚽ Phase 7: A Scapegoat Is Found

The scapegoat is never an outfield player who has 'battled' all match. Even if he directly caused the elimination by missing a penalty, he is a 'hero'.

Beckham was scapegoated for the defeat against Argentina in 1998 only because he got a red card after forty-six minutes. Writer Dave Hill explained that the press was simply pulling out its 'two traditional responses to England's sporting failure: heralding a glorious defeat and mercilessly punishing those responsible for it, in this case Posh Spice's unfortunate fiancé'.

Beckham wrote in one of his autobiographies that the abuse continued for years: 'Every time I think it has disappeared, I know I will meet some idiot who will have a go at me. Sometimes it is at matches, sometimes just driving down the road.' He added that he kept 'a little book in which I've written down the names of those people who upset me the most. I don't want to name them because I want it to be a surprise when I get them back.' One day they will all get upset stomachs.

Often the scapegoat is a management figure: Wright as captain in 1950, Joe Mears as chief selector in 1958, and many managers since. Sometimes it is a keeper, who by virtue of his position just stood around in goal rather than battling like a hero. Bonetti spent the rest of his career enduring chants of 'You lost the World Cup.' After retiring from football, he went into quasi exile as a mailman on a remote Scottish island.

In 2006 Cristiano Ronaldo was anointed scapegoat. Only after a defeat to Brazil is no scapegoat sought, because defeats to Brazil are considered acceptable.

⚽ Phase 8: England Enters the Next World Cup Thinking It Will Win It

That's what we wrote in 2009. We are not usually this prescient. If we predicted England's experience in South Africa in 2010 precisely, it's only because over the decades the route map of England's eliminations had become perfectly clear.

In phase 1 of our sequence, England flew to South Africa expecting to win the World Cup. That expectation wasn't particularly ludicrous: Fabio Capello's team had qualified with more dash than ever before, winning nine out of ten qualifying games.

Phase 2 was 'During the Tournament England Meets a Former Wartime Enemy'. Following the 4–1 thumping by the Germans in Bloemfontein, England had exited against Germany or Argentina in six of their last eight World Cups.

We called phase 3 'The English Conclude that the Game Turned on One Freakish Piece of Bad Luck that Could Happen Only to Them'. In 2010 this was of course Frank Lampard's shot that bounced inside the German goal without the referee noticing. As Lampard himself had lamented after England's previous elimination, in 2006, 'It seems to be the English way to lose in bizarre circumstances but it wears you down. It gets to the point where you want to tell Lady Luck to f*** off and take her bad sister with her.'

Phase 4 is 'Morever, Everyone Else Cheated'. FIFA should have been using goal-line technology, and the German keeper should have fessed up that Lampard had scored.

Phase 5 is 'England Is Knocked Out Without Getting Anywhere Near Lifting the Cup'. Had the English somehow beaten Germany, instead of losing by three goals, they would have then needed to beat Argentina, Spain and Holland.

In phase 6, normal life resumed the day after elimination. Riots broke out in English cities in the summer of 2011, not the summer of 2010.

In phase 7, the manager Capello was chosen as the nation's scapegoat. The Italian had raised English hopes by making his players look like world-beaters for two years, before finally pulling off the mask in South Africa to reveal them as the usual losers. Furthermore, as a foreigner he made a perfect scapegoat.

The World Cup as ritual has a meaning beyond football. The elimination is usually the most watched British television programme of the year. It therefore educates the English in two contradictory narratives about their country: one, that England has a manifest destiny to triumph, and, two, that it never does. The genius of the song 'Three Lions', English football's unofficial anthem, is that it combines both narratives: 'Thirty years of hurt / Never stopped me dreaming.'

There is an alternative universe in which Beckham didn't get sent off, Banks's stomach held up, Lampard's goal counted, and so on. In that universe England has won about seven World Cups. Many English people think they would have preferred that. But it would have deprived the nation of a ritual that marks the passing of time much like Christmas or New Year and celebrates a certain idea of England: a land of unlucky heroes that no longer rules the world, although it should.

Yet with that failure in 2010, something changed. To adapt T.S. Eliot, humankind can only take so much reality. England's umpteenth disappointment seems to have finally convinced the nation's fans and media to shed the fantasy of manifest destiny. When the understated Roy Hodgson replaced Capello as manager in 2012, he seemed intent on reducing expectations from low to zero. 'It's difficult to say what would constitute "success" at Euro 2012,' he mused at his first press conference. 'I'd like people to cut us a bit of slack.' People did. When his team lost the quarter-final on penalties to a former wartime enemy, Italy, nobody was very surprised. In 2014, when the pollsters YouGov conducted surveys in nineteen participating countries before the World Cup, the most pessimistic fans (jointly with Costa Ricans) were the English: only 4 per cent expected to win in Brazil. (The most optimistic supporters, incidentally, were Brazilians, 64 per cent of whom expected victory.) English pessimism proved justified. And at Euro 2016, the only surprise was that England went out to Iceland in the second round when everyone had been expecting them to stick to the usual script and go out on penalties in the quarter-final against France.

Finally, the English have become realistic. Perhaps helped by a general decline in national status, they are beginning to realize they are just another country, without any manifest destiny to triumph. (The vote for Brexit in 2016 was in part a last-ditch attempt by the older generation to preserve the idea of national exceptionalism.)

A PERFECTLY DECENT TEAM

Any mathematician would say it's absurd to expect England to win the World Cup.

England wins just over two-thirds of its matches. To be precise, from 1990 to 2010 (counting from the end of the 1990 World Cup to the end of the 2010 World Cup) England played 224, won 122, drew 57 and lost 45. If we treat a draw as half a win, this translates into a win percentage of 67.2 per cent. If we then break this down into five four-year World Cup cycles

England's win percentage has ranged between 65 and 76 per cent, except for the 1998–2002 cycle, when it slumped to 60 per cent. In other words, its performance for most of recent history has been fairly constant.

Yes, these statistics conceal some ghastly mishaps as well as some highs, but the statistics tell us that the difference between anguish and euphoria is a few percentage points.

On the face of it, winning two-thirds of the time – meaning bookies' odds of 1–2 on – is not too shabby in a two-horse race. Of course, some countries do even better. Brazil's win percentage is nearly 75 per cent. But against most teams, England is the deserved favourite. In the 1990–2010 period, England's win percentage was ninth best in the world.

The problem comes when we try to translate this achievement into winning tournaments. England's failure to win anything since the holy year of 1966 is a cause of much embarrassment for British expatriates in bars on the Spanish coast.

It is tricky to calculate the exact probability of England qualifying for a tournament, because it requires an analysis of many permutations of events. However, we can reduce it to a simple problem of multiplicative probability if we adopt the 'must-win' concept. For example, England failed to qualify for Euro 2008 by coming in third in its group behind Croatia and Russia. In doing so it won seven matches, lost three and drew twice (for an average win percentage of exactly 66.66 per cent). It was narrowly beaten by Russia, which won seven, lost two and drew three times (a win percentage of 70.83 per cent).

Suppose that to guarantee qualification you have to win eight games outright. Then the problem becomes one when you have to win eight out of twelve, where your winning probability in each game is 66 per cent. Calculating this probability is a bit more complicated, since it involves combinatorics.

The answer is a probability of qualification of 63 per cent. That means that England should qualify for fewer than two-thirds of the tournaments it enters. In fact, from 1970 to 2018 England qualified 74 per cent of the time: for nine out of twelve World Cups and eight out of eleven European Championships. Given that the number of qualifying matches has risen over time, England's performance is a touch better than you might expect.

The sad fact is that England is merely a good team that does better than most. This means it is not likely to win many tournaments, and it doesn't. When we first published this book, we called it *Why England Lose*. Going into the 2010 World Cup, English people often asked us: 'Aren't you worried about your title? What if England win?' We weren't very worried. Later we changed the title anyway, to *Soccernomics*, because it turned out (amazingly) that few English people wanted to buy a book called *Why England Lose*.

Until 2010, the English tended to think that England should do better. The team's usual status around the bottom of the world's top ten was not good enough. The national media, in particular, felt almost perpetually let down by the team. England were 'known as perennial underachievers on the world stage', according to the tabloid the *Sun*; its history 'has been a landscape sculpted from valleys of underachievement', said the *Independent* newspaper; the former England captain Terry Butcher grumbled in the *Sunday Mirror* in 2006 that 'historical underachievement has somehow conspired to make England feel even more important.'

'Why do England lose?' is perhaps the greatest question in English sports. In trying to answer it, we hear strange echoes from the field of development economics. The central question in that field is, 'Why are some countries less productive than others?' Some of the reasons why England lose would sound familiar to any development economist. So would the most common reason falsely cited for why England lose. Here are five reasons for England's eliminations – first two false ones, then three correct ones.

BRITISH JOBS FOR BRITISH WORKERS? WHY THERE ARE TOO MANY ENGLISHMEN IN THE PREMIER LEAGUE

When pundits gather to explain why England lose, their favourite scapegoat of the last few years is imports: the hundreds of foreigners who play in the Premier League. Here is England's midfielder Steven Gerrard speaking before England lost at home to Croatia and failed to qualify for Euro 2008: 'I think there is a risk of too many foreign players coming over, which would affect our national team eventually if it's not already. It is important we keep producing players.'

After all, if our boys can barely even get a game in their own league, how can they hope to mature into internationals? After England's defeat to Croatia, FIFA's president, Sepp Blatter, Manchester United's manager, Alex Ferguson, and UEFA's president, Michel Platini, all made versions of Gerrard's argument. In 2013 Greg Dyke, then chairman of England's Football Association, warned: 'In the future it's quite possible we won't have enough players qualified to play for England who are playing regularly at the highest level in this country or elsewhere in the world. As a result, it could well mean England's teams are unable to compete seriously on the world stage.'

These men are effectively blaming imports for the English lack of skills. The reasoning is that our own workers don't get a chance because they are being displaced by foreign workers. Exactly the same argument is often made in development economics. Why are some countries not very productive? Partly because their inhabitants don't have enough skills. The best place to learn skills – such as making toothpaste, or teaching maths, or playing football – is on the job. To learn how to make toothpaste, you have to actually make it, not just take a class to learn how to make it. But if you are always importing toothpaste, you will never learn.

That is why, for more than half a century, many develop-ment economists have called for 'import substitution'. Ban or tax certain imports so that the country can learn to make the stuff itself. Import substitution has worked for a few countries. Japan after the war, for instance, managed to teach itself from scratch how to make all sorts of high-quality cars and electrical gadgets.

The idea of import substitution in the Premier League has an emotional appeal to many English fans. Britons often com-plain about feeling overrun by immigrants, and few spots in the country are more foreign than a Premier League field on match day. Some clubs have wisely dispensed with English-men almost altogether. All told, Englishmen accounted for only 37 per cent of the minutes played by individual players in the Premier League in the 2007–2008 season before Croatia's night at Wembley. In 2017 that figure was almost exactly the same. To some degree, English football no longer exists.

'It is my philosophy to protect the identity of the clubs and country,' Platini said when he was president of UEFA. 'Man-chester United against Liverpool should be with players from Manchester and Liverpool, from that region. Robbie Fowler was from Liverpool. He grew up in that city, it was nice, but now you don't have the English players.'

Imagine for a moment that, after Brexit, English clubs decided to discriminate against players from other EU coun-tries. If that happened, the people who complain about imports would probably end up disappointed. If inferior English players were handed places in Premier League teams, they would have little incentive to improve. This is a classic problem with import substitution: it protects bad producers. What then tends to happen is that short-term protection becomes long-term protection.

But, in fact, Platini's entire premise was wrong. If people in football understood numbers better, they would grasp that the problem of the England team is not that there are too few Englishmen playing in the Premier League.

You could argue that English players account for 'only' about 37 per cent of minutes in the Premier League. Or you could argue that they account for a massive 37 per cent of minutes. That works out at over seventy Englishmen per match day – more than any other nationality in one of the world's best leagues. The Portuguese, Croatians and Uruguayans dream of accounting for 37 per cent of minutes in the Premier League, or indeed in any big league. If you have over seventy English-men playing regularly at that level, that should be enough to make up a decent squad of twenty-two.

In other words, English players get a lot of regular experi-ence in top-level club football. Even if we lump together the world's three toughest leagues – the Premier League, Spain's Primera División and Germany's Bundesliga – then only Ger-mans, Spaniards and possibly Brazilians play more tough club football. But certainly English players get far more experience in top-level football than, say, Croatians or Uruguayans do.

The experience of competing against the best foreign play-ers every week has probably helped English internationals to improve. Englishmen have had to get better just to stay in their club teams. They now learn about international football every week.

Indeed, since the Premier League has become more interna-tional, England's performances have improved. The switch from a mostly British league to a mostly foreign one can be dated to 1995, the year of the 'Bosman ruling' that allowed European players to play anywhere in Europe. Let's compare England's performances in the era of a British league, from 1968 to 1992, to its performances from 1998 to 2016. (We have consciously excluded the World Cup of 1966, which was an anomalous event given that England were playing at home.) In that first 'British' period to 1992, England reached one World Cup semi-final, in 1990. However, that was an exception. In the years when it had a national league, England reached the quarter-finals of major tournaments only four times in thirteen attempts.

By contrast, in the 'international' period since 1998, it has reached four quarter-finals in just ten attempts. Moreover, its win percentage at major tournaments rose from 52 per cent in 1968–1992 to 57 per cent in the 'international' period 1998–2016 (counting a draw as worth half a win.) The figures suggest that, if anything, the international league has been good for the England team.

In any case, English fans want to see teams full of foreign players. Platini wondered whether Liverpudlians could identify with a Liverpool team full of foreigners. Well, they seem to manage. Judging by the Premiership's record crowds despite its record ticket prices, fans still identify enough. England can have an excellent league, or it can have an English league, but it can't have both. Given the choice, fans seem to prefer excellence. In that sense, they are typical consumers. If you try to substitute imports, then, at least at first, consumers have to put up with worse products. They generally don't like that.

TIREDNESS: THE CHEAP-BATTERY PROBLEM

In every World Cup ever played, most goals were scored in the second halves of matches. That is natural: in the second half players tire, teams start chasing goals and gaps open up on the field. But England is the exception. Its scoring record is very unusual. Overall, in England's last nine big tournaments since 1998, it scored a slight majority of its goals – 29 out of 49 – in the *first* half. But the team's record in crucial games is much starker: in the matches in which it was eliminated from tournaments, it scored nine of its ten goals before half-time, and four of those ten in the opening ten minutes. (Think of the calamitous defeat to Iceland at Euro 2016: Rooney's penalty put England 1–0 up after four minutes.) In other words, England perform like a cheap battery.

The typical pattern (recall the 2–1 defeat by Brazil in Shizuoka in 2002) is for the English to get an early goal, and then re-create the British army's retreat from Dunkirk in 1940, spending much of the game with their backs to the wall in their own penalty area, before inevitably conceding.

England players and coaches often blame the team's humiliations on exhaustion. When one of the authors of this book asked the team's then manager Eriksson why England lost in the quarter-finals in the World Cup of 2002 and in Euro 2004, he replied that his players were tired after tough seasons. Was that really the only reason? 'I would say so,' Eriksson said. 'If you're not fit enough . . . In Japan, we never scored one goal in the second half.'

Ashley Cole, reflecting on the World Cup of 2006, noticed the same phenomenon but could not explain it: 'We had to be honest . . . and recognize something was amiss in the second halves. We just didn't know what.' However, some of his more thoughtful teammates did seem to know. Here is Lampard looking back on 2006:

> Throughout the tournament we had suffered in the heat. Our second-half performances were invariably below the standard of the first period and at its worst – against Paraguay in Frankfurt – most of us could barely walk, never mind run, in the latter stages of the match.

This echoes Gerrard's account of the previous tournament: 'The truth was that England were knackered at Euro 2004. . . .

A long, hard season took a terrible toll.' In 2010 in South Africa, too, England never scored in the second half.

Of course the English would blame tiredness. It sounds better than admitting that they just weren't good enough. But they can also seek support in a widely held belief in football: that an overcrowded schedule harms performance.

Lorenzo Buenaventura, Pep Guardiola's longstanding fitness coach, says: 'Medical studies in Italy have shown that the speed of post-match recovery depends entirely on the players' diet,' he told the writer Martí Perarnau. 'If they eat properly then they should have recovered 80 per cent of the glycogen in their muscles within three days. Only 80 per cent! Just imagine what it would be if they ate unhealthily!'

Coaches in particular like to blame tiredness. José Mourinho, in his first spell at Chelsea, even developed the theory that Arsenal controlled the Premier League's fixture list, and rigged it to give Chelsea a tough schedule. ('Is José Mourinho the only one who can look at the fixtures and find something very strange?')

And though the English only play as many league games as the Italians and Spaniards, they like to think that their season is uniquely exhausting. Even some foreigners agree. When Buenaventura was at Bayern Munich, he called the Bundesliga's month-long winter break 'a huge competitive advantage'. By contrast, he said, 'In England . . . they have games every two days during the Christmas break and any doctor will tell you how hard that is on the body. By the middle of January the players are all struggling badly.' Capello once told the FIFA website why he thought England didn't win summer tournaments:

They're the least fresh of any of the competing national sides, because their league doesn't have a break. It's like when you're driving a car: if you stop halfway to put fuel in then you'll definitely get where you want to go, but if you don't there's always the chance you'll be running on empty before you reach your goal. In my opinion the football played in the first half of the English season is much better than in the second half.

The theory that the 'terrible toll' of 'a long, hard season' is hurting England in summer tournaments sounds plausible. The only problem is that this theory isn't backed up by data.

Stefan and Guy Wilkinson went looking for evidence that overburdened players lose more matches. They studied rest days per player, rest days per team and distance travelled to away games for every Premier League season from 1992–1993 to 2012–2013. But in a database of over 10,000 matches, they found no link between number of games played and a club's results. It seems that squads are big enough, and coaches have become sufficiently versed in rotation since the 1990s, that nobody loses club games just because they are tired. 'Scheduling is not the problem it is often made out to be by managers and the media,' the paper concludes. 'If a team loses on the weekend after playing a midweek game a manager might complain that his players are tired but these excuses rarely appear if the team wins.'

It is true, according to Prozone stats, that the Premier League has more high-tempo attacks than other leagues. On the other hand, Prozone also shows that the league features fewer counterattacks – and those tend to be particularly exhausting, as they force both forwards and defenders to cover lots of space quickly.

Also, it turns out that English players don't go into tournaments with an unusually high number of games in their legs. At Euro 2016, for instance, BBC stats showed that England's players had played fewer minutes of club football than the Spanish and French internationals, and only very slightly more than the Germans. Sure, the Germans in the Bundesliga had had a winter break – but that means they would have had to cram more of those extra games into the spring, and so should have been more tired than the English come June.

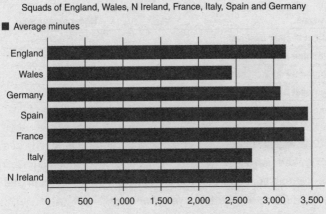

Squads of England, Wales, N Ireland, France, Italy, Spain and Germany

Source: BBC

Average number of minutes played in club football in 2015–2016

It may even be that players who have appeared in more games have an advantage, because experience outweighs exhaustion.

In short, we aren't convinced that the accumulated tiredness of a season is so uniquely damaging to England. Rather, we would focus on what happens during the tournaments themselves. England play an exhausting brand of football: high tempo, low possession. That's tiring, especially in blazing summer heat (it was over 100 degrees Fahrenheit in Shizuoka), in knockout rounds against the better European and Latin American teams who rarely give away the ball. If you're chasing opponents all afternoon in those conditions, you probably won't score many after half-time. So the problem isn't that England arrive at the tournament tired. It's that they exhaust themselves in the course of each game.

HOMEBOYS

Here's the secret to winning at sports: play at home. The book *Scorecasting* gives the percentages of games won by home teams from 2000 to 2009:

League	Home games won
Major League Baseball	53.9%
National Hockey League	55.7%
National Football League	57.3%
National Basketball Association	60.5%
International football in Europe	61.9%

Scorecasting argues that home-field advantage is mostly due to biased referees. However, psychological factors probably matter too. We know that you will generally sleep better in your own bed, and dive better in your own pool.

In an international tournament, every team except the host is playing away. But not every team is equally affected. Many national teams now consist chiefly of players who emigrated young to play abroad. That's true even of a country as rich as France: Antoine Griezmann moved to Real Sociedad in Spain aged 14, and Paul Pogba to Manchester United at 16. These players join the international 0.1 per cent, and soon feel more at home in a first-class airport lounge than on the average street in their home country. Playing abroad becomes routine for them: if it's Wednesday, this must be Azerbaijan.

But none of that is true for British (i.e. not just English) players. When FIFA TMS analysed international transfers of different nationalities from 2011 to 2013, it found that only 26 per cent of transfers involving British players were to a club outside Britain. The only two countries in the world with a more insular transfer history in that period were Myanmar and Nepal: over that period, both reported a grand total of zero foreign transfers (and just two domestic ones each). In short, few leading English players have much experience playing outside England. That hurts England at tournaments abroad.

This is another case of English insularity undermining English competitiveness. Most leading English players only get their first experience of football abroad in their twenties, when they start to play in the Champions League and for England. But even in the national team, they build up only limited foreign experience, because England from 2000 to 2014 played just 40 per cent of its friendlies abroad. That's in the lowest decile of all the countries on earth.

The decline of the away friendly is a relatively new phenomenon. In every decade from the 1920s to the 1980s, England played more away friendlies than home ones. But the annual Home Nations tournament against the other British teams was abandoned in 1984, and other away fixtures were dropped around that time for fear that English hooligans would destroy foreign cities. Then, in the 1990s, when money poured into football, a fixture at Wembley became more lucrative than almost any game abroad. Today an Englishman's home is his castle. Sure, England plays qualifying games abroad, but travelling to Andorra or Estonia is not a good substitute for a workout in front of a full-throated crowd in Berlin, Madrid or Rome. Friendlies are typically the only stage outside the knockout rounds of major tournaments where England can get used to playing the world's biggest teams.

There is some evidence from international data that teams that play more away friendlies perform better in competitive games, even if it's not clear why that is. Looking at data for the 2000–2014 period, we estimate that if England had played 50 per cent of its friendlies away (i.e. 10 percentage points more than it actually does), its win percentage would rise by three percentage points. Just by coincidence, those three points would entirely close the gap with Germany's performance. If England wants to win more, it would do better scheduling some foreign friendlies than barring foreigners from the Premier League.

Instead its main strategy for winning World Cups lately has been to bid to host the thing. Had England been awarded the 2006 or 2018 competition (which knowing what we now know about FIFA was never going to happen), that might well have paid off. Of the two tournaments the English have hosted, they won the 1966 World Cup and went out of Euro '96 only on penalties in the semi-final. That bodes well for Euro 2020, when the semi-finals and final will be played at Wembley. (Of course actually getting to the semi-final has been the tricky bit for England in recent times.)

For now, when England have to spend a month in a foreign country for a summer tournament – in effect, when they have to dive every day in someone else's pool – it's a shocking new experience for most of the squad.

EXCLUSION: HOW ENGLISH FOOTBALL DRIVES OUT THE MIDDLE CLASSES

The Romans built their empire with an army drawn from every part of society. Only when the militia became an elite profession open just to particular families did the empire start to decline. When you limit your talent pool, you limit the development of skills. The bigger the group of people you draw from, the more new ideas that are likely to bubble up. That's why large networks like the City of London and Silicon Valley, which draw talent from around the world, are so creative. So is the Premier League.

The problem of English football is what happens before the best English players reach the Premier League. The Englishmen who make it to the top are drawn very largely from one single and shrinking social group: the traditional working class. The country's middle classes are mostly barred from professional football. That holds back the national team.

There are many ways to classify which social class someone was born into, but one good indicator is the profession of that person's father. Joe Boyle, with some help from Dan Kuper, researched for us the jobs of the fathers of England players at the World Cups of 1998, 2002 and 2006. Boyle ignored jobs the fathers might have been handed after their sons' rise to stardom. As much as possible, he tried to establish what the father did while the son was growing up. Using players' autobiographies and newspaper profiles, he came up with the list below. It doesn't include every player (asked, for instance, what Wayne Bridge's dad did for a living, we throw up our hands in despair), but most are here. Another caveat: some of the dads on the list were absent while their boys were growing up. That said, here are their professions:

Player	Father's job
Tony Adams	Roofer
Darren Anderton	Ran removals company; later taxi driver
David Batty	Dustbin man
David Beckham	Heating engineer
Sol Campbell	Railway worker
Jamie Carragher	Pub landlord
Ashley Cole	None given, but in his autobiography he describes 'a grounded working-class upbringing in East London'
Joe Cole	Fruit and vegetable trader
Peter Crouch	Creative director at international advertising agency
Stewart Downing	Painter and decorator on oil rigs
Kieron Dyer	Manager of Caribbean social club
Rio Ferdinand	Tailor
Robbie Fowler	Labourer; later worked night-shift at railway maintenance depot
Steven Gerrard	Labourer (bricklaying, tarmacking, etc.)
Emile Heskey	Security worker at nightclub

Paul Ince	Railwayman
David James	Artist who runs gallery in Jamaica
Jermaine Jenas	Soccer coach in US
Frank Lampard	Footballer
Rob Lee	'Involved in a shipping company'
Graeme Le Saux	Ran fruit and vegetable stall
Steve McManaman	Printer
Paul Merson	Coalman
Danny Mills	Coach in Norwich City's youth academy
Michael Owen	Footballer
Wayne Rooney	Labourer, mainly on building sites; often unemployed
Paul Scholes	Gas-pipe fitter
David Seaman	Garage mechanic, later ran sandwich shop, then worked at steelworks
Alan Shearer	Sheet-metal worker
Teddy Sheringham	Policeman
Gareth Southgate	Worked for IBM
John Terry	Forklift-truck operator
Darius Vassell	Factory worker
Theo Walcott	RAF administrator; later joined services company working for British Gas

Many of these job descriptions are imprecise. What exactly did Rob Lee's dad do at the shipping company, for instance? Still, it's possible to break down the list of thirty-four players into a few categories. Eighteen players, or more than half the total, were sons of skilled or unskilled manual labourers: Vassell, Terry, Shearer, Seaman, Scholes, Rooney, Merson, McManaman, Ince, Heskey, Gerrard, Fowler, Adams, Batty, Beckham, Campbell, Ferdinand and Downing. Ashley Cole with his 'working-class upbringing' by a single mother is probably best assigned to this category, too. Four players (Jenas, Lampard, Mills and Owen) had fathers who worked in football. Le Saux and Joe Cole were both sons of fruit and vegetable traders. Anderton's dad ran a removals company, which seems to have failed, before becoming a cab driver. Sheringham's father was a policeman. Carragher's and Dyer's dads ran a pub and a social club, respectively. That leaves only five players out of thirty-four – Crouch, James, Lee, Southgate and Walcott – whose fathers seem to have worked in professions that required them to have had an education beyond the age of sixteen. If we define class by education, then only 15 per cent of England players of recent years had 'middle-class' origins.

The male population as a whole was much better educated. Of British men between ages 35 and 54 in 1996 – the generation of most of these players' fathers – a little more than half had qualifications above the most basic level, according to the British Household Panel Study.

English football's reliance on an overwhelmingly working-class talent pool was only moderately damaging in the past, when most English people were working class. In the late 1980s, 70 per cent of Britons still left school at the age of 16, often for manual jobs. But by then the growth of the middle class had already begun. In fact, middle-class values began to permeate the country, a process that sociologists call 'embourgeoisement'. It happened on what used to be the football terraces, which because of high ticket prices are now slightly more middle class than even the country at large.

Nowadays, about 70 per cent of Britons stay in school past the age of 16. Very nearly half of young people enter university. More and more, Britain is a middle-class nation. Yet because football still recruits overwhelmingly from the traditional working classes, it excludes an ever-growing swathe of the population. That must be a brake on the England team.

The shrinking of the talent pool is only part of the problem. Until at least the late 1990s British football was suffused, without quite knowing it, by British working-class habits. Some of these were damaging, such as the sausages-and-chips diet, or the idea that binge drinking is a hobby. 'Maybe in earlier generations the drinking culture carried over from the working-class origins of the players,' wrote Alex Ferguson in his 1999 autobiography. 'Most of them came from families where many of the men took the view that if they put in a hard shift in a factory or a coalmine they were entitled to relax with a few pints. Some footballers seem determined to cling to that shift-worker's mentality. . . . Also prevalent is the notion that Saturday night is the end of the working week and therefore a good time to get wrecked.' Of course, 'problem drinking' exists in the British middle classes, too. Equally, of course, most working-class people have no issues with alcohol. However, Ferguson is explicitly describing a traditional working-class attitude.

Another problem was that the British working classes tended to regard football as something you learned on the job, rather than from educationalists with diplomas. It was the attitude you would expect of an industry in which few people had much formal education. The late Ernie Walker, long-time secretary of the Scottish Football Association, who worked for decades to introduce coaching courses in Scotland, told us that clubs mocked his attempts as 'some new-fangled thing got up by college boys – as if there was shame in being educated'. He recalls that coaching and tactics became 'shame words'. 'People would say, "The trouble with football today is that there is too much coaching." That's like saying, "The trouble with school is that there's too much education."'

It would be crazy to generalize too much about the working classes. There is a strong working-class tradition of self-education. Large numbers of post-war Britons became the first people in their families to go to college. Nonetheless, the anti-intellectual attitudes that Walker encountered do seem to be widespread in the British game.

These attitudes may help explain why English managers and English players are not known for thinking about football.

When the Dutchman Johan Cruyff said, 'Football is a game you play with your head,' he wasn't talking about headers.

Over the past fifteen years these traditional working-class attitudes have begun to fade in British football. Foreign managers and players have arrived, importing the revolutionary notions that professional athletes should think about their game and look after their bodies. Andy Carroll's drinking now marks him out as an exception in the higher reaches of the English game. But one working-class custom still bars middle-class Britons from professional football: what you might call the 'anti-educational requirement'.

Most British football players still leave school at 16. The belief persists that only thus can they concentrate fully on the game. The argument that many great foreign players – Ruud Gullit, Dennis Bergkamp, Tostao, Socrates, Osvaldo Ardiles, Jorge Valdano, Slaven Bilić, Josep Guardiola, Andres Iniesta, Fernando Redondo, Kaká, Juan Mata and Vincent Kompany – finished school or even attended university is ignored. In 2017, four of Athletic Bilbao's squad alone had college degrees. By contrast, when Sunderland's Duncan Watmore graduated from Newcastle University with a first-class degree in economics in 2015, he was discussed in the media as a quasi-Einstein. There is no English international equivalent of the Italian defender Giorgio Chiellini (son of an orthopaedic surgeon and the vice-president of a Norwegian navigation company), who got an MBA in 2017.

Once again, Germany leads the way in making professional football upmarket. Of the twenty-four players in the German squad that won the World Cup in 2014, thirteen had finished the highest stream in the country's school system, the Gymnasium. That wasn't a coincidence. Germany's football academies have about the same proportion of Gymnasium students, about 55 per cent – which is slightly more than for the country's population as a whole. To cap it all, the scorer of the German goal in the final against Argentina, Mario Götze, is the son of a professor of data technology at the Technical University of Dortmund. German football 'has, it seems, become thoroughly middle class,' writes Raphael Honigstein in *Das Reboot*. British football has not. Indeed, many British coaches and players remain suspicious of educated people.

It is true that the clubs' new academies are meant to help players keep studying, but in practice this rarely happens. Some years ago, Simon visited the academy of an English club. It's an academy of some note: two of its recent graduates first played for their countries while still teenagers. But all the boys we met there, bright or otherwise, were sent to do the same single lowly vocational course in leisure and tourism to fulfil the academy's minimum educational requirements. Together the boys caused such havoc in class that all the other students had dropped out of the course. It's not that football players are too busy to study; they rarely train more than a couple of hours a day. Rather, it's that being studious is frowned upon.

English football consequently remains unwelcoming to middle-class teenagers. For instance, Stuart Ford, who at seventeen played for England Schools, gave up on becoming a professional because he got tired of listening to rants from uneducated coaches. Being middle class, he always felt like an outsider. He recalled, 'I was often goaded about my posh school or my gross misunderstanding of street fashion. That was just from the management.' Instead he became a Hollywood lawyer. Later, as a senior executive at a Hollywood studio, he was one of the people behind an unsuccessful bid to buy Liverpool FC.

Or there was the youth trainee at Oldham Athletic, whose teammates hounded him as an intellectual snob after he walked into the club one day carrying a copy of the midmarket newspaper the *Daily Mail*. He told us years later, 'Aside from the club-wide piss-taking, I had Deep Heat rubbed into the lining of my slips. I took so much verbal (and physical) abuse that month that I often wonder what would have happened had it been the *Financial Times*.' This man, incidentally, studied for that same vocational course in leisure and tourism with several future Premier League players.

One of the few remotely middle-class Englishmen to have made the national team in recent decades is Graeme Le Saux. He has a middle-class accent, reads the upmarket *Guardian* newspaper, and when he joined Chelsea looked forward to exploring London's galleries and museums. Naturally, throughout his career in football Le Saux was abused by his fellow professionals. So far, so typical. What's curious is the particular slant the abuse took. The heterosexual Le Saux was branded 'gay'. Liverpool's Robbie Fowler once pretended to offer him his bottom on the field during a game. Le Saux has said that during another match, the great metrosexual David Beckham called him a 'poof' (derogatory British slang for gay), though a spokesman for Beckham denied the allegation. But the point is that the class warriors in English football simply decided 'gay' can be a synonym for 'middle class' (and not in a good way).

Some of the more educated foreign players in the Premier League must view these goings-on with dismay. As they have no assigned place in the British class system, they have a touch more freedom to be intellectual. However, Erik Thorstvedt, Tottenham's Norwegian goalkeeper of the 1990s, does recall bread rolls being chucked at his head when he opened a broadsheet newspaper on the team bus.

If the British working classes get little education, that is mainly the fault of the middle-class people who oversee the UK's school system. Nonetheless, the educational divide means that any middle-class person entering British football feels instantly out of place.

Many middle-class athletes drift to cricket or rugby instead. Often, this represents a direct loss to football. For most people, sporting talent is fairly transferable until they reach their late teens. Many English football players, like Gary Neville and Gary Lineker, were gifted cricketers, too. Some well-known rugby players took up rugby only as teenagers, when they realized they weren't going to make it in football. And in the past, several paragons represented England in more than one sport. Only a few sports demand very specific qualities that can't be transferred: it's hard to go from being a jockey to being a basketball player, for instance. But English football competes with other ball games for talent, and it scares away the educated middle classes.

This is particularly sad because there is growing evidence that sporting talent and academic talent are linked. The best athletes have fast mental reactions, and those reactions, if properly trained, would make for high-calibre intellects.

Interestingly, some people inside English football have become aware of the game's class discrimination. Daniel Hargreaves, who in 2013 was working for Everton's academy with the remit to make sure its decisions were evidence-based (the sort of job that didn't exist in English football a few years earlier), spotted the club's tendency to scout mainly in working-class neighbourhoods. 'Traditionally we have core areas where we think we find players,' he said. 'But there's a growing middle class, there are more green spaces in the middle-class areas.' Has Everton operated an unintentional bias against the middle classes? 'I think evidence would suggest that's the case.'

But for now, this class bias helps explain why even though the academies of English clubs are the richest in the world, England doesn't produce better players than poor nations. Instead of trying to exclude foreigners from English football, it would be wiser to include more middle-class English people. Only when there are England players with educated accents might the national team maximize its potential.

CLOSED TO INNOVATIONS: ENGLISH FOOTBALL'S SMALL NETWORK

When the internet arrived, many pundits predicted the decline of the city. After all, why live in a small flat in Hackney when you could set up your laptop in an old farmhouse overlooking a sheep meadow?

The prediction turned out to be wrong. Cities have continued their growth of the past two hundred years, which is why flats in Hackney became so expensive. Meanwhile, the countryside has turned into something of a desert, inhabited by a few farmers and old people and used by the rest of us mostly for hiking. It turns out that people still want to live in dirty, overcrowded, overpriced cities. And the reason they do is the social networks. To be rural is to be isolated. Networks give you contacts.

Someone you meet at a party or at your kids' playground can give you a job or an idea. Just as the brain works by building new connections between huge bundles of neurons, with each connection producing a new thought, so we as individuals need to find ourselves in the centre of the bundle to make more connections.

Networks are key to the latest thinking about economic development. Better networks are one reason that some countries are richer than others. As it happens, networks also help explain why some countries have done better at football than England. English football's biggest problem until very recently was probably geography. The country was too far from the networks of continental Western Europe, where the best football was played.

Once upon a time, England was at the centre of football's knowledge network. From the first official football international in 1872, until at least the First World War, and perhaps even until England's first home defeat against foreign opposition (a largely forgotten 0–2 against Ireland in 1949, which came before the famous 3–6 against Hungary in 1953), you could argue that England was the dominant football nation. It was the country that exported football know-how to the world in the form of managers. The English expatriate manager became such a legendary figure that to this day in Spain and Italy a head coach is known as a 'mister'.

Many English people clung to the belief in England's supremacy long after it had ceased to be true. The astonishment each time England didn't win the World Cup ended only with the team's abject failures in the 1970s.

The gradual British decline in football echoes the decline in Britain's economic status. The country went from supreme economic power under Queen Victoria to having its hand held by the International Monetary Fund in the late 1970s. Admittedly, in football as in economics, most observers exaggerated Britain's slide. The country's position in the top ten largest economies was never much in doubt. But in football it became clear by 1970 at the latest that dominance had shifted across the Channel to the core of Western Europe. For the next forty years, that part of the Continent would be the most fertile network in football. And Britain was just outside it.

Western Europe's grip on global football probably peaked at the German World Cup of 2006. The region has only about 400 million inhabitants, or 6 per cent of the world's population, yet only once in that entire tournament did a Western European team lose to a team from another region: Switzerland's insanely dull defeat on penalties to Ukraine, a match that was the nadir of 10,000 years of human civilization.

In 2006 even Brazil couldn't keep up with Western Europe. Argentina continued its run of failing to beat a Western European team in open play at a World Cup since the final against West Germany in 1986 (though it did win two of the eight subsequent encounters against Europeans on penalties). Big countries outside the region, like Mexico, Japan, the US and Poland, could not match little Western European countries like Portugal, Holland or Sweden. If you understood the geographical rule of that World Cup, you could sit in the stands for almost every match before the quarter-finals confident of knowing the outcome.

At the 2010 and 2014 World Cups, the Western Europeans lost more often. In part this must be because they were playing outside their own continent. Still, they ended up on top again.

Western Europe excels at football for the same fundamental reason it had the scientific revolution in the sixteenth and seventeenth centuries and was for centuries the world's richest region. The region's secret is what the historian Norman Davies calls its 'user-friendly climate'. Western Europe is mild and rainy. Because of that, the land is fertile. This allows hundreds of millions of people to inhabit a small space of land. Moreover, as Malise Ruthven, the scholar of Islam, has pointed out, Europe has 'a higher ratio of coast to landmass than any other continent or subcontinent, and a coastline some 23,000 miles long – equivalent to the circumference of the globe'. No wonder Europeans were the first people to sail the world. Geography has always helped them exchange ideas, inside their continent and beyond. In short, they are networked.

From the World Cup in Germany, you could have flown in two and a half hours to any one of about twenty countries containing roughly 300 million people in total. That is the densest network on earth. There was nothing like that in Japan at the World Cup of 2002: the only foreign capital you can reach from Tokyo within that time is Seoul. South Africa, host in 2010, was even more isolated. And the only foreign capital within two hours' flight of Brazil's biggest city, São Paulo, is Asunción in Paraguay.

Admittedly the southern tip of South America has its own fruitful football network. Uruguay and Argentina, in particular, have benefited from their long exchange. Their capitals Monte-video and Buenos Aires are separated only by an easy boat ride, and in 1901 the two countries met in the first international match ever played outside the British Isles and North America (Canada and the US had already played each other twice by then).

Brazil has been playing against both its neighbours for over a century, too. It's no wonder that this is the only region outside Western Europe to have won World Cups. No wonder, either, that every winning country borders another winning country (if you count England and France, separated by 20 miles and a lot of seawater, as bordering each other). If you want to win, you need to be in a good neighbourhood.

But the Western European neighbourhood is unique. For centuries now, the continent's interconnected peoples have exchanged ideas fast. The scientific revolution could happen in Western Europe because its scientists were near one another, networking, holding a dialogue in their shared language: Latin. Copernicus, Polish son of a German merchant, wrote that the earth circled the sun. Galileo in Florence read Copernicus and confirmed his findings through a telescope. The Englishman Francis Bacon described their 'scientific method': deductions based on data. England at the time was very much a part of the European network. As the late British historian Tony Judt noted, cross-Channel ferries have been sailing between the English port of Dover and the French port of Calais for nearly 900 years. Even in the Bronze Age, boats went back and forth between the two coasts pretty much every day.

A typical product of that European network was the lens grinder, a crucial new machine in the development of the microscope in the early 1660s. Robert Hooke in London invented a new grinder, which made lenses so accurate that Hooke could publish a detailed engraving of a louse attached to a human hair. But meanwhile Sir Robert Moray, a Scot in London who knew what Hooke was up to, was sending letters in French about the new grinder to the Dutch scientist Christiaan Huygens. Thanks to Moray, Huygens had previously got hold of details of Hooke's balance-spring watch.

Moray and Huygens 'sometimes wrote to each other several times a week', writes the historian Lisa Jardine. Their letters crossed the Channel in days, or about as quickly as mail does now. Meanwhile, the French astronomer Adrien Auzout in Paris was getting copies of some of their letters. So Hooke's breakthroughs were being spread to his European competitors almost instantly.

All this irritated Hooke. But the proximity of many thinkers in Western Europe created an intellectual ferment. That is why so many of the great scientific discoveries were made there. These discoveries then helped make the region rich.

Centuries later, football spread the same way. In the nineteenth century the game infected Western Europe first, because there it had the shortest distances to travel. Later the proximity of so many peoples brought the region two world wars. After 1945, Western Europeans decided they could live crammed together only under a sort of single government: the European Union. Borders opened, and the region became the most integrated in the history of the world.

Again the best ideas spread fastest there, just as they had in the scientific revolution. The region's football benefited. One of the first men who carried tactical ideas around Europe was the Hungarian-Jewish Holocaust survivor Béla Guttmann, possibly football's leading coach in the 1950s and 1960s. 'In the course of my long career I have been to a lot of countries and have also worked in some of them,' said Guttmann, who coached everywhere from the Netherlands to Uruguay (but mostly in Europe). 'If I saw anything good in football, I stole it immediately and kept it for myself. After a while, I mixed myself a cocktail from these stolen delicacies.'

The tradition continued with Arrigo Sacchi. The Italian's father was a shoe manufacturer in Ravenna, Italy, and the young Sacchi used to accompany him on business trips. He saw a lot of games in Germany, Switzerland, France and the Netherlands. 'It opened my mind,' he later said. As manager of AC Milan in the 1980s, he imported a version of Dutch football that revolutionized the Italian game.

Another great European networker was Arsène Wenger. While growing up in a village in the French Alsace, near the German border, he used to watch the legendary German football programme *Die Sportschau* on Saturday afternoons. He became a fan of Borussia Mönchengladbach, and generally absorbed German football. Later Wenger took a French coaching course and came to admire Dutch 'total football'. The point is that he was taking in influences from all the countries around him. It was easy because they were so close. More recently, Pep Guardiola has borrowed from Cruyff, Sacchi and Capello as well as from Spanish-speaking Latin Americans such as Marcelo Bielsa. Intriguingly, Guardiola uses the same 'theft' metaphor that Guttmann did: 'Ideas belong to everyone and I have stolen as many as I could.'

Ideas spread even more quickly in European football than in other economic sectors, because football is the most integrated part of the Continent's economy. Only about 3 per cent of all Western Europeans live in a different European Union country, because few companies bother hiring bus drivers or office administrators from neighbouring countries. In some professions, language barriers stop workers from moving abroad. But many football players do find work abroad, largely because television advertises their wares to employers across Europe. And so most of the EU's best players have gathered in the English and Spanish leagues or at Bayern Munich, and meet one another on weekday nights in the Champions League. This competition is the European single market come to life, a dense network of talent. There's always much debate about the superiority of one football model over another – the Bundesliga versus the Premier League versus the Spanish league and Italy's Serie A – but the real point is the intensity of competition inside Europe, on the field and in the boardroom. That forces the big clubs constantly to strive for improvements.

The teams in the Champions League can draw talent from anywhere in the world. Nonetheless, an overwhelming majority of their players are Western Europeans. With the world's best players and coaches packed together, the world's best football is constantly being refined there. That's what the German coach Joachim Löw explained at the press conference after the World Cup final in Rio in 2014. Immaculate as ever, and speaking despite the circumstances in his usual thoughtful manner, he reminded us how the Germans rebuilt their football after hitting a low in the early 2000s. They learned passing from the Dutch and Spaniards, speed of play from the English Premier League and minority recruitment from the French. Their leading club, Bayern, imported as head coach first the leading Dutch thinker on football, Louis van Gaal, and then the leading Spaniard, Guardiola. Löw had also sent his assistant to chat with the coach of the Swiss handball team, who had developed the tactic of playing without a goalkeeper – an idea Löw himself has toyed with. In football, you always have to keep innovating even when you are the best.

The German ideas theft paid off in Brazil. The best European countries are moving towards a game in which there are no specialists anymore: no non-passing man-markers or big centre-forwards or ankle-biting midfielders who drop every ball in the feet of a skilled playmaker. Rather in the better teams, especially Germany, every player looks like a passing midfielder – even the German keeper, Manuel Neuer. Lionel Messi completed 242 passes at the World Cup; Neuer completed 244. His team completed 3,754 in total, one more than Spain in 2010, and the most for any team at any World Cup since 1966 (we simply don't know passing totals before then). Spain's tiki-taka isn't dead. It has just been updated by Germany.

There are different ways to play this fast-passing European game. Germany and Spain are in the spirit of Guardiola: hog the ball and pass non-stop. Holland in 2014 were more like José Mourinho's teams: let the opposition have the ball, but when you win it, pass forward immediately, ideally shooting within three seconds of gaining possession. However, both the Dutch and Germans rely on moving the ball quickly and accurately.

Western European football is a passing game played by athletes. Rarely does anyone dribble, or keep the ball for a second. You pass instantly. It's not the beautiful game – dribbles are prettier – but it works best. All good teams everywhere in the world now play this way. Chris Anderson and David Sally showed in their book *The Numbers Game* how statistically alike the top European leagues are. Whether in the English Premier League, Serie A, the Bundesliga or Spain's premier division, the average team completed similar numbers of passes per game, of similar lengths, and had comparable numbers of shots and corners. In all four leagues, the average game produces somewhere between 2.5 and three goals. The differences between these nations 'are cosmetic, shallow', the authors conclude. 'If it was not for the shirts, you would not be able to tell them apart.' All four leagues are producing Western European football. We saw in 2014 that even the Brazilians cannot compete with the Europeans. Brazil has lost dominance in football even as it gets richer, because it is excluded from the knowledge networks of Western Europe. In recent years it hasn't even tried to pass at European pace. The 7–1 defeat to Germany was a one-off, but Brazil's decline is a long-term phenomenon.

Western Europe has discovered the secret of football. More precisely, a core group of Western European countries has, namely, five of the six nations that in 1957 founded the European Economic Community, ancestor of the European Union. (We'll leave out the sixth founding nation, the hopeless minnow Luxembourg.) Germany, France, Italy, Holland and even Belgium don't all play in exactly the same style. Holland and Italy, say, are rather different. But they all adhere to the basic tenets of rapid collectivized Western European football. Here are some results from the period 1968–2006:

⚽ The core five countries won twelve European Championships and World Cups between them.

⚽ The countries at the corners of Europe – the Brits, the Iberians, the Balkans, the former Soviet bloc and Scandinavian nations north of the Baltic Sea – between them won one: Greece's European Championship of 2004, delivered by a German coach.

⚽ Europe's only other trophies in this period went to Denmark and Czechoslovakia. Denmark enjoys an utterly permeable border with the five core countries. Czechoslovakia was the exception, the only Eastern European country to win anything in this period.

Countries separated from the core of the EU – either by great distance, by poverty or by closed borders under dictatorships – often underperform in football. In the vast landmass running from Portugal in the south-west to Germany in the north-east, and including Croatia and Bosnia just east of Italy, every country of more than 2 million inhabitants qualified for the World Cup 2014. The nations that didn't make it were on Europe's margins: the Scots, Irish and Welsh, all the Scandinavians, the Turks and most of Europe's eastern edge. The countries at great distance – and it can be a distance of the mind rather than geographical distance – are often out of touch with core European football. Our point is not that 'Europe' leads the world; it's that continental Western Europe does. Many countries on Europe's margins have traditionally had dysfunctional indigenous styles of football. The Greeks, for instance, dribbled too much. The Brits played mindless kick-and-rush.

Again, this is explained by theories of networks. If you are on the periphery, like the British were until recently in football, it's harder to make new connections, because you have to travel farther. Worse, those not on the periphery see you as only a second-best connection. You are the end of the line, not the gateway to a new set of connections. That's why foreign countries stopped hiring English coaches or even English players. As a result, the people on the periphery become more and more isolated and insular. The Ukrainian manager Valeri Lobanovsky was a football genius, but during the days of the Soviet Union he was so isolated that when a Dutch journalist came to interview him in the mid-1980s, Lobanovsky pumped him for information about Holland's players. As we'll discuss later in the book, Spain had the same problem under General Franco's dictatorship. 'Europe ends at the Pyrenees' was the saying in those days.

Gradually isolation becomes your mind-set: after a while you don't even want to adopt foreign ideas anymore. Anyone who has spent time in England – particularly before 1992 – has witnessed this attitude. Isolation can lead you into your own blind alleys that nobody else appreciates. For instance, the long refusal of English players to dive may have been an admirable cultural norm, but they might have won more games if they had learned from continental Europeans how to buy the odd penalty.

British isolation has gone in phases. The era of extreme separation from Europe began on Sunday, 3 September 1939, when the country's borders closed on the outbreak of the Second World War. In football, that isolation deepened when

English clubs were banned from European competitions after the Heysel disaster of 1985. They lost what modest network they had.

But between 1990 and 1994, British isolation began to break down: English clubs were readmitted to European competitions, new laws enforced free movement of labour and capital within the EU, and Eurostar trains and budget airlines connected Britain to the Continent. London turned into a global city. English became the global language. Southern England, at least, became part of core Europe again, just as it was during the scientific revolution.

The embrace of internationalism from the early 1990s meant, for a while, the end of English football managers managing England or the best English clubs. You wouldn't appoint a Frenchman to manage your baseball team, because the French don't have a history of thinking hard about baseball. And you wouldn't appoint an Englishman to manage your football team, because the English don't have a history of thinking hard about football. After repeated failures with the traditional British style of kick-and-rush, the English embraced European football. England hired a Swedish manager with long experience in Italian football, Sven-Göran Eriksson.

At this, the conservative *Daily Mail* newspaper lamented, 'The mother country of football, birthplace of the greatest game, has finally gone from the cradle to the shame.' It was a wonderful statement of 'English exceptionalism': the belief that England is an exceptional football country that should rule the world playing the English way. However, the obvious statistical truth is that England is not exceptional. It is typical of the second-tier football countries outside the core of Western Europe.

The numbers suggest that England needed foreign knowledge. From autumn 1996 to Euro 2016 England had two foreign managers and seven English managers, including three

caretakers (Stuart Pearce, Howard Wilkinson and Peter Taylor).
The foreigners have the better record:

Manager	WPC* all games	Played	Qualified for finals	Played in finals	WPC* in finals
English	66	124	4/5	18	44
Foreign	73	109	5/5	18	58

* win percentage

The Swede Eriksson should be remembered as the great qualifier: for the first time since the 1960s, he ensured that England
consistently made it to the major tournaments. But foreign
managers have also performed slightly better at the final tournaments themselves: Eriksson's and Capello's England teams
never lost at the group stages, and reached three quarter-finals
and one round of sixteen. By contrast, the English managed
one semi (at home at Euro '96), one appearance in the last
sixteen, and two exits in the first round.

Foreign managers have overachieved with England. This is
not merely because Eriksson and Capello had a 'golden generation' of players to work with. Many of the same men who
played well for the Swede and the Italian performed abysmally
for Steve McClaren and Kevin Keegan. It's painful to imagine how
well England might have done if the FA had stopped discriminating against foreigners decades earlier. In the same way, British
cycling, cricket and athletics have recently become world-class
by stealing foreign ideas (and possibly with the help of a few
steroids). In tennis Andy Murray became the first male Briton to
win Wimbledon since 1936 largely because as a teenager he
had taken himself off to an academy in Barcelona. (If only some
English football players had made the same move.)

When it comes to England's football coaches, it may sound
odd that a foreign passport can make such a difference. After
all, you might think that England's players these days have

enough foreign experience of their own. They play with and for and against foreigners at their clubs every week. Michael Owen, the first England international to play his entire professional career after the border-opening Bosman ruling of 1995, told us that he had grown up a 'European' rather than a purely English footballer. Surely players like him no longer need foreign managers?

Why they do was best demonstrated that miserable night at Wembley against Croatia in 2007. A team of Englishmen managed by an Englishman played like caricatures of Englishmen. Gerrard in particular was a remarkable sight, charging around in the rain at top pace, hitting impossibly ambitious passes, constantly losing the ball. He played like a headless chicken, or like an English footballer circa 1988.

For Liverpool, Gerrard usually played like a European sophisticate. He had mastered the international, globalized style of top-class modern football. The problem against Croatia was that there wasn't a foreigner on the field or the bench to check him. When things began going badly, he shed that cosmopolitan skin, returned to childhood and played like an Englishman of old. He and all the other England players had grown up until about the age of twenty playing an only slightly diluted version of English football. Because of that upbringing, national football cultures continue to exist. That's why England still needs a foreign manager to correct its players' flaws.

Other peripheral countries from Greece to the US have followed the English example, and hired foreign coaches from the core of Europe. Importing know-how turned out to be a reasonably good remedy for the problem of isolation, which makes it even odder that in 2006 England did an about-face and appointed the Englishman McClaren, who had never even worked abroad. The English Football Association didn't realize that England, as a recovering isolationist, still needed foreign help. Rooney, for one, seems to have known better. Here he is in his autobiography, damning the newly appointed McClaren with faint praise: 'But he's a good coach, always smiling. I'm glad he's got the job. I think he was the best Englishman available.'

By hiring Fabio Capello to succeed McClaren in 2007, England accepted the need for continental European know-how. Capello was like one of the overpaid consultants so common in development economics, flying in on business class to tell the natives what to do. His job was to teach the English some of the virtues of Western European football, such as not exhausting yourself before half-time.

Italians know exactly how to measure out the ninety minutes. They take quiet periods, when they sit back and make sure nothing happens, because they know that the best chance of scoring is in the closing minutes, when exhausted opponents will leave holes. That's when you need to be sharpest. In the World Cup of 2006, typically, Italy knocked out Australia and Germany with goals in the final three minutes.

But the English (as opposed to British) vote for Brexit expressed a widespread desire for a bit more isolation. That desire had already become visible in football. Since 2012, England has been hiring English managers again. Roy Hodgson, Sam Allardyce and Gareth Southgate didn't have brilliant coaching CVs, but they had the right passport. No wonder England underachieves.

But hang on a moment: who says it underachieves?

SHOULD DO BETTER: IS ENGLAND WORSE THAN IT OUGHT TO BE?

That England underachieves is usually taken for granted in the British media. After all, the team hasn't won anything since 1966, and sometimes doesn't even qualify for tournaments. Clearly that is not good enough for 'the mother country of football, birthplace of the greatest game'.

But does England really underachieve? Or is it just that the English expect too much of their team? To answer this, we first need to work out how well England should do, given its resources.

Before we are accused of looking for excuses, let's consider what is and isn't possible. A five-year-old can't win the 100 metres finals at the Olympics, and neither can a seventy-year-old. You aren't going to have a career in the NBA if you are only five foot tall, and you'll never ride the winner in the Kentucky Derby if you are six foot eight. It is very unlikely that you will have a career in show jumping if your parents earn less than £40,000 per year, you probably won't win a boxing match if you've never had any training as a boxer and you won't have a shot at being world chess champion unless you can persuade a team of grand masters to act as your seconds. Genetics are beyond our control; training depends partly on our own effort, but partly on the resources that other people give us.

What is true for the individual is also true for the nation. During his tenure an England football manager cannot easily (a) increase the size of the population from which he will have to draw the talent, (b) increase the national income so as to ensure a significant increase in the financial resources devoted to developing football, or (c) increase the accumulated experience of the national team by very much. (England played over 950 games from 1872 to 2016, and currently plays around a dozen games per year, so each extra game doesn't add much to the history.)

Yet in any international match, these three factors – the size of the nation's population, the size of the national income and the country's experience in international football – hugely affect the outcome. It's unfair to expect Jamaica, say, to perform as well as much larger, more experienced and richer Germany. It is fairer to assess how well each country should perform given its experience, income and population, and then measure that expected performance against reality. Countries like Jamaica or Luxembourg will never win a World Cup. The only measure of performance that makes any sense for them is one based on how effectively they use their limited resources. The same exercise makes sense for England, too, if only as a check on tabloid hysteria: does England really underperform given what it has to work with?

In absolute terms England is about tenth in the world. That was the country's average position in the FIFA rankings from 1992 to 2016. England's highest ranking in this period was fourth and its lowest was twenty-first, but most of the time England moved in a fairly narrow band between fifth and fifteenth place. It might be argued that England aren't winning the all-important games (perhaps because of fading legs in the knockout games of major tournaments, and the national penalty neurosis), but the fact is that they rank only a notch below the world's best teams.

But we want to know how well England does in relative terms – not relative to the media's expectations but relative to English resources. Might it be that England performs about as well as it should, given the country's experience, population and income?

To work this out, we need to know the football results for all the national teams in the world. Luckily, we have them. There are a number of databases of international matches, but the best historical database was assembled by Russell Gerrard, a mathematics professor at Cass Business School in London. By day Gerrard worries about mathematical ways to represent the management problems of pension funds. For example, one of his recent papers is snappily titled 'Mean-Variance Optimization Problems for the Accumulation Phase in a Defined Benefit Plan'. It concerns, among other things, Lévy diffusion financial markets, the Hamilton–Jacobi–Bellman equation and the Feynman–Kac representation. As you might expect, Gerrard has been meticulous in accumulating the football data, which took him seven years of his life. His database runs from 1872 to 2001 and includes 22,130 games.

To update Gerrard's database we've used results compiled by Christian Muck on his website Länderspielausgabe, which he very kindly put on spreadsheet for us. Christian also leads a dual life; by day he is a Scrum-Master/software developer for an insurance company in Luxembourg, and by night he runs his database. He started out in 2000 helping collect some data for a computer game, and then started to create HTML pages of results because no searchable databases existed at the time. Now he maintains the site as a way to practise his programming skills. And we say: long may he keep practising.

THE GERRARD/MUCK DATABASE

Later in the book, we will crunch Gerrard/Muck data to discover which is the best football country on earth, and which punches most above its weight. But here, let's limit ourselves to a sneak preview of where England stands. The distant past is of limited relevance. Let's therefore concentrate on recent history, from 2000 to 2014. England played 158 matches in this period. It won 53 per cent of them and drew 28 percent, for a 'win percentage' of 67 per cent (remember that for these purposes we treat a draw as half a win). That is near the middle of the country's historical range.

We want to see how much of a team's success, match by match, can be explained by population, wealth and experience. However, for this purpose win percentage is not the best measure of success, because any two wins are not the same. We all know that the 1–5 away win against Germany in 2001 is not the same as a drab 1–0 against Luxembourg.

Instead we chose goal difference as our measure, since for any match we expect that the greater the difference between the two teams' populations, wealth and experience, the greater will be the disparity in scores. (Of course, a positive goal difference tends to be highly correlated with winning.)

We then analysed the Gerrard/Muck database of matches using the technique of multiple regression. Quite simply, multiple regression is a mathematical formula (first identified by the mathematician Carl Friedrich Gauss in 1801) for finding the closest statistical fit between one thing (in this case success of the national team) and any other collection of things (here experience, population and income per head). The idea is beautifully simple. The problem used to be the endless amount of computation required to find the closest fit. Luckily, modern computers have reduced this process to the press of a button (just look up 'regression' on your spreadsheet package).

For each international match you simply input the population, income per head and team experience of the two nations at that date, and in seconds you get a readout telling you how sensitive (on average) the team's performance is to each factor. We will also take into account home advantage for each match.

Collecting the data is usually the toughest part. Happily, we have the Penn World Tables that provide the best data on historical national income statistics going back to 1950. (They can be downloaded online.*) We have used the Penn data for population and national income of 184 countries. We will unveil our findings about the other 183 countries in the next few chapters. Here, we will focus just on England and its supposed underperformance.

In the first few editions of Soccernomics, we used data from 1980–2001 to estimate performance, but for the present edition we have re-run the entire exercise using international results over the period 2000–2014. While this is a slightly

* Robert C. Feenstra, Robert Inklaar and Marcel P. Timmer (2015), 'The Next Generation of the Penn World Table', *American Economic Review*, 105(10), 3150–3182, available for download at www.ggdc.net/pwt

shorter period, in fact there were more international matches played: just under 22,000 compared with just under 21,000.

We've also tweaked the model a little. As before, we include home advantage, population ratio, GDP per capita ratio and experience ratio, but this time we also included 'fixed effects' specific to each country. These estimate the extent to which the country deviates from the average across the entire period – in other words, whether the country overachieves or underachieves given its resources.

How good is our model? Well, if it could predict the outcome of individual games there would be no point in watching football. It's one of the most random of sports, with lots of victories for underdogs, which is one reason why it's so entertaining. Still, our model is very accurate *on average*. Over the 158 England games in our database, the team scored 133 goals more than its opponents. Our model 'predicted' England's goal difference at +125, or only eight goals fewer than the actual number. That's an average error of just one goal every twenty games. And this is fairly typical for the data: of the 125 nations that played over 100 games in the period, there was only one case where the average error exceeded a goal every five games (the Philippines, who conceded about one goal per four games fewer than expected). Rather than thinking of this as a forecasting model, think of it as a way of accurately summarizing recent history. Our model is pretty good at explaining a country's long-term record. It's less good at predicting any individual match.

Compared with our estimates for the 1980–2001 era, home advantage has become even more important. The difference between playing at home and playing away is now worth one goal. The next most important variable we identify is experience, which we measure by the number of games a country has played in its history. Having twice the international experience of your opponent is worth 0.84 goals per game (or 8.4 goals per ten games). Income and population size are less important. Having double the income per person of the opposing country is worth 0.4 goals per game, or two extra goals every five games. Having double the population of your opponent is worth about the same: 0.42 goals per game. Note that all these effects have diminishing returns. For instance, having four times your opponent's income does not give you an advantage of 0.8 goals, but something less.

In other words, being large and rich helps a country win matches, but having a long football history helps a lot more. This is why the Portuguese and Croats win more than very large but inexperienced China and India. The importance of experience is not good news for the US.

For now, we are interested only in England. Are its resources so outstanding that it should do better than merely ranking around tenth in the world?

First, let's look at experience. England is one of the most experienced countries in football. It played 934 internationals between 1872 and the end of the 2014 World Cup. According to our data, only Sweden (977) and Argentina (951) played more. However, England's much vaunted history is not worth much against the other leading football nations, because most of them have now accumulated similar amounts of experience. Brazil, Uruguay, France, Italy and the Netherlands had all played more than 700 internationals by 2014, as had Germany and Russia if we include their pre-1990 incarnations.

When it comes to our second variable, national income, England scores high, too. It is usually one of the richest of the serious football countries. Where England falls short is in size. What often seems to go unnoticed is that England's population of 53 million puts it at a big disadvantage against the countries it likes to measure itself in football. Not only is Germany much bigger, with over 80 million inhabitants, but France has 66 million and Italy 60 million. Among the leading

European nations, England is ahead only of Spain (47 million). So in football terms, England is an experienced, rich, but medium-sized competitor.

The extra element we added to the model for this edition is England's fixed effect. This is worth minus 0.3 goals per game. In other words, between 2000 and 2014 the 'England' effect was to score three goals fewer every ten games than we would expect based on the country's size, experience and wealth. That's not that bad. Italy – which managed to win the World Cup in 2006 – had almost exactly the same fixed effect. So did Sweden. Overall, England sits just below the middle of the pack of nations so far this century, a touch beneath where it should be given its resources.

To get a feel for how this works, consider England's performance at the World Cup 2014. England lost 2–1 to both Italy and Uruguay, drew 0–0 with Costa Rica, and flew home in disgrace. Our model suggests that the team definitely underperformed. Given their resources, they should have lost to Italy but beaten smaller, poorer, less experienced Costa Rica. Over the three games, the model predicted a goal difference of +1.1, rather than the actual outcome of minus two. Still, it's worth noting that the model expected close results: in none of the three games was the predicted margin larger than a single goal.

But now let's look at Euro 2012. There England slightly overachieved: its predicted total goal difference over its four matches was about +0.75, but its actual goal difference was +2, and it went out to Italy only on penalties.

Whether you think that is 'good enough' for England is a matter of taste. What is clear is that the difference in almost every case is the margin of a single goal or a penalty shootout. Given that on average over the fifteen years England's goal difference is very close to what the model predicts, the statistical margin between success and failure is comparable to the proverbial thickness of the paint on the goalposts. In other words, when we talk about England's performance at a tournament, we are often simply talking about luck.

Later in the book we will reveal our global table for relative performance: a ranking of the teams that did best relative to their countries' experience, income and populations. For now, we'll just say that England came in eleventh out of 182 countries in terms of goal difference per game between 2000 and 2014, almost exactly where the model predicts England should be and in line with the average FIFA ranking

Our conclusion: England is a strong football nation that in recent years has underperformed a bit, though not nearly as much as the English tabloids seem to think. All it needs to bring home a trophy is better timing (it must win fewer friendlies and more World Cup semis), some penalty-taking skills and a few million more inhabitants.

In fact, England's record against Germany is really rather good of late, so long as you don't start out with the expectation that England should always win because we invented the game. Overall from 2000 to 2014, England played Germany seven times. England won three and lost four. Its goal difference over the seven games was zero (the −3 suffered in the 2010 World Cup in South Africa being wiped out by the +4 in the World Cup qualifier in Munich in 2001). Given that Germany is slightly richer and has 27 million more inhabitants, England's expected goal difference was −1.6.

The 'thirty years of hurt' shouldn't be a mystery. A midsized country like England, which has only about the same amount of experience as the world's leading nations, simply should not expect to be world-beaters. As so often, the former England defender Jamie Carragher gets it right:

The psychology of our international game is wrong. England ought to be embracing the idea of being the underdog on

the world stage. . . . We should be revelling in the image of
the plucky outsider trying to unbalance the superpowers of
Argentina and Brazil, while matching the French, Germans
and Italians.

Still, it is true that over its history, England could have been
luckier. A better penalty here, a stronger goalkeeper's stomach there, Darren Anderton's shot rolling home in extra time
against Germany at Euro '96 instead of hitting the post, and
it all could have been different. What we see here is partly
the enormous role of luck in history. We tend to think with
hindsight that a team that did well in a particular tournament
was somehow always going to do well and a team that lost
was doomed to do so. The winner's victory comes to seem
inevitable. This is a common flaw in the writing of any kind of
history.

In fact, though, inevitable victories hardly ever happen in
football tournaments. Perhaps the only recent case was Brazil at the World Cup of 2002. Just how dominant the country was dawned on a leading European club manager a few
months after the final. This manager was trying to sign Brazil's goalkeeper, Marcos. After all, Marcos was a world champion. Marcos visited the club and did some physical tests, in
which he didn't perform particularly well. Never mind, thought
the manager, the guy won the World Cup. So he offered
Marcos a contract. At two o'clock the next morning, the manager was awakened at home by a phone call. It was Marcos's
agent.

The agent said, 'I'm sorry, but Marcos won't sign for you.'

The sleepy manager said, 'All right, but why not?'

Then the agent confessed. A couple of years before the
World Cup, Marcos had broken his wrist. It had never healed
properly. But his old club manager, Luiz Felipe Scolari, became
manager of Brazil and put Marcos in the team. Suddenly

Marcos was going to a World Cup. Every day at the tournament, the agent explained, Marcos was in pain. He could barely even train. In matches he could barely catch a ball. Every day Marcos told himself, 'I really must tell Scolari about my wrist.' But he could never quite bring himself to. So he went on, day after day, until he found that he had won the World Cup. Brazil was so superior that it won the World Cup with a crocked goalkeeper.

However, such dominance is very rare. Normally, the differences between teams in the final stages of a World Cup are tiny. The difference between an England team being considered legendary or a failure is two to three games, each generally decided by a single goal, over two years. After all, the difference between making a World Cup and spending the summer on the beach can be just a point. Sometimes it's a point that you lost by hitting the post. Sometimes it's a point garnered by a rival in a match you didn't even play in.

Once you're at the World Cup, the difference between going home ignominiously in the first round and making the semi-finals is often a matter of a few inches here or there on a couple of shots. The greatest prize in the sport hinges on a very few moments. Jonathan Wilson puts it well in his *Anatomy of England*: 'One moment can shape a game, and one game can shape a tournament, and one tournament can shape a career. Football is not always fair.' Wilson points out 'one of the major problems of international football: that there is so little of it huge conclusions are drawn from individual games'. As Arsène Wenger once noted, European Championships are over in about three weeks, and any team in a league can be top of the table after three weeks.

In those short tournaments, England have probably been unluckier than most. Over lunch in London in 2013, the FA's then chairman Greg Dyke, who had spent a lot of time asking people in the game why England lose, told Simon: 'There's another argument. The guy who owns Brentford [the small London club that Dyke supports] is Matthew Benham, right? He's very rich. He's made all his money gambling on football. He employs top-quality graduates, maths graduates. All they do is study football around the world. He does everything on statistics. Everything is on probabilities. He says, the single biggest factor why England haven't done well is because they've been unlucky.'

Simon interjected that luck is particularly important in World Cups.

'And also,' said Dyke, 'the number of times you're knocked out on penalties.'

Of the ten tournaments for which England had qualified from 1990 until our conversation, they had exited six on penalties.

Dyke continued: 'He [Benham] says you can alter the chances of winning or losing on penalties, but not by a lot. So if the luck had gone the other way, his argument is that we'd have won one or two of those and we wouldn't be sitting here having this conversation.'

Yet there we were, having this conversation.

There is a similar issue with luck in major league baseball, notes Michael Lewis in *Moneyball*: 'The season ends in a giant crapshoot. The playoffs frustrate rational management because, unlike the long regular season, they suffer from the sample size problem.' Lewis means that because there are so few games in the play-offs – because the 'sample size' is so small – random factors play an outsize role in determining the winner.

Most football fans understand that luck matters, even if they construct a post-fact story about the tournament that makes either victory or humiliation seem fated from the start. But our data point to an even scarier truth than the existence of fluke: namely, there is barely any difference between 'brilliant' and 'terrible' England teams. It looks suspiciously as if England for most of its modern history – at least before Capello arrived – has been more or less equally good.

This may sound hard to believe. Fans feel strongly about the qualities of managers and players. There are periods of national optimism and national pessimism, associated with the view that the England team is either strong or disgraceful.

But in fact, watching England play resembles watching a coin-tossing competition. If we focus on outright victories, then England on average wins just over 50 per cent of its games; the rest it either draws or loses. So just as a coin has half a chance of landing heads up and half tails up, England in the average game has about half a chance of winning and half of not winning.

We assigned a '1' for each win and a '0' for a loss or a draw, and examined the sequence of England's 400 games from 1980 to 2014. Before we discuss this sequence, let's look at coin tossing. If you tossed a coin 400 times, you would expect on average to get 200 heads and 200 tails. However, there is no reason to think that the outcomes would alternate (heads, tails, heads, tails . . .). Sometimes you will get sequences of a few heads, sometimes a few tails. Crucially, though, there would be no relationship at all between the current coin toss and the last one. If you toss a fair coin there is always a fifty–fifty chance of heads, whatever sequence has occurred up to this point. There is no statistical correlation between current coin tosses and past coin tosses, even if the average of any sequence is always around 50 per cent.

Here is our finding: England's win sequence over the 400 games is indistinguishable from a random series of coin tosses. In that period they had 199 unbroken sequences of consecutive wins, losses or draws; theory would have predicted 200. There is no predictive value in the outcome of England's last game, or indeed in any combination of England's recent games. Whatever happened in one match appears to have no bearing on what will happen in the next one. The only thing you can predict is that over the medium to long term, England will win about half its games outright. We have seen that the outcome of matches can be largely predicted by a country's population, income and experience. However, this explains only the average outcome. In other words, if England were smaller, poorer or less experienced, it would have a lower percentage of wins, but the sequence of those wins would still be unpredictable.

To make sure that our finding was right, we constructed a few random sequences of 1s and 0s to see if they looked like England's results. Often we found more apparent correlation in our random sequences than in England's results.

Contrary to all popular opinion, it may be that for most of modern football history the strength of the England team has barely ever changed (which would make the vast apparatus of punditry attached to the team instantly redundant). The figure below shows the win percentage of the England team from 1950 to 2016 (again counting draws as worth half a win):

Games played

England win percentage

Apart from a few moments in the 1950s it has not risen above 70 per cent, and it has never fallen below 67.5 per cent. The overall picture is one of steady but extremely slow decline, punctuated by two eras of exceptional performance. One of those eras was the late 1960s, when England were world champions. The other period of clear improvement began in the early 2000s and continues today.

The following table shows the record of England managers since 1946 (excluding caretaker managers):

Manager	Tenure	Played	Wins	Draws	Losses	Goals scored	Goals conceded	Win percentage	Average goal difference
Winterbottom	1946–1962	138	77	33	28	369	192	67.8	1.283
Ramsey	1963–1974	112	67	28	17	212	97	72.3	1.027
Revie	1974–1977	29	14	8	7	49	25	62.1	0.828
Greenwood	1977–1982	55	33	12	10	93	40	70.9	0.964
Robson	1982–1990	95	47	29	19	154	60	64.7	0.989
Taylor	1990–1993	38	18	13	7	62	32	64.5	0.789
Venables	1994–1996	24	12	9	3	35	14	68.8	0.875
Hoddle	1996–1999	28	17	4	7	42	13	67.9	1.036
Keegan	1999–2000	18	7	7	4	26	15	58.3	0.611
Eriksson	2001–2006	67	40	15	12	128	61	70.9	1.000
McClaren	2006–2007	18	9	4	5	32	12	61.1	1.111
Capello	2008–2012	42	28	8	6	89	28	76.2	1.452
Hodgson	2012–2016	56	33	15	8	109	44	72.3	1.161

One thing that is clearly visible is the improvement in the national team performance since 2000, under two foreign managers (Eriksson and Capello) and an Englishman with a lot of overseas coaching experience (Hodgson). With hindsight, McClaren's brief and sorry tenure looks like a return to the slightly less successful era of the 1980s and 1990s.

Capello is in fact, by these statistics, the most successful England manager in history. Most obviously, his win percentage of 76 (counting draws as half a win) was higher than anyone else's (and 15 percentage points above McClaren's). Capello also won a higher proportion of games outright than any of his predecessors. True, he had the good luck of coaching in the aftermath of the break-ups of the Soviet Union and Yugoslavia. There are now far more weak little countries in European football, the likes of Slovenia and Kazakhstan, which England generally beats. But the previous five regular England managers enjoyed the same advantage, and none of them has stats to match Capello's. As we've seen, Capello was the nominated scapegoat for the World Cup of 2010. But it is unfair to judge him on just four matches. Over his four-year reign, his results stand out.

What's also noticeable is how freely his teams scored. They beat their opponents by an average of 1.45 goals a game, about half a goal better than the typical modern England manager. Scoring was easier for pre-war England sides, and for Walter Winterbottom's teams in the immediate post-war period, because many international sides in those days were rubbish: in May 1947, for instance, Winterbottom's England won 0–10 away to Portugal, not a result that England have threatened to match since.

Match for match from 2012 to 2016, Hodgson did pretty well too. His England career win percentage was 72 per cent – marginally higher than World Cup-winning Alf Ramsey, and the second-best of all time after Capello.

On the whole, though, very little has changed in England's results over sixty years. A star player might fade or retire, but in a country of about 50 million people, there is always someone coming up who is near enough his level to make almost no difference. Over the long term, the three key factors that determine a country's performance are very stable. The British economy boomed in the 1990s and is now dropping down the global wealth rankings, but measured over the past century Britain has always been one of the wealthiest nations in the world. Equally, its share of the football population changes only glacially. And while the England team gains experience, so do its main rivals. The only key factor that changes is home advantage. Given that playing at home is worth a lead of one goal per game in global football, it's little wonder that England won the World Cup in England in 1966.

Otherwise, England's performances in good or bad times are much the same. It's just that fans and the media seek to see patterns where none exist. Nicholas Taleb, the financial investor who wrote *The Black Swan: The Impact of the Highly Improbable*, famously explained that we are constantly fooled by randomness. In neuroscientific terms, our rational brains are egged on by our emotional brains to find patterns even if there aren't any. In the end, the best explanation for the short-term ups and downs of the England team is randomness.

MADE IN AMSTERDAM:
THE RISE OF SPAIN
AND THE TRIUMPH
OF EUROPEAN
KNOWLEDGE
NETWORKS

In another universe, Ignacio Palacios-Huerta's penalty report would have won the World Cup for Holland in 2010. Still, for all our best efforts, Spain's win was about as inevitable as World Cups get. The country once derided as eternal losers had not merely become world champions; it was also the best team in the world. (Many world champions are not.) In fact, Spain had probably been best in the world for nearly a decade before 2010. Then, in 2012, it completed an unprecedented triple of European title, world title, European title. In 2014 it was humiliated in Brazil, and it has now been overtaken by Germany, but for about five years or so, Spain was perhaps the best national team ever. Crucially, the country owed its triumphs in large part to its location in interconnected

Western Europe. The rise of Spain is the perfect example of our network theory: why the countries of Western Europe still rule football.

*   *   *

Spain hadn't always been so connected. General Francisco Franco, Spain's fascist ruler from 1936 until his death in 1975, had isolated the country from the rest of Europe. Jimmy Burns, the Anglo-Spanish writer born in Madrid in 1953, recalls in his *When Beckham Went to Spain*:

> Spain was virtually a closed economy. I spent part of my childhood between England and Spain, smuggling things from London to Madrid, never the other way round – clothes, gramophone records, books and magazines. While England seemed to be very much part of the world, Spain even to my young eyes struck me as something of a world of its own, where kids of my age all seemed to be taught by either priests or nuns.

The cosmopolitan Real Madrid of Burns's childhood, studded with imported stars such as Alfredo di Stefano (from Argentina), Ferenc Puskás (Hungary) and Raymond Kopa (France), was very much the exception in Franco's Spain. Few foreigners wanted to join lesser clubs in this poor country, and those who tried to come were often blocked. For most of the 1960s Spain officially let in only foreign players of Spanish descent. In fact many Latin American players invented Spanish ancestors to get in – one Argentine claimed his father had come from 'Celta', which isn't a town at all but the name of the club in Vigo – but even these imports didn't transform Spanish football. There weren't many of them, and they mostly weren't very good. Nor did Spanish players of the Franco era go abroad to learn new tricks.

Spain's isolation in those years was usually reflected in the national team's results. Though the country won the European Championship at home in 1964, in the period before Western Europe made its great leap in football know-how, for the next forty years the Spaniards did almost nothing in international tournaments.

What saved Spain's football was the country's opening to Europe and the world. Spanish isolation began to break down in the last years of Franco's life. In 1973, just after Spain reopened its borders to foreign football players, FC Barcelona imported the great Dutchman Johan Cruyff. It is possible to draw a direct line between Cruyff's arrival in Barcelona and Spain's victory in Johannesburg thirty-seven years later.

Signing Cruyff had not been easy. Franco's regime often obstructed Spanish companies from making foreign payments, and Barcelona ended up having to register the player as a piece of agricultural machinery. In another mark of the isolationist climate of the time, an elderly Barça director lamented to the club's secretary Armand Carabén, 'A Dutchman in the Nou Camp! What's the world coming to? This is pure madness. A man from the land of butter comes to the land of olive oil. Does nobody understand that even if he plays nicely, his stomach will be a mess within four days?'

But Cruyff was more than just stomach and legs. Possibly more than any other great player, he was brain, too. He was a philosopher of football, and the most important thing about football, for Cruyff, was the pass. He could (and often did) spend hours talking about the pass. You never passed into a teammate's feet, he lectured, but always a metre in front of him, to keep the pace in the game. While the first man was passing to the second man, the third man already had to be in motion

ready to receive the second man's pass. Cruyff talked people
silly about the pass.

In the early 1970s he and Barcelona's Dutch manager,
Rinus Michels, introduced Spaniards to a form of Dutch 'total
football'. The two men had arrived at just the right time.
Besides opening to the world, Spain was then beginning its
long economic rise.

Cruyff played his last game for Barcelona in 1978, but
Spain would hear from him again. Much later, he would bring
his ideas on football back to Catalonia. They would provide the
underpinnings first of the great Barça sides, and eventually of
the Spanish world champions of 2010.

Cruyff had planned to retire as a player after leaving Barcelona. However, he lost his money in a series of ill-advised ven-
tures, most notably a pig farm, and had to start playing again.
After a spell in the North American Football League with the
Washington Diplomats and the Los Angeles Aztecs, he finished
playing at Ajax in 1984. He stayed in Amsterdam, and a year
later became manager of the club that he had first entered in
the early 1950s as a toddler from down the road. As manager
he went to the fields where Ajax's boys' teams played, fields
that had practically been his backyard, and said that everything
had to change. Years before Cruyff transformed Barcelona's
academy, he transformed Ajax's.

Everything he did there was the sum of a lifetime's thinking
about football. Cruyff once said that before he was thirty, he
had done everything on instinct; but after thirty, he began to
understand why he did it. No longer would Ajax's youth teams
aim to win matches, the club's new manager told a surprised
set of volunteers. From now on, the only purpose of the youth
teams would be to turn talented boys into adult stars. That
meant, above all, creating two-footed players who were masters of positional play and the pass. The boys in Ajax's academy would spend much of their time playing passing games,

especially Cruyff's favourite, six against three. Cruyff's long-time assistant Tonny Bruins Slot recalled in 2011, 'Making triangles, getting a numerical advantage in midfield, speed of action in a small space, putting pressure on an opponent: everything was in there.'

For Ajax's boys' teams, even matches became practical classes. Sometimes kids were put in older age groups, where they could no longer get by on natural brilliance or speed and had to develop guile, too. Often the coaches deliberately played boys out of position. 'That began with [Dennis] Berg-kamp,' said Bruins Slot. 'He was a wonderful attacker anyway and the right-back in the under-18s just wasn't good enough. So we put Dennis in that position for a while. He managed it with his fingers in his nose [a Dutch phrase meaning 'without any trouble']. Also, Dennis could now put himself inside the mind of a defender, which would be useful to him as a striker. That was a success, so we began to do it more often.'

Cruyff was always looking for lessons from other disciplines. An opera singer, Lo Bello, was brought in to teach Ajax's play-ers how to breathe. In winter, when pitches were frozen, the boys attended lectures: a great female ping-pong player taught them how to deal with stress; a groundsman told them how to look after their gear; and a onetime promising youngster who had never made it explained where he had gone wrong.

Cruyff drew a connecting thread through the entire club, from the youngest boys' eleven to the first team. Every Ajax team in every age group played the same 4–3–3 formation as the great Holland and Ajax teams of the 1970s. (Cruyff said that only with 4–3–3 could every zone on the field be occupied.) When the opposition's left-back had the ball, Ajax's players from the under-eights to the first team knew exactly which positions they had to occupy to press him. When the outside-right from the under-eighteens made his professional debut, he felt entirely at home. That's one reason Cruyff happily threw kids into big

European games: the seventeen-year-old Bergkamp turned a Swedish full-back and part-time policeman inside out one night, and returned to school in Amsterdam the next day.

And partly, it was simply that Cruyff was a born teacher. One of us, Simon, experienced it himself. When Simon interviewed the great man in his Barcelona mansion in 2000, Cruyff rose from his sofa and taught him how to kick with his left foot. 'Look' – he demonstrated – 'whether you kick with your right or left, the point is that you are standing on one leg. And if you stand on one leg, you fall over. So you need to adjust your balance, and the only way to do that is with your hand, your arm.' And he kicked an imaginary ball with his left foot, flinging out his right arm. Simon's left foot improved instantly.

Cruyff left Ajax in 1988 after yet another argument, and stayed away until 2011, when he returned to the club as a director and spiritual godfather. However, Ajax's youth academy has always stuck to the Cruyffian model. It works pretty well. Over the past twenty years, home-grown Ajax players (also counting foreigners who joined the club as teenagers) have included Bergkamp, Edwin van der Sar, Frank and Ronald de Boer, Edgar Davids, Clarence Seedorf, Patrick Kluivert, Nwankwo Kanu, Zlatan Ibrahimovic, Maxwell, Steven Pienaar, Cristian Chivu, Rafael van der Vaart, Wesley Sneijder, Nigel de Jong, Jan Vertonghen and the Dane Christian Eriksen. In the Europa League final against Manchester United in 2017, Ajax fielded a team whose average age was 22 years and 282 days, the youngest for any European finalist in history.

Back in 1995, after a largely home-grown Ajax team had beaten Milan in the Champions League final, Simon visited Amsterdam to find out how the world could copy Ajax's model. After all, football progresses largely through international copying. Co Adriaanse, then the head of Ajax's youth academy, sat in the metal container that was his office and scoffed, 'It's not a recipe for pancakes! Other clubs don't have a club style.

They don't start with kids at eight years old. They don't have the quality. And there's no continuity.'

Indeed, not even Arsène Wenger at Arsenal has managed to replicate Ajax's recipe. Something is lacking. In Wenger's years in London since 1996, Arsenal's youth teams have produced very few future stars: Ashley Cole (already nearly sixteen when Wenger inherited the club), Cesc Fàbregas and Héctor Bellerín (both sixteen when Wenger nabbed them from Barcelona), and the two Frenchmen Gaël Clichy and Francis Coquelin (both seventeen when they came to London from France).

Only one club has learned Ajax's recipe: Barcelona. No wonder, because Cruyff carried the recipe across in person. It's the perfect case study of intra-European knowledge transfer. When the Dutchman moved from Amsterdam to the Nou Camp as head coach in 1988, he did something that few Barça coaches had ever done before: he went to the fields where Barcelona's youth teams played. There he saw a skinny kid in central midfield hitting perfect passes. 'Take that boy off at half-time,' he told the boy's coach. 'Why?' asked the coach. 'Because I'm putting him in the first team,' said Cruyff. The skinny kid, whose name was Pep Guardiola, spent a decade in Barcelona's first team. From 2008 to 2012, Guardiola managed the Spanish, European and world champions. He once said, 'Johan Cruyff taught me the most. I worked six years with him and learned a terrific amount.' Guardiola was only the latest in a line of Cruyffians in the Nou Camp. Guardiola's predecessor, Frank Rijkaard, was an Amsterdammer and an Ajax man. Rijkaard got the Barcelona job on Cruyff's recommendation despite having just been relegated from the Dutch Premier Division with Sparta Rotterdam.

Louis van Gaal, Barcelona's coach from 1997 to 2000, was also an Amsterdammer and Ajax man, though he absolutely did not get the job on Cruyff's recommendation. Van Gaal had played for Ajax in the early seventies, at the same time as Cruyff, but only in the second team. Van Gaal appears to have harboured a jealousy of Cruyff ever since. Though the personal feud between the two men amused Dutch fans for years, both of them thought almost exactly the same way about football. When Van Gaal came to Barcelona, he cemented the club's veneration of the pass. He advanced the careers of great passing kids like Xavi and Iniesta. Van Gaal and later Rijkaard didn't always win on the field, but they continued the transfer of Dutch know-how to Catalonia that Cruyff had begun in 1973.

When Guardiola became Barcelona's head coach, he restored and updated Cruyffism. How this works was explained to us in 2009 by Albert Capellas, then coordinator of Barça's youth academy. We met Capellas over beers in a Swiss hotel bar. A couple of weeks later, he was giving us a tour of the Masía, or farmhouse, the unlikely headquarters of Barça's academy until the little brick building with the sundial on the front was finally closed in 2011.

The day we visited the Masía, ten months before Spain won the World Cup, you could simply walk in off the street. There were no guards. Inside you got a coffee and a friendly welcome at the bar. It felt like the house of a large Catholic family. A deliveryman stopped by and carried an enormous ham into the kitchen. There was a room with foosball and billiards tables, but when we visited they were covered, because the boys in the Masía had to study for school. The doors to the garden were open, to let the sun flood in. In the garden stood a sculpture of a female body, which must have provoked the odd stray thought among the Masía's all-male residents.

From the upstairs windows of the Masía, you could look out onto the Nou Camp. You could almost touch it here. The boys of the Masía actually slept in the stadium; the little farmhouse had become too small to house them.

But that morning, nine months before the World Cup in South Africa kicked off, the Masía still felt as cosy as the canteen at the old, now destroyed little Ajax stadium, De Meer. Both places resembled neighbourhood cafés, where men gathered for fellowship and coffee. Part of Ajax and Barcelona's secret is that they are local clubs, run by largely the same bunch of local men for decades. These locals are interested in the talented kids of today, because in ten years' time, when the kids are in the first team, the locals expect still to be around.

When the staff sat down to explain how the Masía worked, you felt as if you were being transported back to Amsterdam in 1985. For a start, said Capellas, Barça's youth teams all played the same 4–3–3 as the first team. When the opposition's left-back had the ball, Barça's players, from the under-eights to the first team, knew exactly which positions they had to occupy to press him. When the outside-right from the under-eighteens made his professional debut, he felt entirely at home. That was one reason Barcelona happily threw kids into big games: Iniesta, Xavi and Leo Messi were all playing regularly in the world's biggest stadium while still in their teens.

There were a lot of things the Masía didn't worry about. Until players reached their mid-teens, said Capellas, 'we don't think about competition, or not so much.' Boys' matches were treated as practical classes. The Masía didn't care about size, either. Nobody minded that Messi and Iniesta were short. Capellas said, 'If he's small or if he's tall, for us that is not important. We don't test for physical capacities. We are always thinking about the technical and tactical capacities of each player.' The players barely ever did fitness training without the ball. Even speed was of limited relevance. Guardiola, a slow runner, had moved the ball fastest.

Nor did the boys train much. Ninety minutes a day was enough, Capellas told us. Schoolwork took up much more of their time, because like Ajax, Barcelona knew that most of its players would never turn pro. This was not a ruthless corporation. 'We treat our fifty boys like our family,' said Pep Boade, Barça's grizzled old chief scout, and this didn't appear to be cant. Many youth academies are ruled by militaristic brutes, but Barça's coaches sounded like traditional Catholic mothers. When a boy was cut from the Masía, sometimes his rival would cry from guilt at having been better. Capellas said, 'Messi and Iniesta don't live here anymore, but this is their home, they come by to eat, if they have a problem they come to talk to us, as they would to a mother or father. For us they are not stars. It's Leo, it's Bojan, it's Andres. Andres is humble. We say, "You are a good man, you are an incredible person, don't lose your values."'

In one regard, though, the Masía was hyper-professional. What mattered to Barça, as to Ajax, was passing. Both academies fetishized the pass. Football, to Cruyff, was about making passing 'triangles' on the field. If a player could do that, Cruyff picked him. That remains Barça's principle. Capellas recited the mantra, 'Always the players must find triangles.' Training, then, is a deep study of passing.

To pass, or to stop the other team from passing, you also need to know exactly where to be. The average player has the ball for only 53.4 seconds every game (according to Chris Carling, the English performance analyst at Lille in France), so any player's main job is to occupy the right positions for the other eighty-nine minutes and 6.6 seconds. The boys in the Masía spend a lot of time playing four against four, with two touches of the ball allowed, and with three 'joker' players who join whichever team has the ball. You win this game by being in the right position: football as a sort of chess, rather than football as physical combat. In the sun of the Masía, just as at Ajax's youth complex De Toekomst ('The Future'), where the chill wind sweeps in off the highway, some great future players spent the mornings of their youth making Cruyffian triangles.

Our tour of the Masía ended in the dining room, where in late morning you could already smell a tasty lunch. 'Home cooking,' Capellas noted. On the plain whitewashed walls were pictures of Masía teams past. Capellas and Boade found the picture from 1988, with an absurdly skinny young Guardiola. Two other boys in the photo later became his assistant coaches at Barça. One of them, Tito Vilanova, would succeed him as head coach in 2012 before resigning a year later suffering from the throat cancer that would soon kill him.

Guardiola was another part of the Masía's secret. The academy produced the boys; he sent them on in the stadium next door. Capellas said, 'When we play Real Madrid's youth teams, we are equal. Don't think Real doesn't have good youth players.' Yet Real's boys rarely make the first team, because Madrid keeps buying stars. By contrast, Guardiola, like Cruyff, was a man of the club who knew exactly what was cooking in the Masía, even in the second-string youth teams.

'You have to have someone up there who says, "Go in,"' said Capellas. That was easy when the kid was as good as Messi or Iniesta. But Guardiola had done the same with Pedro, not an obvious star, and he had stuck in the first team. In the sun outside the Masía, Capellas used his foot to draw a circle on the ground: Guardiola went from the Masía to the first team and then recruited from the Masía again. The circle was round, said Capellas.

Barça has been lucky, the club's then chief executive Joan Oliver admitted to us in 2009: 'Yeah, good fortune exists always in the world, in every kind of industry. It's not possible always to guarantee that we will have a Messi or an Iniesta or a Xavi from the academy. Perhaps you could not get the best player of the world from your academy, but we get six, seven first-team players.' That is not to mention Masía exports such as Thiago Alcántara (Bayern Munich) and José Reina (Napoli).

FROM THE MASÍA TO JOHANNESBURG

In short, once Spain's isolation had been lifted in the last years of Franco, Barcelona began building a style based on knowledge transfer from Amsterdam. Eventually Spain adopted this made-in-Amsterdam game. At Euro 2008 and again at the World Cup in South Africa, the Spaniards often looked as if they were still making their triangles at morning practice at the Masía. They passed the ball up and down like little men filling in a crossword puzzle at top speed. Whenever they went 1–0 up, they simply made sure the opponent never got the ball again. The 2010 World Cup final was the forty-fourth straight game in which Spain had won after scoring first. Everyone knew exactly how the men in red played, yet it was impossible to beat them because they had become Cruyffian masters of the pass.

Spain became a great football nation because it joined European knowledge networks. This might sound like too neat a theory – the sort of thing you get when you let academics loose on something as mysterious and intuitive as football. Luckily, though, the facts seem to match our theory. Let's look at Spain's results, decade by decade:

THE RISE OF SPAIN

Decade	P	W	D	L	% Won	Win %*
1920s	32	23	4	5	72	78
1930s	25	13	5	7	52	62
1940s	19	8	6	5	42	58
1950s	44	20	13	11	45	60
1960s	60	28	13	19	47	58
1970s	59	29	18	12	49	64
1980s	103	49	28	26	48	61
1990s	98	57	26	15	58	71
2000s	128	91	25	12	71	81

*Including draws as half a win

We'll take the 1920s as an illustration of what this table shows. Spain won twenty-three of its thirty-two matches in the decade, or 72 per cent. It also drew four games. If we count a draw as worth half a win, then Spain's total win percentage for the decade was 78 per cent. The figure in the last column for each decade is the most telling one. It provides the best measure of Spain's success decade by decade.

The table demonstrates how closely Spain's football success tracks the country's integration with Europe. In the 1920s, before the civil war of the 1930s, Spain performed very well. But then isolation descended under Franco. From the 1930s to the 1980s, Spain's win percentage hovered around a disappointing 60 per cent. The team were winning about half their games, and drawing another quarter. That European Championship of 1964 was an anomaly. The broader story was that a poor, shut-off Spain was struggling to access the world's best football know-how. In these sorry decades Di Stefano, the Argentinian, turned Colombian, turned Spanish international, summed up Spain's football history in a phrase: 'We played like never before, and lost like always.'

But in 1986 Spain joined the European Union – a sort of formal entry into European networks. Soon afterwards, the Spanish national team improved sharply. We have seen that a country's success at football correlates with its wealth. And Spain from the 1980s was growing richer fast. In the 1960s and 1970s its income per capita had been stuck at about 60 per cent of the average of the core fifteen member nations of the EU. In the 1980s and 1990s Spain began to catch up. The Barcelona Olympics of 1992 nicely captured the rise: the Games showcased a 'new Spain', and a young Spanish football team guided by twenty-one-year-old Pep Guardiola won gold.

Yet during this period the Spaniards continued to be mocked in international football as 'notorious underperformers'. Like England, they just couldn't match the big nations in big tournaments. However, the criticism was wrong. It was clichéd and misguided to label Spain 'perennial underachievers' in these 'bad' decades. In fact, given the country's modest resources of people and wealth, it was overachieving even then. It was simply not big or rich or connected enough to expect to match the leading nations in football.

Let's take the relatively recent period of 1980 to 2001. For Spain this was a fallow period: failure in a World Cup hosted at home, and no performance of note save an appearance in the final of Euro 1984, which is remembered chiefly for goalkeeper Luis Arconada's fumbling of Michel Platini's free kick.

In absolute terms Spain's win percentage (counting draws as half a win) of about 66 per cent in that period ranked it somewhere near the bottom of the global top ten, around the same level as England. But we want to measure Spain's relative performance: how it achieved relative to its resources.

First let's look at experience. By 2001 Spain had played 461 internationals in its history. That itself is a marker of isolation. We've seen that according to Russell Gerrard's data, Sweden by 2001 was the most experienced country in international football, with 802 internationals. England, Argentina, Hungary, Brazil and Germany (including West but not East Germany) had all played over 700 each. Spain – cut off for so many years – lagged.

When it comes to our second variable, wealth, Spain still fell short of most of its rivals. In the 1980s and 1990s it was significantly behind Germany, France, England and even Italy.

And Spain was small. When people complain that the country underperforms, they usually mean it does worse than the giants of international football. Well, no wonder, given that Spain is much smaller than they are. Not only did Brazil in 1990 dwarf Spain's then population of 39 million people, but so did Germany, France, Italy, and even that other 'notorious underachiever', England.

We calculated that Spain, given its population, income and experience in the 1980–2001 period, 'should' have scored on average 0.3 goals per game more than its opponents. But Spain did much better than that: it outscored opponents by nearly 0.9 goals, averaging nearly 0.6 goals more than expected. Of the teams that played at least one hundred games in this period, Spain was the eighth-best overperformer in the world. The country was an overachiever long before it began winning prizes. Until very recently, it just wasn't quite big or rich or experienced or lucky enough to win anything.

Consider, for instance, its record against Italy in the 1980–2001 period. In those years Spain's population, income per head and international experience were on average about 30 per cent inferior to Italy's. Given that, we would have expected Spain's goal difference to be about minus two over its four games against Italy. Instead Spain overachieved, notching a win, two draws and a defeat with a goal difference of zero.

In short: Spain's bad times were not bad at all. It always was overachieving. But in the past twenty years or so, Spain's resources have improved. Since Spain joined the EU, and despite its recent economic crisis, the country's average income has risen to about three-quarters of the core EU's average. Its population has grown to 46 million. Spain has also become fully networked in Europe. Its best football players now experience the Champions League every season. A richer, more populous, more experienced and more networked Spain became first a serious contender, and finally (thanks to its continued overachievement) the best team on earth. As we discussed in the previous chapter, learning through European networks then helped Germany succeed Spain as world champions.

Spain's post-Franco wealth, size and integration translated into goals. In the 1990s Spain's win percentage (still treating draws as worth half a win) shot up to over 70 per cent. In the 2000s it was over 80 per cent, with Spain losing just 12 per cent of its games. From 2000 to 2009 the country won

71 per cent of its matches outright, a long-term performance about as good as any other national team's since international football took off in the 1930s. Brazil never managed it. Even the all-conquering Italy of the 1930s won just 70 per cent of its games that decade. Spain had become a great team long before it won titles. Here is Wayne Rooney in his autobiography describing a Spain–England exhibition game in 2004, a time when the Spaniards were still considered eternal losers:

> Spain had been taking the mickey, passing the ball back and forth, and showboating which upset me. When that happens, you have to try and break up your opponents' passing game by getting stuck into them, tackling hard and quickly. Perhaps I overdid it because I was so frustrated, but we couldn't get a kick of the ball. Not nice.

Of course the emergence from isolation cannot by itself explain Spain's success. Intangibles matter too – the sudden emergence of several great individuals, such as Xavi and David Villa. Spain were the only team at the 2010 World Cup with as strong a personnel as the best club sides. No other country in the tournament fielded eleven players who were starters at big clubs. Spain was massively overperforming its size and wealth, but that overperformance was possible only because of the end of isolation. Nor did the financial crash of 2008 hurt Spain's national team. Despite the recession, the collapse of property values and unemployment of over 20 per cent, Spain remained networked with the rest of Europe.

It was wonderfully appropriate that the Spaniards sealed their rise in a World Cup final against their mentor country. This was the Cruyff versus Cruyff final. Probably for the first time, both teams in football's biggest game were, in their origins, the product of one man. It was a triumph of intra-

European knowledge transfer. That night in Johannesburg, the old Amsterdammer living in Barcelona must have felt like the proud father of twins – albeit that the Dutch twin behaved like a fratricidal delinquent.

Seven of the fourteen Spaniards who played in the match had spent time in the Cruyffian Masía; seven of the fourteen Dutchmen had come from Ajax's Cruyffian academy. One of those seven Dutchmen, Eljero Elia, had never even made it into Ajax's first team. Khalid Boulahrouz and André Ooijer, who sat on the Dutch bench that night, were also rejects of the Ajax academy. When even your dropouts are staffing the second-best national squad on earth, you are doing pretty well. Not as well as the Spaniards, though. Had Spain been able to field just one other product of the Masía – and when the Argentine Messi was a boy the Spaniards had begged him to play for their national youth teams – FIFA could have dispensed with the World Cup altogether and simply handed Spain the trophy at a quick ceremony in Zurich.

The Holland–Spain final was best understood as 'Jungian mirroring', summed up David Winner, author of *Brilliant Orange: The Neurotic Genius of Dutch Football*: 'Holland's path to the world title is blocked by the more authentic version of their better selves. It is now Spain who play Dutch football.' That is how Cruyff saw it, too. 'I thought my country would never dare to play like this and would never give up its own way of playing,' he said after the game. He continued:

Even without great players like in the past, a team has its own style. I had the wrong end of the stick. . . . They didn't want the ball. And unfortunately, and it's hard to say so, they played dirty. So bad that they really should quickly have been down to nine men. Then they made two such mean tackles that I felt the pain myself. This nasty, vulgar, hard, closed game that wasn't watchable and was barely football anymore – yes, with that they could trouble Spain. They played anti-football.

But perhaps Holland had to, because the Spaniards were now better at football. The Dutch had taught the Spaniards how to play, just as in the Dutch–Spanish Eighty Years' War (1568 to 1648) the Dutch had sold the Spaniards arms. In Johannesburg, Holland paid for it.

TOM THUMB: THE BEST LITTLE FOOTBALL COUNTRY ON EARTH

In 1970, when Brazil won its third World Cup, it got to keep the Jules Rimet trophy. The little statuette of Nike, then still known chiefly as the Greek goddess of victory, ended up in a glass case in the Brazilian federation's offices in Rio de Janeiro. One night in 1983 the trophy was stolen. It has never been seen since.

However, the point is that Brazil deserves the Jules Rimet. The five-times world champion is – still, even after that 1–7, for now at least – the best country in football history. Our question here is a different one: which country is best after taking into account its population, experience and income per capita? If Brazil is the absolute world champion, who is the relative one, the biggest overperformer? That overachieving country deserves its own version of the Jules Rimet trophy – call it the Tom Thumb. And which countries are the worst underachievers relative to their resources? Along the way we will have to consider several impressive candidates and make some judgement calls before coming up with our winner and loser.

First of all, if we are dealing with statistics, we have to construct our arguments on the basis of large numbers of games played. There have only been twenty World Cups to 2014, and most of these involved hardly any countries from outside Europe and Latin America. So crunching the numbers from World Cups might at best tell us something about the pecking order among the long-established large football nations. But when the difference between, say, Argentina's two victories and England's one comes down to as little as Maradona's 'hand of God' goal, or the difference between Italy's four and France's one to a comment by Marco Materazzi about Zidane's parentage, then the statistician needs to look elsewhere. Happily, since national teams play a lot of games, we have plenty of data. As in Chapter 17, we will rely on the remarkable Gerrard/Muck database of international matches.

The number of games between countries has soared over time. Between the foundation of FIFA in 1904 and the First World War the number rose quickly to 50 per year. After 1918 growth resumed. By the eve of the Second World War, there were more than 100 international matches a year. But this was still a world dominated by colonial powers, and only with independence movements after the war did international competition mushroom. In 1947 there were 107 international matches; by 1957 there were 203; by 1967, 308. Few new countries were founded in the next two decades, but the number of international matches continued to rise thanks to the jet plane, which made travel less of a pain and more financially worthwhile. In 1977 there were 368 international matches; in 1987 there were 393. At that point the world seemed to have reached some sort of stable equilibrium.

But then the Soviet Union broke up into fifteen separate states, and Yugoslavia collapsed. The new countries flocked into FIFA. At the same time the commercial development of football meant that cash-hungry national associations were eager to play lucrative friendlies. In 1997 there were 850 international games, more than double the figure of a decade before. Since 2000 the number seems to have stabilized around an average of about 940 international games per year.

If we concentrate just on games since the start of the millennium, then a list of the most successful teams features the usual suspects. Let's rank the top ten countries by the percentage of games won, or, given that around one-third of matches are draws, by the 'win percentage' statistic calculated by valuing a draw as worth half a win (between 2000 and 2014):

	P	W	D	WPC*	GD
Spain	182	127	31	78.3	1.220
Brazil	227	141	51	73.3	1.330
Netherlands	172	102	45	72.4	1.076
Argentina	192	113	45	70.6	0.875
France	192	109	50	69.8	0.938
Germany	193	112	44	69.4	1.093
Iran	221	122	60	68.8	0.950
Portugal	176	98	44	68.2	0.983
Egypt	215	124	44	67.9	0.949
England	158	84	44	67.1	0.842

* win percentage

The best teams are much as you would expect. As we saw in the last chapter, Spain in this period was one of the handful of best international teams in the history of football. And even at a time when Brazil was struggling to reinvent its national playing style, its win percentage was almost 75 per cent. That equates to bookmakers' odds of 3 to 1, or about as close as you can get to a sure thing in a two-horse race.

If we look at Brazil's win percentage over time, some interesting insights emerge. Here are the team's results by decade:

	P	W	D	L	F	A	WPC*
1910s	15	6	4	5	28	24	53.3
1920s	24	10	4	10	35	34	50.0
1930s	22	14	1	7	60	49	65.9
1940s	43	23	7	13	127	68	61.6
1950s	96	62	18	16	229	100	74.0
1960s	115	78	16	21	275	134	74.8
1970s	101	65	27	9	188	62	77.7
1980s	117	73	28	16	222	83	74.4
1990s	166	108	38	20	366	137	76.5
2000s	157	96	36	25	323	118	72.6
2010s	102	70	18	14	102	102	77.5

* win percentage

Viewed in the light of history, it's little wonder that Brazil lost at home to Uruguay in the World Cup final of 1950. The Brazilians simply weren't that good then. Their hubris at that tournament had no historical basis. It's only in the 1950s that Brazil turned into football's superpower. Indeed, in the fifty years after that the team's performance was strikingly consistent: Brazil's win percentage (counting draws as worth half a win) hovered between 73 per cent and 78 per cent in each of the past six decades. If you had to pick a particular golden age, it would probably be 1964 to 1985, but our main finding is great stability of performance, even in the supposedly fallow twenty years after 1970. World Cups, as we have seen, usually turn on a couple of crucial matches, which in turn are usually decided by one goal each. The pundits then investigate these crucial matches for meaning, when in fact the best explanation of the outcome of such a tiny sample of games might be chance. The broader story of Brazil between the late 1950s and today is consistent excellence.

Still, Brazil now risks sliding out of the top unless it can plug into the Western European knowledge networks. In the last three World Cups it has often looked slow (or worse) against leading European teams. It ought to consider the revolutionary step of hiring a Western European manager. Imagine a Brazil coached by Pep Guardiola (as a few Brazilians were suggesting ahead of the 2014 World Cup). But it seems that even now, Brazilians are too proud of their own football tradition to try to learn from foreigners.

There's just one other finding of note. Brazil historically performs better in World Cup years. It wins about 5 per cent more often in years with a World Cup, and the difference is statistically significant. That sounds counterintuitive: after all, the team would tend to face tougher competition in those years. However, the sordid truth is that most of the time, Brazilian internationals coast a little. They don't raise their game for qualifiers against Bolivia or Nike-inspired friendlies against Asian countries. In these off years, weary stars sometimes cry off claiming injury, and agents sometimes finagle places in the team for players who need a foreign transfer. But in a World Cup year, when everyone is playing for his place, Brazil is usually at its best.

Portugal deserves particular praise for making the global top ten. The country has only 10 million inhabitants, compared with the 47–82 million of the large European nations and Brazil's 210 million. Portuguese victory in Euro 2016 – which came after the time period in this table – was a deserved reward for longstanding national overachievement. England's spot in the top ten emphasizes that its reputation as 'notorious underachiever' is undeserved.

One thing our table tells us is that Western Europeans have dominated international football. The region provides six of the ten best countries. We have seen that this is partly thanks to Europe's unmatched knowledge networks. Those networks rest on tradition: European nations are generally older, and have played international football longer, than the rest of the world. It may also help that, until very recently, control of global football largely remained in Europe. FIFA makes the rules of the game from a posh suburb of Zurich, and although Western Europe has only 5 per cent of the world's population, it has hosted ten out of twenty World Cups. (A mark of how power in global football is shifting is that the 2006 tournament in Germany may turn out to have been the region's last in decades.)

But tradition does not in itself secure dominance. If it did, then British companies would still dominate industries like textiles, shipbuilding and car making. Dominance is transitory unless producers have the resources to stay ahead of the competition. The key resource in football is talent. Generally speaking, the more populous countries are more likely to have the largest supply of talented people. We have also seen that rich countries are best at finding, training and developing talent. In short, it takes experience, population and wealth to make a successful football nation.

The easy bit is recognizing this. The hard work is assembling the data to answer our question: which countries do best relative to their resources of experience, population and wealth?

Thankfully, Russell and Christian's data can help us with the issue of experience. Between them they have recorded every single international game since the start of the sport's history. That allows us to measure the cumulative number of games a country had played up to any given date. We have seen that the most experienced football countries had played more than 900 international matches to 2014. Pedants might dispute some of the exact numbers – identifying international games is often a judgement call if we go back more than fifty years, when arrangements could be quite informal – but even if our figures were off by 5 per cent, it wouldn't significantly affect the statistical analysis.

We also have data on each country's income. The measure typically used is gross domestic product. GDP is the total value of all goods and services bought and sold within an economy. (It includes imports and exports but excludes income from assets owned overseas and profits repatriated to foreign countries.) The best sources for GDP figures are the Penn World Tables (www.ggdc.net/pwt), the authoritative source for international economic comparisons.* For the current edition we used version 9. The centre has estimates of GDP for 182 countries going back as far as 1950. To measure the economic resources available to each person, it divides GDP by population. Admittedly, there are all sorts of finicky issues involved in making comparisons across countries and across time, not to mention worries about measurement error and statistical reliability. Nonetheless, these data are the best we've got.

Now we run the multiple regressions we described in Chapter 16. Our aim is to find the connection between goal difference per game and our three key inputs – population, wealth and experience – while also allowing for home advantage.

After all these pyrotechnics, we can make another ranking. But this time we can compensate all the world's national teams for that trio of factors beyond their control: experience, population and income per head. Here are the top ten overachieving national teams in the world, allowing for population, wealth and experience, all games 2000–2014 (countries with more than 100 games):

Country	P	W	D	WPC*†	GD	GD outperformance
Palestine	114	27	30	36.8	−0.605	1.564
Rwanda	142	43	35	42.6	−0.310	1.117

* Robert C. Feenstra, Robert Inklaar and Marcel P. Timmer (2015), 'The Next Generation of the Penn World Table', *American Economic Review*, 105(10), 3150–3182, available for download at www.ggdc.net/pwt.

Jordan	217	78	75	53.2	0.249	1.114
Czech Republic	147	75	32	61.9	0.714	1.059
Spain	182	127	31	78.3	1.220	1.042
Portugal	176	98	44	68.2	0.983	1.025
Croatia	150	77	44	66.0	0.567	0.975
Ivory Coast	170	91	43	66.2	0.865	0.884
Syria	188	72	49	51.3	0.394	0.852
Panama	188	66	52	48.9	−0.074	0.807

† win percentage

Who would have predicted Palestine in first place? The poor country, mostly occupied by Israel, is still fighting just to be recognized as a state. Yet against all odds, it has succeeded in football.

In 1998, very soon after becoming president of FIFA, Sepp Blatter recognized Palestine. It was 'a bold move', comments James Montague, author of *When Friday Comes: Football, War and Revolution in the Middle East*, because at the time the Palestinian Authority was merely counted as an 'observer entity' (not even a 'non-member observer state') at the United Nations.

Palestinians have long been crazy about football (more later about the general Arab love of the game). But their national team's success also has something to do with the quest for statehood. There is a famous parallel in club football: Catalonia isn't a state, and so Catalans have invested a lot of their emotion and resources into FC Barcelona. De facto, the club flies the Catalan flag around the world. The Palestinian national team does the same for Palestine. So seriously does the country's elite take the sport that Jibril Rajoub, often touted as the Palestinian Authority's future president, heads the national football federation. A lot of private money has gone into coaching, facilities and into the West Bank's professional clubs, which fly the flag every time they play in an Asian competition. Some players in the Palestinian league now earn $3,000 a month, a very decent wage by local standards, says Montague.

After joining FIFA, Palestine did what many small national teams do: it recruited from its diaspora. Before the qualifiers for the 2006 World Cup, the country's football federation put an advertisement in the German magazine *Kicker* appealing for Palestinian-origin players. The team could also draw on an entire Chilean professional club: Palestino, started by Palestinian immigrants in 1920, plays in the Palestinian colours and is committed to a Palestinian state in the pre-Israeli borders.

But in recent years Palestine has come to rely more on local players – or at least on some of them. The team's big problem (and arguably the country's) is Israel's blockade of the Gaza Strip. Gaza is Palestine's football hotbed, with a long tradition of beach games. Yet Gazans now have a terrible time just getting to the Palestinian West Bank. One talented young Gazan, Mahmoud Sarsak, travelling to the West Bank to join a professional team there, was arrested by the Israelis, accused of being linked to Islamic Jihad (which he denied), spent two and a half years in prison, and almost died after going on a hunger strike. He was finally released in 2012 after Blatter and former players including Eric Cantona and Lilian Thuram appealed on his behalf, but his football career never recovered.

It's so difficult for players to travel that Palestine has sometimes even struggled to put a team together for World Cup qualifying matches. Then there are the Israeli raids that have destroyed Gazan stadiums. (Israel says the stadiums had been used as launch sites for rockets aimed at Israeli civilians.) Even watching a game on TV can be dangerous. During the 2014 World Cup, an Israeli missile killed nine young Palestinians enjoying the Argentina–Holland semi-final in a beach café.

No wonder Palestine's national team in recent years has largely been drawn from the West Bank (a place with its own problems), supplemented by some Israeli Arab players, who don't even all speak Arabic. Palestine's physical proximity to Europe, the leading football continent, is no help anymore. 'It might as well be on the moon,' says Montague.

Given all that, the country's overachievement is astonishing. From 2000 to 2014 Palestine scored 1.5 goals a game more than we would have forecast given its population, its income per capita and its very short experience of international football. In 2015 it qualified for its first ever Asian Cup. We would prophesy the country a bright football future except that there seems to be zero prospect of the Israeli–Palestinian conflict ever sorting itself out.

However, it doesn't feel right to name a team that loses its average match by 0.6 goals as the world's most overachieving football country. Instead, let's limit ourselves to the countries that played more than 100 games between 2000 and 2014 and scored more goals than they conceded:

Country	P	W	D	WPC*	GD	GD outperformance
Jordan	217	78	75	53.2	0.249	1.114
Czech Republic	147	75	32	61.9	0.714	1.059
Spain	182	127	31	78.3	1.220	1.042
Portugal	176	98	44	68.2	0.983	1.025
Croatia	150	77	44	66.0	0.567	0.975
Ivory Coast	170	91	43	66.2	0.865	0.884
Syria	188	72	49	51.3	0.394	0.852
Netherlands	172	102	45	72.4	1.076	0.802
Ukraine	141	61	42	58.2	0.248	0.731
Russia	134	58	44	59.7	0.500	0.703

* win percentage

The final column of the table is the one to notice. It shows what you might call each country's 'outperformance', the gap between the goal difference it 'should' have achieved against opponents given its national resources and experience, and what it actually did achieve (listed in the penultimate column). Jordan, the most overachieving country in football according to this table, scored over a goal per game more than its resources would predict.

Now the evidence for Palestinian football supremacy starts to mount. Jordan is something of a second Palestine. So many Palestinian refugees have fled to the little country since 1948 that today somewhere between 50 and 80 per cent of Jordan's population is Palestinian. (It's impossible to give an exact number, because many families are mixed.)

Anyone who has witnessed anti-immigrant sentiment in Europe and the US will guess that it wasn't always easy to integrate Palestinians and Jordanian 'East Bankers'. Each ethnic group has its own big professional football team (al-Wihdat for the Palestinians, al-Faisaly for Jordanians), and games between the two are often fraught, explains Montague. The two teams provide most of the players for Jordan's national team, al-Nashama ('The Brave'), so tensions sometimes spilled over.

In 1999 Jordan's twenty-three-year-old Prince Ali (an Arsenal fan) took over as president of the country's football federation. (He became famous in 2015 when he stood against Blatter for the FIFA presidency.) The federation didn't have much to spend, he told us. 'We have definitely the lowest budget in our region. That includes Palestine. In Jordan the government always says there are other priorities.' In fact he says that in the 1980s and early 1990s, after the Muslim Brotherhood got hold of the ministry of education, Jordanian schools actively discouraged sports.

Prince Ali says he tried to bring Jordanian and Palestinian players together, and that he got the country investing in grassroots sports. He set up centres around the country for kids from age eight, some of whom were eventually scouted by professional clubs. In 2004 the country reached its first ever Asian Cup, going all the way to the quarter-finals. It repeated the trick in 2011. It also got to the brink of qualifying for the World Cup 2014, but in the play-off, al-Nashama's biggest match ever, it was thumped by Uruguay.

Another surprising overachiever on our list is Syria. In the early 2000s, the country entered a football golden age. Until then the league had been dominated by the army and police clubs. They nabbed all the best players, so other clubs scarcely bothered. But then the Syrian football federation put a stop to this by making the sport professional. Money poured in. Players' salaries rose, facilities improved, and the federation got better at scouting and training youngsters. Syria started to do well in youth World Cups.

Tragically, the country was doomed. In 2011 the Syrian civil war broke out. Some of those talented youngsters made the long dangerous walk to Europe. Others were killed at home.

Syrian football had enough juice left to win the West Asian Championship in 2012. But the team's decline was inevitable (and just about the least important thing going wrong in the country). Syria's win percentage from 2000 to 2010 had been 52.3 per cent (counting draws as worth half a win); from 2011 to 2014 it fell to just 42.5 per cent. Still, Syria did get close to making it to the 2018 World Cup, reaching the fourth round of qualifiers before narrowly going out to Australia.

Some of that Syrian football talent might yet come through, but probably not in the country's national team. Rather, Syrian refugees and their children may soon start popping up in European national teams.

When three neighbouring countries such as Palestine, Jordan and Syria feature among the world's biggest overachievers, these are obviously not simply three separate national stories. There's something about the region that makes it special. Note, too, that Egypt, separated from Gaza only by a steel barrier, is the sole African country in our top ten of the world's winningest teams.

Indeed, when we carried out a similar study covering the period 1990–2010 for an earlier edition of this book, we identified yet another country in the region, Iraq, as a big overachiever. Those twenty years – which featured two Gulf Wars, massacres, sanctions, Saddam Hussein, near-civil war – were not happy ones for Iraqis. Nonetheless, in that period the Lions of Mesopotamia scored nearly a goal a game more than you would expect given the country's resources. As Iraqi supporters used to chant (often while firing bullets into the air), 'Here we are Sunni – yah! Here we are Shiite – yah! Bring us happiness, sons of Iraq!' Even Kurds supported the Lions. Montague calls the team 'arguably the last symbol of national unity left in Iraq'.

The Middle East has a remarkable football tradition. The region's proximity to Europe means that the game arrived here long before it reached bigger, richer East and South Asian countries such as China, Japan and India. (Football may be the one activity in which Jordan can beat China and Palestine can beat India.) The Syrian-French journalist Henri Mamarbachi sent us his memories of the Israeli invasion of Lebanon during the 1982 World Cup:

Day and night for weeks, Beirutis were under constant bombardment by sea, air and land, there was no electricity and therefore no way to watch TV during whatever respite they could get in the evening. And this was worse than the shelling and the unbearable heat, for they were now deprived of watching what was more important than anything else. So, every evening, you could see under each house car bonnets open for the purpose of linking the batteries to whatever

portable generator they could get hold of. Watching the
World Cup in the streets, with colourful foreign flags often
hanging from the windows – those were the only moments
Beirut was not totally isolated, totally desperate and the
enemy almost forgotten.

Nowadays young people around the world have endless distrac-
tions – but not in the Middle East. There's a joke told about most
capitals in the region. A tourist arrives at the airport. He gets
into a taxi, and the driver asks him, 'Would you like to go to a
place where you can have fun?' 'Yes,' replies the tourist. 'Where
there are women?' 'Yes!' says the tourist. 'And where you can
have a drink?' 'Yes, yes, yes!' And the driver says, 'There isn't
one.' Young men in the Middle East have few ways to have fun
except watching and playing football. (Most young women in
the region are deprived even of football.) Prince Ali told us, 'The
real talent well in football in our region [Asia] comes from the
Levant, traditionally: Iraq, Jordan, Syria, Lebanon and Palestine.'

The region's demographic 'youth bulge' may have helped
destabilize governments, but it's an asset to the national football teams. Montague writes (and one must never tire of quot-
ing the classics): 'In the Middle East there was the mosque
and the terrace, and little in between.'

Still, we're not claiming that these Arab nations are
world-beaters. We have merely shown that they punch massively
above their weight inside Asia. After all, they hardly ever play
teams from anywhere else. In the fourteen-year period under
study, Syria played non-Asians just twice (Venezuela and Zimbabwe), while Palestine only met Chile and Mauritania. It's hard to
imagine any of the Arab countries beating the global big boys.

Furthermore, GDP statistics for poorer countries outside
Europe (especially countries in the midst of war or sanctions)
are notoriously unreliable. In general, there is more 'noise'
in all the data for countries outside Europe, meaning that we

struggle to pick up the influence of the factors we are interested in. It's like listening to a radio with poor reception: the meaning of the words is hard to make out.

It therefore makes more sense to focus on Europe alone. Europe is a more homogeneous place than the world as a whole, meaning that differences, especially in income and experience, tend to be smaller. Second, the data are better: Europeans have been collecting them for longer, and they have a relatively long history of transparent record keeping (though there are some very suspicious European statistics too). Last, most of the world's dominant teams are grouped together in Europe, playing against pretty much the same set of opponents. It all adds up to a fairly accurate picture of how well each European team performs.

Let's first rank the best European teams on their absolute performance, without taking into account their population, experience or income. The following table presents the 'absolute' top ten ranked by win percentage (2000–2014):

		P	W	D	WPC*	GD
1	Spain	182	127	31	78.3	1.220
2	Netherlands	172	102	45	72.4	1.076
3	France	192	109	50	69.8	0.938
4	Germany	193	112	44	69.4	1.093
5	Portugal	176	98	44	68.2	0.983
6	England	158	84	44	67.1	0.842
7	Croatia	150	77	44	66.0	0.567
8	Italy	177	87	57	65.3	0.520
9	Czech Republic	147	75	32	61.9	0.714
10	Greece	166	77	46	60.2	0.193

* win percentage

Now let's assess them by their overachievement relative to their resources. The European efficiency table below (the only one of its kind, as far as we know) may be the most telling we have, so we rank every team for which we have data.

RANKING OF EUROPEAN NATIONAL TEAMS, CORRECTING FOR POPULATION, WEALTH AND
EXPERIENCE, ALL GAMES BETWEEN TWO EUROPEAN OPPONENTS, 2000-2014

Country	P	W	D	WPC	GD	GD outperformance
Montenegro	49	15	17	48.0	-0.204	1.289
Croatia	129	69	39	68.6	0.620	1.201
Serbia	65	24	20	52.3	0.354	1.179
Portugal	138	76	34	67.4	0.935	1.078
Bosnia and Herzegovina	92	37	20	51.1	0.098	0.932
Iceland	96	25	21	37.0	-0.531	0.896
Netherlands	134	78	33	70.5	1.119	0.892
Czech Republic	129	65	27	60.9	0.651	0.883
Spain	126	82	25	75.0	1.151	0.804
Albania	119	32	32	40.3	-0.294	0.757
Slovenia	105	37	21	45.2	-0.171	0.559
Ireland	111	42	43	57.2	0.261	0.479
Greece	144	73	38	63.9	0.326	0.419
Israel	105	40	31	52.9	0.190	0.410
FYR Macedonia	107	27	26	37.4	-0.486	0.388
Denmark	135	62	33	58.1	0.363	0.381
Slovakia	124	41	33	46.4	-0.097	0.370
Sweden	145	68	36	59.3	0.566	0.334
Ukraine	126	52	40	57.1	0.183	0.325
Moldova	121	23	30	31.4	-0.760	0.294
Romania	138	65	33	59.1	0.442	0.267
Belarus	116	37	26	43.1	-0.190	0.237
Germany	139	79	32	68.3	1.000	0.234
Georgia	115	25	28	33.9	-0.678	0.203
France	134	81	32	72.4	0.918	0.156
Armenia	103	19	19	27.7	-0.932	0.148
Switzerland	105	42	36	57.1	0.267	0.112

Latvia	123	32	28	37.4	−0.504	0.104
Finland	126	45	31	48.0	−0.032	0.104
Bulgaria	113	43	31	51.8	0.053	0.099
England	120	65	30	66.7	0.850	0.050
Cyprus	105	20	21	29.0	−1.057	0.038
Norway	129	53	30	52.7	0.155	0.017
Belgium	112	46	30	54.5	0.161	0.016
Italy	139	75	43	69.4	0.640	−0.055
Turkey	144	63	38	56.9	0.333	−0.067
Lithuania	111	28	20	34.2	−0.667	−0.093
Russia	118	54	36	61.0	0.542	−0.118
Poland	138	59	38	56.5	0.297	−0.270
Estonia	134	24	33	30.2	−1.030	−0.325
Austria	102	28	25	39.7	-0.363	−0.413
Hungary	124	44	26	46.0	−0.145	−0.425
Malta	117	10	17	15.8	−1.855	−0.598
Azerbaijan	101	10	26	22.8	−1.376	−0.705
Kazakhstan	84	7	17	18.5	−1.429	−1.097
Luxembourg	106	6	15	12.7	−2.104	−1.137

Again, the most important number is in the last column: each country's 'goal difference outperformance'. Four of the top five countries are from ex-Yugoslavia. Their overachievement is remarkable, given that we credited them with the experience of the Yugoslav national teams. (They did after all inherit the country's longstanding football structures when Yugoslavia collapsed into war in the 1990s.) In other words, while these countries are small and poor, we counted them as pretty experienced.

Like western Arabia, this is another troubled region with an exceptional football culture. Yugoslavia benefited from being the most open communist country. The south-eastern bit of the Iron Curtain was porous, and many of the best Yugoslav players moved to Western clubs, gaining useful access to the Western European knowledge networks.

Openness seems to have benefited the high-achieving Czechs, too. Prague before communism was an unmistakably central European city, interlinked with Germany, Austria and Italy. Very soon after the fall of communism the Czechs had re-forged networks with their Western neighbours.

The top of our rankings also show that the starring roles of Iceland and Portugal at Euro 2016 didn't come out of the blue. By contrast, our table is less flattering to most of Europe's trophy-winning nations. Germany and France barely overachieve relative to their considerable resources, whereas Italy actually underachieves slightly. These are large, well-connected countries, all of them richer than the European average. They only do about as well as they should.

Now that we've reviewed all the evidence, who gets the Tom Thumb trophy – the poor, small, inexperienced man's Jules Rimet – for the relatively best team on earth? Which country does best, allowing for experience, population and income? Well, one day we'd like to see this played out on grass. Let's have a World Cup in which teams start with a handicap, settled by a panel of econometricians chaired by Professor Gerrard. But until that great day comes, all we have is our model. It shows that the Middle East, former Yugoslavia and the Iberian Peninsula are the world's overachieving hotspots. Whether you think our award should go to Montenegro, Portugal or Palestine is a matter of judgement.

Only one great question remains: which is the relatively worst team on earth? The following table shows the worst underperformers relative to their population, income and football experience of 124 teams with more than 100 games played (2000–2014):

Country	P	W	D	WPC*	GD	GD outperformance
Luxembourg	115	7	20	14.8	−1.965	−1.463
India	124	43	29	46.4	−0.411	−1.367
Malta	125	14	17	18.0	−1.736	−1.003
Malaysia	166	53	38	43.4	−0.163	−0.919
Hungary	139	49	30	46.0	−0.158	−0.880
Estonia	169	38	40	34.3	−0.864	−0.840
Austria	121	33	33	40.9	−0.306	−0.833
Hong Kong	104	28	23	38.0	−0.673	−0.741
Tanzania	163	50	41	43.3	−0.325	−0.727

* win percentage

Luxembourg is the shocker. The country of just over half a million people ought to be bad at football, but in fact it's much, much worse than it should be. That seems surprising. It's sandwiched between some of the best football nations on earth. If you judge by the map, Luxembourg is smack in the middle of the Western European knowledge network. But networks are never simply geographical. Nobody in football wanted to network with Luxembourg because the country was too small to support a decent league or to produce many good players. Top-class foreign coaches and players were never spotted at the Jeunesse Esch ground passing on their know-how. Admittedly, the nation's dry spell of fifteen years without a win ended with Paul Koch's legendary last-minute penalty save against Malta in 1995, but even after that the Luxembourgeois hardly hit the heights. In 2001 Joel Wolff, secretary-general of the country's FA, confessed to us in a world exclusive interview, 'Let's say that we have arrived at a relative nadir.' Whenever managers recited the verity, 'There are no more minnows in international football,' they were forgetting Luxembourg. This cosy little country gets our *Soccernomics* award for the relatively worst football team on earth.

CORE TO PERIPHERY: THE FUTURE MAP OF GLOBAL FOOTBALL

On a snowy night in Amsterdam, a dozen or so Dutch football writers and ex-players have gathered in a roomy flat in the dinky city centre. Guus Hiddink walks in and grabs someone's shoulders from behind by way of greeting. Growing up with five brothers gave him a knack for male bonding. (Hiddink appears to find women more exotic, and his cohabitation with his then mistress in Seoul shocked Koreans.)

The evening starts with a football quiz, at which the future manager of Chelsea, Russia, Turkey and Holland performs indifferently. Then there is food and football talk until the early morning. Though Hiddink is the senior figure at the table, he never tries to dominate. He likes telling stories – about his former player Romario, or his old roommate at the San Jose Earthquakes, George Best – but when others interrupt he is just as happy to lean back in his chair and listen. He is a solid, soothing, jowly presence. 'You can feel he's at ease,' Boudewijn Zenden, one of his former players, told us, 'so if he's at ease, the others are at ease. He creates this environment where you feel safe.'

Hiddink – a great success as a coach until 2008, less so in his declining years – has a special place in the latest stage of football's history. In the early twenty-first century, he became one of the world's main exporters of football know-how from Western Europe to the margins of the earth. We saw in Chapter 17 that from about 1970 to 2000, five of the six founding members of the European Economic Community dominated football thinking and won almost all the game's prizes. These countries perfected what you might call the continental European style: a fast, physical, collectivist football.

But then these countries began exporting their expertise. Hiddink and other Dutch, German, French and Italian expat managers established themselves in Hiltons and Westerners' compounds around the planet. From around 2000, they helped several new football countries – Russia, Australia and South Korea, to name a few – close some of the gap with the managers' own native countries.

When we first published Soccernomics in 2009, we expected this process to continue. We thought that rising powers would catch up with and outstrip Western Europe and South America in football, just as economic and political power has also moved away from the West. But in football, this hasn't happened. On the contrary: as we write in March 2018, Western Europe looks more dominant than ever. From 2006 to 2014, Western European teams won three straight World Cups, something no continent had managed before. Two of those trophies were won outside Europe, something no European team had ever managed before. Better, continental Western Europeans hogged eight of the nine places on the podium in this period:

World Cup	Winner	Runner-up	Third
2006	Italy	France	Germany
2010	Spain	Holland	Germany
2014	Germany	Argentina	Holland

Notice the region's depth: five different European countries have made it into the top three. Some will inevitably fail sometimes, as Italy and Spain did at the 2014 World Cup, but there is always a neighbour coming through. Only 5 per cent of the world's population lives in Western Europe, yet in 2014 the other 95 per cent of humanity put together produced just one team that could match the best Europeans: Argentina.

In short, the rest of the world began to catch up, but in recent years has stalled. We'll explain why we think that happened, and then discuss the countries that we think have the best chance of closing the gap in future.

FROM THE BACK CORNER TO THE WORLD

Born in 1946, Hiddink grew up close to what was just becoming the epicentre of global football knowledge. He is the son of a village schoolteacher and Resistance hero from a small town in the Achterhoek, or 'Back Corner', about five miles from the German border. The Back Corner is wooded and quiet, one of the few empty bits of the Netherlands, and on visits home from stints in Seoul or Moscow, Hiddink enjoys tooling along its back roads on his Harley-Davidson Fat Boy. 'Pom-pom-pom-pom-pom.' He puffs out his cheeks to mimic the motor's roar.

He grew up milking cows, ploughing behind two horses and dreaming of becoming a farmer. But Dutch farms were already dying, and he became a football coach instead. At nineteen he took an assistant's job at the Back Corner's semi-professional club, De Graafschap, where his father had played before him. He then made an unusual career move: from coach to player. The head coach, seeing that his young assistant could kick a ball, stuck him in the team, and thus began a sixteen-year playing career.

The handsome, round-faced, wavy-haired playmaker was too lazy and slow for the top, yet he was present at a golden age.

The Dutch 1970s shaped Hiddink. Holland, playing what foreigners called 'total football', a new kind of game in which
players constantly swapped positions and thought for themselves, reached two World Cup finals. Dutch clubs won four
European Cups. Off the field, Dutch players of Hiddink's generation answered foreign journalists' questions with sophisticated
discourses in several languages. For a keen observer like Hiddink, the players' constant squabbles provided object lessons
in how to keep stars just about functioning within a collective.

Dutch football's renown at the time helped even a second-rate
player like Hiddink find work abroad, with the Washington Diplomats and the San Jose Earthquakes. 'I was Best's roommate,'
says Hiddink, enjoying the quirky American word, and he mimics
himself fielding the phone calls from Best's groupies: 'George is
not here. George is sleeping.'

It was the start of a world tour whose destinations would
include South Korea, Australia, a suite in a five-star hotel in
Moscow (where, according to the president of the Russian FA,
he spent a fortune ordering cappuccinos from room service),
and Istanbul. Hiddink got the Koreans playing the best football
in their history at the World Cup of 2002, the Australians playing their best ever in 2006, and the Russians at Euro 2008.
But in the last years of his career his teams faltered. (He
retired in 2016 after a final caretaker stint at Chelsea.)

1889–2002: OFF THE PLANE WITH A LEATHER BALL

Football seems to have a quality that enables it eventually to
conquer every known society. The first exporters of the game
were Victorian British sailors, businessmen, missionaries and
colonial officers. In 1889, to cite a typical story, twenty-one-
year-old Englishman Frederick Rea disembarked on the island
of South Uist off the west coast of Scotland to work as a

headmaster. A couple of years later two of his brothers visited, carrying with them a leather football. Within two decades the game had conquered South Uist. Shinty, a stick sport that had been played there for 1,400 years, 'was wiped like chalk from the face of the island', wrote Roger Hutchinson in the British football journal *Perfect Pitch* in 1998, 'supplanted, like a thousand of its distant relatives from Buenos Aires to Smolensk, by a game almost as young and innocent as Frederick Rea himself'. Today football is the dominant sport on South Uist. It conquered because of its magic.

Victorian Britons spread the game to continental Europe, Latin America and bits of Africa. However, for a century Asia and North America remained almost immune. Contrary to myth, football took a long time to become a global game. What people called the 'World Cup' should until the 1980s have been called 'the Euro–Latin American Duopoly'. Though most people on the planet lived in Asia, the continent's only representative at the World Cup of 1978 was Iran. Even in 1990 the British Isles had more teams at the World Cup (three) than all of Asia combined (two). Many Asian countries still barely knew about football. When that year's World Cup final was shown on Japanese television, there was a surprising studio guest: baseball player Sadaharu Oh. 'Mr Oh,' he was asked during the match, 'what is the difference between sliding in baseball and in football?' In Australia, too, football then was still marginal. Johnny Warren, an Australian international and later TV commentator on the game, called his memoirs *Sheilas, Wogs, and Poofters*, because according to Australian myth in the years before Hiddink landed there, women, immigrants and homosexuals were the three core elements of the national football public.

But by 1990 the so-called third wave of globalization was under way. Increased world trade, cable television and finally the internet brought football to new territories. Roberto Fontanarrosa, the late Argentine cartoonist, novelist and football nut, said, 'If TV were only an invention to broadcast football, it would be justified.'

Suddenly the Chinese, Japanese, Americans and many urban Indians could see football's magic. They saw it even more clearly than the people of South Uist had a century before. Football by now had the prestige of being the world's biggest sport, and everyone wanted a piece of its fans' passion. Football is often mocked for its low scores, but precisely because goals are so scarce, the release of joy is greater than in other sports. When the former goalkeeper Osama bin Laden visited London in 1994, he watched four Arsenal matches, bought souvenirs for his sons in the club shop and remarked that he had never seen as much passion as among football supporters.

Just then football was capturing the last holdouts. On 15 May 1993, Japan's J-League kicked off. The next year China acquired a national professional league, and in 1996 the US and India followed. A therapist we met at a football debate in San Francisco nicely described the game's impact on new converts. When she'd first seen a World Cup on TV, her reaction was: 'Why didn't anybody ever tell me about this?' She hadn't stopped watching football since. She stands for millions of Americans (and Indians, Chinese, inhabitants of South Uist, and so on).

From the 1990s the new marginal countries began to hire European coaches who could quickly teach them the latest in football. By the turn of the millennium, Hiddink was an obvious candidate for export. He had won the European Cup with PSV Eindhoven, had managed clubs in Turkey and Spain, and had taken Holland to the World Cup semi-final in 1998. After he passed fifty, he felt his ambition begin to wane. Never a workaholic to start with, the boy from the Back Corner had by now proven himself. He had met with triumph and disaster and treated those two impostors just the same. He had gone from villager to cosmopolitan. He had fallen in love with golf. Football was becoming just a hobby.

He took a break and in 2001 popped up in his first missionary posting, as manager of South Korea. As part of the
globalization of football, the country was due to co-host the
2002 World Cup with Japan. South Korea had played in several
World Cups before but had never won a single match, and in
1998 had lost 5–0 to Hiddink's Holland.

When Hiddink landed in Seoul, history was beginning to work
in his favour. Like many emerging nations, the South Koreans
were getting bigger. Thanks to increased wealth, the average
height of a South Korean man had risen from five foot four in the
1930s to about five foot eight by 2002. That meant a bigger pool
of men with the physique required to play international football.
In an interview during a Korean training camp in the Back Corner,
a year before the World Cup, Hiddink told us he'd caught Koreans
using their smallness as an excuse in football. He added, 'But
I won't allow that. I won't let them say beforehand, "They're a
bit bigger and broader; we're small and sad." And gradually I
notice that some of our players are big, too, and know how to
look after themselves.' The 'height effect' was also quietly lifting
many other emerging football countries, from China to Turkey.

But the Koreans had other problems. The Dutch psychological quirk had been squabbling. The Korean disease, as Hiddink
soon discovered, was hierarchy. In Korean football, the older
the player, the higher his status. A thirty-one-year-old veteran
international was so respected he could coast. At meals, the
group of older players would sit down at the table first, and the
youngest last.

Whereas Dutch players talked too much, Koreans were
practically mute. 'Slavishness is a big word,' Hiddink said that
day in the Back Corner, 'but they do have something like: if
the commander says it, we'll follow it blindly. They are used to
thinking, "I'm a soldier. I'll do what's asked of me." And you
have to go a step further if you want to make a team really
mature. You need people who can and will take the team in

their hands.' Hiddink wanted autonomous, thinking 'Dutch', players: a centre-half who at a certain point in the game sees he should push into midfield, a striker who drops back a few yards. He was teaching the Koreans the Dutch variant of the continental European style.

However, he learned what every successful missionary knows: respect the local way of life, or at least pretend to, because otherwise the locals won't listen to you. That afternoon in the Back Corner he said, 'I don't go to work on the culture of the country. I just leave it; I respect it. I only do something about the conditions that they need to perform on the pitch. And of course there are a couple of things off the field that do influence that.'

At the 2002 World Cup the Koreans played with a fervour rarely seen in football. Helped by bizarre refereeing decisions, the country from football's periphery reached the semi-final. It remains the only team from outside Europe and South America to reach that stage in a World Cup since 1934.

South Korea had craved global recognition, and Hiddink achieved it. Korean cities planned statues in his honour, and a caricature of his face appeared on Korean stamps. Hiddink's autobiography appeared in a Korean print run of half a million, despite having to compete with an estimated sixteen Hiddink biographies. In the Back Corner, Korean tour buses made pilgrimages to the Hiddink ancestral home. Soon after the World Cup, the man himself dropped by to visit his octogenarian parents. 'Well, it wasn't bad,' admitted his father. 'Coffee?'

2002–2004: THE PERIPHERY STARTS BEATING THE CORE

During that World Cup of 2002, other peripheral football countries were emerging, too. Japan reached the second round, the US got to the quarters and South Korea was conquered in the match for third place by Turkey, which hadn't even played in a World Cup since 1954.

Several other countries also began to jettison their traditional football culture. Most countries on the fringes of Europe had dysfunctional indigenous playing styles. The ones on the southern fringe – Greece, Turkey, Portugal – favoured pointless dribbling, while the British and Scandinavians played kick-and-rush. Gradually they came to accept that these styles didn't work. They came to the realization that every marginal country needs: there is only one way to play good football – combine traditional Italian defending with the German work ethic and Dutch passing into the European style. ('Industrial football', some Turks sulkily call it.) In football, national styles don't work. You have to have all the different elements. You cannot win international matches playing traditional British or Turkish football. You need to play continental European football.

Nobody did better out of abandoning their roots and adopting continental European football than Turkey's friends across the water, the Greeks. The Greek national team had traditionally played terrible football in front of a couple of thousand spectators. During foreign trips, its camp followers – friends, journalists and miscellaneous – would hang around the team hotel drinking espressos with players until the early morning. When Greece somehow made it to the World Cup of 1994, it ended up regretting it. At the team's training sessions outside Boston, an outfield player would stand in the goal while the others blasted shots into the bushes. They spent most of the tournament travelling the East Coast of the US to receptions with Greek Americans, though they did find time to be thrashed in three matches. In 2002, Greece gave up on the Greek style and imported a vast chunk of experience in the person of an aging German manager, Otto Rehhagel.

The Rhinelander was the prototypical post-war West German collectivist. He had grown up a healthy drive across the border from Hiddink, amid the ruins of post-war western Germany. An apprentice housepainter and bone-hard defender, Rehhagel was brought up on the 'German virtues' of hard work and discipline. As a coach in Germany for decades, he aimed to sign only collectivist European-type players whose personality had been vetted by his wife over dinner in the Rehhagel home. Everywhere he tried to build an organization. Sacked as manager of Arminia Bielefeld, he sighed, 'At least thanks to me there is now a toilet at the training ground.' On later visits to Bielefeld with other clubs, he always enquired about his toilet.

Rehhagel quickly rooted out Greece's cult of the soloist, introduced core European football and took the team to Euro 2004 in Portugal. There he went around saying things like, 'Now that I am coaching Greece, I want to make one philosophical statement. Please write it down: man needs nothing more than other people.' Banal as this sounded, it must have resonated in post-war West Germany. Certainly the Greek players, who pre-Rehhagel never seemed to have heard of collective spirit, had begun preaching the notion in many languages. 'We was very good organized,' said Zisis Vryzas after Greece beat France in the quarter-finals. Angelos Charisteas, the reserve at Werder Bremen who would become the highest scorer of Euro 2004, eulogized, 'We have a German coach, he has a German mentality, and we play like a German team.' Greece had made the journey from midget dribblers to boring European football thanks to German coaching.

Rehhagel himself called it 'learning from European football'. At the time, becoming 'European' – code for becoming organized – was the aspiration of many marginal European countries, in football and outside. Just as these countries were joining the European Union, they were absorbing European football. The final of Euro 2004 pitted Greece against another recently marginal country. The Greeks beat the Portuguese 1–0 thanks to another header from Charisteas, who soon afterwards would be a reserve again at Ajax. It turned out that with merely half-decent players, a good continental European coach, and time to prepare, almost any marginal country could do well. But with hindsight, the 2002–2004 period was probably the periphery's peak to date.

2005–2006: EVEN AUSTRALIA

In this new climate, the best continental European coaches could pick their posts. Hiddink received many offers to take teams to the World Cup of 2006, but he chose the most marginal country of all: Australia.

In 1974, while Hiddink was still absorbing total football in the Back Corner, Australia had qualified for its first World Cup as Asia's sole representatives. The Socceroos of the day were part-timers, and some had to give up their jobs to go to Germany. The German press was particularly interested in the milkman-cum-defender Manfred Schaefer, who had been born in Hitler's Reich in 1943 and came to Australia as a child refugee after the war. At one point in the tournament West Germany's striker Gerd Müller asked him if he really was an amateur. Well, Schaefer proudly replied, he had earned $4,600 by qualifying for the World Cup. 'That's what I earn a week,' said Müller.

The Australians achieved one draw in three matches at the World Cup. 'However,' writes Matthew Hall in his excellent book about Australian football, *The Away Game*, 'their thongs, super-tight Aussie Rules-style shorts and marsupial mascots endeared them to the German public.'

In the next thirty years, football sank so low in Australia that the country's football federation was sometimes reduced to filming its own matches and giving them to TV channels for free. Australian club football was punctuated by weird vendettas between Balkan ethnic groups. Only in 1997, during the new wave of globalization, were the Socceroos of 1974 publicly honoured in their own country.

Then, in 2005, Hiddink landed with a mission to teach European football. First he gathered the Australian team in a training camp in his native Back Corner. His first impression: 'What a bunch of vagabonds. Everyone came in wearing a cap, or flip-flops. One had on long trousers, another shorts, and another Bermuda shorts. I said, "What is this?" "Well, that's how we live." "Hello, but you probably play like that, too."'

Hiddink spent Australia's first training session in the Back Corner watching his new charges fly into each other like kamikaze pilots. 'You don't have to chase these guys up,' he remarked. After a half hour he stopped the game. When the players' cries of 'Come on, Emmo!' 'Hold the ball, Johnno!' 'Let's go!' and the streams of 'Fucking' had finally faded, Hiddink asked them to shout only when a teammate was in trouble and needed coaching. That would improve everyone's vision of play, he said. The game resumed in near silence. It was Australia's first baby step towards continental European football.

Just as he had with the South Koreans, Hiddink was turning the Australians into Dutch football players. That meant giving them the intellectual discipline needed for the World Cup. The Australian way was to train hard, play hard, but then relax with late-night beers in the hotel bar. Hiddink wanted the players thinking on their own about their jobs. Working hard wasn't enough. Hiddink was teaching them to think like Europeans. The Socceroos tended to run to wherever the ball was. Hiddink forbade them from entering certain zones. In European football, doing the right things is always better than doing a lot of things.

He had noticed that at the Confederations Cup of 2005, shortly before he took over, where the Socceroos had lost all their three games and conceded ten goals, all four Australian defenders would often stay back to mark a single forward. That left them short elsewhere on the field. No semi-professional Western European team would be so naive.

It was striking how quickly the Socceroos learned the basics of European football. In November 2005, only a couple of months after Hiddink had started part-time work with them (he was also coaching PSV at the other end of the globe), they beat Uruguay in a play-off to qualify for the World Cup. Suddenly the Melbourne *Herald Sun* found itself wondering whether the sport of 'Aussie Rules' football could remain dominant in Australia's southern states. Already more Australian children played football than Aussie Rules and both rugby codes combined.

The newspaper's worries appeared justified when a few months later, just before the World Cup of 2006, an Australia–Greece football friendly drew 95,000 people to the Melbourne Cricket Ground. In no city in Europe or Latin America could such a game have drawn such a crowd. Australia had also just become approximately the last country on earth to acquire a national professional football league. (Until 2005 the Australians called it 'soccer', but then the national association renamed themselves Football Federation Australia, provoking a culture war that still rages.)

And then Hiddink led the Socceroos to the second round of the World Cup of 2006. Great crowds of Australians set their alarm clocks to watch at unearthly hours. Soon after the Socceroos got back from Germany, Australia launched its own (disastrous) bid to stage a World Cup. What had happened on South Uist more than a century before is now threatening to happen in Oz. A century from now, Aussie Rules might exist only at subsidized folklore festivals.

2006–2009: HIDDINK TO GHIDDINK IN A MOSCOW HOTEL SUITE

After Australia, Hiddink could have had almost any job in football. In an ideal world, he would have liked to manage England.

Of all the world's marginal football countries, England had the most potential because it was rich and fairly large and had recently re-joined the network of core countries.

Hiddink also relished the specific challenges of managing England. He had the psychological expertise to inspire tired multimillionaires. He loved dealing with difficult characters; Wayne Rooney would be a cinch for him. And he would have improved the thinking of a team that had everything but intellect. As a lover of the bohemian life, he would have been happy in London, and his girlfriend would have been an hour from her beloved Amsterdam. But Hiddink couldn't bear the thought of British tabloids crawling over his family, and so he decided to spread his continental European know-how to Russia instead.

Like England, Russia had always been removed from the best Western European football know-how. The country didn't have much of a tradition. The excellent Soviet side of the 1980s had been largely Ukrainian. But now, after communism, Russia's door to the West had opened slightly. There was potential here.

Admittedly, the country's population was collapsing rather than growing, as Russian men drank themselves to death. However, when Hiddink took the job, the Russian economy was moving the right way. In the decade from 1998, Russian income per capita nearly doubled. The country's new oil money bought Hiddink's brain. (Oil in general has become one of the dominant financial forces in modern football.)

As in South Korea, Hiddink's job was to force his players to be free. Traditionally, Russian football players had the 'I only work here' demeanour of *Homo sovieticus*. They feared their coaches as much as they feared the mafiosi who stole their jeeps. They shoved safe sideways passes into each other's feet, because that way nobody could ever shout at them. There was *zaorganizovannost*, over-organization.

Ghiddink, as the Russians call him, joked with his players, relaxed them. As a 'punishment' in training, a player might have a ball kicked at his backside, while the rest of the squad stood around laughing. The times helped: this generation of Russian players could barely remember the USSR. Armed with iPhones and SUVs, they had left the periphery and joined the global mainstream.

As he had in South Korea, Hiddink practically ordered his players to think for themselves, to give riskier passes, to move into new positions without his telling them to. Marc Bennetts, author of *Football Dynamo: Modern Russia and the People's Game*, said, 'It's as if he's beaten the Marxism-Leninism out of them.' At Euro 2008, Russia's hammering of Hiddink's native Holland was the ultimate triumph of a marginal country over a core one. It also provided the almost unprecedented sight of Russian football players having fun. They swapped positions and dribbled, knowing that if they lost the ball no one would scream at them. After the game, their best player, Andrei Arshavin, muttered something about 'a wise Dutch coach' and cried.

Russia lost in the semis of Euro 2008 to another former marginal country, Spain. By then, after twenty-two years in the European Union, Spain was so networked that it didn't even need a foreign coach to win the Euro.

Spain, Russia and Turkey, another semi-finalist at Euro 2008, were all beneficiaries of the spread of football know-how to marginal countries. When all countries have about the same football information, and converging incomes, the countries with the most inhabitants usually win. Three of the four semi-finalists at Euro 2008 (Russia, Germany and Turkey) had the largest populations in Europe.

It looked in 2008 as if the rise of the periphery was threatening football's traditional order. If a country like England stopped advancing tactically, we thought, it would get overtaken.

2009-?: THE PERIPHERY STALLS

But it hasn't happened that way. The football powers of a generation ago are mostly still the football powers of today.

Until the late 1990s the cliché in football was that an African country would 'soon' win the World Cup. Everyone said it, from Pelé to the 1950s England manager Walter Winterbottom. But it turned out not to be true. Nor can the richer Asian countries compete with the world's best. Look at the figure below, which shows how the 'new' continents have performed against established Europe and South America since 1950:

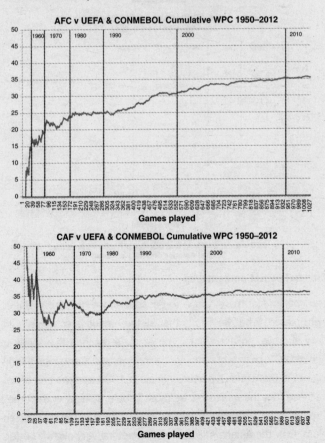

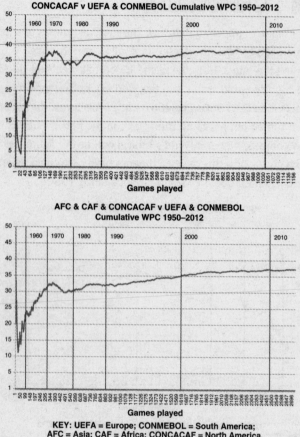

CONCACAF v UEFA & CONMEBOL Cumulative WPC 1950–2012

Games played

AFC & CAF & CONCACAF v UEFA & CONMEBOL Cumulative WPC 1950–2012

Games played

KEY: UEFA = Europe; CONMEBOL = South America;
AFC = Asia; CAF = Africa; CONCACAF = North America,
Central America and the Caribbean

Cumulative win percentages

The charts allot more space to decades in which more matches were played. What we see is that all the emerging continents initially improve, but then stall. The Africans reached their peak in about 1990, before plateauing. (With hindsight, Cameroon's thrilling run to the World Cup quarter-finals in 1990 was the end of Africa's rise, not the start of it, as most people thought at the time.) The North and Central Americans stalled early in the new millennium. Only the Asians still seem to be getting very slightly better.

The US, too, was showing alarming signs of stagnation even before its remarkable failure to qualify for the 2018 World Cup. Here is the US men's national team's win percentage, decade by decade (counting a draw as half a win):

Decade	Played	Won	Drawn	Lost	Goals for	Goals against	WPC
Pre-1950s	39	13	3	23	74	141	37.2
1950s	25	7	1	17	49	96	30.0
1960s	24	6	5	13	35	55	35.4
1970s	71	18	15	38	66	146	35.9
1980s	75	28	23	24	88	84	52.7
1990s	208	82	49	77	270	231	51.2
2000s	173	99	30	44	291	161	65.9
2010s	122	63	24	35	207	141	61.5

The nadir for 'Team USA' was the post-war period up to 1960. This coincided with the peak of American dominance as a superpower and the American Dream. It might sound odd that the world's mightiest country was such a mouse at football, but in fact for most of these years the US felt little need to measure itself against other countries. It had its own games. Pre-war, an American team staffed largely with recent immigrants had played fairly often against Europeans and South Americans, but after the war the number of games slumped.

The table shows that from the 1970s, the US grew more interested in football. The North American Football League took off, and the national team began playing more often. Things kept getting better in the 1980s (when the US started playing more against South Americans), and stayed stable in the 1990s when the country returned to World Cups. American football was coming out of isolation. It's not that the US started scoring more goals; rather, it gradually learned to concede fewer. Defence is always more mechanical than attack, so it appears that in these decades the US was learning from the rest of the world, and from foreign coaches such as Bora Milutinovic. Yet when we calculated the world's worst underachieving nations for the period 1980–2001, the US still made our bottom ten on earth. Given the country's fabulous wealth and enormous population, it 'should' have scored nearly three-quarters of a goal more per game than it did. Its win percentage in those 21 years (counting draws as half a win) was just 52 per cent.

In the 2000s the US's win percentage jumped to 65 per cent, double what it was before 1960. Admittedly that statistic flattered the country. The Americans were playing fewer internationals against teams from Europe and South America. In the decade to 2010, for the first time since the 1970s, the US played the majority of its games against North and Central American teams. That isn't the way to learn best practice. Then from 2010 to 2016 the team declined somewhat even before that shock defeat to Trinidad and Tobago in October 2017. The US has never regained its peak FIFA ranking of eighth place in 2005.

In short, there is a common pattern for football's developing nations: for a while they catch up, but then they stall before reaching the top. Why?

Almost exactly the same question has long been asked about developing countries in a different context: national income. Is the gap between rich and poor countries narrowing or expanding? This research is often associated with the pioneering work of Robert Barro (of Harvard) and Pep Guardiola's friend Xavier Sala-i-Martin (Columbia, and treasurer of FC Barcelona from 2004 to 2010). They reasoned that it's easier for a poor country like Vietnam to grow its economy than a rich one like the US. That's because much of what Vietnam has to do in the early stages is simply copy: if it imports the kind of computers and other machines that are already being used in the US, then its offices and factories will quickly become more productive.

By contrast, if the US wants to grow it has to do new things, which is more difficult. Investors, knowing that, will be keener to invest their capital in Vietnam than in the US. All things being equal, Vietnam's economy will then grow faster than the US's. That's catch-up – at least for countries going from poverty to middle-income.

There are possibly only two topics in this world about which we can gather data for every country over an extended period. Luckily, those topics happen to be national income and national football teams' results. When a country becomes independent it joins the UN, sets up a central bank, collects taxes and starts reporting national income accounts. It also joins FIFA to create a national football team. And if we want to study convergence, arguably football data is better, since we know the score for every game played, while measuring national income is notoriously unreliable.

So what does the data tell us? On national income, there is evidence of convergence of incomes across many parts of the world, notably Europe, Asia and North America. This is good news since we want poorer countries to catch up and enjoy the same standards of living as rich countries. The bad news is that the global economic picture is extremely patchy. For much of the 1980s, 1990s and 2000s, African countries in particular actually fell further behind the developed world. War, political instability, underinvestment in health and education, and bad infrastructure held them back.

The picture for football convergence is different. Stefan, together with Melanie Krause from the University of Hamburg, looked for convergence in two statistics: average goal difference and average win percentage (counting draws as half a win) from 1950 to 2014, averaging over four-year periods ending with a World Cup, for instance from 2010 to 2014.

Their main finding: if your national team started off under-performing, it was likely to get better, regardless of when and where you were in the world. Standards across the world have slowly converged for many years. The poorest countries have improved fastest. FIFA deserves some credit for this. Just by staging World Cups in all age ranges, and running a regulated transfer market, it has helped the weak catch up. Of course, FIFA could have done so much more if only it had put all the billions it earned from World Cups into building facilities in poor countries.

Catch-up seems to be simpler in football than in macroeco-nomics. A developing country can improve its football just by copying the training and tactics used in the best countries. That's easier when much of the know-how you need is broadcast worldwide every evening on TV. Migrant coaches like Hiddink help do the copying. By contrast, copying whole economic sys-tems is much harder and requires extraordinary coordination.

It probably also matters that so many people care deeply about their national football teams' results, and that outcomes are highly visible. Meeting a clear target is often much sim-pler than meeting a complex one. A bad economy can always be blamed on someone else, but the national team is more accountable.

And whereas governments can nationalize or steal foreign investments, they can't easily steal the returns on the skills of football players. (Some officials do try, as witness the quar-rels between African federations and players over unpaid World Cup bonuses.) If a country's football is dysfunctional, the best players will simply go abroad and learn new skills there.

But why do developing football nations stall before entirely catching up with the best countries? Melanie and Stefan have scoured the wider convergence literature for an explanation, and they think they have found a good candidate: the middle-income trap. The idea is that convergence from a low level of income is relatively simple: invest, invest, invest. You just import or copy capital (machines) from more advanced countries. Capital makes people more productive. Almost regardless of the wider economic system, this prescription will work.

However, it only works up to a point. Once a certain minimum of catch-up has been achieved you need to become innovative. The greatest wealth ultimately goes to innovators (in today's world, think Apple, Google, Facebook). A nation's mindset therefore needs to change as national income increases. We see this today in many Asian economies where governments are encouraging more individualism in order to promote a more innovative economy. But it's a hard shift to make.

The same argument applies in football. Teams from Africa, Asia and North America have in recent decades managed to replicate some of the basic patterns of play developed in Europe and South America. In particular, the weak have got fit and learned to defend. They no longer lose 10–0. Yet they now appear caught in football's equivalent of the middle-income trap. They play organized football, but the creative stars and the exciting new tactics (think of German forward pressing) still come from the established nations.

But in the long term, Western Europe's dominance looks unsustainable. When the whole world is playing football, and watching the same games on TV every night, a region with 5 per cent of the planet's population can't keep winning for ever. Some other countries will surely catch up. And given that Palestine and Jordan are small and poor, our best bets for future kings of the world are three large, relatively well-off countries that are now taking football seriously: the US, Japan and China.

As we write, the US is the laughing stock of global football, having failed to make it out of the world's easiest qualifying zone to the 2018 World Cup. However, more than any other non-European country it has the means to close the gap with the world's best. In the last twenty-five years it has regularly reached the last sixteen of World Cups, and it has the most registered young football players of any country. The momentous 2–1 defeat to Trinidad should be the prompt for an overhaul of everything that's wrong in American football.

Japan, for its part, has formulated a plan to host the World Cup again by 2050 and win it. Both countries already dominate women's football: Japan won the World Cup in 2011, and the US in 2015. In the women's game, where no country has much experience, big, rich nations win.

However, as we've seen, both nations seem to have stagnated in men's football. More than twenty years after they set up national competitions, neither the J-League nor the MLS looks capable of nurturing world-class players. In fact, the best advice we can give any aspiring star from either country is: emigrate fast. What would help both leagues is if their champions were invited to participate in a kind of global Champions League. On the face of it, that would make commercial sense. With American or Japanese TV viewers switching on, the global TV audience for Seattle Sounders–Arsenal or Kashima Antlers–Arsenal would be a lot bigger than for Legia Warsaw–Arsenal.

The problem is that the logistics don't work. As long as the Champions League is played on weekday nights, few Americans or Asians will watch. Most Americans are at work at that time, and most Asians in bed. The worst time on average to attract TV viewers is 4 a.m., says the Futures Sport + Entertainment consultancy – and that's what time it is in Beijing during the second half of Champions League games in Europe.

The only way a global Champions League could take off is if it were played at weekends. A game that kicks off in London, say, at 3 p.m. local time on Saturday, would catch Americans at breakfast and Chinese on a night out. But that would entail bumping domestic leagues to midweek. And the English clubs won't buy that, because they now make a lot more money from the Premier League than from the Champions League. They want to keep the Premier League in its prime weekend spot.

So a global Champions League won't happen anytime soon, unless an investor steps up wanting to pay the kind of money that would shift the Premier League, probably something close to what the NFL gets in the US – say £4 billion a year guaranteed for five years. Given the upheaval this would cause in Europe, that seems like a pretty risky call at the moment. For now, the only step in that direction is likely to be staging Champions League finals in places like New York or Tokyo. So the MLS and the J-League are doomed to continuing marginality. The US and Japan have come far since the 1990s, but the final step to excellence is often the hardest one.

China is a different story. It hasn't come far at all. As of March 2018, the country of 1.3 billion people has still only ever qualified for that single World Cup in 2002, and is a humiliating 68th in the FIFA rankings, 24 spots behind Montenegro.

Yet we expect China's rise in football to begin now, stimulated by football-mad President Xi Jinping. The model is its ascent in athletics: going from nothing before 2008 to topping the medals table at the Beijing Olympics.

Most foreign coverage of Chinese football now focuses on the league, but in fact that's a sideshow. Importing ageing has-beens like Carlos Tevez and Ezequiel Lavezzi just creates a gilded elephants' graveyard. Fans often scoff that players are only interested in money, but the Chinese league's failure so far to attract many stars in their prime shows that this is unfair: the best players do like money, but they will generally choose to earn it in a top-class league. As of early 2017, measured by players' estimated transfer values, the Chinese league was only about as strong as the MLS, and below the Belgian league. No doubt the Chinese league will get better. It might soon become the richest in Asia. But it's still far from being the place to groom future stars. Even Chinese sugar daddies don't seem to think the main football action is at home: from 2015 to 2017 they spent over $2 billion buying stakes in European clubs.

Nor will hiring Marcello Lippi to coach 'Team China' do the trick, not even on what is reportedly the highest salary of any coach on earth. Tom Byer, the football adviser to China's education ministry, says the best indicator of whether an Asian country will start qualifying for World Cups is not the fame of the national team's coach. Rather, it's qualifying for the Under-20s World Cup and Asian Under-17s championships. In other words, success is about producing youngsters. And this is where China should start improving.

China has potential: there are over 100 million Chinese children aged under six. But historically, very few Chinese kids have ever been given the chance to play sport. It was seen as a 'distraction' from the serious business of learning. Go around Shanghai or Beijing and you will scarcely see a ball being kicked anywhere. 'You look at Chinese children and you can just tell they are not athletic,' Byer told us in 2016. 'They have basically cut out all physical activity.'

But in 2014, China's State Council issued 'Document No. 46', outlining a policy to build sports into a $770-billion industry by 2025. Xi had made football a national priority. He set China the goal of playing in, hosting and eventually winning the World Cup. His government announced plans to hire 120 foreign coaches to train up to 50,000 Chinese football teachers. In 2016, China unveiled a five-year plan to spend about $220 billion on sports. In theory if not quite yet in practice, football is now compulsory in schools. Many will get artificial fields. And as more Chinese parents get into football themselves, they will start kicking balls with their kids in the crucial under-six age range, predicts Byer.

Over time, all this should pay off. A country the size of China cannot easily continue to perform as badly as it has. We expect that it will soon routinely start to qualify for World Cups.

Something else will help the biggest non-European countries. The expansion of the World Cup to forty-eight teams from 2026 will make the competition more random. In the group phase, teams will play just two matches each, so a lucky win will be enough to reach the second round. If teams are tied, there will be penalty shoot-outs – another randomizer. Then there will be five straight knockout rounds, one more than in the current system. The upshot will be a competition in which luck plays a bigger role, much like in the play-off stages of the NFL. That should favour plausible outsiders such as the US, Japan and soon probably China (especially if the US ends up co-hosting in 2026).

The emerging powers need to become as innovative as the Western Europeans. Until they are, though, their best bet is luck.

THE FUTURE: THE BEST OF TIMES – AND THE SMARTPHONE

When Paris Saint-Germain paid £198 million for Neymar in August 2017, more than double the world's previous record transfer fee, the usual mutterings went up that this was insane. Monchi, AS Roma's sporting director, said, 'I don't want to think we're building an artificial bubble that will explode in the future, like the property bubble, which has done so much damage to the global economy. Personally, this millionaire show makes me uncomfortable and scares me.'

Monchi was expressing a broadly felt disquiet: that football's transfer fees, debts, wages, ticket prices, spoiled players and general hype have got out of hand.

We disagree. We don't think there is a football bubble. On the contrary, we think the game has never had it so good. Viewers from San Francisco to Chennai are tuning in to football, and so players will probably keep getting more spoiled and 'overpaid' for a while yet. But there's one big risk to football on the road ahead: the smartphone.

Over the last thirty years, sports have been the fastest-growing segment of the entertainment business, and football has been the fastest-growing sport. All this happened thanks to TV. When clubs became de facto producers of TV content, the game had to smarten itself up. Run-down stadiums full of misbehaving fans no longer cut it. It's no coincidence that the refurbishing of English stadiums and the first sale of the rights to satellite TV happened almost simultaneously in the early 1990s. In the TV era, with comfortable stadiums, football hooliganism has declined across Western Europe. Since 2002, the build-up to the World Cup has no longer been overshadowed by angst about thugs.

On the field, too, violence has been taken out of the game. In the past, creative players had it hard. The tackles that George Best had to endure on Manchester United's right wing in the 1960s almost resembled the sackings of NFL quarterbacks. In 1966 Pelé limped out of the World Cup; in 1983 Diego Maradona had his time at Barcelona ruined by an assault by Andoni Goikoetxea ('The Butcher of Bilbao'); and in 1992 Marco van Basten's career was effectively ended by injuries at the age of twenty-eight. But in the TV era, the authorities cracked down on thuggish defending. Before the World Cup of 1998, FIFA made the tackle from behind a sending-off offence. These curbs have freed the game's stars. Lionel Messi, Cristiano Ronaldo and Zlatan Ibrahimovic have been able to thrill fans week in, week out into their thirties, almost unhindered by injuries or fear.

No wonder that since about 2000, viewers beyond Europe have been switching onto European games. Manchester United, to cite just one example, started life as a club in Manchester. It soon became a club in England, later a club in Europe, and today it is a global club.

Perversely, the televising of games has made actually going to the stadium even more attractive. Perhaps because people now spend so much of their lives in a virtual world, they are willing to pay a premium for high-class real-life experiences such as attending big football games. Fans do complain about English ticket prices. Yet in twenty years' time, when the stadiums are packed with Asian tourists paying £400 for their tickets, we may well look back and say, 'Can you imagine that in 2018 you could get into a game for £60 and have money left over for pints?'

Football is now, by a large and constantly growing margin, the planet's favourite game. There was a landmark moment in 2009, when the Champions League final overtook the Super Bowl as the world's most watched sporting event: 109 million viewers versus 106 million, according to the Futures Sport + Entertainment consultancy. Even in the Canadian prairie city of Edmonton, crowds swarmed downtown to celebrate Barcelona's victory over Manchester United.

The football economy is not a bubble, because its higher spending is funded by higher revenues, and by rich men desperate to throw money at the game. In 2016, Manchester United could afford to pay £89 million for Paul Pogba, because its annual revenues had jumped sixfold in the previous eighteen years to £515 million. A year later, it wasn't really PSG that signed Neymar; it was Qatar, a tiny state that is the world's largest exporter of liquid national gas. With all that money coming in, of course star players are earning enormous salaries and becoming spoiled. These are the problems of success.

It's perfectly reasonable to make a moral critique of the new football. You can say: 'I remember when my local team consisted of local boys earning the same sort of wages as most people in our town. I don't like the moneyed football of today.' That's fair enough. You can still find the old local football if you drop down a division or two, but perhaps you still want to go to Chelsea or Manchester United and find everything much as it was in 1974, and you can't. It's reasonable to resent that. After all, most of us like football because it connects us with our childhood. But it's illogical to jump from a moral preference ('I dislike the new football') to an economic prediction ('This is a bubble that's going to burst'). You might loathe today's big football, but that doesn't mean it's doomed.

In the 1960s, the football agent Ken Stanley told his client George Best: 'Think about what football will be like when it's truly a world game. Think of the size of America. Think of every boy in Africa having a team shirt and a ball at his feet. Think about China and Japan and the rest of the Far East. There are billions of people out there, George. The game is still growing. They'll be watching you on television in Peking and Calcutta before long.'

Stanley's prophesy is now coming true. Global TV has changed football. To understand what happens next, we have listened to Kevin Alavy, managing director of Futures Sport + Entertainment. Kevin sits in Sydney working out how many people really watch different sporting events, and extracting trends from mountains of broadcasting data, though he's far more charming than that description implies. This is how he defines his work: 'Very simply, are these sports events worth the massive investment that they typically cost, and how can my clients get even more value from their association with sport?' For this edition of *Soccernomics*, he gave us some insight into the usually confidential data that Futures Sport has gathered on World Cups and European Championships since 1998.

Alavy told us: 'Football now touches all countries without exception. That is different to twenty years ago.' However, he adds that football still has great scope for global growth. The game has only just begun to penetrate the world's four most populous countries, China, India, the US and Indonesia, which between them account for about 45 per cent of humanity. But in China and India, says Alavy, as yet less than 10 per cent of the population 'really, really cares about football'.

Indonesia, which in 2000 barely had a football culture, has become 'the world's number one country by English Premier League viewership', according to Alavy. Like most developing countries, it has a fast-growing population (about 255 million people in 2015), a growing share of which is acquiring screens and subscribing to pay-TV.

Then there are the large economies of Japan, Canada and Australia, where football is also growing fast. One measure of the game's unrealized potential is that the Premier League still earns more from TV rights inside England (about £5.1 billion total from 2016 to 2019) than in the rest of the world put together (about £3.2 billion). Those proportions won't stay that way for long. European football has entered the global export business. Gerard Piqué, the Barcelona defender with an interest in economics, told us: 'There are markets to exploit and I think that football will still grow much more. And the big clubs will get much bigger. Barcelona and Real Madrid will increase their revenues.'

* * *

So far, so good for football. But the revolution in people's entertainment habits is inevitably going to affect the sport. Football's big future business risk is a little thing called the smartphone.

Scarily for a sport that has turned itself into TV content, more and more people have stopped watching TV. Global TV viewing of sports peaked in 2012. Since then, Futures Sport notes 'the tendency of especially younger people to consume video content online, via their mobile, tablet or laptop, rather than via a TV set'. Overall, the amount of time spent watching TV typically falls by a few percentage points a year, says Futures Sport. Indeed, this is probably one reason why Donald Trump decided in 2015 to diversify from television into politics.

With ever more channels, and ever fewer viewers, most TV programmes now cater to tiny niches. In fact, says Future

Sports: 'One-third of all sports programmes are watched by no one. That's to say, when the official TV audience reporting bureaus around the world report upon the audience for that event, their best estimate is zero viewers. There simply aren't enough sports fans, or people in the world in general, to go round to watch all televised sport.'

Even the world's most popular sport struggles to charge consumers to watch games. If you can mess around on Facebook for free, and if your smartphone habit has slashed your concentration span, then why pay to sit down and watch a ninety-minute football game that might be boring, especially now that websites package the best bits into free videos? Online football videos generated 23 billion views in the year to May 2017, said a report by Tubular Labs and Brave Bison. Ninety-four per cent of this audience was male, two-thirds of it aged under thirty-four. We doubt that many of these millennials have pay-TV subscriptions. No wonder that Sky TV's British football audiences fell about 14 per cent in 2016–2017 compared with the season before.

For now, football has more than managed to offset these lost Western TV viewers by tapping new markets like Indonesia. But how will the game cope in the longer term?

As Johan Cruyff said, 'Every disadvantage has its advantage.' On the one hand, the shift away from TV is worrying. On the other hand, it's an opportunity: for the first time ever, viewers no longer need a television set to watch football. They can now choose their platform: mobile phones, tablets or Xboxes. Millennials are starting to watch games through online streaming, which tends to be cheaper than pay-TV. That means they can now watch on the subway, in the café or during the lunch break at the office. It's possible that football could eventually make big money out of this kind of viewing.

You could imagine Facebook or Amazon paying billions for the rights to show every goal of a World Cup or the Premier

League. They haven't yet, but in 2017 it was reported that Amazon, Twitter, Facebook and YouTube were all bidding to acquire rights to the NFL's Thursday Night Football. Amazon ended up buying streaming rights. Also in 2017 Facebook announced that it would be live-streaming Champions League football, and Major League Soccer, and was competing for rights to the 2018 World Cup. Social media are entering the sports broadcast markets. Football must hope that they will make up for any waning interest from TV.

Virtual reality is also about to come along and improve football viewing. Pretty soon, you will be able to put on VR goggles and feel that you are standing on the field in Barcelona watching Messi dribble straight at you. You will feel so close that you could touch him. You will see what he sees, and hear what defenders shout at him. VR can put you inside the action in a way that TV can't.

It will be social, too. You will be able to put on your goggles and invite your mate in Australia to join you virtually on your couch for the big game. Or you can 'meet' and hang out with him on the field, chatting and watching Messi run past you without getting in Messi's way. Already some American sports offer highlights in VR. By 2020 this will probably be a routine way for lots of people to watch football, at least some of the time.

True, there are drawbacks. Watching in VR for ninety minutes can make you dizzy. Much of the time, you may want to keep watching in 2D, as we do now. Maybe you will only watch highlights in VR. Still, this innovation will make football even sexier. It just might not be enough to keep viewers paying.

* * *

The most-watched football event of all – and by some estimates, the most-watched human event – is the World Cup. But almost unnoticed, it has been losing viewers so far this century. We expect that trend to worsen, even aside from the global ditching of TV sets.

Until very recently, the World Cup had two great advantages over almost any other big sports event. First, it had a global audience. Second, it was free-to-air: people in most countries could watch it on terrestrial channels, without paying. That was the way FIFA liked it, and anyway, some countries had laws requiring sports events of 'national significance' to be screened free-to-air.

The European Championship has shown the power of putting out games on free-to-air channels worldwide. In China, for instance, the free channel CCTV-5 showed every match of Euro 2016. 'This is the number one channel all sports events want to be shown on, if they want to maximise their Chinese audience,' comments Futures Sport. Channels like these helped the Euros gain viewers for every edition from 2000 to 2016. Tournament audiences jumped 27 per cent just from Euro 2012 to 2016. Admittedly that translates into a fall in viewing per match, given that the tournament expanded in this period from sixteen teams to twenty-four, which meant that the number of games increased. Still, growing your TV audience is a remarkable achievement in the post-TV age.

FIFA could have pursued the free-to-air strategy for the World Cup, and done much better out of it, given that the tournament is global rather than merely European. But FIFA hasn't. Futures Sport explains:

They've been much more willing to sell the rights to at least some of the matches in FIFA World Cups to pay-TV. In major football countries, such as Spain, Italy, Portugal, France and Argentina, only around half of all matches in the 2014 FIFA World Cup were televised free-to-air. Where coverage has shifted to pay-TV, tournament viewing figures have declined, even compared with a baseline of 2002 (when the FIFA

World Cup was held in Japan and Korea, and hence the time zone difference was at its very worst from a European and South American perspective).

Pay-TV decimates your audience. Futures Sport says: 'If a programme were to shift from being aired on the number one most popular free-to-air channel to the most-watched pay-TV channel in a country, as much as 75–90 per cent of its viewership could be lost.' Even when only some games are on pay-TV, viewing also declines for the games that are shown free on other channels. Futures Sport explains: 'Fans demand simplicity and convenience. With so many entertainment options from which to choose, they just don't have an incentive to search hard for content.' And it may be that as fans lose sight of parts of the tournament's story, they lose interest in the story as a whole.

We're not worried that FIFA (or indeed the Premier League) will go bankrupt any time soon. The World Cup will continue to bring in billions. It's just that the tournament is probably going to become less central to planetary life. Having already slashed viewing in pay-TV countries, FIFA has now made another decision that seems almost designed to put off fans: starting in 2026, it is expanding the World Cup from thirty-two to forty-eight teams.

The Euros have already shown that more means worse. In Futures Sport's words: 'An increase in the number of matches means more sub-standard matches in the eyes of the average fan. For example, the unprecedented qualification of Albania for UEFA Euro 2016, whilst a major achievement for the defensive-minded Albanian side, was probably not such an exciting event for non-Albanians.'

The average group game at twenty-four-team Euro 2016 attracted 23 per cent fewer viewers than at sixteen-team Euro 2012, says Futures Sport. That was partly because most of the eight additional qualifiers were weak teams that had come to defend, hoping to scrape into the second round by finishing third in their group.

THIRD-PLACED TEAMS PER GROUP AT EURO 2016

Pos	Grp	Team	Pld	W	D	L	GF	GA	GD	Pts
1	B	Slovakia	3	1	1	1	3	3	0	4
2	E	Republic of Ireland	3	1	1	1	2	4	-2	4
3	F	Portugal	3	0	3	0	4	4	0	3
4	C	Northern Ireland	3	1	0	2	2	2	0	3
5	D	Turkey	3	1	0	2	2	4	-2	3
6	A	Albania	3	1	0	2	1	3	-2	3

Source: Futures Sport + Entertainment

The table shows how few goals these teams conceded: on average, just 1.11 per game, even though they faced some of the world's strongest countries. Overall, Euro 2016 produced 2.12 goals per game, the lowest average since Euro '96 – which was itself the first tournament with sixteen teams. A forty-eight-team World Cup will probably feature a bunch of boring Cinderellas, too. That won't encourage viewers to pay, especially given that by 2026 there will probably be even more free entertainment options.

As we write, in spring 2018, football is richer and more popular than ever before. The one question mark is this: what happens when the object on which today's football economy is built – the TV set – starts to become obsolete?

It's hard enough to predict technological change, let alone to say how it will affect football. The one thing we can predict with confidence is that football will remain the world's most popular sport. It isn't going anywhere. Salaries might possibly deflate (though we don't expect them to) but nobody will look round in twenty years and say, 'The whole thing was a bubble.' This game is bigger and probably more durable even than television. We can put it no higher than that.

ACKNOWLEDGEMENTS

Dozens of people helped make this book possible. We would like to thank Peter Allden, Dave Berri, Victor Bichara, Joe Boyle, Edward Chisholm, Dennis Coates, Bastien Drut, Rod Fort, Bernd Frick, Julien Bracco Gartner, Brian Goff, Sunil Gulati, Jahn Hakes, Pauline Harris, Brad Humphreys, Paul Husbands, Kai Konrad, Dan Kuper, Markus Kurscheidt, Mike Leeds, Ben Lyttleton, Wolfgang Maennig, Issa Martinez, Roger Noll, Andrew Oswald, Holger Preuss, Skip Sauer, Philip Soar, Henk Spaan and Lia Na'ama ten Brink.

We got ideas and information from Kevin Alavy, Rob Baade, Rob Bateman, Joel Becker, Vendeline von Bredow, Carl Bromley, Tunde Buraimo, Pamela Druckerman, Gavin Fleig, Mike Forde, Rod Fort, Russell Gerrard, Matti Goksoyr, Norbert Hofmann, Ted Knutson, Adam Kuper, Hannah Kuper, Marc McElligott, Jean-Pierre Meersseman, Kaz Mochlinski, Christian Muck, James Nicholson, Ignacio Palacios-Huerta, Ian Preston, Antoinette Renouf, Placido Rodriguez, Mark Rosentraub, Andreas Selliaas, Simon Wilson, Axel Torres Xirau and Paul in 't Hout; from Benjamin Cohen, Jonathan Hill, Mark O'Keefe, and Alex Phillips at UEFA; and from David O'Connor and Andrew Walsh at Sport+Markt.

The following were fantastic collaborators: Kevin Alavy, Wladimir Andreff, Giles Atkinson, Tunde Buraimo, Luigi Buzzacchi,

Filippo dell'Osso, Christian Deutscher, Bastien Drut, David Forrest, Pedro Garcia-del-Barrio, Steve Hall, David Harbord, Takeo Hirata, Tom Hoehn, Todd Jewell, Georgios Kavetsos, Stefan Késenne, Melanie Krause, Tim Kuypers, Umberto Lago, Stephanie Leach, Neil Longley, Victor Matheson, Susana Mourato, Susanne Parlasca, Thomas Peeters, Ian Preston, Steve Ross, Rob Simmons, Ron Smith, Tommaso Valletti, Daniel Weimar, Guy Wilkinson, Jason Winfree and Andy Zimbalist.

Gordon Wise and Kate Cooper were hardworking and imaginative agents. For this edition, Jack Fogg at HarperCollins took over the reins with patience and competence.

We also want to thank all the interviewees quoted in the text.

SELECT BIBLIOGRAPHY

BOOKS

Anderson, Chris and David Sally. *The Numbers Game: Why Everything You Know about Football Is Wrong*. London: Viking, 2013.

Andreff, Wladimir and Stefan Szymanski, eds. *Handbook on the Economics of Sport*. Cheltenham: Edward Elgar, 2006.

Andrews, David L. *Manchester United: A Thematic Study*. London: Routledge, 2004.

Ball, Phil. *Morbo: The Story of Spanish Football*. London: WSC Books, 2001.

Bellos, Alex. *Futebol: The Brazilian Way of Life*. London: Bloomsbury, 2002.

Bennetts, Marc. *Football Dynamo: Modern Russia and the People's Game*. London: Virgin Books, 2008.

Biermann, Christoph. *Die Fußball-Matrix: Auf der Suche nach dem perfekten Spiel*. Cologne: Kiepenheuer & Witsch, 2009.

Bose, Mihir. *The Spirit of the Game: How Sport Made the Modern World*. London: Constable & Robinson, 2011.

Burns, Jimmy. *Hand of God: The Life of Diego Maradona*. London: Bloomsbury, 1996.

———. *When Beckham Went to Spain: Power, Stardom, and Real Madrid*. London: Penguin, 2004.

Campomar, Andres. ¡Golazo! A History of Latin American
Football. London: Quercus, 2014

Carragher, Jamie. Carra: My Autobiography. London: Corgi
Books, 2009.

Cole, Ashley. My Defence: Winning, Losing, Scandals, and the
Drama of Germany 2006. London: Headline, 2006.

Conn, David. The Fall of the House of Fifa. London: Yellow
Jersey Press, 2017.

Cox, Michael. The Mixer. London: HarperCollins, 2017.

Dobson, Stephen and John Goddard. The Economics of
Football. Cambridge: Cambridge University Press,
2001.

Dorsey, James. The Turbulent World of Middle East Football.
London: Hurst, 2016.

Drogba, Didier. 'C'était pas gagné . . .' Issy-les-Moulineaux:
Éditions Prolongations, 2008.

Drut, Bastien and Richard Duhautois. Sciences Sociales
Football Club. Louvain-la-Neuve: De Boeck, 2015.

Epstein, David. The Sports Gene: What Makes the Perfect
Athlete. London: Yellow Jersey Press, 2013.

Exley, Frederick. A Fan's Notes. London: Yellow Jersey Press,
1999.

Ferguson, Alex. Managing My Life: My Autobiography. London:
Hodder & Stoughton, 2000.

———. My Autobiography. London: Hodder &
Stoughton, 2013

FIFA TMS. Global Transfer Market 2012. Zurich: FIFA TMS,
2013.

Foot, John. Calcio: A History of Italian Football. London: Fourth
Estate, 2006.

Gerrard, Steven. Gerrard: My Autobiography. London: Bantam
Books, 2007.

Ginsborg, Paul. A History of Contemporary Italy. London:
Penguin, 1990.

Gladwell, Malcolm. *Outliers: The Story of Success*. London: Allen Lane, 2008.

Goldblatt, David. *The Ball Is Round: A Global History of Football*. London: Viking, 2006.

Gopnik, Adam. *Paris to the Moon*. New York: Random House, 2000.

Hall, Matthew. *The Away Game*. Sydney: HarperSport, 2000.

Hamilton, Aidan. *An Entirely Different Game: The British Influence on Brazilian Football*. Edinburgh: Mainstream Publishing, 1998.

Hamilton, Duncan. *Immortal: The Approved Biography of George Best*. London: Century, 2013.

Hill, Declan. *The Fix: Football and Organized Crime*. Toronto: McLelland & Stewart, 2008.

Holt, Richard and Tony Mason. *Sport in Britain, 1945–2000*. London: Wiley-Blackwell, 2000.

Honigstein, Raphael. *Das Reboot: How German Football Reinvented Itself and Conquered the World*. London: Yellow Jersey Press, 2015.

Hopcraft, Arthur. *The Football Man: People and Passions in Football*. London: Aurum Press, 2006.

Hornby, Nick. *Fever Pitch*. London: Indigo, 1996.

Kapuściński, Ryszard. *The Football War*. New York: Vintage International, 1992.

Kok, Auke. *1974: Wij waren de besten*. Amsterdam: Thomas Rap, 2004.

Kolfschooten, Frank van. *De bal is niet rond*. Amsterdam and Antwerp: L. J. Veen, 1998.

Lampard, Frank. *Totally Frank*. London: HarperSport, 2006.

Lever, Janet. *Football Madness*. Chicago: University of Chicago Press, 1983.

Lewis, Michael. *Moneyball*. New York: W. W. Norton, 2004.

Lyttleton, Ben. *Edge: What Business Can Learn from Football*. London: HarperCollins, 2017.

Mandela, Nelson. *The Long Walk to Freedom*. London: Abacus, 1995.

Montague, James. *When Friday Comes: Football in the War Zone*. London: deCoubertin Books, 2013.

Mora y Araujo, Marcela and Simon Kuper, eds. *Perfect Pitch 3: Men and Women*. London: Headline Books, 1998.

Nieuwenhof, Frans van de. *Hiddink, Dit is mijn wereld*. Eindhoven: De Boekenmakers, 2006.

Norridge, Julian. *Can We Have Our Balls Back, Please? How the British Invented Sport and Then Almost Forgot How to Play It*. London: Penguin, 2008.

Oliver and Ohlbaum Associates and Fletcher Research. *Net Profits: How to Make Money Out of Football*. London: Fletcher Research, 1997.

Orakwue, Stella. *Pitch Invaders: The Modern Black Football Revolution*. London: Victor Gollancz, 1998.

Peace, David. *The Damned United*. London: Faber and Faber, 2006.

Perarnau, Martí, *Pep Confidential*. Edinburgh: Arena Sport, 2014.

Rooney, Wayne. *My Story So Far*. London: HarperSport, 2006.

Silver, Nate. *The Signal and the Noise: Why So Many Predictions Fail – But Some Don't*. London: Penguin Press, 2012.

Simons, Rowan. *Bamboo Goalposts: One Man's Quest to Teach the People's Republic of China to Love Football*. London: Macmillan, 2008.

Szymanski, Stefan. *Playbooks and Checkbooks: An Introduction to the Economics of Modern Sports*. Princeton, NJ: Princeton University Press, 2009.

———. *Money and Football: A Soccernomics Guide*. New York: Nation Books, 2015.

Szymanski, Stefan and Tim Kuypers. *Winners and Losers: The Business Strategy of Football*. London: Penguin Group, 1999.

Szymanski, Stefan and Andrew Zimbalist. *National Pastime: How Americans Play Baseball and the Rest of the World Plays Football*. Washington, DC: Brookings Institution Press, 2005.

Taylor, Peter. *With Clough by Taylor*. London: Sidgwick & Jackson, 1980.

Tomkins, Paul, Graeme Riley and Gary Fulcher. *Pay as You Play: The True Price of Success in the Premier League Era*. Wigston: GPRF Publishing, 2010.

Turnbull, John, Thom Satterlee and Alon Raab, eds. *The Global Game: Writers on Football*. Lincoln, NE: University of Nebraska Press, 2008.

Varley, Nick. *Parklife: A Search for the Heart of Football*. London: Penguin, 1999.

Vergouw, Gyuri. *De Strafschop: Zoektocht naar de ultieme penalty*. Antwerp: Uitgeverij Funsultancy, 2000.

When Saturday Comes. *Power, Corruption and Pies: A Decade of the Best Football Writing from 'When Saturday Comes'*. London: Two Heads Publishing, 1997.

White, Jim. *Manchester United: The Biography*. London: Sphere, 2008.

Wilson, Jonathan. *Inverting the Pyramid: A History of Football Tactics*. London: Orion, 2008.

———. *The Anatomy of England: A History in Ten Matches*. London: Orion, 2010.

Wortmann, Sönke. *Deutschland. Ein Sommermärchen: Das WM-Tagebuch*. Cologne: Kiepenheuer & Witsch, 2006.

Zirin, Dave. *A People's History of Sports in the United States*. New York: New Press, 2008.

ARTICLES AND RESEARCH PAPERS

Anderson, Christopher. 'Do Democracies Win More? The Effects of Wealth and Democracy on Success in the FIFA World Cup'. Paper presented at the annual meeting of the Midwest Political Science Association, Chicago, 2011.

Baade, R. 'Professional Sports as Catalysts for Metropolitan Economic Development'. *Journal of Urban Affairs*, 18, no. 1 (1996): 1–17.

Berlin, Peter. 'Playing by the Numbers'. *Financial Times*, 1 February 1992.

Bryson, Alex, Babatunde Buraimo and Rob Simmons. 'Time to Go? Head Coach Quits and Dismissals in Professional Football'. IZA Institute of Labor Economics, Discussion Paper Series, March 2017.

Dickson, Alex, Colin Jennings and Gary Koop. 'Domestic Violence and Football in Glasgow: Are Reference Points Relevant?' *Oxford Bulletin of Economics and Statistics*, 78, no. 1 (February 2016): 1–21.

Feenstra, Robert, Robert Inklaar and Marcel P. Timmer. 'The Next Generation of the Penn World Table'. Available for download at www.ggdc.net/pwt (2013).

Gabaix, Xavier. 'Zipf's Law for Cities: An Explanation'. *Quarterly Journal of Economics*, 114, no. 3 (August 1999): 739–767.

Hicks, Joe and Grahame Allen. 'A Century of Change: Trends in UK Statistics since 1900'. House of Commons Library Research Paper 99/111. London: House of Commons Library, December 1999.

Hirshleifer, J. 'The Paradox of Power'. *Economics and Politics*, 3 (1991): 177–200.

Kavetsos, Georgios and Stefan Szymanski. 'National Well-Being and International Sports Events'. *Journal of Economic Psychology*, 31, no. 3 (April 2010): 158–171.

Kirby, Stuart, Brian Francis and Rosalie O'Flaherty. 'Can the FIFA World Cup Football (Football) Tournament Be Associated with an Increase in Domestic Abuse?' *Journal of Research in Crime and Delinquency*, 51, no. 3 (2014): 259–276.

McGrath, Ben. 'The Sporting Scene: The Professor of Baseball'. *New Yorker*, 7 July 2003.

Palacios-Huerta, Ignacio. 'Professionals Play Minimax'. *Review of Economic Studies*, 70, no. 2 (2003): 395–415.

Peeters, Thomas and Stefan Szymanski. 'Financial Fair Play in European Football'. *Economic Policy* 29, no. 78 (2014): 343–390.

Peeters, Thomas, Victor Matheson and Stefan Szymanski 'Tourism and the 2010 World Cup: Lessons for Developing Countries'. *Journal of African Economies*, 23, no. 2 (2014): 290–320.

Quigg, Zara, Karen Hughes and Mark A. Bellis, 'Effects of the 2010 World Cup Football Tournament on Emergency Department Assault Attendances in England'. *European Journal of Public Health*, 23, no. 3 (2012): 383–385.

Szymanski, Stefan. 'A Market Test for Discrimination in the English Professional Football Leagues'. *Journal of Political Economy*, 108, no. 3 (2000): 590–603.

———. 'Income Inequality, Competitive Balance, and the Attractiveness of Team Sports: Some Evidence and a Natural Experiment from English Football'. *Economic Journal*, 111 (2001): F69–F84.

———. 'Entry into Exit: Insolvency in English Professional Football'. *Scottish Journal of Political Economy* (2017). http://dx.doi.org/10.1111/sjpe.12134.

Szymanski, Stefan and Guy Wilkinson. 'Testing the O-Ring Theory Using Data from the English Premier League'. *Research in Economics*, 70, no. 3 (2016): 468–481

Tapp, A. 'The Loyalty of Football Fans – We'll Support You Evermore?' *Journal of Database Marketing and Customer Strategy Management,* 11, no. 3 (2004): 203–215.

Tapp, A. and J. Clowes. 'From "Carefree Casuals" to "Professional Wanderers": Segmentation Possibilities for Football Supporters'. *European Journal of Marketing,* 36, no. 11 (2002): 1248–1269.

Taylor, Matthew. 'Global Players? Football, Migration and Globalization, c. 1930–2000'. *Historical Social Research,* 31, no. 1 (2006): 7–30.

Van Ours, Jan. C. and Martin A. van Tuijl. 'In-Season Head-Coach Dismissals and the Performance of Professional Football Teams'. *Economic Inquiry*, 54, no. 1 (2016): 591–604

Williams, Damien J. and Fergus G. Neville. 'Sport-Related Domestic Violence: Exploring the Complex Relationship between Sporting Events and Domestic Violence'. In M. F. Taylor, J. A. Pooley and R. S. Taylor (eds), *Overcoming Domestic Violence: Creating a Dialogue around Vulnerable Populations. Social Issues, Justice and Status* (New York: Nova Science Publishers, 2014).

MAGAZINES AND WEBSITES

De Correspondent (Netherlands, with a special mention for journalist Michiel de Hoog, who has produced some of the most intelligent articles on football in recent years. If he were writing in English, you might never have heard of *Soccernomics*)

Hard Gras (Netherlands)

Johan (Netherlands, now defunct)

So Foot (France)

Voetbal International (Netherlands)

INDEX

Page references in *italics* indicate diagrams.